BECOMING WALLA WALLA

BECOMING WALLA WALLA

The Transformation of Cayuse Country, 1805–1879

DENNIS CROCKETT

WSU
PRESS

Washington State University Press
Pullman, Washington

Washington State University Press
PO Box 645910
Pullman, Washington 99164–5910
Phone: 800-354-7360
Email: wsupress@wsu.edu
Website: wsupress.wsu.edu

Library of Congress Cataloging-in-Publication Data

Names: Crockett, Dennis, author.
Title: Becoming Walla Walla : the transformation of Cayuse Country,
    1805-1879 / Dennis Crockett.
Description: Pullman, Washington : Washington State University Press,
    [2024] | Includes bibliographical references and index.
Identifiers: LCCN 2024026615 | ISBN 9780874224337 (paperback)
Subjects: LCSH: Walla Walla Valley (Or. and Wash.)—History—19th century.
    | Indians of North America—Walla Walla Valley (Or. and Wash.) | BISAC:
    HISTORY / United States / State & Local / Pacific Northwest (OR, WA) |
    ARCHITECTURE / Regional
Classification: LCC F897.W2 C76 2024 | DDC 979.5/6903—dc23/
    eng/20240725
LC record available at https://lccn.loc.gov/2024026615

The Washington State University Pullman campus is located on the homelands
of the Niimíipuu (Nez Perce) Tribe and the Palus people. We acknowledge their
presence here since time immemorial and recognize their continuing connection
to the land, to the water, and to their ancestors. WSU Press is committed to
publishing works that foster a deeper understanding of the Pacific Northwest
and the contributions of its Native peoples.

On the cover: Top image: Indian camps, Umatilla Indian Reservation, July 4,
1903 (Lee Moor house photographs, PH036 5923, University of Oregon
Libraries, Special Collections and University Archives) Bottom image: Bird's-
eye view of Walla Walla, Washington Territory, 1876. Lithograph, designed by
E. S. Glover, printed by A. L. Bancroft & Co., San Francisco, published by
Everts & Abel, Walla Walla. (Library of Congress Geography and Map
Division. https://loc.gov/item/75696671/)

Cover design by Jeffry E. Hipp

To my amazing family

And to the staff, past and present,
at St. Mary Regional Cancer Center in Walla Walla

Contents

Illustrations

Maps

Timeline

1805–06: The Sahaptians interacted with Lewis and Clark.

1811: The (American) Pacific Fur Company (PFC) established Fort Astor, received consent to pass through Sahaptian territory.

1813: Word received of outbreak of war with Britain, PFC sold out to the (British) Northwest Company (NWC).

1818: NWC permitted to establish Fort Nez Perce (later Fort Walla Walla).

1818–46: The Anglo-American Convention established temporary joint occupation of the Columbia Department/Oregon Country.

1821: British government forced merger of the NWC into the Hudson's Bay Company (HBC).

1824: Fort Vancouver established as HBC headquarters in the Columbia Department.

1829: First settlement of HBC retirees and their Native wives in the Willamette Valley (French Prairie).

1829–31: Malaria epidemic devastated the Native people of the Lower Columbia.

1830s: Establishment of a "Frenchtown" in the Walla Walla Valley.

1834: Settlement of Methodists in French Prairie.

1836: Settlement of Presbyterians among the Cayuse and Nez Perce.

1840: Arrival of Catholic missionaries in the Lower Columbia.

1842: One hundred and fifteen Americans arrived in Oregon.

1843: The Provisional Government of Oregon established in French Prairie. Start of "Oregon Fever"; ca. 800 Americans arrived.

1844: ca. 1,500 Americans arrived. Increasing tensions among Sahaptians.

1845: ca. 2,500 Americans arrived.

1846: The Oregon Treaty divided the territory along the 49th parallel.

1847: Measles epidemic ravaged the Sahaptians.
Ca. 2,500 American overlanders arrived.
Cayuse attacked Americans, killing thirteen.

1848: Oregon Militia skirmished with Cayuse in the Walla Walla Valley.
Start of California Gold Rush.
Congress established Oregon Territory.

1849: Arrival of the US Army; US Fort Vancouver and Fort Dalles established.

1850: Five Cayuse men tried in Oregon City, found guilty, and hanged.
Congress passed the Oregon Donation Land Act.
Ca. 6,000 Americans arrived.

1853: Washington Territory established.

1855: Walla Walla Treaty.
Start of "the Yakima War."
Skirmishes in the Walla Walla Valley.

1856–57: The Army established Fort Walla Walla in three successive locations.

1858: Large punitive expedition departed Fort Walla Walla into Palus, Spokane, and Coeur d'Alene territories.
The Army declared the territory east of the Cascades open to settlement; merchants and homesteaders arrived from the west.

1859: Rapid growth of the village of Wailetpa/Steptoeville/Walla Walla.
Walla Walla County established.
Establishment of the State of Oregon.
Congressional ratification of the Walla Walla treaty.

1860: The census counted 722 in Walla Walla and 320 at the fort.

1861: Outbreak of the Civil War.

1862: Gold rush to the "Nez Perce mines."
City of Walla Walla established by territorial legislature.

1863: Idaho Territory established by Congress.

1865: End of Civil War. Closure of Fort Walla Walla.

1865–66: Walla Wallans attempted annexation to Oregon.

1868: Bill to vacate and sell the Umatilla reservation passed by Congress.
National economic downturn reaches Walla Walla.

1869: Completion of the transcontinental railroad.
The Walla Walla and Columbia River Railroad (WWCRR) chartered.

1871: Telegraph reached Walla Walla.
Trustees of the WWCRR moved ahead with construction without public support.
Oregon's senators introduced bill to annex Walla Walla County.
Council held on the reservation concluded that Indians had no desire to relinquish their rights to the reservation.

1873: Reopening of Fort Walla Walla.
Onset of "the Great Depression," numerous local bankruptcies.
Establishment of the Wallowa reservation.

1875: Completion of the WWCRR.
Removal of the Wallowa reservation.
Columbia County established from Walla Walla County.
Oregon's senators introduced a bill to annex Walla Walla and Columbia counties.

1877: The "Nez Perce War."

1878: The "Bannock War"; the Umatilla reservation attacked.
Bureau of Indian Affairs (BIA) planned to remove Umatilla reservation.

1879: Umatilla reservation chiefs visited President Hayes.
BIA introduced the allotment plan for the Umatilla reservation.

Population Growth in Washington Territory/state
(according to census records)

	1860	1870	1880	1890
Walla Walla	722	1,394	3,585	4,709
Seattle	0	1,107	3,533	42,837
Olympia	<1,000	1,203	1,232	4,698
Tacoma	0	73	1,098	36,006
Spokane	0	29	350	19,922

Introduction

For two weeks during spring 1855, Isaac Stevens, the newly appointed governor of Washington Territory, and Joel Palmer, Oregon Superintendent of Indian Affairs, assembled the headmen of the Nez Perce, Cayuse, Walla Walla, Umatilla, and Yakama bands to negotiate the terms of a reservation policy for their people. Around 5,000 attended this enormous council, which took place at the present site of the city of Walla Walla (fig. 1). At the time, it was the location of a long-established Cayuse village, in close proximity to important east-west and north-south trade routes, and a geographic middle point for the invitees. The location was insisted on by the Yakama headman, Kamiakin, who declared: "There is the place where in ancient times we held our councils with the neighboring tribes, and we will hold it there now."[1] The site offered sufficient water and grazing land for the 5,000+ horses of the attendees.

Stevens had already identified the valley as one of the most desirable locations for American settlement: "The valley was almost a perfect level, covered with the greatest profusion of waving bunch grass and flowers,

Figure 1. Gustav Sohon, *Walla Walla Council, May 1855* (cropped). Watercolor. (1918.114.9.39, Washington State Historical Society, Tacoma.)

amidst which grazed numerous bands of beautiful, sleek mustangs, and herds of long-horned Spanish cattle belonging to the Indians, and was intersected every half mile by a clear, rapid, sparkling stream."[2] An Army officer noted of the site, "It was in one of the most beautiful spots of the Walla Walla valley, well wooded and with plenty of water." He concluded, "I am not surprised they are unwilling to give [it] up."[3] In fact, due to the illogical manner in which language and maps were employed at the council, it was unclear to the Indigenous people exactly what land they were "giving up." The treaty resulting from the council produced three years of bloodshed and brutal suppression, after which the Walla Walla Valley was declared open to American settlement. The principal occupants of the site, the northern Cayuse bands, were subsequently forced to move onto a reservation to the south, in Oregon Territory, together with the Walla Walla and Umatilla (who were to entirely abandon their ancestral territory).

In 1865, ten years after the treaty council and just six years after ratification of the treaty, the city of Walla Walla was so well established that Phillip Castleman, a resident photographer and entrepreneur, set out to produce a print to celebrate and advertise the city (fig. 2). The project itself was not unique; lithographic bird's-eye views of cities had been popular in the United States for several decades. And since the development of portable photographic technology in the 1850s, such city views were occasionally based on photographs rather than drawings. What is remarkable is that the embryonic city could be the subject of such a celebratory print and, furthermore, that its small population possessed the civic and personal pride necessary to make such an ambitious project profitable. Yet, despite the accuracy in the depiction of the landscape, it is difficult to identify a recognizable landmark or building.

Ten years after the publication of Castleman's print, Eli S. Glover, a professional viewmaker, arrived in Walla Walla to produce a more traditional, imaginary bird's-eye view print of the city (fig. 3). His more expansive image contains not a trace of Indigenous presence. In fact, it could be read as a celebration of the complete conquest of the Cayuse land demographically, architecturally, botanically, and economically.

Countless histories of the Oregon Trail and manifest destiny have narrated the American government's fixation on possessing Oregon, as well as the American people's obsession with acquiring land in the Far West and their "heroic" "triumph" at turning "wilderness" into "civilization." The

Figure 2. *Walla Walla, 1866.* Lithograph, Grafton T. Brown & Co., San Francisco, photographs by Phillip Castleman (Walla Walla Maps Collection, Whitman College and Northwest Archives).

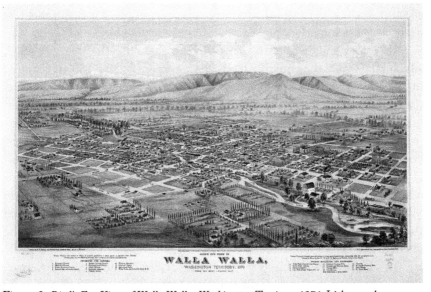

Figure 3. *Bird's Eye View of Walla Walla, Washington Territory 1876.* Lithograph, designed by E. S. Glover, printed by A. L. Bancroft & Co., San Francisco, published by Everts & Abel, Walla Walla. (Library of Congress Geography and Map Division. https://loc.gov/item/75696671/.)

3

focus of this book, however, is the physical, demographic, and cultural transformations of the Walla Walla region in general, and the site of the city of Walla Walla in particular, during the seventy years prior to the production of Glover's print.

––––––

People lived here for millennia. They experienced dramatic cultural transformations during the eighteenth century and then encountered another, entirely different culture at the start of the nineteenth century. By the 1820s, they had allowed these fellow traders to share their territory and ultimately alter their lives. Yet they were completely unaware that their territory had become part of a global, imperial, commercial war. The hostile competitors soon arrived—sometimes as traders, sometimes as teachers, ultimately as conquerors. One goal of this book is to determine exactly where Walla Walla fits into this conquest.

The written documentation of this period was produced exclusively by Euro-Americans. Even the words of Indigenous people—when they do exist—were recorded by Euro-Americans. We will never have an unbiased account of these decades; the best we can do is to present the events and deeds of these imperfect people as accurately as possible.

This story ends with two very different accounts. The treaty of 1855, which established the Umatilla reservation, was ratified in 1859 and expired in 1879. What progress had been made in those twenty years? What was the relationship between the city and the reservation? The second end point is Glover's remarkable visual record of the city, which—unlike Castleman's print—is recognizable today. Walla Walla had rapidly developed into the largest and wealthiest city in Washington Territory. Yet daily life in 1860s–70s Walla Walla is as ambiguous to us as the city portrayed in Castleman's print. Can this ghostlike city be reanimated? Who were these Walla Wallans? What were their wants and fears? To what future did they aspire? Is it possible to address the same questions regarding the residents of the reservation?

This book is divided into two parts, separated by the punitive war carried out by the US Army against the occupants of the Columbia Plateau in 1858. Contemporary voices—letters, newspapers, travelogues, memoirs, and official reports—will lead us through these pages as much as possible. The sections of part 1 (1805–58) are rather traditional, chronological chapters, introducing the Cayuse and the foreigners to the region, each of whom transformed the environment to varying degrees: the fur traders, entrepreneurs, missionaries, colonists, and the US Army. The sections of part 2 (1859–79) are arranged semi-chronologically and treated more as vignettes or themes. There will be no neat conclusions (in fact, there is no chapter titled "Conclusion"). There will be no projections made into the future. This is a broad and intentionally untidy approach to writing history. But by approaching the period in such detail, it is hoped that a realistic picture emerges of the complexities of human existence in this particular place during this particular time.

Part I

"The Most Hostile Spot on the Whole Line of Communication"

E cological anthropologists have observed that hunter-gatherer societies generally have access to adequate and reliable resource harvest
areas, expend minimal energy to provide for their needs, and live free of
persistent anxiety.[1] This scenario may have applied to the primary occupants of the Walla Walla Valley in 1700, but the eighteenth century saw
radical transformations in the region. First, the Cayuse-Nez Perce adoption of the horse ca. 1730 altered the prestige of these people, inevitably
made them more warlike, and ultimately spread their influence between
the great market centers of the Plains and the Lower Columbia River.
The second great transformation came with first waves of pandemic during the last quarter of the century. If the equestrian revolution brought
these people material wealth and intertribal authority, the rapid decimation of their people from unforeseen disease brought about a transformative spiritual crisis.

The nineteenth century opened with their first encounters with Euro-
Americans, who were unaware of the state of spiritual crisis—of the "persistent anxiety"—experienced by these newly "discovered" people. The
Euro-Americans initially sought commercial benefit from the Indigenous
lands and required Indigenous cooperation; the Indigenous people sought
both material and spiritual power from the Euro-Americans. Yet only
the Indigenous lifeways were to be altered. The following nine chapters
attempt to narrate Indian-non-Indian relationships in the Pacific Northwest in general, with particular focus on the Walla Walla Valley and the
Cayuse people.

1

The Cayuse and the Walla Walla Valley

The Walla Walla Valley has been inhabited for at least 10,000 years. Prior to the mid-nineteenth century, the principal occupants of the central and upper valley were a people that identified themselves as *Líksiyu*, commonly known as the Cayuse. Thanks to the central role played by storytelling in Cayuse culture, we possess significant knowledge of Cayuse history and the Cayuse relationship to the land they occupied. Euro-American chroniclers, anthropologists, and historians of the past two centuries have added to this knowledge anecdotes, statistics, and details that are sometimes insightful but too often particularly biased against the Cayuse. In fact, Euro-Americans quickly assigned the Cayuse a reputation as the belligerents among the relatively peaceful Sahaptian people—a reputation that was confirmed within the Euro-American community by a series of incidents in the mid-nineteenth century. These incidents will be outlined in the following chapters. The purpose of this chapter is to shed some light on the Cayuse people.

In the early nineteenth century, the Cayuse comprised as many as nine principal bands located along the Umatilla and Walla Walla rivers and their tributaries.[1] In the most general terms, the area of principal occupancy of the Cayuse in the Walla Walla Valley was bounded by the Touchet River to the west, the Snake River to the north, and the Tucannon River to the east; they shared occupancy—as well as close kinship ties—with the Walla Walla (*Walúulapam*) near the confluence of the Touchet and Walla Walla rivers; with the Umatilla (*Imatalamthláma*) near the mouth of the Umatilla River; with the Palus (*Naxiyamtáma*) along the Snake River; and with bands of Nez Perce (*Nimiipuu*) on the Tucannon and in the Grande Ronde and Wallowa valleys. Their southern territory was far more fluid but generally bounded by the Blue Mountains to the southeast and the Deschutes River to the west.

Alliances with their Sahaptian neighbors were maintained through intermarriage, a common cosmology, shared resource harvest areas, military coordination, long-established traditions of reciprocity, and linguistic communication, despite their wide array of dialects.[2] The practice of polygamy ensured that high-status families were closely connected across the vast territory. The Cayuse language, which has not been spoken in almost a century, is considered by anthropologists to have been either distinct or distantly related to the Sahaptian languages of their neighbors.[3] During the first half of the nineteenth century, through extensive kinship ties, the Cayuse adopted the Nez Perce language as their own, yet Cayuse identity was sustained by exclusive use of their unique language among themselves.[4]

Water was created first, life and land were created next, the land promised to take care of all life, all life promised to take care of the land.[5]

The Cayuse and their neighbors on the Columbia Plateau have followed the "natural" or "divine" laws, *tamálwit* (Cayuse-Nez Perce; *tamánwit* in Columbia River Sahaptin). The laws were handed down from the Creator of the earth and the Animal People. The Animal People, led by Coyote, Fox, and others, manipulated and named the parts of the land, and prepared it for humans. Based on this covenant between the Creator, the Animal People, and the humans, the people are provided with all the resources for life on specific parts of the earth. Therefore, the earth—often referred to as one's mother—and its natural resources are sacred. The seasonal round, the annual migrations to the sites of the First Foods, is guided by *tamálwit*, which is regularly reinforced by various types of stories, songs, dances, and celebrations.[6] The creation stories, memorized and retold generationally (often humorously), unify the people with their particular land and offer lessons in ethical behavior.

Like people throughout the Northwest, individual spiritual identity and uniqueness among the Cayuse were acquired and sustained by the guardian spirit (*Weyekin*) experience. Early adolescents were sent alone to particularly sacred sites to fast and seek contact with a nonhuman spirit. Ideally, the individual would thus be intimately partnered to this spirit and would receive from it unique powers and knowledge. Historian

Christopher Miller writes, "In a very real sense, the spirit provided the steering mechanism that guided a person through the hazards of life, making him or her an important contributor to the groups with which he or she was associated."[7] Historian Larry Cebula similarly emphasizes the Plateau peoples' unceasing quest to "harness" spiritual power.[8]

Pašxápa

Winter village sites were long-established—perhaps for millennia—and situated in prime locations. Although they were partially occupied year-round, the entire band passed the most sacred time of the year at these sites: the winter solstice and the new year.[9] This time was dedicated to storytelling, dancing, and celebrating the guardian spirits. Families may also have traveled to participate in the celebrations with relatives among other bands.

Each band represented a politically autonomous village, often consisting of a broadly extended family, numbering from under one hundred to more than two hundred residents. Like those of their neighbors, Cayuse villages were governed by councils comprising the male heads of the families. Each council named a headman to act as its spokesman, to oversee the well-being of the village, and to provide a model of wisdom, generosity, and diplomacy.

The city of Walla Walla would be established on the site of the central winter village of the Cayuse in the Walla Walla Valley, located on the tributary known originally by Whites as Pasha Creek, and later as Mill Creek (map 1). The site was known to the Cayuse as *Pašxápa* (roughly, pash-KA-pah, "place of the balsamroot sunflower"). Its residents were *Pašxápu* (the Cayuse-Nez Perce suffix *-pu* indicates "people of").[10] The Cayuse name for the broader region is unknown; however, the Cayuse-Nez Perce name *Weyíilet* ("place of waving grass") was applied to at least a section of the valley, near the confluence of Mill Creek and the Walla Walla River. The Nez Perce name for the Cayuse people, *Weyíiletpu*, suggests a broad territory for *Weyíilet*.[11] The Columbia River Sahaptins (Walla Walla and Umatilla) refer to the section of the Walla Walla River where it joins its major tributaries—the Touchet River, Dry Creek, and Mill Creek—as *Walúula* or *Walawála* ("multiple, diminutive rivers").[12]

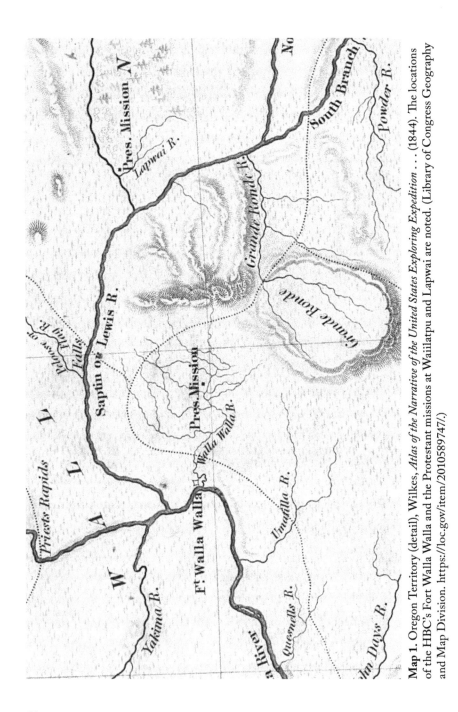

Map 1. Oregon Territory (detail), Wilkes, *Atlas of the Narrative of the United States Exploring Expedition . . .* (1844). The locations of the HBC's Fort Walla Walla and the Protestant missions at Waiilatpu and Lapwai are noted. (Library of Congress Geography and Map Division. https://loc.gov/item/2010589747/.)

It has long been assumed that the idiom "Cayuse" is an anglicization of the French term *cailloux* (roughly, "people of the rocks") by which Canadien fur trappers supposedly identified the *Líksiyu*. *Cailloux* certainly made more sense as a designation for these people than did *Tête Plat* (flathead) or *Nez Perce* (pierced nose) for the people labeled by those terms. Exactly how French terms, or English translations of French terms, or odd pronunciations of French terms came to be affixed to specific Indigenous people is often a mystery.[13] For the sake of clarity, common English designations will be used for self-identified Indigenous people.

The Equine Revolution

The Cayuse are attributed with being the first of the Sahaptians to acquire the horse—around 1730, through interaction with their ancestral enemy to the south, the Northern Shoshone. Through breeding and raiding, the number of animals in their herds multiplied quickly, and the Cayuse and Nez Perce became both outstanding equestrians and producers of a valuable commodity. The horse allowed the Cayuse to expand their subsistence economy significantly; their ability to travel greater distances efficiently vastly increased their access to the plants and animals on which they survived. At the same time, they had to accommodate the foraging needs of their immense herds of horses. This need for vast, well-watered grasslands may have led the Cayuse to establish (through reciprocity or conquest) their relatively large territory of principal occupancy.

The adoption of the horse brought about a cultural revolution in the West. The Cayuse and Nez Perce became valuable intermediaries at the great markets of the Plains and the Columbia River, establishing a prominent presence at the megamarket of the Columbia Narrows, where they traded with the Chinookan people slaves, horses, and products from the Plains for fish, beads, dentalium, and—prior to direct contact with Whites—items of European manufacture (e.g., metal cooking vessels, glass beads, and clothing). They also sent large expeditions east to the upper Yellowstone River to hunt bison and trade horses, slaves, and objects acquired from the Chinookans. The Walla Walla and Grande Ronde valleys also developed into important centers of this trade network. The Grande Ronde Valley was a long-established summer trading and shared resource area for all

Sahaptian people (and in times of peace, also for the Northern Shoshone and Paiute). Aside from breeding horses, the Cayuse were primarily traders and raiders rather than producers. Salmon played an important part in the Cayuse diet, yet among the Sahaptians, they were less focused on fishing.

Contact with the people of the Plains—the Crow (*Apsáalooke*), in particular—led to further dramatic transformations in Cayuse-Nez Perce culture. Prior to 1800, they had adopted material elements of Plains culture, such as the tipi, the horse-drawn *travois* to haul goods, leather horse tack, feathered headdress, and ornamented leather garments and parfleche.[14] At the same time, they assumed aspects of Plains war culture. Councils would appoint individuals of exceptional skill to direct war parties, and during times of warfare, they would serve as the bands' single authorities.[15] Social prestige for men came to be based on war experience, which was made visual by the display of coups (representing successful actions such as a kill, a scalp, stealing a horse, taking a slave, making physical contact with an enemy, or taking an enemy's weapon).[16] With the domestication of the horse, adversaries were established at distances unthinkable to pedestrian cultures. The Sahaptians, including the Palus across the Snake River and the Wanapam (*Wánapam*), and Yakama (*Mámachatpam*) up and across the Columbia River, organized raiding parties against the Shoshone and Paiute, and into the Willamette Valley and Alta California. The ultimate prizes of these raids were horses and slaves. The captives became possessions of the warriors' families or were treated as commodities. Some became assimilated as wives or warriors.[17]

The Cayuse-speaking population during the first half of the nineteenth century is usually estimated at five hundred.[18] Based on accounts by outsiders, however, the influence of high-status Cayuse men over their neighbors to the west was far out of proportion with their numbers. Daniel Lee, a missionary at The Narrows (1838–43), pointed out, "From the Dalls Indians the [Cayuse] used formerly to take an annual tribute of salmon, alleging that the fishery belonged to them. Whether or not their claims were well founded, their superior power in war kept their tributaries in abject submission. . . . They buy at their own price, compelling them to sell even their own stock of provisions, so as to have little left to subsist on themselves."[19] Lee's colleague Henry Perkins made a similar observation in December 1843: "This is the month when the Kaius, WallaWallas & Nez

Perces make their yearly gathering here to pass the winter. The former of these are the elite of the country. They are few in number but exert a very great influence. They are a brave, & enterprising people, & command a great deal of respect from the surrounding tribes."[20] The American explorer Thomas J. Farnham, who trekked to the Northwest in 1839, anointed the "Skyuse" as "the imperial tribe of Oregon." According to his sources, the Cayuse "formerly claimed a prescriptive right to exercise jurisdiction over the country down the Columbia to its mouth [i.e., the Pacific Ocean]; and up the North and South Forks to their sources [i.e., the Rockies]."[21] A century and a half later, this image of the Cayuse was embraced by Robert Ruby and John Brown, authors of *The Cayuse Indians: Imperial Tribesmen of Old Oregon*. However, Farnham's observations regarding Indigenous people are often unreliable. More recent studies have rejected this "Imperial Tribesmen" interpretation. Robert Boyd, for example, notes that there was no need to travel so far and for such a prolonged period for salmon, suggesting that their presence at the Cascades had more to do with social interaction. Eugene Hunn suggests, "Cayuse political control of Celilo residents may have been only a misconception by Whites who did not comprehend reciprocity." He adds, "Hunter-gatherers do not create empires, they tend rather to mind their own business."[22] Nonetheless, written accounts of the Cayuse prior to the reservation period invariably made note of their independence, military prowess, fearlessness, and spectacular horsemanship (as well as their love of gambling and horse racing).

Cayuse Architecture

[W]e encamped on the lower side of this creek at a little distance from two lodges of the [Nez Perce] nation . . . one of these lodges contained eight families, the other was much the largest we have yet seen. it is 156 feet long and about 15 wide built of mats and straw. in the form of the roof of a house having a number of small doors on each side, is closed at the ends and without divisions in the intermediate space this lodge contained at least 30 families. their fires are kindled in a row in the center of the house and about 10 feet assunder. all the lodges of these people are formed in this manner.
—Meriwether Lewis, May 5, 1806[23]

By 1800, the primary winter dwellings of the Cayuse were the mat lodge or longhouse and the mat or hide tipi, which were both versatile and portable and thus well suited the various climatic and mobility demands of the Cayuse seasonal round. Variations of the lodge existed throughout the Northwest and were determined by both available resources and usage. The seminomadic Sahaptians required flexible, transportable structures with interchangeable parts. On the other hand, stationary people, like the Chinookans along the lower Columbia, built permanent, cedar plank lodges, which could last for generations. Women and slaves were exclusively responsible for assembling, maintaining, striking, and hauling the dwellings. A team was required to assemble a lodge, and it is assumed that individual women within each band possessed special skills in particular aspects of production or assembly.[24]

The tipi, the primary dwelling of the Plains Indians, was adopted by the Cayuse and their allies in the second half of the eighteenth century. Ideally suited to a seminomadic lifeway, the tipi provided good insulation from both cold and heat, it could be assembled and dismantled relatively quickly, and its parts could be transported with a horse-drawn travois. The tipi framework was covered with either overlapping layers of tule mats or a prepared, sewn cover of (summer) bison hides.

The Seasonal Round

Guided by *tamálwit*, the Cayuse followed a consistent annual migration to their sacred resource areas. Each arrival called for a First Foods ceremony and celebration. In early spring the women, children, and slaves harvested cow parsnip and bitterroot (for which they may not have had to travel far from the winter village). Later in the spring the band would travel in smaller groups to higher elevations to harvest highly prized blue camas bulbs and cous biscuitroot. (Arriving among the meadows of violet camas lilies certainly would have been something worth celebrating.) Throughout the summer and early fall, numerous berries ripened sequentially, and temporary shelters were required during these harvests. Tipis could have been struck, hauled, and reassembled at these camps. Also, some of the structural elements of tipis or lodges from the winter camps could have been reemployed to build lean-tos or arbors at temporary camps. Specially skilled men may have focused on the spring and fall salmon runs. Others would have focused on hunting specific animals at specific times. The bands would return to the winter village at regular intervals throughout the year, where women would have dried and prepared foods for the winter.

Like Indigenous people throughout the West, the Cayuse managed their resource areas by burning after the harvests, particularly in the late summer. Boyd writes, "We now know that the 'lawns' that Vancouver observed on Whidbey Island, the prairies that early trappers and explorers described in the Willamette Valley . . . had been actively manipulated and managed, if not actually 'created,' by their Native inhabitants. . . . Native Americans understood the concept of plant succession. They knew that the creative use of fire reverted the successional sequence to its early stages."[25] Euro-Americans in the region regularly complained of the smoke from these controlled burnings and of having to traverse black, lifeless prairies. It took decades before the vast expanses of meadows were equated by Whites with this systematic burning.

First Encounters

Before ever seeing a White person, the people of the Columbia Plateau were dying in catastrophic numbers from their diseases. The arrival of Western-manufactured goods at the markets of the Northwest coincided with the region's first "virgin soil" epidemics. Transmission originated with the coastal peoples, who were involved with the European and American sea otter trade in the late eighteenth century. Diseases spread along the trade routes to the great market of the lower Columbia. The first waves of smallpox during the 1770s and '80s are estimated to have killed from a third to more than half of the Indigenous population of the Northwest.[26] The horror and confusion generated by these epidemics brought about—in Hunn's words—a "spiritual apocalypse."[27] The guardian spirit cosmology could account for individual illness but not for the wholesale ravages of an epidemic. Infected individuals died or survived regardless of their spiritual power. It is unclear how the epidemics were perceived; however, based on the widespread response, it seems that they were understood as a spiritual crisis brought about by the people's behavior. A number of prophets appeared throughout the region urgently calling for spiritual purification, or preparation for the end of the world, the return of the dead, or the renewal of the world. All efforts involved dancing.[28] An eruption of Mount St. Helens in 1800 resulted in an ash cloud that dropped up to six inches of "dry snow" on parts of the plateau. This event could only have intensified the dancing. The first Euro-American visitors to the plateau in the early nineteenth century observed mass-dancing spectacles (which they invariably believed to have been performed in their honor).

The first physical encounters between the Sahaptians and British-subject fur trappers occurred during the former's bison expeditions to the Plains. Competition between the London-based Hudson's Bay Company (HBC) and the Montreal-based North West Company (NWC) in the North American fur trade led the NWC to send trapping and exploration parties into and beyond the Rocky Mountains. In 1792, the NWC commissioned Alexander Mackenzie to chart an overland route from Montreal to the Pacific Ocean. Mackenzie's published notes and charts (London, 1801; Philadelphia, 1802) concluded with a plea to the British government to act quickly to fully exploit the economic resources of the Northwest before the Americans could.[29]

Thomas Jefferson and others within the US government were keenly aware of recent international publications regarding exploration and trade in the Pacific Northwest, particularly Mackenzie's book. Within a year of his inauguration as president in 1801, Jefferson initiated negotiations with France for the purchase of its territory at the mouth of the Mississippi River; the result was the purchase of the entirety of French Louisiana in December 1803. During these negotiations, Jefferson also initiated plans with his personal secretary, Meriwether Lewis, to lead an expedition across Louisiana to the Pacific Ocean "for the purposes of commerce." Among other things, Jefferson charged Lewis with learning everything he could about the people encountered, including "the articles of commerce they may need or furnish." He continued: "And considering the interest which every nation has in extending & strengthening the authority of reason & justice among the people around them, it will be useful to acquire what knolege you can of the state of morality, religion, & information among them; as it may better enable those who may endeavor to civilize & instruct them, to adapt their measures to the existing notions & practices of those on whom they are to operate."[30] From the very beginning, therefore, the mission was about much more than commerce.

Lewis and Clark's "Corps of Discovery" was on the brink of starvation in fall 1805 when they came upon a large band of Nez Perce in the Weippe Prairie. To their surprise, they were warmly embraced by the "Chopunnish." In fact, the highlight of the next nine months of their journey was the treatment they received among the Sahaptians. All chroniclers in the party concluded that they were the friendliest, most hospitable, honest, and sincere people encountered. On their return trek, they spent several days at the village of "Yel-lep-pet [Tamatapam] . . . the principal Chief of the Wal lah wal lah Nation" on the west side of the Columbia, opposite the river that they referred to as the "Wal lah wal lah."[31] William Clark conducted a medical clinic for Tamatapam's people. In particular, they were afflicted by eye inflammation due to the constant wind and blowing sand of the Wallula Gap. At night the two explorers and their companions witnessed a spectacular dance of 300 Sahaptians.

The expedition had bypassed the Walla Walla Valley on its westbound trek; however, during their return journey, they were advised by Tamatapam to take the shorter route to the Clearwater ("Kooskooskee") River. Together with twenty-three horses and several Walla Walla guides, they followed a trail along the Walla Walla and Touchet rivers to the Tucannon ("Ki-moo-e-nim Creek"). At this territorial border the Walla Wallas departed, and some Nez Perces arrived to escort them to the Clearwater. Based on a brief encounter with a small number of Cayuse, Lewis and Clark noted they were a band of the Nez Perce and attempted to transcribe the Nez Perce designation for them: "Y-e-let-pos."[32]

The Sahaptian people were eager to maintain trade relations with the Americans. Above all, they desired access to the American weapons, and perhaps their medicine. Clark conducted another busy medical clinic during the Corps' extended stay among the Nez Perce. Sahaptians traveled long distances to receive his care for all types of afflictions. Equipped with only rudimentary medicine, ointments, and medical training, Clark established an almost superhuman reputation as a healer among the Sahaptians.[33] Based on his notes, Clark failed to associate the elaborate displays of honor bestowed on him with the recent "spiritual apocalypse" experienced by his patients.

———

In response to the Lewis and Clark expedition, the NWC commissioned David Thompson in 1807 to expand its operations beyond the Rocky

Mountains. Over the next four years, Thompson and his party charted the entire Columbia River and established trading posts (or claimed sites for future posts) in the name of Britain and the NWC. And so, the Cayuse and other peoples of the Pacific Northwest were caught between the imperial ambitions of Britain and the United States, both of whom would soon demand behavioral and cultural transformation of the occupants of the region and would establish their unique footprints on the environment.

2

The Fur Trade in the Walla Walla Region

O n July 9, 1811, at a site near the confluence of the Snake ["Shawpa-tin"] and Columbia rivers, David Thompson met Tamatapam, "the principal chief of all the tribes of Shawpatin Indians." After a long discussion and a sufficient presentation of gifts, Tamatapam invited Thompson to establish a trading post at the site. Thompson then erected a pole with a sheet of paper affixed, on which he wrote, "Know hereby that this country is claimed by Great Britain as part of its territories, and that the N.W. Company of Merchants from Canada . . . do hereby intend to erect a factory in this place for the commerce of the country around."[1] Thompson's note-on-a-stick may have been easy to overlook and may have gone unnoticed by his hosts, yet according to the "doctrine of discovery," it was a legal procedure, intended to carry great weight. Based on fifteenth-century papal decrees, non-Christian lands could be "discovered" and claimed in the name of Christian European rulers; the planting of a flag or other such indicator established an exclusive right of preemption for a ruler. According to the original decrees, the inhabitants of the newly discovered land were to subject themselves to their new sovereign and to the sovereign's religion, under penalty of enslavement, extermination, and so on. By the late eighteenth century, this God-given right of dispossession had become international property law (yet the missionary imperatives of the original decrees were largely ignored).[2]

At that very moment, another group of fur traders was laboring to set up shop—thanks to the doctrine of discovery—near the mouth of the Columbia. In 1792, the American Capt. Robert Gray navigated up the river, planted an American flag on a riverbank, buried some US coins, and named the river Columbia, after his ship. In New York in 1810, John Jacob Astor, who had already made a fortune in the fur trade, created the Pacific Fur Company (PFC), which was intended to dominate all trade between

North America and China. Part of Astor's PFC party traveled overland, roughly following the footsteps of Lewis and Clark; the other members of the party sailed around Cape Horn and arrived at the mouth of the Columbia in April 1811. The latter portion of the party was a remarkably international company, composed of Scots, Canadiens, Hawaiians (hired *en route*), Iroquois, and a few White Americans.

To protect their commercial stake, to cast a bright spotlight on their (and the United States') claim to authority in the region, and to demonstrate their domination of the landscape, the PFC selected a site on the south side near the river's mouth, gruelingly cleared some dense forest, and constructed a fortified trading post. It was christened Fort Astor. The clerk Gabriel Franchère noted the fort "had a sufficiently formidable aspect to deter the Indians from attacking us."[3]

Slowly, the Astorians, as they soon became known, established a working relationship with the local Chinookan headman, Concomly. Alexander Ross, a Scottish clerk, observed that the Chinookan people "are a commercial rather than a warlike people. Traffic in slaves and furs is their occupation."[4] Ross and his colleagues were impressed by both the quantity and variety of Euro-American goods in their possession and their bargaining prowess. It is generally understood that the major players in the pre-contact trade network along the north Pacific coast and the Lower Columbia—Nootkan and Chinookan speakers, respectively—had developed an interlanguage. The traders and trappers soon adopted this lingua franca and injected it with English and French words for items previously unknown to the Chinookan people. This evolving pidgin language came to be called "Chinook Wawa." Commercial and diplomatic ties were soon firmly established with the first of many blanket marriages, or *marriages à la façon du pays* (according to the custom of the country) between a PFC partner and a daughter of Concomly.[5]

Looming over the broad mouth of the Columbia, Fort Astor signaled the commercial and territorial aspirations of the American PFC—both to the Chinookan people and to other Euro-American traders. While awaiting the arrival of the overland party, the Astorians instead were shocked to receive a visit from David Thompson and his party in July 1811. Thompson did his best to discourage the Astorians from interfering in the NWC's enterprise. However, several of the Astorians were former employees of the NWC and welcomed the challenge.

The Astorians and the Sahaptians

During their first difficult, twenty-four-day voyage up the Columbia, the Astorians were regularly harassed and intimidated, particularly by the Chinookan Wasco-Wishram people at the Narrows.[6] They came to learn that these professional traders—in the busiest marketplace in the Northwest—demanded tribute for the privilege of passing through, camping in, or using resources in *their territory*. However, when the Astorians reached the mouth of the Walla Walla River, they encountered an enormous, friendly camp of "the Walla-Wallas, the Shaw Haptens [Nez Perce], and the Cajouses; forming together about fifteen hundred souls." Ross noted, "altogether, their appearance indicated wealth. . . . The plains were literally covered with horses, of which there could not have been less than four thousand in sight of the camp." Ross identified the principal headmen as Tamatapam [Walla Walla], Quill-Quills-Tuck-a-Pesten [Nez Perce], and Allowcatt [Cayuse]," and noted that Tamatapam was subservient to the other two. The Sahaptians and PFC men camped at the mouth of the Snake River, where they discovered Thompson's British flag and note declaring the spot in the name of Britain. According to Ross, after presenting the headmen with a greater quantity of gifts than Thompson had, "It was then finally settled that we might proceed up the north branch, and that at all times we might count upon their friendship."[7] The PFC party then progressed up the Columbia, where they established two small trading posts in close proximity to NWC posts: Fort Okanogan and Fort Spokane. (It was a tradition among the fur trading companies to name posts after the principal occupants of the sites.) To the delight of the PFC, the Okanogans (*Syilx*) and Spokans (*Sqeliz*) agreed to participate in the collection of beaver pelts.

Like Lewis and Clark's experience in the Weippe Prairie, the PFC's destitute overland party, which had split into several groups, were rescued by the Sahaptians. The group led by the Scottish partner, Donald McKenzie, encountered the Nez Perce on the Clearwater River in December; they were fed and given horses to ride to the Columbia. Another party, led by the American partner Wilson Price Hunt, was rescued by a band of Cayuse after crossing the Blue Mountains in January 1812. Three months later, the Americans John Day (hunter) and Ramsay Crooks (partner) were discovered on the brink of death by the Umatillas.

After recuperating at Fort Astor, McKenzie returned to the Clearwater to set up a small trade post constructed from driftwood among the Nez Perce. The Nez Perce were disappointed, however, to learn that he was primarily interested in trading his vast stock of desirable goods for beaver pelts. They had no interest in trapping beaver and preparing pelts; such activity would have severely interfered with their seasonal subsistence round. Ross noted, "Their occupations were war and buffalo-hunting. . . . They spurned the idea of crawling about in search of furs; 'Such a life,' they said, 'was only fit for women and slaves.' They were, moreover, insolent and independent. I say independent, because their horses procured them guns and ammunition; the buffaloes provided them with food and clothing; and war gave them renown. Such men held out but poor prospects to the fur trader."[8] On receiving word from the NWC in 1813 that war had been declared between the United States and Britain, the heads of the PFC decided to sell out to the NWC and return east. (Fort Astor was rechristened Fort George, for George III, and established as the center of NWC operations west of the Rockies.) However, before departing, the Astorians ignorantly generated hostilities with the Sahaptians and transformed their relationship with the fur traders. While camping at the mouth of the Palouse River, two prized silver goblets belonging to the partner John Clarke were stolen. By this time, the Astorians were well aware that theft was something of a game among Indigenous boys. The one who "found" and returned a missing possession generally expected some small reward. When Clarke's goblets were finally recovered, Clarke—to the astonishment of everyone present—ordered the thief hanged. Ross noted, "The deed was, however, no sooner committed than Mr. Clarke grew alarmed. The chief, throwing down his robe on the ground, a sign of displeasure, harangued his people, who immediately after mounted their fleetest horses, and scampered off in all directions to circulate the news and assemble the surrounding tribes, to take vengeance on the whites."[9] When Clarke's party joined McKenzie's at their rendezvous point among the Walla Walla a few days later, they were greeted by a great deal of agitation and aggression. Tamatapam rode to their camp at full speed, berated the Astorians, and insisted that they leave immediately.[10]

On their final voyage up the Columbia, the PFC partners, trappers, and *voyageurs* passed through the Narrows without being attacked—for the first time. Perhaps the people of the Narrows were aware of the Sahaptian army waiting for the traders upriver: near the mouth of the Snake River, they encountered an army of warriors—estimated by Ross as 2,000 strong. Ross claimed the Astorians were only saved by showing off their assortment of weapons.

————

FUR TRADE ARCHITECTURE

The accounts by the Astorians devote far more space to descriptions of Indigenous buildings than to their own. Like the Lewis and Clark chroniclers, they were impressed by the Chinookan plank houses; however, they also had no intention of employing Chinookan construction techniques for their structures. Nor were the fur companies interested in utilizing Sahaptian construction techniques at their forts. However, as blanket marriages were established between fur trappers and women of the Plateau, the transportable tipi (thanks to the skills of the women) often became part of the couples' migratory existence.

Fort Astor was constructed in the techniques of all fur trade posts (figs. 4 & 5). The walls of the buildings were assembled with grooved-post construction (known to the Canadiens as *pièce sur pièce en coulisse* or *poteaux et pièce coulissante*). The foundation consisted of long, square-hewn logs set on stones, tied by dovetail or lap joints, and fixed with dowels, forming a sill. Square mortises were carved at the corners and about 8 feet apart along the sill. Tenoned vertical posts with grooved sides were secured into the sill, and horizontal planks with tongued ends were slid in between the posts and secured with wooden pins or nails. Spaces for doors and windows were created between posts set just a few feet apart. Once all the horizontal elements were in place, the wall plate—a mirror image of the sill—firmly locked the walls together. The wall plate could support joists for a second story, or it could serve as the base for the roof trusses. The roofs were shingled with cedar bark. Floors were generally composed of boards affixed to hewn joists that were attached to the sill. This technique allowed for large, two-story buildings (which were inconceivable with the corner saddle post technique used by Lewis and Clark at their winter camp, Fort Clatsop). The buildings were generally whitewashed with a mixture of water and lime, known as *lait de chaux* ("lime milk"). This gave the buildings within the forts a more unified and perhaps "civilized" look, and the lime preserved the wood.

Figure 4. Granary, Fort Nisqually, 1843. (Moved in 1933 to Point Defiance Park, Tacoma.) Originally, it would have been painted with *lait de chaux*. (Library of Congress, Historic American Buildings Survey, HABS WA-37-C.)

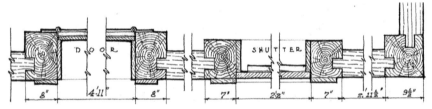

Figure 5. Grooved-post wall section, Granary, Fort Nisqually. (Library of Congress, Historic American Buildings Survey, HABS WA-37-C.) n.d. (c. 1934).

Fort Nez Percés/Walla Walla: "The Gibraltar of Columbia"

The site at the mouth of the Snake River had long been an important trade and meeting place for all the Sahaptian people. Since 1812, this midpoint between Fort Astor and Forts Spokane and Okanogan had also been the PFC's rendezvous point. For both of these reasons, a monumental fort on this site would physically and symbolically establish Euro-American commercial and territorial authority—or at least, co-authority among the Sahaptians. However, construction near this site was postponed for years because it was, according to Ross, "the most hostile spot on the whole line of communication."[11] Relations between the Euro-Americans and the Sahaptians changed with John Clarke's violent spectacle. The Sahaptians were numerous, apparently fearless, possessed exceptional memory, and inhabited the geographic center of the NWC operation in the region. However, Donald McKenzie, who became a partner with the NWC in 1816, was fixated on the beaver-rich Snake River country (which Ross called the "Valley of Troubles"[12]) and lobbied for a supply/trade post there to support his Snake River trapping expeditions. McKenzie spent two years establishing good relations with the people of the Narrows, greeting and offering gifts to the headmen of every sizable band. (McKenzie was a large man, 312 pounds according to Ross, so he stood out as the headman among the White traders.) In summer 1818, he led a large party (thirty-eight Iroquois, thirty-two Hawaiians, twenty-five Canadiens) that set out to build a fort among the Sahaptians.[13] He selected a site a half mile north of the mouth of the Walla Walla River. Alexander Ross was to be in charge of the fort after it was built. Like all heads of the fort, his major responsibility was to procure horses for the Snake River trapping expeditions (the Snake brigade). Of course, they received a cold reception on arriving at the site. Tamatapam, their one high-status ally, was with a war party in the Snake country. The number of curious and cautious Sahaptians rapidly increased, but they made no contact with the fur traders. This tense situation went on for "many anxious days and sleepless nights." When Tamatapam finally arrived with his huge, victorious war party and nine slaves, the assembled masses were distracted by days of celebration. This was a bad time to bring up the subject of establishing peace between the Sahaptians and the Shoshone-Bannocks—which was essential to McKenzie's plans. Tamatapam was incredulous. The Cayuse headman Alokwat asked for a promise that McKenzie would not supply the Shoshone-Bannocks with weapons. Eventually, after weeks of tension, great quantities of gifts were distributed to fifty-six headmen and warriors, who consented to allow the fur traders free passage through their lands under the condition that the Shoshone-Bannocks agreed to the peace.[14] McKenzie and Ross then purchased 280 horses to support the Snake brigade and to haul building materials for Ross's fort. "The place selected was commanding," Ross noted, "On the west is a spacious view of [the Columbia] in all its grandeur, resembling a lake rather than a river. . . . On the north and east . . . boundless plains. On the south . . . a striking contrast of wild hills and rugged bluffs on either side of the water, and rendered more picturesque by two singular towering rocks . . . called by the natives 'The Twins,' . . . To effect the intended footing on this sterile and precarious spot was certainly a task replete with excessive labour and anxiety."[15] Unlike the construction of Fort Astor/George, there were no readily available construction materials; timber had to be harvested in the Blue Mountains and carried by horses. Ross's description of the fort—originally christened Fort Nez Percés—emphasized its defensive elements:

> For the purpose of protection, as well as of trade among Indians, the custom is, to have each establishment surrounded with an inclosure of pickets some twelve or fifteen feet high. [Normally,] the natives have free ingress and egress at all times, and within its walls all the business of traffic is transacted. A little more precaution was, however, necessary at the Nez Percés station, on account of the many warlike tribes that infest the country. . . . [T]he natives were never admitted within the walls, except when specially invited on important occasions. All trade with them was carried on by means of an aperture in the wall, eighteen inches square, secured by an iron door. . . . The fort was defended by four strong wooden towers or bastions, and a cohorn, or small mortar, above the gate; it was, therefore, at once the strongest and most complete fort west of the Rocky Mountains, and might be called the Gibraltar of Columbia. . . . Thus, in the short period of a few months, as if by enchantment, the savage disposition of the Indians was either soothed or awed; a stronghold had arisen in the desert, and the British banner floating over it, proudly proclaimed it the mistress of a vast territory: it was a triumph of British energy and enterprise, of civilisation over barbarism.[16]

Virtually every chronicler to visit the fort made note of its extreme location (fig. 6). The head of the HBC remarked, "A more dismal situation than that of this post can hardly be imagined." The ornithologist John Kirk Townsend noted that it stood "in a bleak and unprotected situation, surrounded on every side by a great, sandy plain, which supports little vegetation, except the wormwood and thorn-bushes." The chief traders at the fort were partly responsible for the bleakness of the site, as another visitor noted: "The sage brush, willow, and grease-wood had been cut and cleared away for a considerable distance around, to prevent any Indians getting near the fort without being discovered."[17]

Figure 6. *Fort Walla Walla.* Lithograph, designed by John Mix Stanley, 1853 (cropped). The fort was largely rebuilt with adobe walls after a fire in 1841. (Stevens, *Reports of Explorations . . .* , plate 42, Whitman College and Northwest Archives.)

Despite the brutality of the environment and the frequent violent episodes that Ross experienced during his five years at the fort, three decades later he recalled moments of bliss there:

> In the charming serenity of a temperate atmosphere, Nature here displays her manifold beauties; and, at this season, the crowds of moving bodies diversify and enliven the scene. Groups of Indian huts, with their little spiral columns of smoke, and herds of animals, give animation and beauty to the landscape. The natives, in social crowds, vied with each other in coursing their gallant steeds, in racing, swimming, and other feats of activity. Wild horses, in droves, sported and grazed along the boundless plains; the wild fowl, in flocks, filled the air; and the salmon and sturgeon, incessantly leaping, ruffled the smoothness of the waters. The appearance of the country on a summer's evening was delightful beyond description.[18]

Our authority for the fort's original name and its change of name is, of course, Ross, who explained, "When the first traders arrived in the country, they generally distinguished all the natives along this part of the communication indiscriminately by the appellation of 'Nez Percés.' . . . The appellation was used until we had an opportunity of becoming better acquainted with their respective names. It was, therefore, from this cause that [Fort Walla Walla] derived its name."[19] The occupants of the land on which a post was built—known as the Home Guard (*Gardins*)—developed unique relationships with the post. The headmen were regular recipients of gifts from the chief traders, and they and their families stood out among their neighbors by wearing more English-manufactured clothing. Although the Home Guard at Fort Walla Walla were Walla Wallas, the fort was regularly visited by more belligerent Cayuse and Nez Perce headmen, and jealousies among the various headmen required that the traders possess unique diplomatic skills.

The Hudson's Bay Company

The competition between the NWC and the HBC had grown violent in the 1810s—so violent that in 1821, the British government intervened and forced a merger of the NWC into the HBC. The HBC assumed control of all British concerns in the Columbia Department.[20] It also retained most of the NWC clerks, trappers, and laborers. George Simpson, governor-in-chief of the Northern Department of the HBC (which extended from Hudson Bay to the Pacific), decided in 1824 to replace Fort George as its main factory in the region with Fort Vancouver, which was established on the north side of the Columbia near the mouth of the Willamette River (see fig. 9). He also placed John McLoughlin in sole charge of all HBC interests west of the Rocky Mountains. From Fort Vancouver, Chief Factor McLoughlin came to oversee a trade empire that included twenty-three fortified trading posts stretching from Alta California (Mexico) to Russia. In addition to furs, McLoughlin diversified the company's interests to include the production and export of lumber, salted salmon, beef, and grain.

Fort Vancouver received at least one annual shipment of supplies from London; however, the HBC posts needed to be self-sustaining. Orchards and farms were established nearby. As Fort Vancouver was under construction, a sawmill, gristmill, and a tannery were also constructed. A sizable village quickly developed outside the fort, operated by current and former employees. Blanket marriages arranged between HBC employees and Native women improved the fur traders' relationship with particular bands. John Dunn, a former HBC clerk, wrote of Fort Vancouver in 1844, "Six hundred yards below the fort, and on the bank of the river, there is a neat village, of about sixty well built wooden houses, generally constructed like those within the fort; in which the mechanics, and other servants of the company, who are in general Canadians and Scotchmen, reside with their families. They are built in rows, and present the appearance of small streets."[21] For his British audience, Dunn omitted the facts that the village was referred to as "Kanaka Village" due to its large Hawaiian population and that its primary population comprised Indigenous women and the children of their unions with Whites, Hawaiians, and Iroquois.[22] Joseph Drayton of the American Wilkes expedition into the Northwest in 1840–41 noted in regard to settlements outside the forts: "Very few of those who embark or join [the HBC's] service ever leave the part of the country they have been employed in; for after the expiration of the first five years, they usually enlist for three more. This service of eight years in a life of so much adventure and hazard, attaches them to it, and they generally continue until they become old men; when, being married, and having families by Indian women, they retire under the auspices of the Company, to some small farm, either on the Red or Columbia rivers."[23] Against official HBC policy, McLoughlin began supporting the settlement of retirees in the Willamette Valley in 1829. (In 1846, McLoughlin himself retired to Oregon City—which he had established in 1829.) The homes and buildings of these "Frenchtowns," as they came to be known to the Americans, were generally constructed in the fur trade techniques. The land on which these families settled was divided into *rangs*, or "long lots," which extended from a river in long rectangles (as was common in most of francophone America). Of course, these settlements were far more diverse than the term Frenchtown implies.

Fort Walla Walla and the Hudson's Bay Company

The fort was occupied by the chief trader and a staff of five to seven, including an interpreter. The staff generally comprised Hawaiians and Métis (mixed parentage) sons of HBC employees. The families of the trader and staff also lived at the fort. When the Snake brigade would depart for Fort Vancouver, the wives and children of the trappers often remained at the fort until their return.[24] Despite this degree of domesticity, Fort Walla Walla remained "the most hostile spot on the whole line of communication" throughout the entire period of the HBC's activity on the Columbia (1821–55). Aside from their horses, the Sahaptians were of minimal commercial benefit to the HBC. Yet Simpson and McLoughlin repeatedly emphasized the need to remain on good terms with these warlike people, and "to maintain a Post for their accommodation whither it pays or not."[25]

Hostilities between the Sahaptians and the Shoshone-Bannocks continued throughout the 1820s and '30s. Each Sahaptian killed or abducted was blamed on the HBC, which was accused of arming the enemy. Following raids, regardless of the aggressor or the outcome, the fort became the scene of chaos. Even during times of relative peace, the trader manipulated jealousies among the headmen—according to Simpson, to "have them in a certain degree under our control."[26] Yet this game generated a constant degree of tension. Ross recalled,

> I have never experienced more anxiety and vexation than among these people. Not an hour of the day passed, but some insolent fellow, and frequently fifty at a time, interrupted us, and made us feel our unavoidable dependence upon their caprice. "Give me a gun," said one; "I want ammunition," said another; a third wanted a knife, a flint, or something else. Give to one, you must give to all. Refuse them, they immediately got angry, told us to leave their lands, and threatened to prevent our people from going about their duties. . . . In their own estimation they are the greatest men in the world. The whites who labour they look upon as slaves, and call them by no other name.[27]

The major trading period at the fort coincided with the winter festivities, during which the trader judiciously bestowed gifts on high-status Sahaptians who arrived from near and far. (The trader generally received horses in return.) Perhaps nothing better symbolized the impact of the fort on the lives of the Sahaptians than this incorporation of the fort—the new focal point of the region—into the sacred winter activities. Yet some headmen saw the need to make a show of exerting their will over the fort.

Ross was replaced as chief trader by John Warren Dease in 1822. When Simpson visited the fort in 1825, he found it surrounded by 300 hostile warriors. The troubles were generated by the fort interpreter, who had conspired with the Cayuse prince Hiyumtipin to take over the fort. Simpson managed to appease the headmen with gifts, but Dease, fearing for the safety of his family, demanded reassignment.[28] He was replaced by Samuel Black (1825–30), who Simpson described as "a cold blooded fellow who could be guilty of any Cruelty. . . . Has not the talent of conciliating Indians by whom he is disliked, but who are ever in dread of him, and well they may be so."[29] Black's tenure was unsurprisingly contentious, and his relationship with Hiyumtipin was violent. Within three years, McLoughlin sought to have Black removed, writing, "Nez Percez is such a hell I don't know what to say about it."[30] McLoughlin repeatedly requested that the traders reimpose the company's standard rates in trading with the Sahaptians—which contradicted the policy of manipulating of jealousies—and was the source of much of the violence at the fort.

Relations at the fort became far more hostile during 1829–31 due to a malaria epidemic that devastated the people of the Columbia River, and which claimed the life of the Cayuse leader Wilewmutkin (Alokwat's successor)—who had maintained a good relationship with the fort. Leadership among the Cayuse bands of the Walla Walla Valley passed to Hiyumtipin. In 1830, Black was replaced by George Barnston (1830–31), who resigned after being beaten unconscious by Hiyumtipin's men. His replacement, Simon McGillivray (1831–32), was removed for his own safety following the murder of an Indian slave attached to the fort by a nephew of Hiyumtipin. McGillivray was replaced by the Canadien Pierre Pambrun (1832–41). In 1836, just months after Pambrun and his interpreter were violently assaulted by the headmen Tawatoy (Umatilla Valley Cayuse) and Looking Glass (Alpowai Nez Perce), McLoughlin noted that Pambrun "has managed the affairs of Walla Walla, one of the most troublesome posts (if not the most troublesome) in the Country, with the utmost skill and judgement."[31]

Despite the constant tension and occasional violence, under Pambrun's direction the fort developed to a state of self-sufficiency. With the consent of the headmen, he enlarged an irrigated farm near the post and established a 50-acre farm several miles up the Walla Walla River, where his staff raised corn, potatoes, turnips, and carrots. Additional land was procured for the company's horses, cattle, pigs, and sheep. With Pambrun's encouragement, some high-status Walla Wallas and Cayuse became small-scale farmers and cattlemen (although the actual labor was supplied by women and slaves). Pambrun also oversaw the development of a "Frenchtown" in the Walla Walla Valley. Former HBC employees settled down with local women, built houses, and established small farms along the Walla Walla River and its tributaries between Pine and Mill creeks (*Weyíilet*). This was done with the consent of the heads of the wives' bands; of course, buildings were constructed using Canadien techniques, and the farms were established in long lots. The 50-square-mile settlement was like a smaller version of the farming community of French Prairie in the Willamette Valley. By the early 1840s, about fifty families comprised the community.

In 1825, George Simpson set in motion a plan to introduce the Native people of Oregon to Anglican culture by sending two young, high-status Salishan men—christened "Spokane Garry" and "Kootenai Pelly"—to be educated at the Mission School of the HBC's Red River colony (near current Winnipeg). In 1830, he sent five Sahaptian boys, including "Cayuse Halket" and "Nez Percé Ellis." After returning to their people, they were intended to become influential Christian, English-speaking leaders. Although most died from diseases at Red River, due to the early influence of these scholars and Pierre Pambrun—who introduced Catholicism to some local elites—a number of Sahaptians embraced Christian prayers and observed sacred services on Sundays.[32] Simpson had considered having three missionary parties sent to the Columbia Department, but mostly for business purposes: "I believe [Christian conversion] would be highly beneficial thereto as they would in time imbibe our manners and customs and imitate us in Dress; our Supplies would thus become necessary to them which would increase the consumption of European produce & manufactures and in like measure increase & benefit our trade. . . . [T]hey might likewise be employed on extraordinary occasions as runners Boatsmen &c and their Services in other respects turned to profitable account."[33]

By this time, Americans were increasingly being drawn to the Pacific Northwest with dual—yet not mutually exclusive—objectives: one was to break the HBC's commercial monopoly on the region's natural resources; the other was to save souls.

3

American Colonization of Oregon 1832–40: Commerce and Christ

In 1821, a number of disgruntled congressmen, journalists, and entrepreneurs began calling for the establishment of an American colony in Oregon Territory. It had been three years since the Anglo-American Convention had settled on a temporary joint occupation of the territory,[1] but, above all, it was the year the HBC was appointed the British authority there. Chief among those supporting American colonization to counter British interests in the territory were Sen. Thomas Hart Benton of the new state of Missouri, and Hall Kelley, an author of spelling textbooks in Boston. Benton immediately began to argue for colonization in Congress and in letters to papers throughout the country. He also used his *St. Louis Enquirer* to (baselessly) accuse the HBC of plotting violent encounters between Indians and the fledgling St. Louis-based fur companies. In 1829, Kelley established and widely promoted the American Society for Encouraging the Settlement of the Oregon Territory, whose goal was to establish a colony of 3,000 members. In a memorial to Congress in 1831, Kelley stated: "The uniform testimony of an intelligent multitude have established the fact, that the country in question, is the most valuable of all the unoccupied parts of the earth." He requested military support, "power to extinguish the Indian title," and authority equal to that given to the HBC by Parliament.[2] While his memorials found insufficient support in Congress, Kelley and Benton generated increasing interest in the Pacific Northwest.

Capt. Benjamin Bonneville had become gripped by the writings of Kelley and Benton while stationed in St. Louis. With funding by New York investors, including John Jacob Astor, he traveled west in 1832 with military orders to gather information for the government regarding Oregon's topography, geology, people, and so on while posing as a fur trader. His party traveled extensively but was shunned by the HBC and barely survived. Bonneville was joined on his overland trek by Nathaniel Wyeth, an entrepreneur and member of Kelley's Society. Wyeth's objective was strictly commercial: to explore the possibilities of establishing depots on the Columbia for the exportation of salted salmon to Boston. However, his initial plans failed when his supply ship from Boston never arrived. He journeyed home to plan for his return to Oregon, convinced that he could make a fortune there.

As Wyeth was on his way back to Boston, Kelley was attempting an arduous journey to Oregon via New Orleans and across Mexico. Near San Diego, he encountered a group of American trappers led by Ewing Young, who operated a trade business based in Taos. Kelley convinced Young and his party to guide him to Oregon. On their arrival, however, John McLoughlin refused to accommodate them due to Kelley's attacks against the HBC. Kelley was soon put on an HBC ship to Hawaii and was back in Boston in 1836. His colonial dream had failed. Yet Young and his companions were among the first American colonists in the Willamette Valley.

Wyeth and an overland party returned to Oregon in 1834 to launch his Columbia River Fishing and Trading Company. He established an inland fur post, Fort Hall (near current Pocatello, Idaho). And, after formalizing a trade agreement with McLoughlin, he constructed Fort William, which was to be the base of his operation (on current Sauvie Island). The island, which just a few years earlier had contained a large Chinookan population, was desolate since the pandemic of 1829–31. Seventeen Hawaiians assisted in the construction of Wyeth's posts. Despite his enormous labor and expense, Wyeth's trading enterprise faced one disappointment after another; just a year into the venture, he declared it a failure. In 1836, he sold Fort Hall to the HBC and soon left Oregon for good.

However, Wyeth left one important legacy in the Northwest (aside from the nineteen American employees who remained in Oregon): his Hawaiian laborers introduced adobe construction—which was widespread in Hawaii—at Fort Hall.[3] Sun-dried mud bricks were used to reinforce the fort's stockade and buildings. In the dry inland Northwest during the 1830s and '40s, the HBC and some new arrivals made quick use of the technique.

The Second Great Awakening's "Macedonian Call"

Another plan to colonize Oregon was conjured in 1833, based on a confusing recent event. In fall 1831, a party of four Indigenous men—supposedly two Nez Perces and two "Flatheads"—arrived in St. Louis. They may have intended to meet with William Clark, now superintendent of Indian Affairs. However, Clark was unable to communicate with the visitors. Two of them soon succumbed to illness; neither of the survivors returned home alive. In one of the few firsthand accounts of their time in St. Louis, the city's bishop wrote, "Unfortunately there was no one who understood their language. . . . It was truly distressing that they could not be spoken to."[4] Subsequently, however, accounts appeared claiming to explain the objectives of the mysterious visit. The most sensational of these appeared in the March 1833 issue of the widely read Methodist *Christian Advocate*. The secretary of the Methodist Board of Foreign Missions, G. P. Disoway, published a fictitious account of the visit, claiming the men were instructed to go east in search of directions for "the true mode of worshipping the great Spirit." Disoway concluded with an urgent appeal to send missionaries to "these wandering sons of our native forests."[5] Two weeks later, Wilbur Fisk, president of Wesleyan University, responded to the article with a plan to send two men "possessing the spirit of martyrs" to live among the "wandering sons," to preach, and to "introduce schools, agriculture, and the arts of civilized life."[6] Fisk recommended his former student, Jason Lee. He rallied the Methodists to fund and organize the mission, to which Lee was appointed superintendent. He was to be accompanied by his nephew, Daniel Lee, and by a teacher. In spring 1834, they departed from Missouri with Wyeth's second overland party.

Near Fort Hall the Methodists were surprised by their welcome among the Sahaptians and by their familiarity with Christianity. Jason Lee assured them that "there was a prospect of our locating at Wallah wallah." However, once there, he found the Home Guard to be "filthy and indolent."[7] Besides, as he wrote repeatedly, the site of his mission was left to Providence.

John McLoughlin warmly greeted the Methodists at Fort Vancouver and turned out to be Providence: he directed them to the Willamette Valley. The Methodists gave up their planned mission among the Salish or

Sahaptian people for the security of the Willamette Valley. Ten years later, Daniel Lee betrayed their concern for colonization in their selection of the mission site: "A larger field of usefulness was contemplated as the object of the mission than the benefiting of a single tribe." Evidence of the recent decimation of the Kalapuyan people of the Willamette Valley—which recently numbered about 13,000—was visible everywhere in abandoned villages and haphazard graves. Jason Lee found the small bands of Kalapuyan people to be "a filthy, miserable-looking company."[8]

Thanks, in part, to centuries of Kalapuyan seasonal anthropogenic fires, the Willamette Valley was now a highly desirable region for agricultural colonists. There were vast prairies, ideal sites for water mills seemingly everywhere, and a harmless, apparently disappearing Indigenous population. The Lees decided to carry out their missionary work among the "prosperous and happy" colonists of the valley and settled on a site to the south of French Prairie (near current Salem).

From the start, the mission maintained a closer relationship to its Canadien and American neighbors than to the Kalapuya. In fact, the mortality rate was so high among the Kalapuya children at the mission that the adults soon kept their distance—and their children—from the mission. The mission school catered almost exclusively to the Métis children of French Prairie.

In 1836, Jason Lee wrote to Fisk emphasizing the need for tradesmen and farmers to relieve the staff of temporal duties. Methodists in New England responded by assembling a party of seven adults and four children under the leadership of Elijah White, which arrived by ship in May 1837. A second group of four adults and three children arrived by ship four months later. In 1838, Daniel Lee and Henry Perkins were assigned to a second mission station at the Narrows, known as Wascopam. Although the Methodist presence lasted only nine years, this station established a permanent American foothold at the most important site of the Lower Columbia, forming an essential link between the plateau and the Willamette Valley.

The Presbyterian Mission

Established in 1810, the American Board of Commissioners for Foreign Missions (ABCFM) was the missionary organization of the Congregational and Presbyterian churches. The ABCFM had plans for the Northwest from the beginning: "As to the north-west of our own continent, the duty of sending a mission thither has been the subject of conversation and reflection from the origin of the Board. It is now time to act."[9] The ABCFM finally acted in 1834, in response to the "Macedonian Call." It assigned Samuel Parker, a Presbyterian minister from Ithaca, New York, to "an exploring mission" to Oregon. The following spring, Parker and his associate, Marcus Whitman, a physician and church elder from Wheeler, New York, traveled to the Rockies with the American Fur Company (AFC).

Parker and Whitman, like the Lees, first encountered Sahaptians at the rendezvous on the Green River. Based on "conversation and prayer" with Flathead and "Napierses" "chiefs," they concluded these people "present a promising field for missionary labor, which is white for the harvest."[10] (Just months earlier, Bonneville had noted of the same people, "They are, certainly, more like a nation of saints than a horde of savages."[11]) Whitman returned east to make arrangements with the ABCFM to return with a missionary party the following year. Whitman took two Nez Perce boys, with the permission of their fathers, back to New York. He named them Richard and John and planned to have them learn English to serve as mission interpreters. Parker proceeded to Oregon, agreeing to meet Whitman at the next rendezvous.

Under the protection of the HBC, Parker took detailed notes of his travels on the Columbia and Willamette. Jean Toupin, the interpreter at Fort Walla Walla, accompanied Parker on his visits with the Cayuse and Nez Perce. According to Toupin, Parker explained to the Cayuse headmen at *Pašxápa*—specifically, Hiyumtipin, his brother Feathercap ("Tamsucky"), and his brother-in-law Teloukaikt—that a doctor would soon arrive to build a "preaching house" and a school on their land. Toupin quoted Parker as saying, "I do not intend to take your lands for nothing. After the Doctor is come, there will come every year a big ship loaded with goods to be divided among the Indians. Those goods will not be sold, but given to you. The missionaries will bring you ploughs and hoes, to learn you how to cultivate the land, and they will not sell but will give them to you."[12] Confident that he had acquired sufficient information about the region, Parker departed for home, via Hawaii, in June 1836.

At the same time, the ABCFM missionary party was on its way to Oregon: Marcus Whitman was joined by his wife, Narcissa; Henry and

Eliza Spalding; the carpenter William Gray; and the Nez Perce boys Richard and John. Henry Spalding was the Presbyterian minister of the party. Of course, Parker failed to meet them at the rendezvous.[13]

In September, they were greeted by John McLoughlin at the bustling Fort Vancouver, dubbed by Narcissa "the New York of the Pacific Ocean." Whitman, Spalding, and Gray then went back up the Columbia to locate sites for their missions. Due to personality clashes during the overland trek, it was decided that Spalding and Whitman would establish separate missions. A party of Nez Perce arrived at Fort Walla Walla to escort the missionaries to the Clearwater. However, Whitman chose to live among the Cayuse (and the Frenchtown community). He was encouraged to do so by Hiyumtipin and against the advice of the Nez Perce, who warned: "[We] do not have difficulties with the white man as Cayous do and [you] will see the difference."[14] Whitman settled on a spot at the mouth of Mill Creek, about 25 miles from the fort. The site was a short distance to the west of *Pašxápa*, among the people known to the Nez Perce as *Waiilatpu*. Whitman called the mission "Wiiletpoo," because it "was originally the name of the Kayuse people."[15]

Spalding selected a site near the mouth of Lapwai Creek on the Clearwater. His station was remote from the forts and White settlements; however, Spalding was among welcoming people. In particular, he had the support of two important headmen: Tamootsin and Twitekis (christened Timothy and Joseph, respectively—the latter was the son of the Cayuse leader Wilewmutkin and father of the more famous Joseph). Whitman, on the other hand, would never attract such figures of authority among the Cayuse to his side. The Whitmans were hopeful that Cayuse Halket, a son of the younger Wilewmutkin, would return soon after five years of schooling at the Red River colony and serve as an interpreter and assistant to the mission.[16] Halket's uncles included the brothers Tawatoy and Five Crows (Umatilla Valley Cayuse), their half-brother Joseph (Wallowa Nez Perce), and their brother-in-law Peo-Peo-Mox-Mox (Walla Walla).

The first house at Waiilatpu, built with the assistance of two Hawaiians hired at Fort Vancouver and some Frenchtown neighbors, was a hastily constructed grooved-post structure. The style and scale of this house—unlike his subsequent buildings—would have blended in among those of Whitman's Frenchtown neighbors. The most readily available green cottonwood was used; there was no time to cure the lumber. The walls were reinforced with adobe bricks, a technique familiar to the Hawaiians, of course, but the decision to use adobe may already have been made at Fort Hall, where adobe was used extensively.

It is hard to imagine the Whitmans at this point had much time or energy for missionary work. In March, Narcissa gave birth to a daughter, the house was still under construction, and virgin soil needed to be cleared and tilled. The missionaries' instructions from the ABCFM were contradictory: on the one hand, preaching in English was emphasized; it was believed that the word would reach the hearts of their audience. On the other hand, they needed to become self-sufficient as soon as possible.[17] Additionally, Whitman was determined to introduce the Cayuse to farming, but instead he was introduced to both the dispersal of his flock with the spring migration and—when they *were* present—the social convention that manual labor, like digging, was the work of women and slaves (which contradicted both Whitman's social and moral conventions). Nonetheless, Whitman wrote overoptimistically to the ABCFM in 1837, "I think there can be no doubt of their readiness to adopt cultivation & when they have plenty of food, they will be little disposed to wander."[18]

Arguably, Whitman's one accomplishment was to sell some Cayuse on farming. Teaching agriculture and demonstrating its advantages were the easy part of Whitman's mission; everyone in the region was already aware of the flourishing farms and gardens around Frenchtown. And small-scale farming *could* be incorporated into the seasonal rounds. However, conveying to the Cayuse the Presbyterian concepts of atonement and salvation was unthinkable without command of a common language. Descriptions of how Whitman later delivered sermons in pseudo-Nez Perce or with the assistance of interpreters show that he fell far short of the language requirement. Nonetheless, initially, when the Cayuse were in their winter villages, the school was well attended, and large groups gathered for Sunday sermons.

Whitman either disregarded or was unaware of the fundamental promise of annual gifts made by Parker to Hiyumtipin. Certainly, the ABCFM had no intention of carrying out such a policy. And from the start, Whitman seemed oblivious to the essential etiquette of reciprocity. Perhaps his greatest failure was to never understand that the land on which he lived, the water that he consumed, and the trees that he harvested were not simply gifts of the Cayuse headmen. The anthropologist Theodore Stern noted, "fort and mission station were not categorically distinct" to the Cayuse, and suggested that the headmen hoped "that with encouragement these Americans might develop into a full-fledged trading opposition [to the HBC]."[19] Whitman reported to the ABCFM in 1837, "the only thing which has given me trouble among them is this wish for us to become an oposition Trader among them. They have seen a little of oposition in trade [i.e., Bonneville] which has caused them to think more of large prices for their beaver & horses than anything else."[20] Whitman, however, was not a trader. And Hiyumtipin was displeased with him from the start. After just two weeks at Waiilatpu, Narcissa wrote, "The old Chief Umtippe has been a savage creature in his day. His heart is still the same, full of all manner of hypocrisy deceit and guile. He is a mortal beggar as all Indians are. If you ask a favour of him, sometimes it is granted or not just as he feels, if granted it must be well paid for. A few days ago he took it into his head to require pay for teaching us the language & forbid his people from coming & talking with us for fear we should learn a few words from them."[21] Only the friendly Nez Perce headman Lawyer (Hallalhotsoot), who lived near Spalding, offered to assist Whitman with the language.

Prior to his first harvest, Whitman possessed only one trade item: medical care. And Hiyumtipin quickly made use of this. In February 1838, many Cayuse developed a lung inflammation. Hiyumtipin ordered Whitman to attend to his ailing wife. Narcissa wrote, "Umtippe got in a rage about his wife & told my Husband while she was under his care that if his wife died that night he should kill him. The contest has been sharp between him & the Indians. . . ." The Whitmans quickly learned the word *te-wat* and came to understand the precarious existence of the healer. Hiyumtipin relied on both Whitman and a Walla Walla *te-wat* for his family's ailments. Narcissa continued,

> Last Saturday the War Chief died at W Walla he was a Cayuse & a relative of Umtippe was sick but six days, employed the same W. W. Tewat Umtippe sent for but he died in his hands. The same day ["Frank Escaloom"] a younger brother of Umtippe went to W W arrived about twilight & shot the Te-wat dead. Thus they were avenged. . . . It has been & still is the case with them that when one dies in your care they will hold you responsible for his life, & you are in great danger of being killed.[22]

Whitman also cared for Itstikats ("Stickus"), a Cayuse headman from the Umatilla Valley. Itstikats was cured and remained a friend of the mission. However, his village was 30 miles away.

Contrary to their optimistic correspondence, missionary life became increasingly painful and intolerable for the Whitmans. In May 1837, with so much work to be done at the missions, William Gray, who irritated everyone he met but whose labor the Whitmans required, departed overland for New York. That fall, as the Whitmans anxiously awaited the arrival of Cayuse Halket, word reached Waiilatpu that he had died at Red River. In December, the Walla Walla River rose and flooded their house. A second flood in March forced Whitman to plan a move to higher ground. Jason Lee visited Whitman and Spalding in spring 1838, during his overland trek to New England with a plan to return by ship with a much larger reinforcement. Naturally envious of Lee's apparent success, Whitman and Spalding appealed to the ABCFM to send a large supply of trade goods (including weapons and ammunition) and their own reinforcement of 220! Both requests would be denied. However, as they were drafting their letter, a reinforcement of nine had already embarked on their overland journey. The reinforcements arrived in September 1838, consisting of William Gray, returning with his wife; the Congregationalists Cushing and Myra Eells, Elkanah and Mary Walker, Asa and Sarah Smith; and a volunteer, Cornelius Rogers. During their overland trek, the party also struggled with personality clashes. The Walkers and Eellses decided to establish a mission together among the Spokan.

The entire mission party shared the original house, of which Cushing Eells wrote, "It is built of adobe. . . . I can not describe its appearance as I can not compare it with anything I ever saw. There are doors and windows, but they are of the roughest kind; the boards being sawed by hand and put together by no carpenter, but by one who knew nothing about such work."[23] Sarah Smith added, "One side of it has partly fallen down & [is] propped up with large poles."[24] That fall, without the consent of Hiyumtipin, the Whitman house and grounds were occupied by at least twenty White and Métis people. Fortunately, Whitman had a good harvest (wheat, corn, potatoes, melons, and vegetables) to complement the mission's primary diet of horse meat. Asa Smith noted that "near 300 bushels" of corn had been harvested and hauled to the mission by the Cayuse women (probably slaves, but the missionaries made a point of omitting mention of slavery in their correspondence).

After the harvest, the mission community focused on the erection of a new adobe mission house. Construction of the building continued for almost a decade and developed organically. It was designed in the form of a **T**. The main section (the short side of the **T**) was oriented north-south, with the ell extended to the east. The rooms were about 20 feet wide. Additional rooms could be added as necessary in any of three directions by extending the walls and roof. In 1847, the "Doby house" was 61 feet wide and the ell extended 80 feet.

Asa Smith's decision to go to Oregon had been based on the glowing letters Spalding had written to the ABCFM, which were extracted and published in the *Missionary Herald*. Smith felt deceived and became a harsh critic of Spalding and Whitman, and the Smiths soon left to live among the Nez Perce, specifically to learn the language. In 1841, after three miserable years and numerous letters complaining about Whitman, Spalding, and Gray, the Smiths left for Hawaii.

During the tumultuous period following the arrival of the reinforcements, the Whitmans considered moving to the Willamette Valley. As they agonized over this decision, in June 1839, their two-year-old daughter drowned in the Walla Walla River. Somehow, this shocking, horrific event convinced them to remain at Waiilatpu. Whitman later wrote to the ABCFM that they would have left the mission "had not the Providence of God arrested me in my deliberate determination to do so by taking away our dear child in so sudden a manner by drowning."[25] To such an extent was the world of the Whitmans governed by Providence.

Construction of the new mission house resumed in summer 1839 with the arrival of a number of American overlanders, including the carpenter Asahel Munger. (The number of White occupants at the mission site was in a constant state of flux.) Narcissa had Munger sketch a plan of the expanded mission house, which she notated and included in a letter to her parents in 1840 (fig. 7). The building was fitted with sash windows (some with twenty panes) and even a sash door. Unlike Whitman's first house, this new complex was far out of scale among the buildings of Frenchtown. In fact, only Fort Walla Walla—which, significantly, bestowed annual gifts on the headmen—was larger (fig. 8). Additionally, no mention is made of Whitman requesting or being granted permission from a headman to build

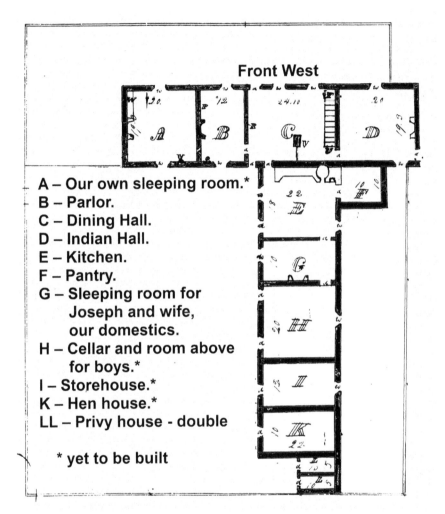

Figure 7. Plan of the mission house by Asahel Munger with Narcissa Whitman's notation, 1840. Despite her plans for a parlor, dining hall, and so on, every room became a dormitory for overland families. She noted the house "will look better when it is whitewashed on the outside." (Adapted from Mss1203 B1F6 010, Oregon Historical Society.)

such a structure. The Whitmans committed a further breach of etiquette by limiting the Cayuse access to just one room. Narcissa emphatically noted that they "shall not permit them to go into the other part of the house at all. They are so filthy they make a great deal of cleaning wherever they go."[26]

The insistence that all other rooms were off-limits to the Cayuse quickly led to problems. When notified of this policy, Teloukaikt—who had succeeded Hiyumtipin as the primary headman in the region—insisted that they pay him for living on his land. He quickly became a bigger threat than the despised Hiyumtipin had been. (Hiyumtipin died the following winter.)

Narcissa's letter to her parents noted, "A tide of immigration appears to be moving this way rapidly. What a few years will bring forth we know not. A great change has taken place even since we first entered the country. . . . We are emphatically situated on the highway between the states and the Columbia River, and are a resting place for the weary travelers." Here is the seed of an additional problem: weary, White overlanders would be welcome inside their house. Narcissa then introduced yet another difficulty: "A Catholic priest has recently been at [Fort] Walla Walla and held meetings with the Indians and used their influence to draw all the people away from us. Some they have forbidden to visit us again, and fill all of their minds with distraction about truths we teach. . . . The conflict has begun—what trials await us we know not."[27]

Figure 8. Paul Kane, *The Whitman Mission at Waiilatpu*, 1847. Graphite on paper. This is the only known image of the mission farm complex. The view is toward the southwest. The rooms were more like individual attached houses, with individual roofs. Based on Narcissa's key (see Figure 7), visible from left to right are rooms G, E, F, and D. Kane, a Toronto-based artist, visited Waiilatpu in July 1847. (Courtesy of ROM [Royal Ontario Museum], Toronto, Canada. ©ROM.)

The Catholic Missionaries

By request of the Canadiens of French Prairie, the HBC provided for the arrival of two Canadien priests: François Norbert Blanchet and Modeste Demers.

The ABCFM missionaries had come of age in a climate of zealous anti-Catholicism. During the 1820s and '30s, journalists and preachers generated an escalating and increasingly venomous flow of propaganda regarding Irish immigration, mistreatment of Protestant girls at convent schools, licentious behavior of priests, and papal schemes to conquer the United States, politically. Anti-Catholicism was a common denominator among the various revival movements that came to be known as the Second Great Awakening. Organizations like the American Bible Society and the American Society to Promote the Principles of the Protestant Reformation supported a series of anti-Catholic—or "No-Popery"—newspapers (e.g., *The Protestant Magazine* and the *American Protestant Vindicator*) and other publications. Traveling lecturers spread the word to rural regions. Boston, the seat of the ABCFM, was a hotbed of "nativist" activity and the scene of their most violent act: the burning of a convent school in 1834. Anti-Catholicism was also widespread in western New York, the birthplace of Spalding and the Whitmans, which came to be known as "the Burned Over District" for the fervor of its revivalist activity. The Congregational minister Lyman Beecher was among the most influential anti-Catholics of the era. During his ministry in Boston (1826–32) and as president of the Lane Seminary in Cincinnati (1832–52), Beecher's strong opinions on temperance, abolition, and Catholicism were widely read and discussed. In 1835, his anti-Catholic rants were compiled into his widely circulated book *A Plea for the West*. He warned of the growing threat posed to the United States by European "popery," which he insisted went hand in hand with European despotism and was thus antithetical to American principles of liberty and democracy. Beecher asserted, "the religious and political destiny of our nation is to be decided in the West. . . . [T]he conflict which is to decide the destiny of the West, will be a conflict of institutions for the education of her sons, for purposes of superstition, or evangelical light; of despotism, or liberty."[28] The Oregon missionaries had direct ties to Beecher: the Spaldings had studied with him at Lane, the Whitmans and the reinforcement party spent time with him in Cincinnati, and Cornelius

Rogers had been a member of his church. The *Missionary Herald* regularly attacked Catholic missionaries as "wicked" and "poisonous."

Canadien Catholicism was a particular focus of the No-Popery literature, which reached a crescendo in 1836 with the publication of *Awful Disclosures of Maria Monk*. Supposedly penned by a former nun at a convent in Montreal, the book offers eyewitness details to support numerous nativist claims against Catholicism—above all, accounts of the systematic rape of nuns at the hands of priests and the ritualistic baptism and murder of the resulting babies. Within months, the book underwent numerous reprintings, reeditions, and expansions, and soon made its way to Oregon.[29]

––––––––

Blanchet and Demers arrived in Oregon with orders from the Bishop of Quebec "to withdraw [the Indians] from barbarity," to serve "the wicked Christians who . . . live in licentiousness," and "to take possession of [the populated] places in the name of the Catholic religion."[30] The priests had significant advantages over the Protestants. Above all, they did not need to concern themselves with farming; they were provided for by their congregation and the HBC; and they benefited from the kinship ties of the Canadiens and their Indigenous wives. They quickly learned Chinook Wawa, and, with the use of visual aids, were able to more effectively convey the basic tenets of their faith. They had no qualms about bestowing the sacrament of baptism on anyone who so requested. Because they were not bound to a mission complex, they were free to expand their field of operation, and Blanchet relished competition with the Protestant missionaries.[31] And, as Stern noted, "Here was another opposition for the Cayuse to play to advantage."[32]

Demers was the priest mentioned in Narcissa's letter. He had baptized a number of Cayuse at Fort Walla Walla during summer 1839. The number of priests in the Far West was just beginning to surpass that of the Protestants. During 1840, the Belgian American Jesuit Pierre-Jean De Smet traveled among the Salish people. A year later, he returned with assistants to establish a string of missions. In 1842, he met with Blanchet at Fort Vancouver. The anxiety among the Protestant missionaries was well summarized in a letter by Narcissa in 1842: "Romanism stalks abroad on our right hand and on our left, and with daring effrontery boasts that she is to prevail and possess the land. . . . The zeal and energy of her [priests] are without a parallel."[33]

———

During late summer 1840, some Americans passed through Waiilatpu. With the dissolution of the AFC, a number of former employees, including Robert Newell, Joe Meek, and William Craig, settled with their families in Oregon.[34] En route, they led the first overland families into Oregon. Gray was building a tub mill, a large house for his family, and a blacksmith shop at Waiilatpu. The scale of Whitman's complex now eclipsed Fort Walla Walla. And again, there is no mention of permission for the expansion being requested or granted from a headman. At the same time, the Cayuse were growing disinterested in Whitman's sermons and increasingly threatening in their encounters with Whitman and Gray. Different headmen were demanding payment for the use of their land. Spalding and Smith were similarly being threatened by once-friendly Nez Perces.

The greatest boost to American colonization appeared in 1841 with the arrival of the United States Exploring Expedition under the command of Lt. Charles Wilkes. The expedition's Joseph Drayton briefly visited Waiilatpu in July, with an eye on future colonization. While Drayton, like all members of the Wilkes party, was unimpressed with the missionary work being conducted in Oregon by the Protestants, he was impressed by Whitman's farm.

4

Oregon Fever

A merican colonization of Oregon became an increasingly urgent issue in the late 1830s, primarily due to the relentless lobbying efforts of Missouri's senators, Thomas Hart Benton and Lewis Linn. Unlike the small-scale, private commercial and missionary interests in the territory, they proposed bills to authorize the president to occupy Oregon militarily and to open it for settlement to American farmers. Congress consistently rejected these bills, however, citing the insignificant size of the American population there and fear of inciting an unnecessary war with Britain. However, the Panic of 1837 and the ensuing depression hit farmers, merchants, and laborers particularly hard in the South and the Mississippi Valley. The proposals of Benton and Linn, which focused on free land and military protection against Indians and "foreign forces," gained increasing support in Congress. And, more significantly, newspapers across the country came to regularly publish and republish letters and articles promoting colonization and congressional action. Yet the administrations of Martin Van Buren and John Tyler paid little attention to Oregon.

Elijah White, Subagent of Indian Affairs for Oregon

White had been a major critic of Jason Lee's leadership since arriving with the second Methodist reinforcement in 1837. After being dismissed by Lee in 1840, he sailed back to the United States and used his connections in Congress to receive an appointment as subagent of Indian Affairs for Oregon. Thus, White was the first government official appointed to Oregon. In May 1842, with the blessing of Linn and Benton, White departed from Missouri for Oregon with a party of 114, many of whom he had personally recruited. He was also carrying an important letter from the ABCFM to its missionaries in Oregon.

When the party arrived at Waiilatpu on September 9, Whitman found an eager market for his livestock and crops. However, the letter from Boston informed Whitman and his colleagues that, based on several years of troubling reports from the missionary party, the board had decided to close both the Waiilatpu and Lapwai missions, to recall the Spaldings, Smiths, and Grays, and to have the Whitmans join the Spokan mission. Whitman weighed this news together with news of the inevitable settlement of the Oregon Question. After conferring with his colleagues, he decided to trek overland to Boston—despite the onset of winter—to save his well-situated farm. He departed October 3.

White's governmental authority was immediately put to the test. On his arrival in the Willamette Valley, he found the colonists in a state of alarm, convinced of an imminent attack by the Sahaptians. The procession of overlanders followed by the sudden departure of Whitman generated great anxiety among the Cayuse and Nez Perce. One overlander noted in his journal the day after camping near Whitman's mission: "Having recd verry bad treatment from the Indians we concluded to get away from here as soon as possible."[1] Various rumors were spread among the Cayuse and their allies, none of which suggested a happy future. A few days after Whitman's departure, someone attempted to break into Narcissa's room while she slept. This led to her removal to Wascopam—which only generated more ominous rumors among the Cayuse. A few weeks later, one of Feather-cap's sons burned Whitman's grist mill and grain supply (perhaps in reaction to Whitman's insistence that Indians never touch the mill). Additionally, a number of Delawares (*Lenape*) were living among the Sahaptians and relating stories of how their families had been forcibly removed from their lands. In November, White set out with a group of HBC men to assert his authority on the plateau. With the Cayuse unwilling to meet with him, the party traveled to Lapwai, where White assembled twenty-two Nez Perce and Cayuse headmen for the first US-Indian council in the territory. He asked the various bands to select individual head chiefs and to abide by a set of laws, the "Nez Perce Laws," as he called them. Among the eleven Hammurabi-like articles to which the appointed chiefs were asked to agree were:

1. Whoever willfully takes life shall be hung.
2. Whoever burns a dwelling-house shall be hung.

10. If any Indian raise a gun or other weapon against a white man, it shall be reported to the chiefs, and they shall punish him. If a white man do the same to an Indian, it shall be reported to Dr. White, and he shall punish or redress it.
11. If an Indian break these laws, he shall be punished by his chiefs; if a white man break them, he shall be reported to the agent, and punished at his instance.[2]

The Nez Perce eagerly accepted the laws and selected Ellis, the Red River scholar, as their head chief. In spring, after further reports of Cayuse threats, White held a council at Waiilatpu. (While awaiting the arrival of the headmen, Feathercap gave him a tour of about sixty individual Cayuse farms at *Pašxápa*.) A temporary 75-foot lodge covered with bison hides was constructed for the council. Teloukaikt and the recently baptized Catholic, Tawatoy, spoke for the Cayuse and Peo-Peo-Mox-Mox (fig. 12) for the Walla Walla. All expressed doubts that Whites would honor any agreement, and all were confused to learn that the position of head chief came without economic benefits. Nonetheless, despite much apprehension, the laws were adopted. Tawatoy was elected head chief. However, hoping to unify the deeply divided Cayuse, he nominated his brother Five Crows (fig. 11), who was then elected in his place.[3] The council concluded with a feast attended by 600 men, women, and children. It soon became apparent, however, that Indians and Whites were not treated equally under the laws. By the time he returned east in 1845 (to lobby for colonization), it was clear that White's brief tenure as Indian agent had only escalated anxieties among Indigenous people throughout Oregon.

The Overlanders of 1843

Aside from visiting the ABCFM in Boston and family in New York, little reliable information exists regarding Whitman's activities in the States. However, soon after entering Missouri, Whitman would have found himself in the midst of "Oregon fever." Parties were organizing throughout the western states in preparation for a departure from Missouri in the spring. Peter Burnett, a lawyer and bankrupt merchant in Weston, Missouri, was perhaps the most enthusiastic and influential recruiter in the country. His speeches were printed and reprinted in papers everywhere. The reintroduction of Senator Linn's Oregon bill at the end of December 1842 and the subsequent deliberations in the Senate were widely—and optimistically—covered in the press. (The bill passed the Senate but was then held up by the House Committee on Foreign Relations.) *"The Oregon fever has broken out, and is now raging like any other contagion."* Beginning that winter, this phrase was printed so often that it does not seem to have an origin.

Numerous papers carried reports of both hard times and the formation of migration companies—often in the same article. The St. Louis correspondent of the *New York Herald*, for example, wrote in April 1843, "There is very little business of any kind doing in St. Louis at this time. Hundreds of mechanics may be found here idle and in a state of absolute penury. . . . There are several expeditions to leave here on or about the 1st of May for the Oregon Territory, Rocky Mountains, &c. There are hundreds of young men anxious to accompany them—many of whom will be unable to go for the want of means to fit themselves out."[4] Thomas Farnham's *Travels in the Great Western Prairies . . . and in the Oregon Territory* appeared in winter 1843 and was extensively discussed throughout the spring. Washington Irving's *The Adventures of Captain Bonneville*, published in 1837, also served as something of a guidebook to Oregon. In February, the *New York Tribune* reported on Elijah White's assessment of the migration party of 1842: "He says no doubt exists as to the ultimate success of the colony."[5] Naturally, this article was picked up by papers throughout the states.

Perhaps inspired by the publicity White was receiving, Marcus Whitman called on Horace Greeley, editor of the *New York Tribune*, on March 28. Above all, Greeley was fascinated by Whitman's appearance: "He was dressed in an old fur cap that appeared to have seen some ten years' service, faded and nearly destitute of fur; a vest whose natural color had long since fled; and a shirt—we could not see that he had any; an overcoat every thread of which could be easily seen; buckskin pants, &c.—the roughest man we have seen this many a day—too poor in fact to get any better wardrobe!" Certainly, Whitman *chose* this outfit for his meeting with the media. Interestingly, Greeley pointed out, "We did not learn what success the worthy man had in leading the Indians to embrace the Christian faith." Missionary work seems to have been on the back burner that day. The most important news Whitman provided for many readers was "that the settlers on the Willamette are doing well [and that they] are building a town at the falls of the Willamette."[6] This article was also republished in several papers.

Americans were also well aware that the recently created Corps of Topographical Engineers had been commissioned to explore the overland route to Oregon. A widely republished report from the *St. Louis Reporter* (June 14, 1842) noted, "This expedition is connected with the proposition now before Congress, to occupy the territory about Columbia river, as proposed by Dr. Linn's bill." In fact, the expedition was led by Senator Benton's enormously ambitious son-in-law, Lt. John C. Frémont. The report of the first phase of the expedition—from Missouri to the Rockies—was published by Congress in March 1843 and widely covered and excerpted in the press. The second phase of the expedition in 1843 took Frémont and his well-armed party of forty to Oregon and then into Alta California, Mexico. The final report (published in 1845) regularly made note, optimistically, of the progress and condition of the overlanders.

Along with notices of departures for Oregon, papers carried announcements of the formation of citizen committees to discuss departure for Oregon the following spring. The papers also republished optimistic letters received from Peter Burnett and other overlanders during their trek. The *New York Herald* published several excerpts from Frémont's report in September and gloriously concluded, "[T]he evening hymn of the white settlers, risen from the banks of the Wallamette, and the echo is caught and repeated from the advancing bands in the mountain passes. And when . . . railroad communication across the prairies [is completed] a new empire will be at once created on the shores of the Pacific, the twin sister of our glorious Union a new field for the enterprise of starving thousands, a new step to the advancement of the human race, a new era in its history."[7] (Of course, this too was republished widely.) In fall 1843, Henry Sager sold his farm and blacksmith shop in eastern Missouri and made preparations to trek to Oregon in the spring with his wife Naomi and their six children. Hundreds of families were making similar preparations.

Waiilatpu 1843–45

Perhaps 800 Americans straggled into Oregon in late summer 1843. Some were escorted to Fort Walla Walla by Whitman's friend Itstikats.

Whitman returned to Waiilatpu with his nephew, Perrin Whitman, at the end of September. Narcissa, who had spent the year at Wascopam and in the Willamette Valley, was in poor health and had no desire to return to the mission ("I felt such a dread to return to this place of moral darkness, after enjoying so much of civilized life and Christian privileges."[8]). The mission period had fully come to an end with Whitman's departure in 1842. His primary concern became Protestant American colonization. His attitude regarding Indians and colonization was best articulated in a letter to his parents in 1844:

> Although the Indians have made and are making rapid advance in religious knowledge and civilization, yet it cannot be hoped that time will be allowed to mature either the work of Christianization or civilization before the white settlers will demand the soil and seek the removal of both the Indians and the Mission. . . . I am fully convinced that when a people refuse or neglect to fill the designs of Providence, they ought not to complain at the results. . . . The Indians have in no case obeyed the command to multiply and replenish the earth, and they cannot stand in the way of others in doing so.[9]

(During his time in the East, Whitman seems to have become a convert of the racial theory soon to be dubbed "manifest destiny.") Once back at Waiilatpu, he drafted a memorial and long letter to the secretary of war spelling out an elaborate plan of colonization. He called for the construction of a string of adobe forts along the overland route, which would eradicate the HBC "desparadoes," and would be empowered "to execute summary justice" on the Indians. He closed his letter, "Hoping that these suggestions may meet your approbation and conduce to the future interests of our growing Colony."[10]

Whitman's anti-Catholicism was reinforced during his trip with his acquisition of Father de Smet's recently published memoir. He was especially enraged by a letter included by Blanchet. Just before departing for his return journey, Whitman wrote to the secretary of the ABCFM encouraging him to read the book, particularly Blanchet's letter, to fully understand the effort to win Oregon for European Catholicism. Blanchet wrote,

> We are in the mean time surrounded by sects who are using all their efforts to scatter every where the poisonous seeds of error, and who try to paralyze the little good we may effect. . . . In the midst of so many

adversaries we try to . . . increase our numbers, and to visit various parts, particularly where the danger is most pressing. . . . The conflict has been violent, but the savages now begin to open their eyes as to who are the real ministers of Jesus Christ. Heaven declares itself in our favor. . . . It is here that we should have a college, convent, and schools. . . . Here is the field of battle, where we must in the first place gain the victory.[11]

De Smet's book also included a tipped-in, 24 × 7–inch Catholic ladder of de Smet's design.[12] Whitman must have stewed over this book throughout his grueling trek. His subsequent letters rarely failed to mention the evil doings of the "the Papists." In his first letter to the ABCFM after his return to Waiilatpu, he wrote, "I feel that this country must either be American or else foreign and mostly papal. . . . I cannot feel that we can look on and see foreign and papal influence making its greatest efforts and we hold ourselves as expatriated and neutral."[13] By the time the last overlanders had passed in fall 1843, the population of Whitman's farm had ballooned to more than forty. A school was opened for fifteen White children. (It became Whitman's practice to annually hire overlanders to run the school.) Neither Whitman nor the Cayuse demonstrated any interest in reestablishing the Indian school. Overlanders' accounts of passing through Cayuse territory mention peacefully trading for livestock, fruits, and vegetables but also of threats and isolated acts of violence.

As many as 1,500 trekked to Oregon in 1844. By winter, about seventy Whites were living at Whitman's farm. Among the residents were the seven Sager children, including a newborn, whose parents had died *en route*. Whitman used his new boarders, including a millwright, to begin construction of a new grist mill and a sawmill 20 miles up Mill Creek. Despite the size of the Whitman colony, fall and winter 1844–45 was a time of quiet; a large party of Sahaptians had traveled to Alta California to trade for weapons and cattle at John Sutter's fort, New Helvetia, and probably to collect slaves in Northern California. However, the situation at Waiilatpu changed forever with their return in spring. Following a dispute at New Helvetia, Toayahnu ("Elijah Hedding"), son of Peo-Peo-Mox-Mox and nephew of Five Crows and Tawatoy, was murdered by an American.[14] The Protestant missionaries throughout the territory had high expectations for Elijah, who had been educated among the Methodists. Naturally, Peo-Peo-Mox-Mox needed to be avenged. Overton Johnson and William

H. Winter left a remarkable account of the tense situation on the plateau in spring 1845. They were overlanders of 1843, who journeyed back east after two years in Oregon. Their travelogue offers this account from May 1845:

> While we were encamped in the neighborhood of the Mission, a party of twenty or thirty Chiefs and braves, a deputation from the Walawala, Nex Pierce, and Kious Indians, came, and met in council with Dr. Whitman, Mr. Spaulding, and other gentlemen connected with the Mission. They told the Missionaries that the hearts of some of their people were bad; and the object of the council proved to be a trial, to ascertain whether Dr. Whitman was not worthy of death. . . . [Because Peo-Peo-Mox-Mox's] son had been killed by an American in California, the Walawala Chief demanded the life of Dr. Whitman. He argued that it would be no more than just and equal, since his son was a preacher, to take the life of a preacher for satisfaction. . . . Dr. Whitman reasoned with them, and appealed to them, by every means, which he thought would tend, in the least, to affect them in his favor; and so did all the others; but it was in vain. After a long consultation, by which they appeared to be not the least shaken in their opinions, they went away, saying that they could not help what their young men might do.[15]

Johnson, Winter, and their small party were harassed until they left Sahaptian territory.[16] Whitman, under the urging of his colleagues, left his farm for a trip to Oregon City (where, among other things, he gained legal guardianship of the Sager children).

Whitman probably came to appreciate the seasonal rounds and the bison expeditions that removed his adversaries from the area. Nonetheless, the threats only increased with the arrival of about 2,500 overlanders into Oregon in 1845. That fall, Whitman was assaulted by Tomahas, a younger brother of Feathercap and a prominent Cayuse farmer. The altercation resulted from what Tomahas perceived to be Whitman's monopolistic control of the gristmill. Tomahas was restrained by Teloukaikt (perhaps his uncle). Whitman was far more troubled by a conversation a few weeks later with Tawatoy, who noted that Whites had killed Elijah Hedding and were responsible for the death of Cayuse Halket. Both were his nephews. And both had been educated at White schools. He also blamed the Americans for the deaths of some of his people by either poison or infection and accused Whitman of possessing poison. According to Whitman, Tawatoy left the decision of abandoning Waiilatpu to him.[17]

John McLoughlin may have intervened on Whitman's behalf in meetings with Peo-Peo-Mox-Mox, Five Crows, and Ellis at Fort Vancouver, and he may have convinced them to not retaliate against Sutter. Peo-Peo-Mox-Mox led another party to the Sacramento Valley in fall 1846 to trade and visit his son's grave. It remains unclear to what degree vengeance was part of his plan.

The Provisional Government of Oregon

The Willamette colony had begun holding organizational meetings in 1841. Augmented by the overlanders, in 1843, they established the Provisional Government of Oregon and enacted the Organic Laws of Oregon. Two years earlier, Senator Linn had unsuccessfully proposed to extend the Organic Act of the Territory of Iowa (of 1839) to Oregon. These laws were now adopted to serve the colonists until the United States formally established jurisdiction over the territory.

The laws of the Provisional Government initially struck a benevolent tone regarding the vast majority of the region's population: "The utmost good faith shall always be observed towards the Indians. Their lands and property shall never be taken from them without their consent; and, in their property, rights, and liberty, they shall never be invaded or disturbed, unless in just and lawful wars."[18] However, the benevolence of the Organic Laws stopped at citizenship, which was offered to "every free male descendant of a white man." While explicitly banning slavery, the Laws also barred Blacks from settling in the territory.

The overlanders of 1843 and 1844 dramatically transformed the Provisional Government. In 1845, the Laws were revised to establish an elected governor, a house of representatives, and a judicial system. In 1844 and 1845, parties were sent to Washington with petitions requesting ratification of their government by Congress and calling again for both US territorial status and military protection.

The territory's first newspaper appeared in Oregon City in 1846: the fortnightly *Oregon Spectator*, established by an organization of Methodists and recent arrivals. Carrying the seemingly timeless motto "Westward the Star of Empire takes its Way," it served as the mouthpiece for the legislature, printing its laws, its amendments, and all speeches by the governor. It also published advertisements, letters by subscribers, and stories from American papers (up to eight months after their initial publication). The "Act to Establish the Territorial Government of Oregon," passed by the US House of Representatives on April 19, 1846, appeared in the *Spectator* on October 1, 1846. However, passage of the bill required conclusion of the Oregon Treaty, which was finally signed June 15. The November 12 issue carried excerpts of letters by Elijah White to the *Washington Union*, written since his return there to present the memorial from the Provisional Government. He attested to the Oregon colonists' strong devotion to the United States, criticized Congress for dragging its feet regarding Oregon, and praised "the red men of that region" who "seem to be of a different order from those with whom we have been in more familiar intercourse." White focused his admiration on the "Keyuse," who "raise all the commodities peculiar to our western states, and live in a comfortable manner. Their country is a verdant and beautiful one, and their prospects for ultimate civilization encouraging."[19] He attributed this surprising development to the missionaries and the HBC (perhaps the last compliment paid to the HBC by an American for decades). Despite White's optimism, the *Spectator* had, from the start, abandoned the Laws' benevolent attitude regarding Indians in general. It regularly printed rumors and accounts of atrocities inflicted on overlanders by "savages," particularly on the Great Plains—despite the fact that only a tiny percentage of overlander deaths were caused by Indians.[20] These rumors increased in number and brutality in 1847 as the number of overlanders swelled to more than 4,000.

Racialism and Manifest Destiny

The overlanders brought with them a new ideology regarding Indians that radically differed from that of the missionaries of the 1830s. The missionaries had conveyed an Enlightenment belief to their relationship with the people of the Northwest; Indians could be civilized, they believed, by adopting agrarianism and Christianity. Despite the failure or disregard of this theory in the East, these missionaries possessed an unyielding assurance that they were tools of Providence. This optimistic belief in redemption of the Indian was sustained primarily in the cities of the Northeast, where Indigenous people either were invisible or posed no economic threat. On the other hand, in areas where Americans were pushing into valued Indian land—in the Mississippi Valley, for example—violence and hatred were manifested on both sides (just as it had been in early colonial New England). The image of the noble savage did not exist at the western borderlands. Many Whites there stemmed from families that had battled for Indian land for generations. They viewed all Indians in their path as subhuman, as annoying and dangerous. In 1834, Hall Kelley traveled through Alta California and into Oregon with a party of American "Indian hunters," indiscriminately raping, killing, and plundering.[21] Of course, those Indian hunters became the first American colonists in Oregon.

John Frémont's third expedition (1845–46)—which officially had nothing to do with territory west of the Rockies—carried out a series of massacres at Indian villages in Northern California and southern Oregon that were unprecedented in scale and callousness.[22] Frémont's party murdered about 1,000 Wintu men, women, and children in a single attack in April 1846 (near current Redding). A retaliatory attack by the Klamaths resulted in the deaths of two of Frémont's men. Frémont retaliated by attacking random Klamath villages.

John Beeson, an overlander of 1853, was outraged by the determination of the young men in his party "to shoot the first Indian they see."[23] Beeson settled in southern Oregon and quickly established himself as the most active critic of the genocidal mindset of many of his neighbors. Threats by these neighbors forced him to return East two years later.

During the 1830s and '40s, American "scientists" increasingly embraced the European studies of ethnography and phrenology. Ethnographers, led by Samuel G. Morton, introduced to the American public the concepts of (1) polygenesis, which held that God had created not one but multiple original species, including Caucasian, Mongolian, Indian, and African; and (2) inequality among these "races." Their theories claimed to explain the domination of the world by Anglo-Saxons and to justify both the enslavement of Africans and the extermination of Indigenous peoples. Phrenologists claimed that the study of skulls and the "reading" of heads supported their theories of racial inequality. These theories were explained in general terms and widely disseminated in mass-produced magazines and newspapers. By the time of the first overlanders to Oregon, racialist concepts supporting the intellectual and moral superiority of Germanic

Euro-Americans were general knowledge.[24] This racialism was embraced even by many abolitionists and people sympathetic to Indian affairs. Politically, racialist theory provided a justification for Andrew Jackson's Indian Removal Act (1830); for subsequent genocides in Florida, California, and Southern Oregon; and for the United States' annexation of all of North America and Mexico. Unsurprisingly, the term "manifest destiny" first appeared in 1845, in an essay titled "Annexation."[25] And in popular literature, by 1840, the sympathetic treatment of the Indian found in James Fenimore Cooper's *Leatherstocking Tales* was eclipsed by Robert Montgomery Bird's enormously popular book *Nick of the Woods* (1837), featuring a Kentucky Indian-slaughtering hero.

The rhetoric of racialism and manifest destiny made early appearances in the *Spectator*. A letter published in May 1846 stated, "Who will dispute the characteristic boldness of the Anglo-Saxon race in America? It certainly cannot be done in this age. . . . Who may dare to say that this little heroic party, directed hither by Providence, has not carried with it to the shores of the Pacific, the germ of republicanism or self-government, whose limits may be bounded by the Frozen ocean on the north, and Cape St. Luca or Cape Horn on the south?"[26] The language of the official speakers grew increasingly aggressive at Oregon City's Fourth of July celebration of 1846. In a long, venomous speech, William Green T'Vault declared, "[T]he children of education are too powerful for the tribes of aborigines that inhabit this continent. As a race, they have withered, and will continue to do so until their arrows are all broken—their springs all dried up; their wigwams returned to the dust; their council fires will go out; their war-cry will not be heard; they have been long sinking before the mighty tide which has been pressing them from the rising of the sun to the setting; they will soon hear the roar of the last wave that will settle over them forever."[27] T'Vault had served briefly as the first editor of the *Spectator*. The speech of the paper's current editor, Henry A. G. Lee—significantly titled "Annexation"—loudly offered more of the same: "[E]vents seem to denote the extension of the race of the north—the descendants of Saxon blood over the whole continent; and this will be the result not of policy or calculation, but of necessity."[28]

As noted above, even Marcus Whitman had bought into manifest destiny. Tensions between Indigenous and settler communities, fueled by the theories of racialism and dreams of manifest destiny, eventually boiled over at Waiilatpu in 1847.

5

1847–48: All Eyes on Waiilatpu

The Cayuse nation is divided into three camps, entirely distinct from each other, each camp having its own chief, who governs his young people as he pleases; each one of the chiefs is independent of the others; and these three camps form, as it were, three independent states of a small federal republic, each of them administering their own private affairs as they please without interference from the others. They were the camps of Tilokaikt, Camaspelo, and Young Chief and Five Crows together.

—J. B. A. Brouillet[1]

———

Marcus Whitman may not have ignored the wise advice offered by people concerned about his safety and the safety of his family and guests, but he certainly moved slowly in moving on from the intensifying hostility surrounding Waiilatpu. Perhaps he was lulled into believing the hostilities had melted away during the relative calm between the summers of 1846 and 1847. The calm was due to the absence of Peo-Peo-Mox-Mox and many Cayuse warriors. Shortly after they returned, however, the situation for everyone in the region became horrifying.

Peo-Peo-Mox-Mox again led a large Sahaptian party into the Sacramento valley in summer 1846. They arrived just as the US Navy, in collaboration with John Frémont's party and some American colonists, had conquered Northern California. In mid-August, the commander at Sonoma Barracks, Lt. Joseph Warren Revere, received word that "the Sacramento valley had been invaded by a force of one thousand Wallawalla Indians." Revere wrote in his memoir, "The prospect of an engagement with a strong force of warlike savages, at a time when we were threatened with a most tedious tranquillity, was extremely welcome and cheering." However, a deeply disappointed Revere soon discovered that the Sahaptians had come in peace, with only "forty warriors, with their women and little children." On his visit to Peo-Peo-Mox-Mox's camp, Revere "found most of his party sick" and noted, "Most of my men, both whites and Indians, as well as myself, caught the ague and fever from this visit up the Sacramento valley."[2] The Sahaptians were suffering from a disease—perhaps measles—already in late summer 1846. Any plans for vengeance would have been abandoned, either due to illness or on seeing the military strength of Fort Sacramento (formerly New Helvetia). Instead, eleven Sahaptian warriors were hired as scouts for Frémont's California Battalion and were soon commended for their bravery and fighting prowess.[3] After the Mexican surrender of the territory, the warriors rejoined their families and resumed plundering the region's Natives. In May 1847, Peo-Peo-Mox-Mox was given satisfactory compensation at Fort Sacramento, the warrior-scouts were paid in clothing and horses, and the party headed home.

————

About sixty Americans spent the exceptionally brutal winter of 1846–47 at Waiilatpu. At the time, Whitman was grappling with the logistics of actually expanding the ABCFM mission in Oregon. The superintendent of the Methodist mission had offered their Wascopam buildings and farm to Whitman at minimal cost. In the spring, Whitman wrote to the ABCFM, "This will open a new field for our Mission and one we can by no means fail to occupy. For if we allow the Papists to take [the Wascopam] station we might as well give up [Waiilatpu] also."[4]

Whitman was unaware of the important developments of the Catholic missionaries during this relatively quiet period. They had been without their leader, François Blanchet, since December 1844. On receiving word that the pope had established the Oregon territory as an apostolic vicariate and that Blanchet was to be elevated to bishop, Blanchet went by ship to Montreal for his consecration. He then sailed for Europe, where he was celebrated for over a year by the pope and the Catholic aristocracy. In 1846, the papacy established three dioceses within the vicariate, each headed by a bishop: Augustin Blanchet, brother of François, was appointed Bishop of Walla Walla (comprising everything between the Rockies and the Cascades). Archbishop Blanchet returned by ship from France in August 1847, with generous funds and a "religious colony" of twenty-two priests, nuns, and lay brothers.[5] Augustin Blanchet traveled overland from Missouri in

1847, with an entourage including eight priests and oblates from France and Quebec.

––––––––

The fur trade was fading away; the era of the beaver skin hat had ended. The HBC only desired a smooth liquidation of its assets in Oregon. However, the relative calm in the region ended abruptly in July 1847, when an advance messenger from Peo-Peo-Mox-Mox's California party arrived at Fort Walla Walla with news of the illness that was killing members of the party. In fact, the returning party may have carried a measles epidemic to the plateau. They infected both Indians and non-Indians, who in turn infected more Indians and non-Indians, including the arriving overlanders, who then carried the disease down the Columbia.[6] Tensions increased on the plateau like never before. Among the new arrivals was the Blanchet party, which initially moved into Fort Walla Walla.

The measles epidemic of 1847–48 is well documented in letters and firsthand accounts. Among the Cayuse, people of all ages were infected, but the disease may have been most lethal among infants and young children. Multiple deaths occurred daily; ultimately, the disease decimated up to 40 percent of the Cayuse population.[7] Although it may not have been the worst epidemic experienced by the Cayuse, it was the most traumatic event to occur since the arrival of the Whitmans.

In the midst of the epidemic, Augustin Blanchet and his vicar general Jean-Baptiste Brouillet arranged to establish a mission among the Cayuse. Tawatoy had offered the Catholics the house that Pierre Pambrun had built for him in 1840 as a diplomatic gift. However, he was hunting bison when they arrived. According to Brouillet, an enraged Marcus Whitman met Blanchet and his entourage at Fort Walla Walla on September 23: "[Whitman] made a furious charge against the Catholics, accusing them of having persecuted Protestants, and even of having shed their blood wherever they had prevailed. He said . . . that he should oppose the missionaries to the extent of his power. . . . He spoke against the *Catholic Ladder* and said that he would cover it with blood, to show the persecution of Protestants by Catholics." Whitman then visited Peo-Peo-Mox-Mox, Brouillet claimed, to urge him to influence his allies against the Catholics. (Despite Peo-Peo-Mox-Mox's initial reluctance, in

October the oblates established the mission of Saint Rose near the mouth of the Yakima River.) On his return to the region, Tawatoy recommended that the Catholics establish their mission near Whitman instead, "saying that there was more land there than near his house, and that it was more central; that, by his wife, he had a right to the land of Teloukaikt, and that he was disposed to give it to the mission, if Teloukaikt was willing; that he would go and live there himself with his young men, if the mission could be established there." Several meetings were held with Teloukaikt and his headmen in November. According to Thomas McKay, who lived among the Umatilla Cayuse, Feathercap accused Whitman of having robbed and poisoned the Cayuse. McKay added that shortly before these meetings, Whitman had asked him "to go and pass the winter with him, saying that he was afraid of the Indians." He also claimed that Whitman told him "several times . . . that he would leave certainly in the spring for the Dalles." On a tour of his land, Teloukaikt told Brouillet "that he had no other place to give me but that of Dr. Whitman's, whom he intended to send away." The Catholics refused to take Whitman's station, so Tawatoy's house became the seat of the mission of Saint Anne.[8]

The rumor that Whitman was systematically poisoning the Cayuse was fostered by Joe Lewis, a young Métis of mysterious origins (described as either half-Iroquois or half-Delaware), who had recently arrived with the overlanders and worked briefly for Whitman (who found him to be a troublemaker). In November, Lewis informed a Cayuse council that he had overheard Whitman and Spalding discussing plans to acquire *more* poison to kill off all the Cayuse and take their land and possessions. An attack was planned at this time, and the Cayuse headmen and several Métis laborers at the complex were privy to the plans. Itstikats later stated that he had warned Whitman on November 28 that "the bad Indians would kill him."[9]

Meanwhile, Whitman seems to have frantically made rounds to care for the sick among the Cayuse bands, and the Catholics made rounds to baptize and administer last rites. According to Boyd, the epidemic was near its peak in late November. Teloukaikt lost three of his own children. Feathercap, who had lost two children at the Methodist mission in 1837, now lost his wife. On November 29, after Teloukaikt buried his third child and a day after the death of Feathercap's wife, a group of about a dozen Cayuse attacked the Whitman complex. The killings that followed have been described countless times in gruesome yet contradictory detail.[10] According to most witnesses, Tomahas and Teloukaikt entered Whitman's house, Tomahas struck him in the head with an axe, and Teloukaikt shot him. It is unclear whether Teloukaikt had consented to the killing of anyone other than Whitman; only his killing seems to have been planned. However, those outside then began assaulting the adult American male residents— Canadiens and Métis men were unharmed. Seven men were killed or mortally wounded, including the two teenaged Sager boys. Narcissa was the only woman killed. Among the identified attackers were Teloukaikt's sons Edward and Clark; Tomahas's brothers Feathercap, Frank Eskaloom, and Klokamas; and Feathercap's son, Waiecat. (The younger men had all attended the Whitmans' Indian school.)

According to the Cayuse messenger who brought the news of the incident to Lapwai, Joe Lewis had convinced Teloukaikt several days earlier that Whitman needed to be killed to save the Cayuse.[11] Lewis also participated in the attack. Some, including women, plundered the mission house, while others pleaded on behalf of the Americans. On the following day, two bedridden men were killed. Teloukaikt then demanded an end to the violence and restoration of the plundered items. The fifty-four remaining Americans were considered slaves. After learning of the incident, Five Crows had a teenage girl brought to his lodge on the Umatilla. She had been the object of his obsession since he encountered her family on crossing the Blues. Several other girls and women agreed to, or were threatened to, "marry" the killers. Brouillet, who arrived on the 30th, helped bury the bodies and sent notice of the killings to William McBean, the new clerk at Fort Walla Walla. McBean then relayed the news to Fort Vancouver.

Unfortunately, the most important figure of authority in the territory since 1824—John McLoughlin—had been forced into retirement in 1846 and settled in Oregon City. No one would ever command such universal respect of all people in the region. McLoughlin was replaced by two chief factors: James Douglas and Peter Skene Ogden.

The first accounts of the incident to reach the colonists appeared in the *Spectator* on December 10. Among the letters printed in this issue were McBean's to Fort Vancouver and Douglas's to the new provisional governor George Abernethy. McBean affirmed that "the sole cause of the dreadful butchery" was the belief that Whitman was poisoning the Cayuse, a belief that was "unfortunately confirmed by one of the Doctor's party."[12] McBean included the names of the dead and those of "the ring-leaders in this horrible butchery Teloquoit, his son [Edward?], Big Belly [Qemátspelu], Tamsuchy [Feathercap], Esticus [Itstikats], Toumoulish [Tomahas], &c." This was a confusing list; neither Itstikats nor the old war chief Qemátspelu were involved. And what was implied by the "&c."? All the high-status Cayuse? Douglas wrote that "Mr. Ogden with a strong party will leave this place as soon as possible for Walla Walla, to endeavor to prevent further evil."

The newly elected provisional legislature acted quickly on December 8 to authorize the governor to raise a militia and to dispatch it immediately. The First Company of Oregon Riflemen, numbering forty-six, departed the following day under the command of Cornelius Gilliam. Lacking an Indian agent in the region, Henry A. G. Lee, Joel Palmer, and Robert Newell were charged with maintaining peace with the allies of the Cayuse (it was assumed that all the Sahaptians would unite to form an overwhelming force). On the morning of their departure, the governor called for raising a militia of 500, "for the purpose of chastising the Indians engaged in the recent horrid massacre at Waiilatpu." The legislature also prohibited the sale or exchange of weapons or ammunition with Indians.

No one seemed to know exactly what they were responding to. It didn't sound like a demand for justice. And the Provisional Government certainly had no legal jurisdiction in Cayuse territory. Nor did they have an official system of justice in place in the territory. Above all, it was an improvised call for large-scale vigilante action against an imaginary Sahaptian army.

Because of Joe Lewis's deception, the killings were carried out in a desperate attempt at self-preservation. Believing what they were told, the Cayuse genocide was being perpetrated by the long-despised Marcus Whitman on behalf of the Americans. This was not a traditional killing of a *te-wat*, as has often been claimed; to Teloukaikt and his followers, it was the eradication of a mass murderer and fully justified.

Ogden arrived at Fort Walla Walla with an army of sixteen HBC men and a large quantity of trade goods. He was well known to the people of the plateau. In his meeting with Tawatoy, Teloukaikt, Peo-Peo-Mox-Mox, and others, he clarified—in Nez Perce—that the HBC would not take sides in their quarrel with the Americans. He scolded the headmen for losing control of their young warriors and for foolishly believing that Whitman was poisoning them. His sole concern was the release of the hostages. On December 29, after a few days of negotiations, they were released to Ogden in exchange for a great ransom in blankets, clothing, rifles, ammunition, and tobacco. The Spaldings arrived two days later from the custody of some hostile Nez Perces, accompanied by his Nez Perce allies. The following day, the freed hostages, the HBC men, the Spaldings, and Bishop Blanchet all headed down the Columbia, leaving Teloukaikt, Feathercap, and their families to figure out their next move. At The Dalles, Ogden strongly advised the assembled militia against attempting to fight the Cayuse in winter. Spalding, on the other hand, urged them to exterminate the Cayuse.

The January 20 issue of the *Spectator* printed pleas for peace by Blanchet, the Cayuse, and Spalding (to his subsequent embarrassment). The issue led, however, with editor George Curry's announcement of the safe arrival of the hostages to Oregon City, pointing out that "a portion of them have been subjected to further outrage and insult—the basest—the deepest that can possibly be conceived, and from which our mind recoils with horror. . . . [W]e dare not chronicle the terrible story of their wrongs." He demanded a bloody retribution: "But for the barbarian murderers and violaters let there be an eternity of remembrance; let them be pursued with unrelenting hatred and hostility, until their life blood has atoned for their infamous deeds; let them be hunted as beasts of prey; let their name and race be blotted from the face of the earth. . . . Oh, how terrible should be the retribution."[13]

The "Cayuse War"

By February 1848, the Wascopam mission was fortified with a stockade and renamed Fort Wascopam. Almost 500 militiamen assembled and passed through there. The militia was looking to kill Indians, to destroy and plunder villages, and was ordered to confiscate cattle and horses. However, it was burdened by unreliable intelligence, ignorance of Sahaptian military tactics, ignorance of the terrain, concern about being away from home, concern about being paid, and they were cold.

The hostile Sahaptians seemed to have been most concerned with sizing up their enemy. Among the first reports of violence, Lee wrote from the Deschutes River on January 28, "We proceeded this morning up the river some twenty miles, when we discovered a considerable party of Indians with their families, removing across the plains, and evidently to station themselves higher upon the canyon. We charged upon them, killed one, took two (female) prisoners and several horses, the rest escaped into the canyon."[14] It is unclear who these *families* were. Obviously, any Indians moving away from the militia were considered hostile. A skirmish took place near Willow Creek on February 24 with a large force of river Sahaptins, supposedly led by Edward. Thomas McKay shot Five Crows, shattering his arm. Gilliam claimed there were 418 (!) warriors in the area and requested that Abernethy send more troops.[15] It seems that some had joined the Cayuse based on a claim that the Americans had killed the HBC men and the priests. Once the truth became apparent, they abandoned the hostile Cayuse. And once they witnessed the firepower of the militia, many others departed.[16] After the militia pillaged and burned a Cayuse village on the Deschutes, the buildings at Waiilatpu were set ablaze in retaliation. The mission of St. Anne was also burned (by one side or the other). As the militia advanced, various headmen sent messages declaring their peaceful stances.

At Waiilatpu, the militia built an adobe fortification from the ruins, utilizing the lumber that Whitman had prepared for an additional house. They christened it Fort Waters, after their commander. From this point, a small party led by Joe Meek was dispatched to Washington with news of the killings and another memorial requesting congressional jurisdiction and protection in Oregon. On March 7, the three peace commissioners held a council with several hundred Sahaptians. A letter from Abernethy was read, demanding that Teloukaikt, Feathercap, and those who had raped the hostages "be given up to us, that they may be punished according to our law."[17] He also demanded restitution of livestock stolen from the overlanders and from Waiilatpu, and guarantees that overlanders would not be molested. The commissioners received assurances that the attendees would not support the hostiles. With the departure of the peace commissioners, Gilliam and his 268 soldiers took off to kill Indians. Running skirmishes took place on the Snake and Touchet rivers. Afterward, many militiamen headed home, their terms of enlistment over and demoralized by their lack of success.

In April, nearly 300 new troops departed Oregon City under the command of Lee, who was also appointed superintendent of Indian Affairs by

Abernethy. Lee and James Waters then pursued Teloukaikt, but their advance must have looked more like a cattle drive, as they collected livestock. Lee proposed to maintain a garrison at Fort Waters in June, writing to Abernethy that to ensure a garrison, "I found it necessary to pledge myself to some responsible men, that I would give them a written authority to colonize the country immediately. . . . A call was then made for fifty volunteers to remain until September 15th, next, with a promise from Capt. Thompson, that he would return by that time with families to settle the country. I am truly glad to say that this offer proved successful, and more than the required number of volunteers were obtained."[18] Abernethy agreed with Lee, and on July 13, 1848, readers of the *Spectator* were notified that the Cayuse territory was open to colonization:

> [F]or the information of any who may wish to join the Colonizing Company, there are now, in the Cayuse country, grist and saw mills, blacksmith's anvil and bellow, with some tools, a quantity of iron, plows, harrows, hoes, a crop of wheat, pease, potatoes and corn—with almost every convenience and facility for forming a settlement. . . . [T]he climate, for health, and the scenery for beauty, cannot be excelled by any spot of earth. In consideration of the barbarous and insufferable conduct of the Cayuse Indians . . . and with a view to inflict upon them a just and proper punishment. . . . [I] hereby declare the territory of said Cayuse Indians forfeited by them, and justly subject to be occupied and held by American citizens, resident in Oregon.

The editors applauded the decision. An editorial titled "Colonization" described the Cayuse lands as "immensly valuable for the purpose of grazing," adding, "Probably this valley can nowhere be surpassed for the growing of wheat."[19]

Of course, Abernethy and Lee held no authority to make such a declaration. It was a punitive action on their part, born out of frustration. It was also ineffectual; the *Oregon Free Press* (Oregon City's new journal, edited by George L. Curry) noted that the entire garrison of Fort Waters had returned to Oregon City on September 29: "and so passes out of existence the 'First Regiment of Oregon Riflemen.'"[20] These men had more important things to do.

6

Oregon Territory

Everything changed in the Far West in summer 1848. On August 10—five weeks after the annexation of Alta California to the United States—the *Spectator* carried news of "a terrible fever" in California: "It is not exactly the yellow fever, but a fever for a yellow substance called gold. An exceedingly rich gold mine has been discovered in the Sacramento valley, and all classes and sexes have deserted their occupations and rushed *en masse* to the mines to make their fortunes. The gold taken from this newly discovered mine is not gold ore, but pure virgin gold. . . . We can assure our readers there is no hoax in this."[1] A week later, the *Free Press* reported, "[T]he 'necromancer' gold has bewitched almost every body lately. Nothing else is talked of—nothing else, apparently, is thought of. . . . 'Hurrah for California!' We're off immediately, if not sooner."[2] On September 2, the *Free Press* predicted that "By far the larger portion of our male population will have left to 'dig for gold' before the expiration of the present month. . . . Nothing like the present 'furor' has been known to our age."[3]

The opening of Cayuse territory to colonization could wait. Fort Waters was abandoned. The governor and most of the legislators got the fever and headed south. The final edition of the *Free Press* appeared on October 28. It never got to report that Oregon Territory had been formally established by Congress on August 14 (map 2). In January 1849, the *Spectator* announced the arrival of Orville C. Pratt, the appointed supreme court justice of the territory. Within a month, however, the editors of the *Spectator* also suspended publication and left for California. There was no newspaper in Oregon to announce the arrival of Joseph Lane, President Polk's appointed governor and superintendent of Indian Affairs on March 2.

In his first address to the Territorial Assembly, in July (and only published three months later), Lane presented a position on Indian affairs that

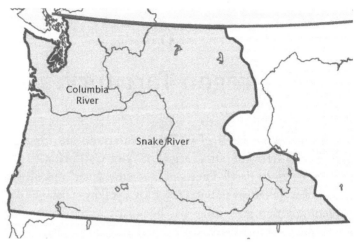

Map 2. Oregon Territory, 1848–53. (Adapted from map by Uwe Dedering, used under creativecommons.org/licenses/by/4.0.)

may have been out of step with most Oregonians: "Widely separated and exposed as are our people . . . peace and harmony with the natives is of vital importance to the security and success of our settlements. The well being of the inhabitants of Oregon, no less than the cause of humanity, requires that we should always encourage relations of the most friendly character with our red brethren." With the exception of the Cayuse, of course: "The Cayuse nation remain unpunished for the massacre at Waiilatpu, but the whole tribe will be held responsible until those, whoever they may be, concerned in that melancholy and horrible affair are given up for punishment. A fine regiment of troops commanded by officers who have distinguished themselves in the service of their country [in Mexico] are *en route* for Oregon and may be expected to arrive by the middle of September. It will then be in the power of the government to make this tribe accountable for their wrongdoing." The future of Oregon, he pointed out, lay in California: "[T]he extraordinary emigration to California, in consequence of her gold mines, will in a short time, result in adding largely to our numbers, so that our population, now only about nine thousand, will be doubled in the next twelve months. . . . It is estimated, that upwards of two millions of dollars, in gold dust, have been brought into Oregon, since their discovery. This new element of prosperity, invested in agriculture and other branches of industry, must have a most cheering effect upon the prosperity of the country."[4]

The gold rush suddenly brought enormous numbers of wealth-obsessed non-Indians into contact with remarkably numerous and diverse Indigenous bands on both sides of the California-Oregon border. For the most part, these people previously had not been in close contact with Whites. Mining activities severely impacted Indigenous food and water supplies as well as seasonal movement. In a region devoid of governmental oversight, miners often killed, raped, and pillaged Native people along their path. Retributions naturally resulted, only to be followed by more violent assaults, often on random Native noncombatants. The hatred generated and focused on the Cayuse since December 1847 was now turned against Indigenous peoples in general.

In California, some newspapers—particularly the *Daily Alta California* and *Sacramento Transcript*—published regular calls for wars of extermination. Yet even more temperate papers were colored by racial science. The first number of Sacramento's *Placer Times* in April 1849, for example, called for "a more humane and christianized course of action":

It is now that the cry of extermination is raised—a thirst for indiscriminate slaughter rages, and men, women and children, old and young, vicious and well-disposed, of the Indian race, wherever met with, are to be straightway shot down or knocked on the head, their villages plundered and burned and frightened fugitives forced deeper in to the mountains, to starve. . . . It does not become us, enlightened Americans of the nineteenth century, to sally forth against a weak and ignorant people, burn their villages, butcher women and children and return at night with our saddle horns loaded with scalps! . . . Let it be borne in mind we do not render ourselves a whit more secure from Indian depredation by indiscriminate slaughter, than by pursuing a humane method of treatment. A check upon the vicious inclinations of the worst, will arise with the rapid growth of society, and gradualy they will recede before the advances of the white man, as is destined the Indian race in general. Thus shall a degraded and worthless people vanish from the face of the land; it is in vain to attempt their extermination by other means—let us not think of it.[5]

This widespread attitude of inevitable extinction and/or extermination was also embraced by the first elected governor of California, Peter Burnett, the most celebrated overlander of 1843, who had served in Oregon's provisional legislature from 1844 to 1848. He stated in an address to the California legislature: "That a war of extermination will continue to be waged between the races until the Indian race becomes extinct must be expected. While we cannot anticipate this result but with painful regret, the inevitable destiny of the race is beyond the power or wisdom of man to avert."[6]

The Cayuse Five

Joseph Lane continued to focus on bringing the Cayuse to justice and managing Indigenous relations more broadly. In April 1849, a month after his arrival, he traveled to The Dalles to bribe the Wasco people into vowing neither to molest the overlanders as they passed through their territory nor to ally with the Cayuse. Lane continued the policy of not pursuing the Cayuse but having their neighbors capture them for a bounty.

The troops that Lane had noted in his inaugural address "were en route for Oregon" arrived in fall 1849. Two companies of the Regiment of Mounted Riflemen (ca. 600 soldiers, with 160 wagons) arrived in Oregon Territory as most White Oregonians were caught up in the gold rush. Their commander, Col. William Loring, had three immediate responsibilities: to establish barracks at Vancouver, to retrieve the large number of soldiers that had quickly deserted for the gold mines, and to assist Lane in apprehending the accused Cayuse. The military force in Oregon was soon enhanced by two artillery companies.

Perhaps as a result of seeing and meeting the long trains of the Mounted Riflemen as they traversed the Grande Ronde and Umatilla valleys, a party of Nez Perce and Cayuse warriors, led by Tawatoy, set out after Teloukaikt and his followers.[7] The latter were shunned by their cousins and former allies, and forced into hiding in the Blue Mountains. A series of skirmishes occurred during fall and winter 1850. Feathercap, Edward, and Clark were killed. In April, William McBean arranged for Tawatoy to turn over three accused attackers to Lane at The Dalles. Tawatoy, with a large entourage, delivered two more Cayuse men to Lane at Oregon City a few weeks later. The five prisoners were Teloukaikt; Feathercap's brothers Tomahas, Frank Eskaloom, and Klokamas; and the little-known Kiamasumkin (perhaps a nephew of Tawatoy).[8] (In all court documents Tomahas's full name was recorded as "Tomahas otherwise called the Murderer," which was, in fact, the meaning of his name.)

The Cayuse Five were not the first Indigenous men to be tried for murder in the new Oregon Territory. In April 1849, an American was killed during a failed attack on Fort Nisqually by Snoqualmick warriors. For a generous reward, six men were turned over by their people. A trial was held; two were found guilty and hanged. The extension of punitive US laws to people with no interest in having any US laws bestowed on them is an issue too complicated for these pages. However, unlike the Snoqualmick men, the crimes with which the Cayuse were charged were committed prior to the establishment of Oregon Territory.

It is unclear exactly when the Cayuse Five were made aware of their legal jeopardy. In an often-quoted but poorly documented statement, Teloukaikt claimed that he was sacrificing himself for his people, as Christ had.[9] Kiamasumkin alone insisted that he took no part in the violence—nor did any witnesses identify him as one of the killers. Although legally absurd, the five were indicted on nineteen charges on May 13, 1850. Their trial for the one charge of murdering Marcus Whitman before judge Pratt began on May 21. A defense team was hastily appointed, but it took its charge seriously. They first made a legitimate motion stating that *ex post facto* the US government lacked jurisdiction to try the case. When the motion was rejected, they requested a change in venue given the attitude of the people of Oregon City. Motion rejected. They then motioned for additional time to prepare a sufficient defense. Pratt again rejected the motion and ordered the trial to proceed the following morning. Deliberations between the Cayuse and their defense team were carried out in Chinook Wawa. Despite attempts by Pratt to follow the outward procedures of a legitimate jury trial, it was a sham. All five were found guilty on May 24, and Pratt sentenced them to death by hanging. Reasonable motions of appeal were denied. The five were hanged before a large crowd by Joe Meek, now US Marshall, on June 3.[10] Lane, who had been replaced as governor, was on his way to California at the time of the trial, having pre-signed the five death warrants.[11]

Indian Affairs in Oregon Territory 1850–53

Meanwhile in Washington, Oregon Territory's first congressional delegate, Samuel Thurston, was working on what would be his single accomplishment: the drafting and passage through Congress of the Oregon Donation Land Act in September 1850. This law allowed for American citizens to claim parcels of 320 acres (640 acres for married couples) for free and recognized the claims made by White Americans (or Métis men of White fathers) prior to 1849 (thus *officially* prohibiting Indigenous people, Blacks, and Hawaiians from claiming land in the territory).[12] The act was scheduled to expire on December 1, 1855, which would become a critical issue. Only three months earlier, Congress had created the office of superintendent of Indian Affairs for Oregon Territory and appointed Anson Dart of Wisconsin to the position. Dart was charged with removing all the Indians from the west side of the Cascades, establishing intertribal peace, diminishing the Indians' relationship with the HBC, and encouraging them—regardless of the landforms they inhabited—to embrace agriculture. In exchange for their land, the Indians were to receive gifts in annual installments. Three agents and three commissioners were assigned to assist Dart in this enormous undertaking.

During his year in Oregon, Dart labored tirelessly to work out treaties with nineteen tribes in western Oregon. However, his plan to relocate all these people across the Cascades was fiercely opposed by the Sahaptians, who refused to surrender land or to allow the "diseased" western Indians to share their lands. Instead, he formulated treaties that allowed the various tribes to reserve relatively small areas of their own territories. Dart then built the Utilla Agency on the Umatilla River (near current Echo, Oregon) and departed for Washington in fall 1851. However, for a variety of reasons, the treaties were never ratified by Congress. Dart resigned in frustration in 1852.

The Utilla Agency primarily served as a trading post for arriving overlanders, as it was ideally situated on the emigrant road between the Blue Mountains and the Columbia. All was peaceful here; Frenchtown was repopulated, and overlanders were greeted by Sahaptians who were only aggressive as traders.[13]

———

In 1853, President Franklin Pierce appointed George Washington Manypenny as commissioner of the Bureau of Indian Affairs (BIA) and Joel Palmer as Dart's replacement. Both were proponents of the assimilationist, civilization-through-agriculture-and-Christianity ideology. Palmer was immediately overwhelmed by escalating, unchecked carnage near the California border. The discovery of gold in southern Oregon in 1851 had created a new gold rush; miners from Oregon and California raced to the region. Violent eruptions followed each new gold discovery. Vigilante mobs were organized (known to history as "volunteers") and attacked all Indians, including those on a temporary reservation established by Palmer. Both Palmer and Gen. John E. Wool, commander of the US Army's newly established Department of the Pacific, blamed the Whites for always initiating the violence. Yet Wool was reluctant to use the small garrisons in the territory to protect the Indians. Palmer's plan was to move all the Indians west of the Cascades onto a large, imaginary reservation on the Oregon coast (which he had yet to visit).[14] Arguably, Palmer's one success was to convince Congress, via Manypenny (in 1854), that no further settlements should be established east of the Cascades until the Indians there could be moved to reservations by treaty.

The US Army in Oregon Territory

The Army command post for the territory, Fort Vancouver, was established on a ridge just to the north of the HBC's Fort Vancouver (fig. 9). (According to the Oregon Treaty, the HBC was permitted to continue its trade and navigation operations in the American part of the territory.) A smaller fort was also ordered to be constructed on the site of the improvised Fort Wascopam at the Narrows.

The evolution of Wascopam and its architecture from 1840s mission to 1850s fort illustrates the broader transition of White settler activity, and its accompanying projections of imperial authority, from commercial and missionary to settlement and state-building. In rapid succession, between the summers of 1847 and 1848, the Methodist Wascopam mission was sold to Marcus Whitman, abandoned by Perrin Whitman, transformed by the militia into Fort Wascopam, then abandoned. In summer 1848, Augustin Blanchet established the seat of his diocese just to the west of the fort. By

Figure 9. *Fort Vancouver, W. T.*, 1853, detail. Lithograph designed by Gustav Sohon. View from the northwest, US Army base to the left, HBC fort to the right, Mount Hood in the distance. (Stevens, *Reports of Explorations . . .* , plate 44, Whitman College and Northwest Archives.)

———

December 1849, two priests and a carpenter had completed a cabin and a chapel with a small "bishop's palace."[15] In May 1850, a detachment of Mounted Riflemen were sent to establish a post on the site of the fort, to serve as a base of operations for the protection of the coming overlanders. However, unlike Vancouver, there was neither a sawmill nor a civilian labor force to employ—until the overlanders began to arrive in late summer. A sawmill was then constructed, and barracks were hastily raised. The region around Fort Dalles was said to be "a most desolate place . . . with nothing to recommend it except wolves, coyotes, rattlesnakes and skunks."[16] Nonetheless, a number of overlanders and settlers from the Willamette Valley and California saw the benefits of living adjacent the military reserve and supplying both the fort and the floods of overlanders with provisions.[17] Among the first merchants to set up shop outside the fort were Perrin Whitman, Henry P. Isaacs (who had met with success in California), and James McAuliff (who had been discharged from the Army in 1855). Ignited by the Donation Land Act, an enormous number of immigrants—perhaps 10,000—passed through the site in late summer and fall 1852.

7

Washington Territory

O lympia—the largest American settlement north of the Columbia—comprised a White population of under 400 in 1852, when its first newspaper appeared. At the outset, the editors of *The Columbian* had one objective: to establish a territory independent of "South Oregon." Their complaints and demands focused on their electoral marginalization within the territorial government, the lack of appropriation for establishing roads north of the Columbia, and the great distance between Salem and the Puget Sound.[1] Olympians petitioned Congress to establish "the Territory of Columbia." Their memorial was eagerly supported by Joseph Lane—now the territorial congressional delegate—who sought statehood for the rapidly growing "South Oregon." The memorial received broad support in Congress, and "Washington Territory" was formally established on March 2, 1853 (map 3). The name was confusingly altered by Congress to *avoid* confusion with the District of Columbia. Nonetheless, *The Columbian* retained its name. The tiny White minority in the territory rejoiced: "Henceforth Northern Oregon has an independent existence, and a destiny to achieve separate and distinct from that of her Southern neighbor. She has been baptized by the Congress of the United States, into a new name—a name GLORIOUS, and dear to every American heart."[2]

The new territory stretched from the Pacific Ocean to the Rocky Mountains. The southern border followed the Columbia from its mouth to the 46th parallel north, then continued to its eastern border. To the surprise of even the signers of the memorial, the northernmost section of the Snake River was incorporated into Washington Territory, rather than serving as a natural (and rational) border. Thus, most of the Walla Walla Valley was joined with Washington Territory, including the HBC's Fort Walla Walla and Frenchtown. Of course, there was no concern for Indigenous areas of principal occupancy; the 46th parallel bisected Cayuse, Walla Walla, and Nez Perce territory.

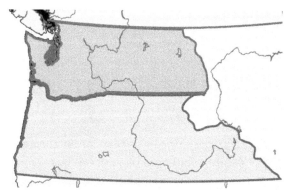

Map 3. Washington and Oregon Territories, 1853–59.
(Adapted from map by Uwe Dedering, used under
creativecommons.org/licenses/by/4.0.)

Isaac I. Stevens

Two weeks after the establishment of Washington Territory, President
Pierce named Maj. Isaac Stevens as both its governor and ex officio super-
intendent of Indian affairs. George Washington Manypenny instructed
Stevens to do what he could to break the influence of the HBC on the
Indians of the territory; all gifts offered to the Indians were to be
American-made, and this fact was to be made explicit.[3] The ambitious
Stevens also successfully lobbied the secretary of state and the secretary of
war to lead a survey of a railway route from Lake Superior to the Puget
Sound during his overland trek.[4] Stevens and his talented survey team
produced an extensive report, remarkable for its detailed descriptions of
the geology, botany, topology, and natural resources of the vast area
covered.

A highlight of Stevens's journey was his stay in the Walla Walla Valley:

November 3 to 8 [1853]. I remained in the Walla-Walla country during
these days, spending two days up the valley, and the remainder at the
[HBC] fort. . . .

November 4. [The HBC] farm is 18 miles from [Fort] Walla-Walla,
and is a fine tract of land, well adapted to grazing or cultivation, it is
naturally bounded by streams, and is equivalent to a mile square. There

is the richest grass here that we have seen since leaving [Kansas] . . .
From this went to McBane's house, a retired factor of the company, from
whence we had a fine view of the southern portion of the valley, which
is watered by many tributaries from the Blue mountains. The land here
is very nutritious. McBane was in charge of Fort Walla-Walla during
the occurrence of the Cayuse difficulties. Thirty miles from Walla-Walla,
and near McBane's, lives Father Chirouse, a missionary of the Catholic
order, who, with two laymen, exercises his influence among the surrounding tribes. . . . From Chirouse and McBane I learned that the
emigrants frequently cast wishful eyes upon the valley, but having made
no arrangement with the Indians they are unable to settle here . . .

November 5. We remained with Mr. McBane over night and returned
to the fort to-day by the way of the Whitman's mission, now occupied
by Bumford and Brooke. They were harvesting, and I saw as fine potatoes as ever I beheld—many weighing 2 pounds, and one weighing 5.
Their carrots and beets, too, were of extraordinary size. . . . From [Bom-
ford's] to the mouth of the Touchet are many farms mostly occupied by
the retired employes of the Hudson Bay Company. On our return we
met Pu-pu-mux-mux, the Walla-Walla chief, known and respected far
and wide. . . . He is of dignified manner, and well qualified to manage
men. He owns over 2,000 horses, besides many cattle, and has a farm
near that of the Hudson Bay Company. . . . He has the air of a substantial farmer.[5]

Lloyd Brooke, George Bomford, and John Noble were civilians who
came to Oregon with the Army. In 1853, they received permission from
the quartermaster at Fort Vancouver to trade in the area of Waiilatpu, Fort
Walla Walla, and the Utilla Agency. They took over Whitman's farm,
where they grazed livestock. Father Chirouse had recently arrived to rees-
tablish the mission of Saint Anne among the Cayuse near the mouth of
Yellowhawk Creek.[6] Stevens also spent time with Andrew Pambrun, son
of Pierre, who had succeeded McBean at Fort Walla Walla (1852–54).
Pambrun received permission to build a house at *Pašxápa* on land once
farmed by Tilokaikt. (However, his workers were regularly harassed by young
men of that band.)

Stevens made no mention of the situation of the Cayuse in fall 1853.
They were still coming to terms with the horrors of 1847–50 when Tawatoy died that September. After the Indian agent made clear that the agency

would not accept Five Crows, an enemy of the Americans, as his successor, Tawatoy's nephew, Weatenatemany (fig. 10) was recognized as head chief. Like his uncle, Weatenatemany was known to the Whites as Young Chief. And like his uncle, he was wary of the Americans. Itstikats and Qemátspelu remained respected headmen in the Umatilla Valley. Howlishwanpum and Tintinmitse were soon established as leaders of the troubled and troublesome Walla Walla Valley Cayuse.

Stevens was greeted warmly in Olympia. He would continue to be appreciated and admired there for his commitment to attracting settlers, to developing the territory, and for combatting HBC influence in the territory. He demonstrated his seemingly boundless energy on his arrival in formulating a territorial government, arranging for elections, and assessing the most pressing needs of the territory (above all, treaties, roads, and military protection). Given his limited contact with Indigenous people, HBC personnel, and settlers between the Rockies and the Cascades, Stevens came to some remarkably strong conclusions. His end-of-the-year report to Manypenny stated:

> The Indian title to lands east of the Cascade mountains should at once be extinguished. . . . [T]he number of settlements already commenced in the Indian country, confirmed me in the opinion of its great necessity. The tribes east of the Cascade mountains have much better organization than the tribes west of the mountains. All of these have chiefs who are well disposed towards the whites, and some of whom have great authority, not only with their own people, but with the surrounding tribes. . . . There is already a flourishing line of settlements in the Colville and Wallah-Wallah vallies, and the settlers are on excellent terms with the Indians. The missions among the Pend d'Oreilles, Cour d'Eleine, Colville, Yakamah, and Wallah-Wallah Indians, are all calculated to lead to early settlements in their vicinity, and should be encouraged. . . . There is much valuable land, and an inexhaustible supply of timber, east of the Cascades; and I consider its speedy settlement so desirable that all impediment should be removed.[7]

Stevens returned east in June 1854 to lobby Congress for funds and to collect his family. He was back in Olympia in December and quickly set out to tackle the most pressing duty: treaty-making. It was in this regard that his deficiency in the essential skills of patience and diplomacy became fully apparent.

Unlike his counterparts in Oregon Territory, Governor George L. Curry and Superintendent of Indian Affairs Joel Palmer, who were struggling with a war of extermination near the California border, Stevens had found the Indians in Washington Territory to be peaceful. However, the Donation Land Act was scheduled to expire on December 1, 1855, and he wanted to ensure that Americans were able to settle as much land as possible. He divided the vast territory into districts and assigned agents to identify tribal leaders among the numerous bands with whom to hold treaty councils. Before embarking on his whirlwind treaty tour, Stevens reported to Manypenny, "It is obviously necessary that a few reservations of good lands should be set apart as permanent abodes for the tribes. These reservations should be large enough to give to each Indian a homestead, and land sufficient to pasture their animals, of which land they should have the exclusive occupation. The location and extent of these reservations should be adapted to the peculiar wants and habits of the different tribes."[8] Unfortunately, these were only words. In late December 1854, Stevens first put into practice his method of "drafting" treaties. He assembled the designated leaders of nine southern Puget Sound peoples, including the Nisqually, Puyallup, and Steilacoom. He arrived with prepared terms and mapped reservations to which the tribal leaders were to agree. An interpreter explained the terms of the treaty as best he could—in Chinook Wawa. The headmen had opportunities to speak, but there were no negotiations. After three days, Stevens collected all the necessary Xs beside the names of the headmen, and the Medicine Creek Treaty was concluded. On ratification by Congress the following year, the United States received over 2 million acres of choice land for farming, grazing, and oyster and clam digging. In exchange, the nine tribes were given three 1,280-acre reservations, a promise of $2,500 worth of gifts annually for twenty years (in buildings, farming equipment, clothing, etc.), and fishing, hunting and foraging rights "on any of the lands not occupied by settlers." (These were not "rights" granted by the treaties; Indigenous rights of access were, in fact, restricted.) Although it may not have been explained at any of Stevens's councils, the treaties contained the proviso that the president reserved the right to move Indians to other reservations (consolidation), to decrease the size of reservations, and to eliminate reservations.

From the start, Stevens rejected the opinion stated in his report to Manypenny that "reservations should be adapted to the peculiar wants and habits of the different tribes." The Nisqually, for example, were removed entirely from their territory of principal occupancy, the Nisqually River Basin.[9] They expressed their displeasure from the start. (And Leschi, one of their headmen, would soon go to war against Stevens.) Four hastily dictated treaties in the Puget Sound area and on the Olympic Peninsula in January and February left thousands of people angry and confused. In some cases, peoples were forced onto common reservations regardless of shared cultural traits or kinship ties. And in many cases, reservation land was not conducive to established forms of American agriculture; the BIA's theory of converting Indigenous people to agrarianism was often negated by the American desire to possess the choicest parcels of arable land.

The Walla Walla Council

In January 1855, Stevens sent his secretary, James Doty, and Indian agent Andrew Bolon to meet with the Sahaptian people to identify leaders and to assess their interest in surrendering parts of their land. Doty's report to Stevens was positive. Arrangements were made for a council with Nez Perce, Cayuse, Walla Walla, and Yakama leaders at the traditional location for Sahaptian councils: *Pašxápa*. The Stevens-Palmer entourage arrived on May 20, followed by an Army escort of forty-seven from Fort Dalles (including Lt. Lawrence Kip, who produced an insightful memoir of the treaty proceedings). Over the next ten days, large war parties arrived from different directions, some producing spectacular processions. Stevens wrote of the arrival of the Cayuse: "The haughty carriage of these chiefs and their manly character have, for the first time in my Indian experience, realized the descriptions of the writers of fiction."[10] Gustav Sohon, Stevens's official artist/cartographer, produced numerous drawings of the events and participants (figs. 1, 10–13). The council began on May 30 and proceeded for twelve days. Stevens and Palmer hired seven interpreters for this extremely complicated council, including Andrew Pambrun, William Craig, and "Delaware Jim" Simonds.[11] Each sentence spoken by Stevens and Palmer was translated to two criers, who then loudly relayed the statements, one into Nez Perce, the other into Sahaptin. (Given the laborious method of communication, relatively little was actually said in twelve days.) Stevens hoped to move all the Sahaptians onto one of two large reservations in Nez

Perce and Yakama territory. After three days of explanations and history lessons—including a heroic retelling of Andrew Jackson's Indian Removal Act ("he said I will take the red man across a great river into a fine country where I can take care of them")—Weatenatemany requested they take a day off before resuming. The request was granted.[12]

After another speech by Palmer on the fifth day, the headmen were invited to speak. The first to speak was Five Crows (who, like Peo-Peo-Mox-Mox, stood a foot and a half taller than Stevens[13]). "We are tired," he said. He then made a brief statement about the creation of the earth, the creation of Adam, and hell, which demonstrated how little the sole Presbyterian among the Cayuse had retained from the teaching of Spalding and Whitman.

Throughout the council, the Cayuse, the Yakama, and Peo-Peo-Mox-Mox (the sole spokesman for the river Sahaptians) displayed a lack of trust in the promises and statements of the Americans. Peo-Peo-Mox-Mox, for example, repeatedly insisted that Stevens and Palmer "speak straight" to the chiefs, "If you would speak straight then I would think you spoke well." He concluded his first statement, ironically, "I should feel very much ashamed if the Americans should do anything wrong." (We may assume that much of the nuanced Sahaptian verbal irony was lost in the transcription of the speeches.[14])

On the seventh day, June 4, the Nez Perce head chief Lawyer was the first to speak in favor of the treaty. He was supported by other Nez Perce headmen. Eagle from the Light, however, offered his own history lesson regarding Sahaptian memory of American deception and violence: "A long time ago they hung my brother for no offense. . . . And Spalding sent my father to the East—the states—and he went. His body was never returned."[15] He had harsh words for Spalding, saying he came as a preacher but became an exploitative trader. Nonetheless, he was optimistic about the treaty, "We will come straight here—slowly, perhaps—but we will come straight." Stevens spent the rest of the day explaining the boundaries of his two reservations.

On the eighth day, Stevens presented a large map of the proposed Nez Perce reservation and explained that the Nez Perce, Spokan, Walla Walla, Cayuse, and Umatilla would each "have its own place on the Reservation." Everyone would have access to at least one blacksmith, farmer, school, sawmill, and flour mill. He explained the role of the head chief of every tribe,

Figures 10–12. Gustav Sohon, portraits of Weatenatemany (upper left), Five Crows (upper right), and Peo-Peo-Mox-Mox (lower left), 1855. Graphite on paper. (1918.114.9.48, 1918.114.9.45, 1918.114.9.64, Washington State Historical Society, Tacoma.)

Figure 13. Gustav Sohon, *Chiefs at Dinner, Walla Walla Council 1855*. Watercolor. Andrew Pambrun's house is visible in the background. (1918.114.9.38, Washington State Historical Society, Tacoma.)

---

noting they would receive $500 annually for twenty years. "You will be allowed to go to the usual fishing places," he assured, "and fish in common with the whites, and to get roots and berries and to kill game on land not occupied by the whites; all this outside the Reservation." He emphasized that the government would provide $100,000 in goods and improvements at each reservation during the first year, and that the government would sell goods to them much cheaper than the HBC. He said the same before a large map of the Yakama reservation.[16] Palmer then gave a long lecture on the telegraph and the railroad! Lieutenant Kip recorded in his journal, "It was sufficiently amusing to listen to this lecture . . . but it probably would have been much more diverting could we have known the precise impressions left upon the minds of his audience, or have heard them talk it over afterwards in their lodges."[17] Stevens attempted to end the session but was halted by Itstikats. Like all the chiefs, he was concerned about being understood. "[I]nterpret right for me," he demanded of the interpreters, then attempted to offer Stevens and Palmer a succinct introduction to the

Tamálwit worldview: "How is it I have been troubled in mind? If your mothers were here in this country who gave you birth, and suckled you, and while you were sucking some person came and took away your mother and left you alone and sold your mother, how would you feel then? This is our mother this country, as if we drew our living from her." Addressing the map—that excluded all Cayuse land—he stated, "I name three places for myself, the Grande Ronde, the Touchet towards the mountains and the Tucannon." After a long pause, the council adjourned for two days. On the following evening, Kip sensed a change in the attitude of the Cayuse: he and a friend rode to their camp (which they established one mile south of the council site) and noted, "if savage and scowling looks could have killed, we should both have ended our mortal career this evening in this valley of Walla Walla."[18] (On June 2, Lawyer had advised Stevens that the Cayuse were planning to massacre his party and were only awaiting the support of the Yakamas and Walla Wallas. Lawyer then moved his family into Stevens's camp, signifying the Nez Perce would defend the Americans.[19])

On the tenth day, Lawyer delivered a history of the United States as he understood it. At one point he gestured to Delaware Jim to emphasize that *his* people were among those forced away by the Americans. He then made some recommendations for his reservation. Weatenatemany spoke next and elaborated on Itstikats's earlier statement:

> I wonder if this ground has anything to say: I wonder if the ground is listening to what is said. I wonder if the ground would come to life and what is on it: though I hear what this earth says, the earth says, God has placed me here. The earth says, that God tells me to take care of the Indians on this earth; the Earth says to the Indians that stop on the Earth feed them right. God named the roots that he should feed the Indians on: the water speaks the same way: God says feed the Indians upon the earth: the grass says the same thing: feed the horses and cattle. The Earth and water and grass say God has given our names and we are told those names: neither the Indians or the Whites have a right to change those names: the Earth says, God has placed me here to produce all that grows upon me, the trees, fruit, etc. The same way the Earth says, it was from her man was made. God on placing them on the Earth during then to take good care of the earth and do each other no harm. God said. You Indians who take care of a certain portion of the country should not trade it off unless you get a fair price.

The last sentence of this statement of faith certainly took a strange turn. However, he concluded, "Lawyer understood your offer and he took it I do not understand it and I do not yet take it." He was seconded by his uncles, Five Crows and Peo-Peo-Mox-Mox. The old Yakama war chief Owhi next made a passionate statement about breaking the covenant between the creator of the earth and the people: "God named this land to us. . . . I am afraid of the Almighty. Shall I steal this land and sell it? or what shall I do? this is the reason that my heart is sad. . . . I am afraid I would be sent to hell. I love my friends. I love my life, this is the reason why I do not give away my lands." In a long-winded response, Palmer revealed both his lack of comprehension of *tamálwit* and his concern for the truth: "I too love the earth where I was born. I left it because it was for my good. I have come a long way. We ask you to go but a very short distance. We don't come to steal your lands, we pay you more than it is worth. Here in this little valley and the Umatilla valley that affords a little good land, between these two streams and all around it is a partched up plain. What is it worth to you or to us? Not one half of what we have offered for it." Howlishwanpum replied, "Your words since you came here have been crooked." As if to prove him correct, Palmer proceeded to insist that they would live better on reservation land in Nez Perce or Yakama territory than where they currently lived.

Kip, who had served as a transcriber that day, noted, "it was melancholy to see their reluctance to abandon the old hunting grounds of their fathers and their impotent struggle against the overpowering influences of the whites." That night he found everyone "very much incensed against the Nez Perces for agreeing to the terms of the treaty," adding, "but fortunately for them, and probably for us, the Nez Perces are as numerous as the others united."[20]

On the eleventh day, a frustrated Weatenatemany pointed south to the Umatilla and Grande Ronde valleys and said, "I think the land where my forefathers are buried should be mine. That is the place I am speaking for. That is what I love, the place we get our roots. The salmon comes up the stream." Palmer responded to the concerns of the Cayuse headmen by offering to establish a third reservation for the Cayuse, Walla Walla, and Umatilla together on Cayuse land in Oregon. For surrendering all of their land, Peo-Peo-Mox-Mox and his son were offered additional perks, including a trading post at the mouth of the Yakima River. After further deliberations, and incapable of hiding his impatience, Stevens stated, "I have offered you more than your country is worth, more than you know how to count." The council was abruptly concluded for the day with the heroic arrival of the increasingly influential Nez Perce war chief Looking Glass. He and about twenty warriors had just returned from a bison hunt, where they battled with the Blackfeet. Looking Glass carried a pole with a scalp dangling from it. To Stevens's dismay, the thousands of Indians spent the night celebrating the return of the warriors.

The twelfth day of the council belonged to the young, dynamized Looking Glass, who assumed the role of the great chief of all the assembled headmen. He demanded a much larger reservation for the Cayuse because "they want more room for their horses and cattle." This became the major issue of the day. Weatenatemany repeatedly recognized Looking Glass as *his* head chief. A flustered Palmer responded: "If we change the line to where he says we would have to stay here two or three days more to arrange the paper. We are all tired."

Lieutenant Kip recorded "a great deal of great excitement through the Indian camps" the following day, Sunday, June 10. Whatever was going on led to certain agreements; on Monday the treaties were signed. Only Lawyer and his supporters seemed to be satisfied in the end. In retrospect, Stevens and Palmer's major accomplishment may have been to break any future alliance between the majority of Nez Perces and any hostile Sahaptians.

––––––––

The Americans and the Sahaptians knew this day would come. The US government had been devising and revising sloppy Indian treaties since 1778. Inevitably, once the federal government reached Washington Territory, lines would be drawn on maps and slipshod treaties would be drafted and sent for the approval of congressmen who understood little to nothing of the people and the land marked out on the maps.[21] For two decades, the Sahaptians had been warned by the Iroquois and Delawares that "the Great Father" would eventually take their land; however, they could not have anticipated Stevens and Palmer's hasty method of making such life-altering arrangements. Some headmen obviously believed that they would yield to reason—that they would come to understand that these valleys, rivers, hills, and meadows were not commodities. On the other hand, many were clearly confused by the overwhelming sense of defeat associated with this treaty. All but a few had been on friendly terms with the Americans since Lewis and Clark. They had never been at war with the Americans—in fact, some at the council had served with the American forces in Alta California during the invasion of Mexico. Some had kinship ties with Americans. Yet there was also abundant distrust of the Americans stemming from a pattern of deception. A number of burning questions required time and honest responses. For example, exactly what government authority had Whitman and Spalding possessed? They seemed to set this whole thing in motion. Why were *all* the Cayuse people hunted and threatened after the Whitman killings? Exactly why were five Cayuse men hanged in the Willamette Valley, and why were they refused the courtesy of a proper burial? Why did the American murderer of Peo-Peo-Mox-Mox's son go unpunished? Neither adequate time nor honest responses were provided by Stevens and Palmer.

According to a remarkable report compiled during 1855–57 by Capt. Thomas J. Cram, the chief topographical engineer for the Department of the Pacific, the council was doomed from the start for a number of reasons, above all:

> The *tout ensemble* of each tribe, on this occasion, was magnificence in the extreme; while that of the whites, on the contrary, was meagre and insignificant. It was humiliating to witness the contrast, so unfavorable to the success so earnestly hoped for. The Indians, as they advanced in bodies of from three to twelve hundred warriors from their distant homes, were all mounted upon fine horses, having their equipments, though of Indian taste, most richly and gorgeously ornamented. The riders strode their steeds with grace and skill. Not so with the whites; the retinue of the commissioners was shabby, diminutive, and mean in appointments generally, and deficient in all those points of show, in particular, that are so well calculated to strike the fancy or command the respect of an Indian.

Cram noted that the headmen were entirely unprepared at that time to consider such a life-altering plan to abandon their territories. "Unmistakable repugnance to the treaty was evinced throughout, not only by the chiefs, but by the individuals composing the tribes, almost to a man. . . . No disinterested witness to the proceedings believed that a single chief signed that treaty with the slightest possible intention of abiding it."[22]

8

The Governor Stevens Wars

In one of his greatest blunders, Stevens immediately sent notice of the treaties to the newspapers of Olympia and Oregon City, adding "By an express provision of the treaty, the country embraced in the cessions and not included in the reservations, is open to settlement." This notice appeared in papers throughout the territories continuously, for months. Of course, there could be no legal settlement of these lands until the treaties were ratified. In this case, ratification took four years. However, Stevens was racing against the expiration of the Donation Land Act in December. Instead of sticking around to assist the Sahaptians or to attempt to gain the trust of the skeptical leaders, Stevens traveled eastward to collect more treaties as quickly as possible. Stevens's cursory treaties, his sloppy public notices, and his neglect in preparing the Indians for the enactment of the treaties resulted in what has come to be known as the "Yakima Indian War": three years of unprecedented and unnecessary violence throughout Washington Territory.

Stevens's public notices may have instilled a false confidence in parties of miners traveling to the recently discovered Colville gold mines in summer 1855. Roads to the mines passed through Yakama, Palus, and Spokan territory. Incidents of rape, assault, and theft led to the retaliatory killings of six prospectors in two instances by Yakama warriors. Captain Cram noted, "The bare recital of some of the crimes committed by these Anglo-Saxon devils, in human shape, is sufficient to cause the blood of every virtuous man, whether of red or white skin, to boil with deep indignation. They were not satisfied with stealing the horses and cattle of the Indians, but they claimed the privilege of taking and ravishing Indian women and maidens *ad libitum*."[1] In September, agent to the Yakama Andrew Bolon investigated the killing of the miners and was himself killed.

When word of Bolon's death reached acting governor Charles Mason, he wrote to Fort Vancouver requesting troops. Punitive detachments from Fort Dalles and Fort Steilacoom were ordered into Yakama territory. On

October 5–7, the infantry unit from Fort Dalles under Maj. Granville Haller was attacked at Toppenish Creek and retreated. Haller wildly overestimated the number of enemy warriors at between 1,500 and 3,000.[2] Word of this defeat caused terror among the settlers and demands for the extermination of all Indians, in biblical terms. Olympia's *Pioneer and Democrat*, for example, stated: "We trust they will be *rubbed out—blotted from existence* as a tribe . . . the old Levitical law should have free and full force."[3] A letter to *The Oregon Argus* may have best articulated the attitude of the American settlers: "Who are the original aggressors it is not worth while to inquire, for in a great measure it is true that we are in possession of the whole continent by force, but it is the force of good against evil, and God has sent us with the sword to exterminate a people who have nothing in common with humanity save the form, as He sent the children of Israel against similar tribes of old."[4] Word of the momentary victory against the uniformed Army certainly spread rapidly among the Sahaptians and certainly inspired young warriors to join the revolt against the Americans. Additional regular troops were dispatched. Mason called for the raising of two mounted militia companies, and Governor Curry called for eight companies. Skeptical of the Army's commitment to fighting, Curry specifically ordered his militia to act independently of the Army. Such was the attitude of many in the territories after years of feeling ignored by the federal government.

Rumors spread of an all-out Indian war of extermination against the Americans. Palmer recklessly confirmed the rumors in letters to the press.[5] Newspapers generated fear that the settlements were in danger because the Army forts were now virtually abandoned. In his call for volunteers, Curry warned, "Say to our fellow-citizens that unless they ACT NOW, and that RESOLUTELY AND PROMPTLY, *the war will be transferred to their firesides!*"[6] Indian agent Nathan Olney did nothing to cool the situation. In letters to the *Argus*, he described a desperate situation: "I have just arrived at [Fort Walla Walla], and find the most alarming state of affairs existing as to the friendly relations heretofore existing between the Americans and Walla Wallas, Palouses, Umatillas, and Cayuses. . . . I fear nothing but a large military force will do any good towards keeping them in check. . . . One thousand volunteers should be raised immediately. . . . These Indians must be taught our power. They must be humbled."[7] Even the Army's official correspondence conveyed a sense of panic: "[T]he Indian war has become general, and a combination for purposes of hostility to the whites been formed on a scale which those most intimately acquainted with Indian character have heretofore believed impossible. Upon the east of the Cascade range, it may be now assumed that every tribe in Washington Territory, as far as the Rocky mountains, is engaged in the war."[8] Olney advised all Whites in the Walla Walla Valley to leave the area for the security of Fort Dalles. The HBC abandoned Fort Walla Walla. Some residents of Frenchtown left with Olney; others, together with some Cayuse, sought security among peaceful Nez Perce bands.

It is unclear exactly when, or to what degree, plans were made to unite the warriors of the plateau in a war against the Americans, but such plans had been discussed.[9] After the skirmish with Haller, Kamiakin dispatched messengers to the Cayuse, Nez Perce, and Walla Walla. According to Itstikats, their message was: "we all had to fight, in every place; all must go."[10] Howlishwanpum stated that he, Itstikats, and Tintinmitse were opposed to war: "The chiefs were for war. Most of the young men were for war. I tried to talk with them; they would not listen to me; their hearts were bad." Among the leaders of the hostile Cayuse were Weatenatemany, Five Crows, Qemátspelu, and Waiecat.

On November 16, General Wool arrived at Fort Vancouver to assess the situation and to personally oversee the operations.[11] In his reports to Army headquarters, he criticized every military action ordered since hostilities commenced. He called for a halt to all military movements and chastised the Oregon militia for its reckless actions, its atrocities inflicted on peaceful Indians, and its enormous expenses (which were charged to the federal government). He concluded that the Army could not achieve its goals by engaging in skirmishes against Indians with faster horses and knowledge of the terrain. "They can only be conquered or brought to terms by occupying their country, and such positions as would command their fisheries and valleys, where their cattle and horses must graze." His plan was to wait until spring and then to starve the hostiles into submission.[12] The Oregon militia, however, was a monkey wrench in Wool's plan. Curry ordered several companies to the Umatilla, to establish a small fort (Fort Henrietta, on the site of the burned Utilla Agency) and to launch a preemptive attack on Peo-Peo-Mox-Mox, believed to be the leader of the hostile Sahaptians. On December 3, the militia advanced to Fort Walla Walla, which, two weeks earlier, had been looted and partially destroyed by Peo-Peo-Mox-Mox's warriors. Two days later, Peo-Peo-Mox-Mox and five guards approached the militia under a white flag. He insisted to Nathan Olney that he wanted peace. They were taken as hostages. On December 7, the militia was attacked by about 300 well-armed warriors in the vicinity of Frenchtown. A chaotic running skirmish ensued. The militia looted and used the sturdy abandoned houses of Frenchtown as bastions. During the battle, Peo-Peo-Mox-Mox and four of his guards were murdered by the militia. James Sinclair, the last factor of Fort Walla Walla, wrote, "The whole scalp was taken from [Peo-Peo-Mox-Mox's] head and cut into twenty pieces. His skull was divided equally for buttons, his ears preserved in a bottle of spirits, and large strips of his skin cut off along his back to be made into razor strops. Such is Indian warfare!"[13] Accounts of the murder in the Oregon papers boasted that some of these "souvenirs" were sent to family members in the Willamette Valley.

On December 8, a larger force of Sahaptians attacked the militia. Skirmishes continued for two days. On the third day, as ammunition was running low for both sides, reinforcements arrived from Fort Henrietta, and the Sahaptians retreated. With the Walla Walla Valley apparently clear of hostiles, the militia established a new winter fort, named Fort Curry, from the remains of the Brooke, Bomford, and Noble farm at Waiilatpu (which had been looted and burned by Waiecat and his band despite Howlishwanpum's attempts to protect it). Seven militiamen had been killed in the four days of skirmishes.

The Northwest papers mixed in news of the militia's "victory" in the Walla Walla Valley with mockery and condemnation of Wool's decision to keep the Army garrisoned in the forts for the winter. Stevens arrived at Fort Curry in December, after completing his treaty-making marathon. Angry, embarrassed, and exhausted, he wrote to Manypenny, "My plan is to make no treaties whatever with the tribes now in arms; to do away entirely with the reservations guaranteed to them; to make a summary example of all the leading spirits, and to place as a conquered people, under the surveillance of troops."[14] In his address to the Olympia legislature in January, Stevens repeated his new policy regarding Indians and treaties, praised the militia, and denounced Wool.[15] The legislatures of both Oregon and Washington territories then petitioned Congress to have General Wool removed.

Wool wrote to Stevens in February, after his return to California:

[Father Chirouse] informs me that the friendly Cayuses are every day menaced with death by Gov. Curry's volunteers. The writer says that they have despoiled these Indians . . . of their provisions. Today, he says, these same volunteers, without discipline and without orders, are not satisfied with rapine and injustice, but wish to take away the small remnant of animals and provisions left. Every day they run off the horses and cattle of the friendly Indians. . . . The writer further says, if the volunteers are not arrested in their brigand actions, the Indians will save themselves by flying to the homes of their relatives, the Nez Perces, who have promised them help, and then all Indians of Oregon and Washington will join in the common defense.[16]

The hostility between Stevens and Wool only escalated and became increasingly public. The *Pioneer and Democrat* was quick to respond to Wool's letter to Stevens: "The most charitable conclusion that we can arrive at, as explaining the remarkable, unjustifiable, and, in one sense of the word we might say, *criminal* conduct of Gen Wool, is to assume that he is *insane*."[17] Joseph Lane and James Anderson, the congressional representatives of Oregon and Washington territories, aggressively supported their fellow Democrats, Curry and Stevens, in their war against Wool in Congress. They were supported by the pro-Democrat press, including the *New York Herald* and the *New York Times*. On the other hand, Wool's assessment of the situation was supported by the pro-Whig press, including the *National Intelligencer* and the *New-York Daily Tribune*.

On March 26, a party of Yakama and Klickitat warriors attacked a blockhouse built to protect two small settlements on the north side of the cascades. Fourteen civilians and three US soldiers were killed in the attack, and the blockhouse and other buildings were burned. Two days later, Col. George Wright arrived at the scene of the "Cascades Massacre," and Wool's somewhat humane approach to the Indians was temporarily abandoned. Nine Wasco warriors surrendered without a fight; Wright charged them with treason (!) and ordered them hanged.

In May, Wright led a large force into the Yakima Valley. In his councils with the headmen, he determined the source of the hostilities to be Stevens's Walla Walla treaty and the manner in which it was forced on them.[18] Wright concluded that an overwhelming majority of Yakama wanted peace and to have a reservation that could support them. He reported to Wool in mid-July, "The whole country should be given to the Indians; they require it; they cannot live at any one point for the whole year. The roots, the berries, and the fish make up their principal subsistence; these are all obtained at different places and different seasons of the year."[19] In this same report, Wright declared that "the war in this country is closed." However, Wool advised Wright, "[Y]ou cannot be too cautious or wary of your double enemy . . . the whites in your rear, from whom . . . you have as much to apprehend as the Indians in your front."[20]

Sure enough, Stevens was directing his own war. He dispatched 200 militiamen under the command of Benjamin Shaw to the Walla Walla Valley with orders to "strike the hostiles wherever he finds them."[21] Shaw marched to the Grande Ronde Valley and attacked a large Cayuse camp on July 17. Forty to sixty were killed, primarily women, children, and elderly men. The camp was pillaged, more than one hundred lodges were burned, and hundreds of horses were stolen or killed. Shaw, Stevens, and many historians called it the "Battle of Grande Ronde." In response to this atrocity, Wool ordered the closure of the territory east of the Cascades to civilians on August 2, 1856.

The US Army in the Walla Walla Valley

The Army's original plans called for the construction of a fort in the vicinity of the abandoned HBC Fort Walla Walla. However, while it was an ideal location for river transportation, it was far from ideal for observing hostile movements. In August 1856, Wright ordered Maj. Edward J. Steptoe and his three companies to establish a post in the Walla Walla Valley. Shaw's militia was still camped in the valley, and Stevens was on his way to join Shaw with the intent of holding another Sahaptian council. On August 29, Stevens's party was attacked before meeting up with Shaw. On Steptoe's arrival in the valley on September 2, he encountered not only Shaw's militia, low on provisions, but also Stevens, and a growing number of hostile Indians (who had been summoned by Stevens's agents): about 4,000 ultimately arrived. Stevens opened his council at Shaw's camp just weeks after the Grande Ronde massacre and demanded "unconditional submission." Stevens wanted everyone moved to their assigned reservations prior to ratification. The headmen that were willing to speak demanded retention of their lands; Stevens fruitlessly lectured and refused to yield. Only Lawyer, who was to retain all of his territory according to the treaty, again spoke in favor of it. After a week of futile meetings, the council broke up. In his report to Secretary of War Jefferson Davis, Stevens unsurprisingly blamed General Wool for the council's failure.

On September 10, Steptoe established his initial camp on Mill Creek.[22] Aside from good observation, this site offered access to grazing lands and pine trees for construction of a blockhouse. On the last day of Stevens's council, Steptoe met with some of the headmen and explained that his fort—consisting of a partially built blockhouse and a large number of tents—was intended to protect the Indians. He reported to Wright: "I attended [the council] yesterday, and was satisfied that Governor Stevens had effected no good by assembling the tribes. The Nez Perces showed generally a disposition to annul the treaty of last year, while the Cayuse chiefs were almost defiant in tone. . . . I cannot help feeling gratified that the treaty of Walla-Walla has not yet been ratified, because it is plain to me that an attempt to execute it now would be attended by resistance at once on the part of most of the Nez Perces, and ultimately by combined resistance amongst the surrounding tribes."[23] Soon after Stevens and the militia departed for Fort Dalles, they were attacked by a combined force of Sahaptians. One militiaman was killed. Steptoe's camp was also fired on. The following day, Steptoe and a large force relieved Stevens and escorted him to Fort Dalles. Steptoe returned to the Walla Walla Valley, accompanied by Wright and additional forces. Wright had two primary tasks: to establish a more permanent fort and to hold his own council. Both were in progress on October 30 when he reported to Pacific Headquarters: "I have . . . in my camp about forty, embracing the principle chiefs of the Nez Percé, Cayuse, &c. [including Itstikats, Howlishwanpum, and Tintinmitse]. I have had several talks with them, all very satisfactory. . . . From appearances I apprehend no serious difficulties with any of these Indians. The council of Governor Stevens was unfortunate; the Indians, many of them, are hostile to the governor; they are opposed to the treaty. . . . I am fully satisfied it should not be confirmed."[24] The next day Howlishwanpum offered Wright an account of the Grande Ronde massacre.[25] Wright assured the Cayuse that the treaty had not been ratified and that the land was still theirs. He again expressed his wish that the treaty would never be ratified. "Peace and quiet can easily be maintained," he wrote. "The Indians are perfectly satisfied with the establishment of a military post here. All they want is quiet and protection."

When Stevens received word of Wright's peaceful council, he wrote to Jefferson Davis to denounce Wright's attempt to usurp his authority.[26] He delivered his own history of the warfare in his address to the legislative assembly on December 3: "[A]bove all, we have waged the war with humanity, with moderation, with honor to our country and honor to ourselves. The dignity, the justice, the mercy of the government, has been vindicated at our hands." He concluded by calling for settlement of the Sahaptian lands.[27]

On December 27, the *New-York Daily Tribune* included both a long editorial on the Stevens/Curry-Wool controversy and a letter from Stevens condemning Wool and attacking all the governor's critics. Three weeks earlier, the seventy-two-year-old Wool had requested to be relieved of his command. His final report to Headquarters as commander of the Department of the Pacific noted:

> [A]ll is peace and quiet in the two Territories. Under present arrangements, I do not believe that war can be renewed by the whites. The posts are well arranged to preserve peace, and to protect the inhabitants from any hostility on the part of the Indians residing in the Territories. From the latter, however, none are anticipated. If the war should be renewed, it will be brought on by the political and pecuniary speculators of the two Territories, who will spare no efforts to make it appear that the war is not ended, and this, too, to create a sympathy in Congress in favor of their [military compensation] claims, caused by a war brought on by themselves, and for no other reason than to promote their own ambitious ends, under the pretence of enriching the country.[28]

Wool's replacement, Gen. Newman Clarke, maintained the ban on settlement east of the Cascades. Like Wool, Clarke hoped that the Stevens treaties would not be ratified and that the Sahaptians would be more involved in the formulation of new treaties.[29] Wright, Steptoe, and Maj. Robert S. Garnett spread the word among the Sahaptians, which resulted in a relatively peaceful, if tense, 1857. (Military activity in the West was focused against the Mormons in Utah Territory.)

Much of the peace was related to Stevens's absence; in 1857 he was elected to serve as territorial congressional delegate. Yet he did manage to destabilize the relative peace, albeit indirectly. In August, J. Ross Browne arrived for an inspection tour of western Oregon and Washington territories on behalf of the BIA. Browne, an Irish adventurer, had briefly been associated with the BIA in California. His conclusions were influenced primarily by his meetings with Stevens. In fact, his report reads as though it had been authored by Stevens. Without having visited the interior, he wrote of the choice agricultural lands to be settled there. He concluded that the major threats to peace were the HBC (!) and the Mormons (who were arming the Indians and "constantly instigating them to acts of aggression"). Steptoe reported that, despite not crossing the Cascades, Browne had nonetheless caused unrest among the Sahaptians by assuring Lawyer (in the Willamette Valley) that the treaty "would *certainly* be ratified and enforced." Steptoe was outraged that Browne would make such an inflammatory statement.[30]

The Steptoe Disaster

It was well known that the Spokan and Coeur d'Alene people, who had not been included in any of Stevens's treaties, feared they would lose their land entirely. As word spread throughout the plateau that the Americans were planning to take Indian land or to enforce the Stevens treaty, some Sahaptian and Salishan headmen discussed contingency strategies. By April 1858, Steptoe was informed of agitation in the Palus and Spokan lands: "Some forty persons living at Colville recently petitioned for the presence of troops at that place, as they believed their lives and property to be in danger from hostile Indians. . . . Two white men are reported to have been killed recently near Pelouse river on their way to Colville."[31] Steptoe decided to lead a show of force through Palus and Spokan territories. On May 6, he left Fort Walla Walla with about 160 soldiers, a number of Nez Perce guides, 2 mountain howitzers, and a large number of civilian teamsters leading a long pack train with provisions and cattle. No advance warning was issued to the Indians regarding his intentions. On May 16, they encountered a joint Sahaptian-Salishan army (near current Rosalia). The soldiers were threatened and harassed. The next day Steptoe's column was attacked as it retreated. Two officers and a soldier were killed, as were two Coeur d'Alene headmen. By the time the command returned to Fort Walla Walla, four wounded soldiers had died. When accounts reached eastern papers, the country—and Army Headquarters—was outraged. "The Steptoe Disaster" was a national embarrassment.[32] Congressman Stevens, however, was thrilled by the news.[33]

Colonel Wright's Punitive Campaign

Everything had changed forever on the plateau. The relative peace of 1857–58 could be attributed to the absence of Stevens, or to General Wool's insistence on protecting the Indians by keeping the Americans on the west side of the Cascades and by refusing to recognize the unratified treaties. Wool's major misstep, it seems, was to allow *miners* to pass through Indian territory.

On receiving word of the Steptoe debacle, General Clarke amassed 2,200 soldiers—about a quarter of all US Army troops—at the forts of the Columbia. Colonel Wright was ordered to lead a large army on a punitive expedition into Palus, Spokan, and Coeur d'Alene territories. After the killing of an Indian agent, a few miners, and several militiamen, Wright was willing to negotiate with all Indians. However, the killing of US soldiers was a different story; recall the hangings of nine prisoners following Major Haller's defeat in 1855.

Wright was convinced that the Yakama chiefs Owhi, Qualchan, and Kamiakin were the masterminds behind the uprising. These three were mentioned repeatedly in newspapers throughout the country as tormentors of the Army. Yet Wright was also provided the names of Indians throughout the region who were accused of "crimes"—including murder, vandalism, and horse theft. Clarke instructed Wright, "You will attack all the hostile Indians you may meet, with vigor; make their punishment severe, and persevere until the submission of all is complete."[34] With Steptoe left behind, Wright departed Fort Walla Walla on August 6 with 570 soldiers, 30 armed and uniformed Nez Perce warriors, and 100 contractors overseeing a supply train with 800 animals and provisions for thirty-eight days.[35] Wright's campaign is well known for its unflinching brutality and its finality. He dispersed the united plateau army after two skirmishes. He attacked villages, killing those who fled, setting fire to lodges, and destroying or confiscating provisions. The soldiers were outfitted with new rifles (Springfield Model 1855) that inflicted greater damage from greater distances (ca. 500 yards). The new Minié balls they fired were designed to shatter bones (thus the enormous number of amputations during the Civil War). Indians rarely came within the effective range of their own muskets (ca. 50 yards), thus none of Wright's soldiers were killed in battle. Wright's troops infamously rounded up 900 Palus horses and killed most of them to terrify and demoralize the Indians. Wright demanded that each band surrender to his mercy. He dictated common terms of peace with every headman he encountered. When he came upon someone suspected of a crime, he summarily had them hanged. In the midst of all this, Wright reported to Clarke,

> I have this moment finished with the Pelouses. After calling them together in council, I addressed them in severe language, enumerating their murders, thefts, and war against the United States troops. I then demanded the murderers of the two miners in April last. One man was brought out and hung forthwith. Two of the men who stole the cattle from Walla-Walla valley were hung. . . . I then brought out my Indian prisoners, and found three of them were either Walla-Wallas or Yakimas. They were hung on the spot. One of the murderers of the miners had been hung on the Spokane. . . . I have treated these Indians severely, but they justly deserved it all. They will remember it.[36]

Later that day, Wright reported to Clarke, "Many barns filled with wheat or oats, also several fields of grain, with numerous caches of vegetables, dried berries, and kamas, all destroyed, or used by the troops."[37] (This statement inadvertently offers evidence of the agricultural success of the Interior Salish people, which was a major goal of the BIA.[38]) The wave of brutality came to an end at Fort Walla Walla on October 9, when Wright called a council with the Cayuse and Walla Wallas and randomly hanged four men, including Waiecat, son of Feathercap (who had been identified by Howlishwanpum as a leader of the uprising). The papers in Olympia and Oregon City celebrated every correspondence during the campaign; Colonel Wright was a celebrity.

General Clarke offered his final thoughts on the situation in the Northwest on October 29, which reflected the Army's changed stance regarding

Stevens's treaties: "Some time since I was persuaded that the treaties made by Governor Stevens . . . should not be confirmed. Since then circumstances have changed and with them my views. . . . Influenced by these views I decided to urge on the department the immediate confirmation of these treaties . . . and the opening of the lands to settlers."[39] In September 1858, Gen. William S. Harney was put in charge of the newly created Department of Oregon. He heeded Clarke's advice and on October 31, 1858, declared the interior open to settlement—without ratification of the treaties. Harney did not concern himself with forcing the Indians onto the reservations. He reported to Army Headquarters: "The same improvidence which characterizes the Indian race elsewhere is seen here, attended by the same results; and it is not too much to predict that the red men of America will gradually disappear about the same time from the different sections of our country."[40]

9

US Army Forts on the Plateau

The establishment of the city of Walla Walla was not simply a result of the Army throwing the valley open to settlement in 1858. Merchants, farmers, ranchers, and families required certain guarantees of sustained prosperity. A market, or easy access to a market, was essential for one's agricultural production; a mercantile or a saloon required a steady flow of customers. The new Fort Walla Walla provided all of this, albeit on a limited scale. It also provided security in a recently insecure region.

There was no master plan for Army forts at this time, nor were there specifications regarding the design of buildings. Unlike the HBC trading posts, the Army "forts" in the Northwest required no fortifications; from the start, they were intended as offensive rather than defensive posts. A fort required a parade ground; training grounds; houses for officers, their families and slaves; barracks; stables; supply buildings; mechanic shops; a guardhouse; mess halls; laundry buildings; and privies. Decisions regarding the construction of new Army posts were left to commanding officers, and construction generally was carried out by the soldiers themselves, with locally available materials. Army buildings in the Far West during the 1850s were usually constructed in adobe, or the walls of simple frame structures were lined with adobe bricks. The Army claimed 640-acre reserves for their forts, with additional land reserved for wood and hay.[1]

Fort Dalles and Fort Simcoe

"When last I saw this post, three years since, it seemed to me to be the most unattractive on the Pacific. . . . The change now is a great one. . . . The officers' quarters are in the cottage form, and for taste are superior to those we have seen at any other post."

—Lt. Lawrence Kip, Fort Dalles, 1858[2]

In winter 1855, Colonel Wright assumed command of the 9th Infantry and was instructed by General Wool to establish his headquarters at Fort Dalles, "where all the troops intended for the Indian country will be concentrated."[3] The construction of the expanded fort was left to Quartermaster Capt. Thomas Jordan and his clerk and supervising architect, Louis Scholl. Between 1856 and 1858, they created the most aesthetically remarkable Army fort in the West.[4]

Despite their primary role as intimidating centers for the subjugation of the Indigenous people of the region, the new Army forts in the West took on the appearance of a New England village, built around a central village green.[5] Simple, single-story, adobe or side-gable frame buildings (which could be as long as necessary) were most common by the 1850s. In the case of Fort Dalles, however, the buildings were based on designs from Alexander Jackson Downing's *Architecture of Country Houses*. Prior to his untimely death in 1852, Downing was the foremost theorist of rural architecture. He sought to educate Americans on the morally transformative qualities of domestic aesthetics and the art of architecture. Since the 1830s, the Carpenter Gothic style had been made popular by a number of architects, including Downing, particularly through publications. These "picturesque" houses featured high-pitched roofs and gables, prominent front gables or center gables, elaborate bargeboards, bay windows, sometimes pointed archways, diamond-paned windows, and vertical board-and-batten siding. Downing insisted on board-and-batten siding, as opposed to horizontal clapboard siding, to emphasize the house's verticality—a hallmark of the Gothic style. He further insisted that materials be undisguised. For example, structural elements should be made visible; wood should look like wood and never be rendered to appear to be stone. Downing associated this with truth and honesty.

With the assistance of more than 200 civilian carpenters, masons, painters, and so on, Scholl oversaw the construction of a group of unique frame buildings adapted from Downing's plans.[6] The most opulent designs were reserved for the houses of Wright and Jordan (fig. 14). Of the latter design (fig. 15), Downing wrote, "The construction itself, though simple, is somewhat peculiar. . . . [O]n the exterior the construction shows, and gives additional richness and character to the composition."[7] He was referring to the visible heavy corner posts and the battens, which are fastened to the structural vertical studs. Scholl considered this plan "the finest

Figure 14. Quartermaster's house, Fort Dalles, 1857. Designed by Louis Scholl. Destroyed. Until 1861, Capt. Jordan, a Virginian, lived here with his wife, four children, two Black slaves, and a White domestic. (Oregon Historical Society Research Lib., 66475, pf1039.)

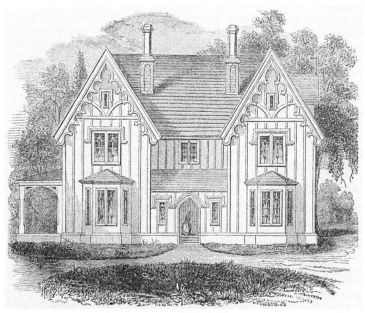

Figure 15. "A Plain Timber Cottage-Villa." (Downing, *Architecture of Country Houses*, design XXV.)

building Downing, our great national architect, ever has [designed]. It is a real beauty."[8] Like all the buildings at the fort, Scholl set this one on an undisguised stone base, which emphasized the irregularity of the terrain.

In August 1856, Wright charged Major Garnett and his two companies of the 9th Infantry to construct a fort in in the Simcoe Valley for the purpose of observing and controlling the Yakama. The house designed by Scholl for Major Garnett, not surprisingly, was based on another design by Downing (figs. 16 & 17). Even the officers' quarters, which were more subdued than those at Fort Dalles, were constructed with board-and-batten siding and diamond-paned windows.

The ultimate purpose of these village-forts was to conquer Sahaptian territory. To Indigenous eyes, they were rapidly built alien cities—unlike any HBC fort, unlike any missionary station, and unlike any town in the Willamette Valley. The regular martial drills and exercises along with the show and demonstration of arms by their identically uniformed soldiers must have been shocking. Could anyone have been confused about their purpose? Word of these hostile cities certainly spread quickly throughout the Columbia Plateau. To many, the forts themselves must have signaled a call to arms.

Cantonment Walla Walla

In January 1856, a month after the militia murdered Peo-Peo-Mox-Mox and apparently cleared the Walla Walla Valley of hostile Indians, General Wool instructed Colonel Wright to establish a permanent post near the HBC Fort Walla Walla "for controlling the surrounding Indian tribes, and to command the river and its crossings."[9] After studying the region, Wright instead instructed Major Steptoe to establish a post in the Walla Walla Valley, which Wright recommended naming Fort Walla-Walla. However, the initial blockhouse that was designated "Fort Walla-Walla" located up Mill Creek may never have been completed. After Stevens's debacle of a council with the hostile Sahaptians, Wright saw the need for a more permanent fort. He reported to Pacific Headquarters in October: "I have selected this position for a winter camp. It is on 'Mill Creek,' six miles from its junction with the Walla-Walla. The troops are busily employed in erecting temporary quarters."[10] The location—the site of *Pašx̣ápa*—was considered

Figure 16. Commanding officer's house, Fort Simcoe Historical Park, Yakama Indian Reservation, 1857. (Library of Congress, Historic American Buildings Survey, HABS WASH,39-WHIT.V,1–6.)

Figure 17. "A Villa Farm-House in the Bracketed Style." (Downing, *Architecture of Country Houses*, design 1850.)

to offer the best view of the valley in all directions and possessed one of the few areas of grass not burned by the hostile Indians (fig. 18). The post was subsequently referred to as "the cantonment."

We are fortunate to have a drawing of this fort; however, there are a number of individual drawings on the sheet, so it should not be viewed as a continuous image.[11] The fort is depicted from the west. According to Michael Kenney, an Irish-born veteran of the 1st Dragoons and longtime resident of Walla Walla, these were crude, windowless buildings constructed of local cottonwood logs, chinked with mud, with pole and sod roofs.[12] The individually drawn buildings in the foreground represent the types of structures comprising the fort and the first civilian buildings: Army-issue cloth tents and rough log buildings with sod roofs.

Although he had no family, Steptoe's existence was made more comfortable by two young slaves: "one black boy, one little Indian boy (whom I bought out of slavery & who is a most promising servant by the way)."[13] Steptoe suggested to Wright that "a good, industrious colony at Walla-Walla" could be beneficial to Indian relations. Wool responded to this

Figure 18. *The Dragoon Cantonment on Mill Creek*, 1857. (*Lyman's History of Old Walla Walla County*, 132.)

request by restating his order banning American settlement east of the Cascades and clarifying his concept of the roles played by the individual forts: "Simcoe and Walla-Walla [are] advanced posts not for the immediate protection of the whites, but to keep the Indians in awe, to be advised of their feelings and intentions, and to check and change these when they become inimical. To permit settlers to pass the Dalles and occupy the natural reserve, is to give up this advantage, throw down this wall, and advance the frontier hundreds of miles to the east, and add to the protective labors of the army."[14] Nonetheless, a small settlement was already developing outside the fort. The ordinance banning White settlement exempted civilian laborers employed by the Army and government-licensed traders, including the fort sutler and others who furnished the fort with supplies and housed, fed, and provided whiskey to the laborers, teamsters, and parties of miners headed for Colville. The merchants generally came by way of The Dalles.

The Final Fort Walla Walla

In January 1857, Steptoe proposed building a more permanent fort in a more advantageous location. Given the paucity of building material in the valley, he recommended constructing the walls of the buildings in adobe brick. Wright approved, and plans for Steptoe's *third* Fort Walla Walla commenced in the spring. At the same time, Pacific Headquarters began expressing concerns over the construction costs of forts Dalles and Simcoe. Already in October 1856, Maj. Osborne Cross, headquarters quartermaster, warned Captain Jordan that his buildings at Fort Dalles were too opulent and expensive. During the relatively quiet 1857 in the Northwest, one of the major military conflicts centered on the cost and style of the fort buildings. Wright argued, "[T]he number of teamsters, packers, herders, and other persons employed in connection with supplying the advanced posts . . . do not justify the statement that 'the expenses of the Post are enormous.'"[15] In June 1857, General Clarke undertook an inspection tour of the Northwest forts together with Deputy Quartermaster Col. Thomas Swords. Clarke then issued orders regarding fort architecture that would impact Scholl's designs for Fort Walla Walla:

II. [S]tructures will be of the plainest kind, according to climate, in view of the health of the troops, and of the most convenient, and economical procurement of materials for construction.

IV. The requisitions for money and materials for erection of Posts, and the necessary buildings appurtenant thereto, will undergo, at Department Head-Quarters, such a scrutiny as a just regard to public economy may seem to require.[16]

Colonel Swords was outraged by Jordan's activities at Fort Dalles. He reported to the Quartermaster General: "In regard to the building operations. . . . I regret that I cannot speak even so favorably, a style of architecture having been adopted, entirely unsuited to a Military post on the frontier. . . . [T]he quarters built for and occupied by Col. Wright . . . a double house with two full stories and attic, [are] such as I have never seen occupied by a private gentleman except at or in the neighborhood of our large Eastern cities; certainly no private residence at all comparable to it can be found on the Pacific."[17] In October 1858, Col. Joseph K. Mansfield, inspector general of the Army, visited the new forts designed by Scholl. Of Fort Dalles, he noted that the officers' quarters "resemble the fancy residence in the country near our large cities. . . . Capt. Jordan is active and ambitious to erect handsome quarters, & deserves credit for his zeal & good intentions: but I cannot agree with him as to the style of buildings for a garrison, in this remote region of country."[18] Of the commanding officer's quarters at Fort Simcoe, Mansfield noted: "A less fanciful building would probably have been quite as comfortable."[19] (The controversy over these forts was at least partly responsible for the War Department's first attempt to regulate fort architecture, which culminated with its 1860 publication *Regulations concerning Barracks and Quarters for the Army of the United States.*[20])

The government funds pumped into Fort Dalles (nearly $500,000 by Mansfield's estimate[21]) fueled the growth of the adjoining town, whose population exceeded 800 in 1860, when it was renamed The Dalles. The city boasted several hotels—including the three-story Umatilla House—regular steamer service to and from Portland, saloons, brothels, restaurants, general stores, and a number of Carpenter Gothic houses. (In 1858, the city was affluent enough to attract the San Francisco lithographic firm of Kuchel & Dresel to produce a lithographic view of the city.) Because emigration from the East had been halted since 1855, the city's rapid growth was the result of migration from California and the Willamette Valley, and from discharged soldiers. James Fulton, for example, had taken his family overland in 1847, settled in the Willamette Valley, mined for gold in California, then settled near Fort Dalles, where he raised cattle and lived on government contracts to supply the fort with beef. (His daughters married Henry P. Isaacs and Louis Scholl.)

Steptoe could only envy Fort Dalles for its proximity to a town. His was nothing more than a hinterland outpost. Scholl sent his plans for the new Fort Walla Walla to his friend Steptoe in April 1857.[22] Certainly, he was instructed to avoid excessive ornament for the building designs.

Steptoe selected a well-watered site on a 30-foot bluff in May 1857.[23] The use of adobe brick as insulation was an essential feature at Fort Walla Walla; after an exceptionally harsh winter in 1856–57, Steptoe was more concerned with comfort than aesthetics. He had been stationed at Fort Kearny, Fort Laramie, and the Presidio in San Francisco, all of which were constructed with adobe brick, and he was well aware of the adobe ruins at the former Whitman farm and at the HBC Fort Walla Walla. The latter was repaired to serve as the quartermaster's warehouse; to avoid confusion with the new fort, it was renamed "Walulla."[24] Lumber for the balloon-frame buildings (with board-and-batten siding over the adobe walls) came from Fort Dalles and from pine harvested up Mill Creek. Years later, Scholl, then a resident of Walla Walla, recalled that "All exterior and interior finished Articles were made by hand planing at [Fort Dalles]. Doors, Sashes, Mantlepieces, Writing Desks, Book cases, Lounges, Wardrobes, &c, Bedsteads for Officers Qrs."[25]

Gustav Sohon's image of Fort Walla Walla (fig. 19) is mostly accurate.[26] The view is from the west, looking across the fort to the stables, with the burgeoning city in the distance. The buildings at the left, the hospital and the quartermaster's storehouse, are two of the more ornate buildings at the fort. The storehouse and some other center-gabled outbuildings seem to have been based on Downing's designs specifically for such buildings. Only the hospital and the soon-to-be-built commanding officer's house were originally designed with dormers. In comparison to those at Dalles and Simcoe, the officers' quarters (depicted at the right of the print, in white) were quite austere: 1.5-story, side-gabled, with verandas running the length of the façade. There were no Downingesque bargeboards, no elaborate

Figure 19. *Military Post & City of Walla-Walla, W.T. in 1862* (detail). Lithograph based on a drawing by Gustav Sohon. The view is from the west. Double officers' quarters were arranged along the south side and barracks on the north side. Behind each barrack was a kitchen and a privy (the officers' quarters each had had their own privy). Facing the parade ground on the west side were the guardhouse and the commanding officer's quarters. The hospital, quartermaster's house, and quartermaster's storehouse were located to the northwest of the quad (left foreground). Stables were located to the east of the quad. Shops and buildings for civilian workers were situated in appropriate sites away from the quad. All the buildings were set on brick foundations. (*Report of Captain John Mullan*, 1863.)

window hoods, no ornate columns nor latticework, no diamond-paned windows. The Downing-inspired elements were limited to bay windows on the officers' quarters, board-and-batten siding, and several prominent center-gables.

After his punitive march, Colonel Wright was named commander of Fort Walla Walla, which Inspector General Mansfield now declared to be—strategically—the most important post in the department, "admirably placed to destroy all combinations this side of the Cascades Mountains, & west of the rocky mountains in this region." He reported that given the fort's proximity to the planned military roads, the roads to the mines, and the overland trail, it should be permanently and "strongly occupied by troops to overawe the Indians, & send out expeditions to punish offenders."[27] General Harney agreed, and until historic events intervened again, the fort was to be garrisoned by two companies each of the 1st Dragoons and the 9th Infantry. Mansfield and Harney suspended construction on Fort Dalles—which was now regarded as only a supply station for Fort Walla Walla—and to turn over Fort Simcoe to the BIA. They also called for a post to be built near the Colville mining area and Fort Boise to be built between Fort Walla Walla and Utah.

The War Department established three reservations for Fort Walla Walla of 1 square mile each: one around the post, one to the northwest for hay, and one up Mill Creek for wood. The remainder of the valley was open to settlement. The area was still populated by "overawed" Cayuse bands and their grazing horses. Some elders could still remember Lewis and Clark; they witnessed and navigated through times of incredible change, mostly traumatic.

While the new fort was under construction (May 1857 to March 1858) a village developed along the ancient trail to the west of the cantonment, across Mill Creek. This town had taken on two names: "Steptoeville" in honor of the man who made it possible, as far as the villagers were concerned; and "Wailepta," which had been recognized by the postmaster general since 1854. William Craig, the Indian agent to the Nez Perce, had built a house a mile to the east of the cantonment and was named postmaster.

From an imperial American perspective, the forts were effective in establishing domination of the Sahaptian people and, in the case of forts

Walla Walla and Dalles, in encouraging settlement. The unratified treaties of 1855 and the planned reservations were the responsibility of the BIA—which was regarded contemptuously by the Army. The Army, the governor, and the vast majority of settlers had only contempt for the Indians, who could only attempt to maintain their antebellum lifeways around the fort and village.

Part II

"Marching Back with Civilization to the Eastward"

Like The Dalles, the initial development of Walla Walla came from the West. The opening of the region to settlement first attracted American and European men (and a small number of women) who were former overlanders from the Willamette Valley and The Dalles, former California gold rushers, or discharged soldiers. Of course, all saw opportunities to improve their lives by claiming free land, by procuring government contracts to supply Fort Walla Walla with provisions, or by establishing essential, if temporary, businesses. The discovery of gold on the Clearwater River in 1861 rapidly transformed the town into a dynamic satellite of San Francisco. By the late 1860s, however, the miners and pack trains had moved on. During the ensuing, increasingly difficult economic times, residents of the city and the valley were forced to become self-sufficient. At the same time, Walla Walla was growing steadily, towns were established across Walla Walla and Umatilla counties, and Sahaptians were increasingly harassed in the valley and on the reservation.

These are only general facts of the early development of the city and region. A nuanced understanding of this place and time requires a detailed approach to a broad range of issues. The following sections are somewhat chronological but are treated more as thematic vignettes than sequential chapters. Some of these sections may even seem disruptive to the narrative. The goal here is a realistic picture, not a neat narrative.

10

Steptoeville 1857–59

"Things are quiet and prosperous at Walla Walla."

—A. J. Cain, summer 1859

"Stores open as usual people Drunk and quarreling."

—A. J. Thibodo, Christmas, Walla Walla, 1859[1]

When General Harney declared the territory east of the Cascades open to settlement on October 31, 1858, the Walla Walla Valley already possessed a significant White population. Fort Walla Walla had taken on the appearance of a village, with more than 400 residents, including a couple dozen families. A few miles to the west, the small farms of Frenchtown were again flourishing. Just to the east of the fort reserve, a few government-licensed traders had built temporary structures. A mile further east, where the old Nez Perce trail crossed Mill Creek on the former site of *Pašxápa*, stood the dragoon cantonment and another group of buildings and tents belonging to government-licensed traders. In what reads like a tourist brochure, Lt. John Mullan described in an official report the appearance of the valley on his approach to Fort Walla Walla from the southwest on a July morning in 1859:

> Gaining the end or crest of the high table-land we enjoyed the magnificent panorama of the Walla-Walla valley that lay at our feet. To our right lay the bold ridge of the Blue mountains; in front the ocean of prairie, beyond which flowed the waters of the Snake river; while to our left was seen the line of the Columbia as it traced itself from point to point by the bluffs and buttes that defined its course; while within their limits lay embosomed the beautiful valley of the Walla-Walla, with the stream of the same name, with its hundreds of feeders pouring down from the mountain sides, flowing midway through the valley; while far in the distance the marks of civilized abodes, and clouds of dust raised by

countless herds, bespoke our approach to thriving settlements. The valley of the Walla-Walla may be regarded as one of the most fertile . . . in this whole region. . . . The valley, if properly cultivated, together with the cultivable section tributary to it, will support a population of not less than 15,000 people.[2]

Isaac Stevens, the territory's congressional delegate, was far more optimistic than Mullan. In an article published in January 1859, he claimed "The Walla-Walla valley . . . is the great key of the interior, and can subsist a farming population of 100,000 souls."[3] Outside of the garrison, perhaps 200 Whites were settled or active in the valley, primarily in Frenchtown. And hundreds of Cayuse continued to occupy sites along the Walla Walla River and its tributaries (although Mullan would not have considered their lodges "civilized abodes").

Aside from the sutler, the official fort merchant, the first traders to set up shop outside the cantonment came from The Dalles by way of California or the Willamette Valley, attracted like pilot fish to the new fort—or, more accurately, to the paymaster. They carried temporary government licenses and were generally attached to the quartermaster. Temporality, indicated by the licenses, was further signified by the construction of commercial buildings: tents, "poles and mud," planks chinked with mud, logs repurposed from the cantonment, all with dirt floors. No one yet owned the ground on which these structures sat; no one could predict the growth of the town and region, thus there was little incentive to erect anything but the most cost-effective structures.

Among the first businesses outside the cantonment—on what would become Main Street—was a log mercantile established by William McWhirk on behalf of the ambitious, far-sighted Dalles merchant, Henry P. Isaacs.[4] Frank Worden, who had also worked with Isaacs, built a frame store in 1857 (on what became the southwest corner of Second and Main; see fig. 46), with lumber milled at The Dalles.[5] Lewis McMorris, who worked as a teamster and carpenter for the quartermaster, supplied these merchants with goods from Portland, and oversaw the construction of some of the first stores and houses.

A number of entrepreneurs decided that once the cantonment was abandoned, the town would move to the west end of the road where it entered the fort reservation (current 12th Ave. between Poplar and Alder).

Harry Howard built a log saloon known as the Half-way House—due to its proximity to both the fort and the cantonment. Three more saloons, a general store, and a bakery were also quickly established. This burgeoning town took on the name Halfway. However, due to the Halfway site's lack of both wood and water, the businesses (and their building materials) soon moved to the Mill Creek site.[6] The Half-way House itself was reconstructed on the main street and rechristened the Gem Saloon. The earliest development of the town was well documented by Alvin B. Roberts, a stonemason who was among the first influx of settlers, arriving from Portland. Like many of his contemporaries, he initially became enamored with the Walla Walla Valley while serving with the militia in 1855.[7]

Despite the gradual decommissioning of the cantonment during 1859, newly arriving businessmen continued to set up shop along the road to the west of the cantonment, called both Wailepta and Steptoeville. Besides businessmen from The Dalles, recently discharged soldiers—particularly recent immigrants—figured prominently among the new residents (similar to the settlement of retired HBC employees).[8] Among the new merchants were James McAuliff (born in Malta of Irish parents), who had established a successful dry goods business in The Dalles after his discharge. On their discharge from the 9th Infantry in 1859, Sgts. Ralph Guichard (Prussia) and William Kohlhauff (Rheinland Pfalz), together with Kohlhauff's wife Johanna (Rheinland Pfalz), had a mercantile store built on what became the northwest corner of Main and Third (which may have been the town's first store with wooden floors and glass windows [fig. 20]). One of the saloons moved from Halfway to Steptoeville was established by Irish-born Sgt. Michael J. Kenney after his discharge from the 1st Dragoons. Other merchants like Elias B. Whitman, a cousin of Marcus Whitman, arrived from California.

In these years, the merchants' clientele consisted of the quartermaster, the garrison (which was paid irregularly), a steady stream of teamsters, parties of miners on their way up to Colville, and the Cayuse that continued to farm and raise horses in the area. The Army's chief paymaster for the District of Oregon carried the vital economic nourishment to the towns that developed around the forts. Small armies of professional gamblers and transient prostitutes followed the paymaster on his rounds.

The town grew at a steady pace in 1859–60. Roads into the valley were improved to assist settlers arriving from the west. Also, for the first time in four years, overlanders began passing through the Walla Walla Valley in late summer 1859, some intending to settle there. Additionally in 1859, the military wagon road from Fort Walla Walla to Fort Colville was completed, and another road from Fort Walla Walla to Fort Benton (the "Mullan Road") was begun. The growth of the town received another boost in April 1859, when the steamer *Colonel Wright* began transporting passengers and freight between The Dalles and Wallula. On receiving word of the *Colonel Wright*'s first successful run, General Harney informed Army headquarters: "The increased facility of communication thus offered can be estimated by knowing that heretofore it occupied from a week to ten days to make the journey to Walla-Walla, which is now done in two days. . . . The valley of the Walla-Walla has already some two thousand industrious and thriving settlers in it . . . with an emigration steadily increasing this number."[9] (Actually, the trip upriver could take three days, but the return to the Deschutes could take a mere six hours.) John F. Abbott, who had established successful stage lines in Oregon, traveled on the *Colonel Wright*'s maiden voyage and soon established a stage line from Steptoeville to the steamer port at Wallula.

From present indications, there will be a population of 2000 persons [in the Walla Walla Valley] before the Spring shall close, chiefly composed of residents of Oregon. The Willamette Valley will be strongly represented there in men and stock, and we learn that quite a number of our citizens will leave Portland within the next month to establish themselves in new homes in the Walla-walla. To this population let there be added the bulk of the heavy immigration expected during the coming season from the older States, and we may not be surprised if before another year that country will favorably compare with the most populous districts of Oregon in numbers and wealth. It is, doubtless, the finest country for stock raising known upon the Pacific slope.

—*Puget Sound Herald*, March 18, 1859

The sense of enduring White settlement in the valley was also signaled by the agricultural economy around the fort and the opportunities it provided for settlement. Within the apparently endless sea of tall, bluebunch wheatgrass, wild sunflower, and other perennial grasses, farms were well established in Frenchtown, and land was being cleared and farmed and live-stock was grazing around the fort reserve for the quartermaster. In spring 1858, for example, Charles Russell, the chief teamster for the quarter-master, was contracted to farm 80 acres of barley on a site just to the north of the fort.[10] Louis and Charles Mullan (brothers of Lieutenant Mullan) and others also farmed for the quartermaster to the west of the reserve. Lewis McMorris was contracted to farm grain, but Cayuse who "felt there were enough farms on their land" forced him to abandon the plan.[11] After his discharge from the 1st Dragoons, Joseph McEvoy, another recent Irish immigrant, ran a cattle ranch for the quartermaster. Like most of the veterans mentioned above, McEvoy and McMorris spent the remainder of their lives in the area.

To supply flour to the fort, in 1859 Capt. Frederick Tracy Dent com-missioned Almos H. Reynolds to build a grist mill on the land claim of John Simms on Yellowhawk Creek. Reynolds, a millwright from New York, had come West with the gold rush, then built several mills in Oregon, maintaining a one-third interest in each.[12] For the mill known originally as Simms's Mill (and later, Pasca Mills), each of the three men owned a third of the business. (According to the federal census of 1860, Reynolds and Simms were among the four wealthiest residents of the county. Only the fort sutler and A. H. Robie, the former assistant to Governor Stevens and Indian agent who established the first sawmill on Mill Creek, listed greater assets.[13])

The majority of overland immigrants arriving in 1859 were interested in acquiring farmland in the established valleys west of the Cascades. Based on the reports of Wilkes, Farnham, Stevens, and others, it was by now gen-eral knowledge that the Walla Walla Valley was ideal grazing land but of limited value for the cultivation of grain. In summer 1859, the *Daily Alta California*, for example, noted, "An exodus has taken place for the Walla Walla country . . . and large numbers of cattle are being driven there, as the country affords rich grazing ground."[14] Ranchers arrived primarily from the Far West, though Hamet Hubbard Case, a surveyor from Illi-nois, was among the new arrivals from the east to settle in the valley. The final entry in his travel diary (September 19, 1859) reads: "Spent the day investigating the virtues of the valley. Visited the Fort and the town of

'Steptoe'—The valley is quite extensive & no doubt the best grazing country in the world. But the good farming soil is only in small patches on the creek bottom."[15] Case was virtually quoting from published reports of the previous two decades.

Aside from numerous reports of the vast grazing land, ranchers from Oregon were lured to the valley by the dryer climate. Some sold their homesteads, acquired through the Donation Land Act, and now sought to procure public land according to the Bounty-Land Act (for veterans of the US military or the territorial militia), the Land Act of 1820 (which allowed anyone to purchase at least 80 acres for $1.25/acre), or the Preemption Act of 1841. Between the ratification of the Indian treaties in 1859 and the passage of the Homestead Act of 1862, the Preemption Act allowed for a "head of a household" or a White man over the age of twenty-one to claim a parcel of up to 160 acres, build a "personal residence thereon," then either purchase the land for $1.25/acre after fourteen months or receive a patent for the land after residing on it for five years.

Squatters' rights may have sounded simple enough to the savvy, experienced ranchers of the Willamette Valley; however, claiming land in the unsurveyed Walla Walla Valley at this time could lead to years of uncertainty and/or litigation.[16] A shortage of qualified surveyors and lawyers, combined with the distance from the land office in Olympia, guaranteed that the government could not keep pace with land claims. Naturally, the newcomers from the West and the recently discharged soldiers had the first shots at claiming choice tracts around the burgeoning town.

William Craig established a homestead in and around current Pioneer Park in 1858 (at which time the cantonment was the seat of the Indian Agency). When Craig moved to Lapwai in 1860, this property was held by his (half-Nez Perce) daughter Martha and her husband, A. H. Robie.[17] Early in 1859, A. B. Roberts claimed 160 acres to the south of Main Street.[18] After assembling a canvas house (near current Colville and Poplar), he planted several hundred fruit trees and fenced the perimeter of his claim. "The pre-emption allowed you to hold all you fenced in until it was surveyed," he noted.[19] Edmund H. Barron staked a claim stretching from the western border of Roberts's claim to the eastern border of the military reserve. In 1860, Roberts sold a section of land bordering Barron's claim to John Sparks. It was common for land to be sold, traded, or bartered, even prior to a patent having been issued for a tract of land.[20] In short, the business of land acquisition was a mess; the land laws seemed to encourage abuse and speculation.[21]

The Seat of Walla Walla County

On April 25, 1854, the superambitious legislature of the new Washington Territory had established Walla Walla County—a region of more than 100,000 square miles, stretching from the Cascades to the Rockies between the 46th and 49th parallels north latitude. Their choice of name for the county would ultimately result in the name of the city. So why did they choose "Walla Walla"? A glance at the official, government-commissioned map of the Oregon Territory of the time may provide the answer (map 4). The map was produced by the US Exploring Expedition of 1838–42 and first published in 1844. The territory on the map north of the Columbia River, stretching from the Klickitat River to the Palouse River, bears the words "Walla Walla" in large, uppercase letters. This actually represented the extent of the Sahaptin language according to Horatio Hale, the linguist of the expedition. However, taken out of context, the Wilkes map offered an obvious name for the enormous county.

The American population of the region was so insignificant in 1854 that the county designation was preposterousness.[22] And, of course, the other 99.9 percent of the county's occupants were unaware that they were now living in a county.

With the non-Indian population in the Walla Walla Valley approaching 1,000, the territorial legislature again attempted to organize Walla Walla County in January 1859. A provisional government was appointed and charged with making arrangements to hold elections.[23] Three weeks later, Olympia's *Pioneer and Democrat* reported, "By a private letter from A. J. Cain, Indian agent for the Columbia river district, we learn that a permanent population is rapidly pouring into Walla-walla country. He states that the Walla-walla county will pole a large vote at the next general election, and that on politics she is *all right*."[24] By "all right," Cain was implying that the electorate would be solidly with the Democratic Party. The county's first Democratic convention was held in Steptoeville on April 9.

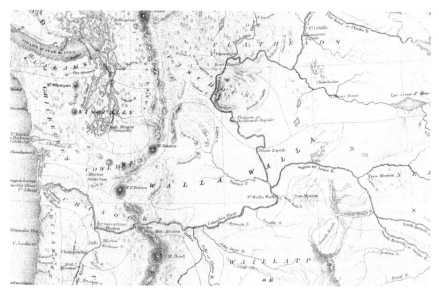

Map 4. The Oregon Territory (detail). (Wilkes, *United States Exploring Expedition,* 1844.)

Unsurprisingly, the men appointed by the territorial legislature in January figured prominently.[25] During the next two decades, Walla Walla County became the bastion of the Democratic Party in Washington Territory.

In June 1859, the provisional government made arrangements to hold elections, to rent a courthouse (initially, I. T. Reese's building), and to levy a property tax. To avoid confusion, just prior to the election, the officials changed the name of the town from Steptoeville to Wailetpa—as it was known to the postmaster general. A small building used for religious services and public meetings (near current Birch and Fourth) was selected as the voting site for Steptoeville. The 16×30–foot wattle-and-daub building had been constructed for Catholic services in 1857–58 by Sgt. William Kohlhauff on orders of Major Steptoe.[26] (It also became the site of the town cemetery.)

Although the city records were lost in a fire in 1865, it appears the majority of those elected had participated in the county's Democratic convention. Thirty-five residents then petitioned the county commissioners to have Wailetpa surveyed and platted. This was followed by another petition requesting that the name of the town be changed from Wailetpa to

Walla Walla, thus embracing the names of both the county and the fort.[27] Both petitions were acted on by the officials on November 17. "Walla Walla" was established as the seat of Walla Walla County. Hamet Hubbard Case was named county surveyor and commissioned to survey and plat the town, which extended west from the point at which the Nez Perce trail crossed Mill Creek (one square half mile originally but expanded and "corrected" by Walter W. Johnson in 1861). One acre was reserved for a courthouse and other public buildings. The street grid followed the course of the main street, originally called Nez Perce, which ran diagonally— southwest-northeast—across the plat (map 5). This resulted in the bifurcation of numerous blocks at the edges of the plat (litigation would follow, of course). Nez Perce and the streets running parallel to it (called Sumach, Rose, Alder, Poplar, and Birch) were to be 100 feet wide. The cross streets were to be 80 feet wide, and were given numerical designations, extending from First St. near the eastern edge of the plat. Lots were established with frontage of 60 feet and depth of 120 feet, and were sold for $5 each plus a $1 recorder's fee, with a limit of two lots per person. Lots were required to be fenced within six months and to be built on within a year. Isham T. Reese, a recent arrival from McMinnville, Oregon, was appointed county recorder and purchased the first lot (on which he already had a building, on the southeast corner of Second and Nez Perce).

A. B. Roberts recalled that the survey team came to his farm in summer 1860 and established Alder, Poplar, and Birch Streets from a large section of his land.[28] Roberts and others were forced to either surrender to the town its claimed sections or enter into litigation against the city. Soon Roberts, the most important orchardist in the region, was almost forced into a real estate side business due to the desirability of his adjoining tract for residential lots. Roberts reserved a 10-acre lot for his family between Alder and Birch.[29]

Oregon Statehood

Oregon statehood was being vehemently debated in Congress when Gen. Harney declared the interior open to settlement. Slavery was the major issue. The constitution drafted in Salem a year earlier had banned slavery (and, radically, excluded free Blacks from residing in the state). However,

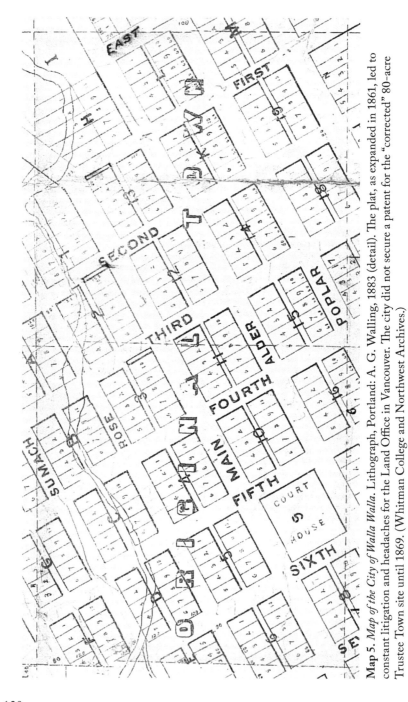

Map 5. *Map of the City of Walla Walla.* Lithograph, Portland: A. G. Walling, 1883 (detail). The plat, as expanded in 1861, led to constant litigation and headaches for the Land Office in Vancouver. The city did not secure a patent for the "corrected" 80-acre Trustee Town site until 1869. (Whitman College and Northwest Archives.)

a far less heated debate concerned the constitution's proposed northeast boundary of the state. The northern boundary followed the Columbia from its mouth to the Snake River, then followed the Snake to the Owyhee River. Thus, the constitutional convention claimed a small part of the vast Washington Territory, embracing the whole of the Walla Walla Valley, arguing that the Snake River boundary was "not only natural in itself, but natural in uniting the political destinies and social feelings of a people residing in the [Walla Walla] valley."

However, due to the concerted efforts of congressional representative Isaac Stevens, Congress rejected the incursion into Washington Territory and set the boundary along the Columbia "to a point near Fort Walla-Walla, where the forty-sixth parallel of north latitude crosses said river; thence east on said parallel to the middle of the main channel of the . . . Snake River"[30] (map 6). President Buchanan signed the statehood bill into law on February 14, 1859. However, the boundary was not surveyed until 1866. (In fact, for a time in 1865, the surveyor claimed that the city of Walla Walla was actually in Oregon.[31])

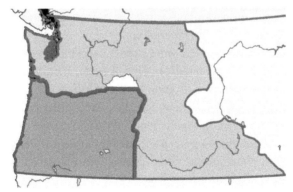

Map 6. The state of Oregon and Washington Territory, 1859–63. (The disputed territory in white.) Congress declared, "Until Congress shall otherwise direct, the residue of the Territory of Oregon shall be and is hereby incorporated into and made a part of the Territory of Washington." (Adapted from map by Uwe Dedering, used under creativecommons.org/licenses/by/4.0.)

The Census of 1860

The first census to include Walla Walla subdivided the county into four precincts: Fort Walla-Walla, Dry Creek, Touchet, and Walla Walla. The census ignored "Indians not taxed," certainly undercounted the Chinese and "Free Colored" residents, and included many transient White laborers. Nonetheless, it offers substantial statistics on the number of families in the area and their places of origin. With a counted population of 722, Walla Walla was suddenly the largest of the "cities, towns, or other definable subdivisions" in Washington Territory.[32] And despite being understaffed at the time of the census, Fort Walla Walla ranked fourth with a population of 320, including 50 women and children. Walla Walla precinct was 77 percent male, and only half of the females were over the age of eighteen. (Lewis McMorris later recalled, "girls were scarce articles here in the early days." Stag dances seem to have been common.[33])

Of the fifty-six families settled in Walla Walla, forty-six had either moved from Oregon or California, or were already residents prior to 1858. In December, the *Pioneer and Democrat* declared: "[W]e are steadily marching back with civilization to the eastward."[34] Only ten families, including one from Ireland, had arrived from the East during the previous year.[35] The vast majority of Walla Wallans listed their occupation as "farmer" (120). There were twenty-eight merchants and twenty-seven teamsters in town. As for building the town, there were twenty carpenters, two painters, a "nail cutter," a glass blower, and a mason. One "Free Colored" man, two Chinese men, and seventeen "Indian" women (wives of White men) were counted.

At the fort there were thirteen families, each with one to four children, and thirteen wives of soldiers were working as laundresses (which was common). Not surprisingly, 64 percent of the fort's garrison was born in either Ireland (122) or the states of the German Confederation (52). The fort's slave population was not recorded.

11

The Cayuse in Limbo 1858–61

Treaties are written out conveying away millions of acres, not one word of which the Indians understand; and complicated articles involving the most abstruse legal provisions, furnishing subjects for interminable litigation, are fully explained and elucidated by some ignorant half-breed interpreter, who does not know one letter from another, but who acts under the direction of some politician, who desires to win his way to public favor by perpetrating a huge swindle upon those who have neither the power or intelligence adequate to their own protection. While the Indians are lost in admiration in listening to the florid eloquence of some sharp commissioner, who dilates in the most extravagant hyperbole upon the justice and magnanimity of their "great father at Washington," they are quietly robbed of their patrimony.

—Senator James Nesmith of Oregon, 1862[1]

When the region was opened to settlement in October 1858, White American soldiers may have been the principal occupants of the valley. Yet the number of Cayuse in the valley had increased, in the wake of a devastating attack on the Umatilla River Cayuse by the Shoshone. Indian agent A. P. Dennison reported, "The Cayuse tribe have recently had a fight with their old enemies, the Snake Indians, in which they were badly beaten, having their principal chief [Weatenatemany] killed, and several men and women. The Snakes also succeeded in capturing a large number of their horses, camp fixtures, &c., and taking several of their women prisoners."[2] Five Crows, Qemátspelu, and perhaps Itstikats spent their last years in the Wallowa Valley among Old Chief Joseph's band of Nez Perce (known to the Nez Perce as "the Wilewmutkin band" to emphasize their close ties with the Cayuse).[3] The new Cayuse leaders were headmen of the Walla Walla Valley: Howlishwanpum and Tintinmitse.[4] Both had been friendly with the Americans, although Howlishwanpum was particularly skeptical at the 1855 treaty council. Qemátspelu was succeeded as war chief by Hyumhowlish.

In December 1858, Andrew J. Cain was commissioned to head the Nez Perce Agency and to temporarily serve as agent to the Cayuse, Walla Walla, Palus, and Spokan people.[5] Among his primary duties were to take a census of the Indians, to assess their condition, and, after receiving word in July 1859, to inform them of the ratifications of the 1855 treaties. Lacking fluency in a Sahaptian language, he was not an ideal candidate for such an important position. However, he worked relentlessly and traveled extensively to carry out his charge. His reports to the superintendent of Indian Affairs for Oregon and Washington, Edward R. Geary (1859–61), offer important glimpses into the condition and attitudes of the Sahaptians in the Walla Walla region. In summer 1859, he noted that the Cayuse (with an estimated population of 400) were living exclusively in the Walla Walla Valley. Cain continued:

> They have been much reduced in numbers from war and disease, and, with the exception of a few of the principal men who have some horses and cattle, are very much impoverished. Some of the principal men who have families cultivate small gardens. . . . The tribe have lost many of their tribal characteristics, and the chiefs have but little influence over their young men, who are much addicted to liquor, and wandering over the country creating disturbances with other Indians. The whole tribe have been much averse to removing from [the Walla Walla] valley, and desire, when compelled to remove, to go to the [Wallowa Valley], (and some have avowed a determination to go of their own accord, as they foresee that the rapid influx of whites will compel their speedy removal) to be enabled to subsist their stock. I will most earnestly recommend their removal at the earliest practicable period, as they cannot remain in their present condition long without being reduced to a state of vagabondism which will render them entirely dependent upon the government for subsistence.

Throughout the 1860s and '70s, Cayuse are documented living and harvesting on the periphery of Walla Walla, and regularly selling and trading horses and cattle on Main Street.

Cain noted of the Walla Wallas,

> with but very few exceptions, [they] are in a very destitute and impoverished condition. Their numbers have been greatly reduced from war,

disease, and starvation, about fifty having died during the last winter from the two latter causes, and many of their influential men, who were instigators of hostilities, have left their tribe, and are living amongst the [Nez Perce]. In my first intercourse with this tribe during the last winter, I discovered strong indications of disaffection. . . . Since the receipt of information in regard to the confirmation of the "treaties," they have been scattered over the country securing roots and fish, and I have had no opportunity of explaining the change that would be made in their condition. They have no cattle, but few horses, and do but little gardening, owing to the unsettled life they have led for the past four years: their subsistence is principally upon roots and fish.[6]

The unstable and insecure conditions of the Cayuse and Walla Wallas are markedly contrasted in Cain's report with the generally positive and healthy condition of the Nez Perce.

Interestingly, Cain always put the word *treaties* in quotes. After spending more time with the people assigned to the Umatilla reservation in summer 1859, he openly criticized the treaties in his correspondence with Geary, arguing that the plans for the reservation should be abandoned because none of the Indians would be satisfied there and because the emigrant road passed *through* the reservation. Based on cultural and kinship ties, he recommended that the Umatilla join the Warm Springs reservation, the Cayuse and Palus join the Nez Perce, and the Walla Walla join the Yakama.[7] In his report of 1860, Cain more emphatically stated the need to rethink the Umatilla reservation, noting that the Cayuse were still residing exclusively in the Walla Walla Valley,

where they have cultivated their usual garden spots. But their attention is principally directed to the care of their horses and cattle. Owing to the rapid increase of the white settlers, daily conflicts occur in regard to their respective rights, and all my energies have been taxed to preserve friendly relations. . . . They would much prefer to go to the Nez Percé reservation, as they have intermarried, speak the same language, and have been mostly absorbed by that tribe . . . The few that remain to be removed are the remainder of a once haughty and powerful tribe, who still claim that the whites are the aggressors, and whilst they profess a desire to be friendly, they wish to be removed as far as possible from the white settlements.[8]

Ignoring Cain's pleas, Geary expressed satisfaction with the Umatilla reservation in his annual report to the Commissioner of Indian Affairs.[9] He was primarily concerned with the availability of alcohol among the Indians and the impractical plans to get payments and supplies to the reservations. Cain himself was soon too overwhelmed with the gold rush on the Nez Perce reservation to concern himself with the Umatilla.

Establishing the Reservation

If demoralization of these wards had been designed by the Government, it is doubtful if the scheme to accomplish it would not have given better satisfaction to them than the past treatment by political Indian agents.

—T. W. Davenport, Indian agent[10]

The BIA had been largely dysfunctional since its creation within the War Department in 1824. After its transfer to the Department of the Interior in 1849, the agency continued to suffer from a lack of continuity, plus it entered into a hostile relationship with the War Department. The BIA was particularly ineffectual during the 1860s, when it was understaffed and overwhelmed by the flood of treaties ratified or not ratified during the previous decade. The Civil War and its aftermath only added to its chaotic state. Six individuals held the position of commissioner of Indian Affairs during the 1860s. Superintendents were appointed by the president based on recommendations of the commissioners. Reservations were managed by agents, who were appointed on recommendation of the superintendents. The position of Indian agent was not a profession; in the 1860s, appointees were often merchants, and, not surprisingly, their appointments were often favors based on personal acquaintance with the superintendent or some regional politician. For a meager annual salary, the agent's responsibilities were to remove the Indians under their charge to the reservation, to explain the terms of the treaty (which existed only in English, of course), to carry out those terms, to see to the well-being of the people, and to manage a large budget. In the case of the Umatilla reservation, the treaty called for the agent:

- to hire and create housing for two millers, a farmer, a superintendent of farming operations, two teachers, a blacksmith, a wagon and plough maker, and a carpenter

- to oversee the construction of a sawmill, a flour mill, a hospital, two schools, shops for the blacksmith, and so on
- to expend "$50,000 during the first and second years after its ratification, for the erection of buildings on the reservation, fencing and opening farms, for the purchase of teams, farming implements, clothing, and provisions, for medicines and tools, for the payment of employés, and for subsisting the Indians the first year after their removal"
- to oversee the construction of houses for the head chiefs of the three tribes, and to pay to each $500 annually (for twenty years)
- to establish a wagon-road around the reservation to replace the Emigrant Road that passed through the reservation
- to administer and control permits for Indians to leave the reservation

The Indians retained "the exclusive right of taking fish in the streams running through and bordering said reservation, . . . and at all other usual and accustomed stations in common with citizens of the United States, . . . [and] the privilege of hunting, gathering roots and berries and pasturing their stock on unclaimed lands in common with citizens." (A number of stipulations in the treaty were not mentioned at the treaty council, including: "Whenever in the opinion of the President of the United States the public interest may require it, that all roads highways and railroads shall have the right of way through the reservation.")

According to the treaty, the Indians were given one year after ratification to settle on the reservation. However, by fall 1860—over a year after ratification—no improvements had been made on the reservation to accommodate the agency. Nor were there any incentives for Cayuse, Walla Walla, or Umatilla bands to settle there. The temporary agent, George H. Abbott, claimed that the BIA had failed to allocate appropriate funds to staff the agency and to construct buildings.[11] It was also unclear to Abbott exactly *who* belonged on the reservation; bands of the three tribes were scattered throughout a large territory. For example, some Walla Wallas were reported to have settled on the Yakama reservation, while others were at Priest Rapids with the charismatic Wanapam prophet known to the Americans as Smohalla.[12] And there was little knowledge or concern for the Cayuse families living among the Nez Perce.

While the reservation was largely ignored by its agent, settlers in the Umatilla and Walla Walla valleys began demanding the removal of "renegade" Indians to the reservation. However, Abbott insisted, "[I]n view of the fact that I am only temporarily in charge of this district, I deem it inappropriate in me to offer any suggestions relative to any subject of future policy for this agency."[13] Meanwhile, A. J. Cain was concerned about the inevitable invasion of miners that would traverse the Umatilla reservation the following spring. Regardless of Abbott's lack of interest in his job and the complete lack of planning for the reservation—which, among other things, had yet to be surveyed—Abbott's hand was forced in winter 1860–61. Maj. Enoch Steen, commander at Fort Walla Walla, wrote to him on December 23: "There is some difficulty between your Indians in this valley and the citizens. They have two of the Indians in confinement and will hang them unless you come up immediately and remove the Indians who wish to move and are to leave in 7 days. I wish you to come up as soon as you can. The Indians say that they want about 6 wagons to haul their corn and potatoes and one for their sick."[14] Steen provided the wagons and drivers, and Abbott reported to Geary two weeks later, "the difficulty is happily settled." He added, "I take pleasure in reporting all the Indians on this reserve perfectly friendly."[15] Yet "all the Indians" is quite vague. Such a move within traditional Cayuse territory may not have been a great imposition for the Cayuse of the Walla Walla Valley. However, the Walla Walla and Umatilla people were asked to completely abandon their ancestral villages and to take up available village sites on Cayuse land. Throughout the 1860s and '70s, agents estimated that at least half of the Walla Wallas and Umatillas were living off the reservation.

As would be asked of agents throughout the period, Abbott attempted to rank the three tribes according to their potential for civilization. He was very impressed by the Cayuse (of which he counted 384) and their newly elected head chief, Howlishwanpum. "The Cayuse tribe," he wrote, "are an industrious and wealthy people, and, intellectually, are superior to the great mass of Oregon Indians. . . . Under proper instruction in the industrial pursuits and a well-regulated school, they will make rapid advancement in civilization." He found the Walla Wallas to be "indolent, superstitious, drunken, and debauched," and added, "little can be done for the moral and intellectual improvement of the present generation at least." The Umatillas were "neither so high in the scale of intelligence, wealth, and industry as the Cayuse, nor so debased and poor as the Walla-Wallas."[16] It is not surprising that the agents would favor the Cayuse; during the first decades of the reservation, they lived in closest proximity to Howlishwanpum's band. Howlishwanpum was personable, savvy, eager to live in a house "with windows," wore "civilized" clothing, ate with flatware, drank coffee with cream and sugar, and was committed to farming and ranching; he was an ideal Indian in the eyes of the BIA. (Historian Elizabeth Vibert notes that Euro-Americans had always regarded the equestrian, bison-hunting Nez Perce and Cayuse as superior in every way—that is, more masculine—in comparison to the river-dwelling, fishing-based Walla Wallas.[17])

The first improvements to the reservation were made in summer 1861, when temporary buildings were constructed of green cottonwood logs to house Abbott and the friends he had hired to run the nonexistent school, mills, hospital, and so on. Abbott then reported that the reservation lacked mills, schools, a hospital, and proper lodgings for his employees due to "the failure of the department to remit the one-half of the funds appropriated under treaty stipulations." He claimed to be $20,000 in debt. William H. Rector, Geary's successor (1861–63), reported in 1862 that he was shocked by the dearth of improvements during a recent visit to the reservation. He was unable to calculate how many thousands Abbott had pocketed during his brief appointment.[18] Timothy W. Davenport, who served as interim agent to the reservation in 1862–63, noted that $66,000 had been expended in the previous two years, of which he could account for only a tiny fraction.[19]

12

The Gold Rush Town

H. P. Isaacs, a well-known citizen of the Dalles, has just returned from Walla Walla and has in his possession a small package of gold, the result of two pansful of earth, taken from the neighborhood of Robie & Co.'s saw mill. The specimen is declared by judges to be direct from the quartz vein. We should not be surprised were we to hear of the discovery of rich diggings in that quarter. The saw mill of Robie & Co. is in successful operation; and after next harvest, Simms & Co.'s grist mill will manufacture flour in sufficient quantity to supply the requirements of the upper country. It is said by those who have seen the crops of the present year, that the Walla Walla Valley is destined to be par excellence, a wheat country.

—*Pioneer and Democrat*, January 6, 1860

So much is packed into this brief, prophetic, and somewhat propagandistic notice. Isaacs, a Philadelphian, had had success mining gold in California and then went into the more secure mercantile business. His store in The Dalles was housed in the city's first brick building, and he had already expanded his business to Walla Walla, the launching point for miners to the Colville region. A. H. Robie's was a state-of-the-art sawmill, established to supply lumber for the region's more permanent houses, barns, and commercial buildings. He was planing standardized pine lumber for balloon-frame construction. It is unclear which farmers had convinced the editors in Olympia of the region's promise as "a wheat country," but prior to 1862, only a handful of farmers were sufficient to satisfy the needs of Fort Walla Walla, the local community, the miners, and the arriving immigrants. Isaacs's report certainly sent a few parties to pan around Robie's mill, up Mill Creek, but it did not result in a gold rush there. However, gold would soon play *the* major role in the early development of the city of Walla Walla.

Gold

On May 8, 1860, A. J. Cain wrote to Edward Geary: "Rumors have reached me to the effect that parties are organizing for the purpose of seeking gold upon the Nez Perces Reservation. I will most respectfully request instructions for my guidance in the case such rumors are true."[1] The rumors were true. Tens of thousands of men in the Far West had never overcome their gold fever. There were still hordes of them—settled down on farms, running businesses, raising families—that would drop everything to explore the latest gold strikes. Politics and gold were the two most vital topics of 1859–60, based on letters to Far West newspapers. Except for mid-winter lulls, every paper carried multiple letters from the various mines. Four days after Cain wrote about the gold rumor, the *Oregon Argus* reported: "Some one, a Capt. Pierce, a trader, I believe, came down a few days ago to W. W., and reported great gold discoveries and plenty of quartz. Plenty ready to bite at the bait. A number have left Walla Walla, and several returned Similkameeners have gone to this new humbug's nest. . . . Time will tell whether this last humbug will live or not."[2] Elias D. Pierce would have been known to many readers of the *Argus*. He had arrived in California in 1850, found some gold, and briefly served as a state representative, but by 1852, he had become infatuated with stories of enormous gold reserves along the Clearwater River. As soon as hostilities subsided on the plateau, he was in Steptoeville. During winter 1858–59, he made several excursions into Nez Perce territory with small parties, negotiated with friendly headmen, and convinced them that he was interested only in gold, with no intention of settling on their land.

By summer 1860, Indian Affairs was agitated by references to Pierce's "lawless invasion" in the newspapers. In July, Geary was notified by his superior: "[I]nstruct the local agents to give public notice to all parties concerned that the treaties with the Indians are paramount and the Government is determined to exercise its full authority to prevent intrusions upon the Reserves of the Indians, under all circumstances, as no person except the proper officers of the Department have any right whatever under any pretense to go upon said reservation." Cain was ordered "to prevent an invasion of the reservation by an armed band of gold hunters."[3] He feared another violent outbreak.

Pierce and his party returned to Walla Walla in October to show off the gold they had acquired and to gain the financial support of the town's merchants. The miners were outfitted on credit by the merchants Kyger & Reese. Word of their initial success was mentioned in the *Dalles Weekly Mountaineer* when Wilbur Bassett, a member of Pierce's party, showed off his gold dust on his way to an assayer in Portland. His trip was intended to be something of a publicity campaign. In Portland, Bassett generated much excitement, particularly among the editors of the *Times* and the *Advertiser*. Beginning in early November, they carried regular firsthand accounts from the miners and initiated the largest gold rush since 1849. The November 6 edition of the *Advertiser* carried a letter, most likely by Pierce: "These mines are at our very door, consequently our merchants entertain bright hopes of the future for Walla Walla. . . . A portion of this company are old miners, and they say that these new discoveries exceed in extent and richness anything north of California. The Indians are very peaceable and do not feel disposed to retard the emigration of the 'Bostons'; on the contrary, they rather encourage their presence."[4] Within two weeks, this and other letters published by the *Times* and the *Advertiser* were republished and discussed in papers throughout the Far West. All papers began carrying regular reports of "the Nez Perce Gold Mines" that shared space on front pages with the presidential election.

On November 25, 1860, Cain requested Major Steen at Fort Walla Walla to provide military protection for the Nez Perce reservation. On the following day, Steen assured Cain that his orders from Colonel Wright, now commander of the Department of Oregon, were "to use all force at the post if required" to remove the miners from the reservation. Cain then advised Geary that in the spring, "miners will be pouring into the country from all quarters and whenever the right of the Indians are invaded, war is inevitable." He recommended "that immediate steps be taken by the proper authorities to modify the treaty with the Nez Perce so as to give the government all the gold bearing country" for the protection of the Indians and the prosperity of the country. Cain included a map of the territory that he proposed to remove from the reservation (north of the Clearwater River). He was frustrated by the federal government's apparent lack of commitment to the Indians. "To ameliorate the conditions of the Indians," he continued, "is an obligation that our people owe the race and should be fulfilled if for no other consideration than placing ourselves right upon the records of the age." Cain was exhausted, frustrated, and in poor health. He concluded, "I hope soon to be relieved from such terrible responsibilities."[5]

Meanwhile, the miller John A. Simms headed to Olympia to represent Walla Walla County in the legislature's winter session, where the county's business focused on the new mining venture: a charter was granted to "E. W. Pierce and others, for Road from Walla Walla into the Clearwater mining country," and a memorial was sent to Congress requesting a new treaty council with the Nez Perce.[6]

During a bitter winter, the miners established the Oro Fino Mining District, encompassing Oro Fino Creek (so named by Pierce) and its tributaries, with headquarters in the newly constructed Pierce City. With no jurisdiction whatsoever, they enacted mining laws based on those in California but specifically banned Chinese miners. In early January 1861, two miners were chosen to travel through deep snow to Walla Walla to show off about $800 worth of gold, and to send letters to the Oregon papers. The Walla Walla merchants were undoubtedly thrilled at the prospect of thousands of miners arriving in the spring on their way to the mines. It was reported that Pierce's men had raised $25,000 on credit in Walla Walla to build the road and ferries from Walla Walla to the mines.[7] Again, the reports published in Portland were widely recirculated. They included directions to the mines. Large numbers of Californians were preparing to leave for the new mines. In March, Joaquin Miller (the future "Poet of the Sierras") and Isaac Mossman turned their mining success into a pony express business, carrying mail between Walla Walla and the mining towns. Suddenly, every Far West paper had its own correspondents at Walla Walla and "the new El Dorado."

It was widely reported that "the town of Walla Walla is being fast depopulated, in consequence of the large number of its inhabitants seeking these mines."[8] Certainly, many, if not most, of the region's idle farm laborers and transients quickly headed for the mines. However, the merchants had no interest in closing their doors. In fact, a number of Walla Walla merchants opened shops in the new satellite towns of Pierce City and Oro Fino. Just as The Dalles had led to American eastward expansion to Walla Walla, so had Walla Wallans extended expansion eastward into the Clearwater Valley.[9] Furthermore, the correspondents from the mines often commented in glowing terms about the Walla Walla Valley and its town. A correspondent for the *Daily Alta California* reported from Walla Walla:

> It has been but three or four years since building was commenced in this place, and the valley around began to be settled up. The present population is variously estimated at from fifteen hundred to two thousand, which includes the whole valley. Every thing is improving rapidly. The farmers have plenty of grain in store to furnish a large mining population, if the Nez Perces country should turn out rich. There is a flouring mill in town, horses are plenty and cheap, such as they are, and everything bids general prosperity . . . The town is growing fast, and some of the sanguine ones predict a future Sacramento for it in greatness. So far as beauty of location is concerned, all agree that it is unequalled on the Pacific coast.[10]

Once the steamers resumed their routes on the Columbia in March, the Portland papers reported the value of gold dust arriving on the steamer *Julia* every Monday (e.g., $28,000 in July; $40,000 in August; $110,000 in September; $100,000 in October).[11] In all but a few of the countless reports from the mines, the Nez Perce are either ignored or described as friendly to the miners. However, while some Nez Perce and Walla Walla Valley Indians benefitted by trading with the miners, conflicts increased as large numbers of miners—with no prior experience with, nor respect for, the Nez Perce—traversed and mined reservation land. Neither the Indian agents nor Major Steen's troops were able to stem the flow of miners onto reservation land. In April 1861, Cain and Geary came to an agreement with Chief Lawyer to cede the portion of their reservation to the north of the Clearwater River to the government in exchange for $50,000 and a promise that no permanent settlements would be established in the area. However, the language was vague. Also, the Nez Perce had yet to receive *any* of the funds and materials promised in the 1855 treaty.[12] Official notice of the "new treaty" appeared in the Olympia papers two weeks later, and reports of the reservation being open to mining spread among all Far West papers.[13] Even the reservation's physician, A. J. Thibodo, sent a letter to the *Portland Times* with detailed directions to the mines.[14]

In May, the steamer *Colonel Wright* made its way up the Snake River to the confluence of the Clearwater. There, a village rapidly developed to supply and otherwise exploit miners. It was given the name Lewiston. The month-old treaty was broken. The situation became completely out of control when exploring miners discovered gold on the Salmon River, deep in Nez Perce country. The boomtowns of Florence, Auburn, and Elk City—more satellites of Walla Walla—appeared almost overnight. With a substantial White population on the Nez Perce reservation, the legislature of Washington Territory established Idaho County in December 1861. By summer 1862, after the discovery of the Boise Basin mines, the reservation's White population exceeded 18,000.[15] In 1863, Congress established Idaho Territory. Its western border with Washington Territory ran briefly along the Snake River and—absurdly—due north from the mouth of the Clearwater (map 7).

Despite the efforts of Geary and Cain, the situation was uncontrollable. During summer 1861, the terms of both men with the agency came to an end. A new treaty was "negotiated" between their replacements and Chief Lawyer in 1863. When the "Thief Treaty," as it is known to the Nez Perce, was ratified in 1867, the Nez Perce reservation was reduced from 7.7 million acres to 785,000 acres, entirely within Idaho Territory (and the Nez Perce still had not received any promised funds).[16] With all of Walla

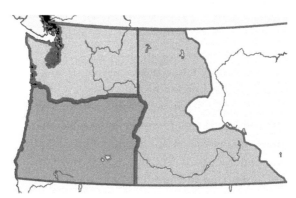

Map 7. The state of Oregon, Washington Territory, and Idaho Territory, 1863–64. (Adapted from map by Uwe Dedering, used under creativecommons.org/licenses/by/4.0.)

Walla County open to settlement, towns, farms, and ranches soon developed along the Walla Walla-Lewiston road.

The *Washington Statesman*, 1861–64

While passing through Walla Walla on his return from Oro Fino in September 1861, Nehemiah Northrop decided that the town—and the miners—required a newspaper. Northrup had arrived on the Pacific coast from New York in 1854 and worked with newspapers in Portland and San Francisco. Once back in Portland, he recruited Raymond Rees, a typesetter with the *Oregonian*, to establish a newspaper in Walla Walla. With used presses obtained in Oregon, they launched the weekly *Washington Statesman* on November 29, 1861.[17] The format was similar to many papers of the time: single-sheet broadside, 24 × 32 inches, four pages, six columns per page (later increased to eight columns). As was standard practice, the first page usually included literary pieces and articles of general interest, taken from various sources, including accounts from eastern papers regarding developments in the Civil War.[18] The second page was dedicated to editorials, stories of local or regional importance, listed prices of goods in Walla Walla and the mining towns, and letters—primarily from the mines. Page three was devoted to local ads and public notices, and page four carried ads for Portland and Dalles businesses.

The editors had no problem finding advertisers; the first issues contain more than one hundred ads. Among these were ads for every merchant, hotel, restaurant, lawyer, physician, blacksmith, photographer, baker, jeweler, and so on in the city. The ads were particularly geared to the transient miners, many of whom had returned to town for the winter: The Oregon Steam Navigation Co. offered passage to the "Nez Perces Mines"; the Walla Walla and Dalles Stage Co. offered triweekly, two-day service between those cities; John F. Abbott offered regular stage service to Wallula; Mossman & Co.'s Express offered mail delivery to and from the mines (with an accompanying image of a steam locomotive!); the merchants offered large supplies of miners' goods, dry goods, clothing, boots, shoes, hardware, liquor; the mercantile businesses of Dorsey S. Baker and Kyger & Reese emphasized their fireproof brick buildings; "Schwabacker [sic] Bros. & Co.

of Walla Walla and Oro Fino City" noted that they "receive goods of the latest styles and use regularly by every steamer and sailing vessel from San Francisco." A few ads were addressed exclusively to permanent residents: J. C. Isaacs noted "Wheat, Barley and Oats taken in exchange for goods"; Moss & Brooks and Way, Bush & Co. were "Contractors and Builders"; W. Philips offered tinware and stoves; Edward E. Kelly's Periodical and News Depot offered newspapers, magazines, and novels; and Edward M. Sammis, "photographist & Ambrotypist," who had just relocated from Olympia, offered "pictures taken in cloudy, as well as clear weather."

Oregon's newspapers were famously partisan, combative, and venomous, particularly during the nationally polarizing 1850s and '60s. Editors in California and Puget Sound of all political stripes came to label their form of malicious journalism "Oregon style." Northrop and Rees certainly retained the racial attitudes of Oregon's Democrat papers, particularly regarding African American suffrage and Chinese immigration, yet with little Republican opposition in the region, they avoided personal attacks.

The third number of the *Statesman* declared "The 'Good Time' has Come":

> The season of prosperity towards which so many in Oregon and Washington have been long and impatiently looking, has indeed come upon us. . . . The hope of a brighter day is no longer merely a picture of the imagination. We have rich and extensive gold fields, which are already pouring their treasures into our marts of business and quickening the pulse of trade and commerce. They promise largely for the future, and may indeed outstrip California in the richness of their yield. We have an almost unlimited country . . . which needs but the exertions of the hardy pioneer in well-directed, energetic effort, to make it produce as abundantly as the fertile valleys of Oregon. We have, in short, all the necessary resources for a great country and a great people; and instead of longer paying tribute to California, we may at once advance to an independent position if we but wisely use these advantages.[19]

The burgeoning town now had an essential booster. And the residents and miners had a home page.

The "Wild West" Town

In anticipation of winter, many hardened miners—along with the gamblers, thieves, and prostitutes who followed them—returned to Walla Walla. Reminiscences of the period clearly recalled the violent transformation of the town since the previous winter. The territorial attorney, Joseph J. McGilvra, noted that in fall 1861, "Every public house was a gambling saloon, and gambling was as open as daylight."[20] An old-timer who spent winters in town recalled,

> Walla Walla was a lively place in those days. . . . It was the winter-quarters for the most of the packers and teamsters, and was full of miners, packers, bull-whackers, mule-Skinners, stockmen, sporting-men [gamblers], etc., intermingled with a good sprinkling of roughs and cutthroats who had been driven out of other localities and came there to winter. To say that it was a pretty hard place at that time, is "hitting it" easy enough. . . . Men were "held up," shot, stabbed, slung-shotted, clubbed, or "doped," very frequently, and the perpetrators of these jokes were in no way delicate in approaching their victims.[21]

A Walla Walla correspondent for the *Oregonian* reported in November, "Walla Walla is emphatically a fast town, carrying one back to the early days of California. Gambling Saloons are as common as 'black berries in bear time.'" Another noted, "There are many hard cases here from California."[22] The *Statesman* carried reports of shootings and violence in each edition during its first three months. A long editorial on January 10, 1862, bemoaned the low state of morality in the town: "The practice of shooting and cutting, upon the impulse of the moment, is too much in vogue."[23]

Winter 1862

The December 20, 1861, edition of the *Statesman* carried a letter by A. B. Roberts explaining the reasons for the valley's mild winters.[24] Two days later, temperatures plummeted. On Christmas day, it began to snow. The *Statesman* noted on January 10, 1862,

> During the past two weeks has been excessively cold. Snow has been lying on the ground to the depth of eight or ten inches, huge icicles hanging

pendant from the eaves, and water freezing into solid ice. On Saturday morning last, the thermometer stood at ten degrees below zero, which was the coldest day we have had, and we think quite cold enough. Whew! how the cold frost bites, and the snow creaks under foot! . . . We don't live in houses constructed for the purpose of keeping the cold out, but to shelter us from the heat and secure at all times a free and healthy circulation of air. Our buildings are not lathed and plastered and ceiled, and stuffed with wool and batting to make them warm.[25]

Another article noted the weather's effect on livestock: "Cattle have died by hundreds from cold and starvation. One gentleman informs us that in going out to search for his stock on one of the small streams in the valley, he found upwards of forty dead cattle in traveling a distance of only three miles. On the Walla Walla, we are informed, dead stock are strewn here and there along the river. . . . Indian stock has suffered greatly, and large bands of horses have perished."[26] Six weeks later the cold had not abated. The *Statesman* noted, "Since the settlement of this country no such winter was ever known before. In fact the Indians have never seen anything like it, if they can be credited. The fact that they have invariably wintered their horses here, while this winter has swept them almost entirely off, is good proof of their assertions." It was estimated that $1 million in livestock had been lost.[27]

The ranchers that had moved their herds from the Willamette Valley had profited greatly during 1861 but now seemed to be ruined. One day in January, the temperature never rose above twenty degrees below zero. All roads to the west were impassable. With little access to fuel, people were forced to burn fence posts and furniture. In February, there were increasing concerns about the scarcity of grain for both people and livestock. The population was at maximum capacity, the miners were running out of money, and some hotels were forced to close.

Finally, on January 23, a stage arrived from The Dalles carrying papers from Portland dated December 30. Two days later, the *Statesman* was stuffed with condensed summaries of war correspondence and of the coming gold rush: "The Portland papers learn from their California exchanges that there will be a very large emigration of Californians to Salmon river in the spring. The probable number of emigrants is estimated in a San Francisco paper at 25,000."[28] With the road to The Dalles partially passable in late February, miners began arriving from Portland, offering the

Statesman firsthand accounts of what was to come: "From persons who have arrived here from the Dalles during the week we learn that there were some four thousand miners in Portland, fifteen days ago, awaiting the opening of navigation to the upper country. Hundreds were arriving by every steamer, and the town was literally filled to overflowing."[29]

Walla Walla was perfectly situated to supply the flourishing satellite mining towns and the large numbers of miners headed to and from the mines. Its merchants, farmers, and millers further benefited from the protection and the government contracts of Fort Walla Walla. With the sensational gold rushes to Montana (beginning 1862) and the Kootenay River area (beginning 1863), it seemed the "Good Time" could be sustained forever.

The City of Walla Walla

During the brutal winter of 1862, news arrived that the territorial legislature had passed the act to incorporate the City of Walla Walla. The cold and isolated people of Walla Walla had work to do. During three meetings held in early March, provisional councilmen were named, and elections were arranged for April 1.

The municipal government was to comprise a mayor, a city council of five, a recorder, a marshal, an assessor, a treasurer, and a surveyor. Among other things, it was granted the power "to prevent and remove nuisances," to "provide the city with good and wholesome water," and "to provide for the prevention and extinguishment of fires." Municipal funds were to be derived from taxing and requiring licenses for auctioneers, pawnbrokers, money changers, theatrical and other exhibitions, shows and amusements, saloons, houses of ill fame, and so on. One-fourth of the funds collected for licenses for saloons were to be set apart for school purposes. The city was officially established as the county seat.

The elections were not particularly competitive: E. B. Whitman was the only candidate for mayor, and there were only five candidates for the council seats. All elected officials, like Whitman, were prominent businessmen, including John Abbott, I. T. Reese, and Bahr Scheideman. In his inaugural address to the city council on April 11, Mayor Whitman outlined the city's top necessities: (1) the establishment of free schools (which

would "attract the better class of emigration"); (2) the enactment of a
.5 percent property tax; (3) the establishment of a police force; (4) support
for the volunteer fire company; (5) the construction of bridges and main-
tenance of the channel of the creek; (6) a jail (the city would share the county
jailhouse recently built on the public square); and (7) the grading of Main
Street.[30] With immediate prosperity guaranteed and rapid population
growth inevitable, the city's immediate future looked brilliant.

13

Commerce

The gold rush quickly attracted established merchants from San Francisco and Portland. By April 1862, thousands of miners were passing through weekly. Long pack and mule trains departed for the mines regularly. Buildings and houses were under construction throughout the rapidly expanding city. The diversity of this population was extraordinary: conversations on Main Street were carried on in various German dialects, in French, Spanish, Yiddish, Gaelic, Cantonese dialects, Nez Perce, Chinook Wawa, and in every version of vernacular English. Based on the attitudes expressed in editorials and letters published in the *Statesman*, White residents—regardless of their country of origin—were valued for their contribution to the order and progress of the city. Nativist humor was ubiquitous; apparently, nothing was funnier than dialogues written in English dialect, particularly "Dutch," Irish, "Chinese," or Minstrel English. Regardless of the large numbers of non-Anglo Walla Wallans, the *Statesman* represented the authoritative voice of the Anglo-American Democratic majority. It was hostile to Blacks in general, to all Indians, and to all Chinese immigrants. And once William Newell of The Dalles purchased it in 1865, the paper went "Oregon style"; its tone became far more partisan and aggressive.

The Merchants

Lots along Main Street quickly filled up with hotels, restaurants, saloon/brothels, livery stables, and so on, and the intersections at Second and Third became particularly busy markets, with mercantile establishments at or near each corner. Second was buttressed by Alpheus Kyger and I. T. Reese's brick dry goods store (northeast corner), opposite Mayer & Co. (southeast corner). On the southwest corner stood the small frame building that had housed Frank Orselli's grocery since 1863. Next door stood Dorsey Syng

Baker's brick general store.[1] In 1865, Dusenbery Bros. had a brick store with cast-iron façade erected next door to Baker (fig. 22). The northwest corner of Second was initially occupied by Emil Meyer's Saloon. Within a few doors of Kyger & Reese were the mercantiles of J. C. Isaacs (Henry's brother) and William Stephens (Baker's former partner).

At the intersection of Third and Main, Kohlhauff & Guichard (fig. 20, northwest corner) was joined by the brick stores of Schwabacher Bros. & Co. (near the northeast corner, next door to Baldwin & Whitman) and

Figure 20. Kohlhauff & Guichard's dry goods store, northwest corner of Main and Third, 1859. Architecturally, Walla Walla's Main Street in the mid-1860s would have been nearly identical to any Western boom town in its first decade. Each side of the broad, earthen street (usually either dusty or muddy) was lined with wood-frame, one-, one-and-a-half, or two-and-a-half story, front-gable buildings with rectangular floor plans. Most would have had whitewashed, minimally ornamented false façades, some with awnings or porches over the plank sidewalks. Once Robie's sawmill was in operation, these buildings would have been assembled in balloon-frame technique with nails and then sided with horizontal clapboards or vertical board and batten. The parapets of the false façades concealed the structures' pitched roofs and presented a more uniform appearance to the street. There would have been plenty of space on the parapet to advertise the business within. (Detail of fig. 2)

Brown Bros. & Co. (fig. 21, southeast corner). Joe Bauer's business was next door to Kohlhauff & Guichard's, and a few doors down stood the two-and-a-half-story City Hotel, the city's largest building and major gathering place. The southwest corner was occupied by another two-and-a-half-story building known successively as Buckley's Saloon, Frank's Hotel, and the Oriental Hotel (1864–65). A few doors below was the mercantile of C. Jacobs & Co.

———

It became routine for Walla Walla's merchants to conduct business in gold dust, to carry tiny scales, and to keep abreast of the value of gold from the different mining regions. Some merchants assumed the role of unofficial bankers: receiving deposits (of gold, greenbacks, valuables), keeping accounts, offering lines of credit, negotiating loans, and, with accumulated capital, purchasing real estate. Of course, success in this form of banking was based on the integrity of the merchant, and, judging by accounts of trade conducted in gold, the Walla Walla merchants were held in high esteem among the miners. However, without someone to accurately assess the value of gold dust or chunks of quartz in Walla Walla, miners and merchants were forced to travel to assay offices in Portland. In 1864, John H. Day, who had received training as a physician, pharmacist, and assayer, went into business with Dorsey Baker, opening "Baker & Day, Assayers" a couple of doors from Mayer & Co. ("Baker was the capitalist, and Day the scientific member of the firm.").[2] At the same time, J. Rosenthal arrived from Corvallis and opened a jewelry store/assay office in the corner building adjoining Schwabacher's.

Prices for manufactured goods increased the farther they were sold from San Francisco. Goods were expensive in Walla Walla relative to Portland, yet miners often preferred to travel light until reaching Walla Walla. And prices skyrocketed in the mining towns, where Walla Walla's merchants were well represented.

The gold excitement attracted new businesses and encouraged existing businesses to expand. Merchants had warehouses constructed, and some adopted more permanent characteristics. In 1861, both Dorsey Baker and Kyger & Reese replaced their frame stores with single-story brick buildings.[3] In 1862 (as soon as a new supply of brick was available), Schwabacher Bros.

Figure 21. Brown Bros. & Co. (1862) stood at the southeast corner of Main and Third. The city's first four brick buildings were almost identical. Visible behind Brown Bros. are the *Statesman* building, in the middle of Third, and the Masonic Hall, on Alder. The rapid proliferation of brick commercial blocks in the United States during the second half of the nineteenth century coincided with the pervasiveness of the Italianate style. The style incorporated ornamental features from Tuscan farmhouses, villas, and renaissance palaces. Italianate commercial building façades featured flat roofs; short parapet walls above decorative, often bracketed cornices; tall storefront windows; and equally tall, double-entry doors with decorative hood moldings or arches. The triple-bay façade was a common treatment for brick Italianate commercial blocks in the Far West. (Detail of fig. 2)

and Brown Bros. did the same. Each of these establishments advertised their "fire-proof" brick building along with their goods. And other advertisers noted *their* location in proximity to the brick buildings.

Of course, women in the city assisted in some family businesses, and many—particularly young, unmarried women—were employed in various occupations (particularly as domestics and teachers). Women-owned businesses, however, were rare in the city during this period. At least one woman ran a brothel for decades (see chapter 19). However, the women-owned businesses advertised in the local papers offered millinery and dressmaking services, exclusively. These businesses needed to effectively compete with the large mercantiles. Maria O'Rourke, an Irish single mother, moved her retail/custom business from The Dalles to a shop on lower Main Street around 1867. Like her competition, she imported the latest fashions from San Francisco, but she attracted a clientele that preferred to conduct such business in an all-female space. According to the 1870 census, she owned $8,000 worth of real estate. She remained in business in Walla Walla for at least another eight years.[4] In 1876, Sarah Cram opened a millinery shop opposite the *Statesman* office, which was taken over by Margaretta Schnebly after a couple of years. Schnebly's shop may have been eclipsed in 1879 by Belle Hessey, "Premier Modiste," whose business was run from three rooms in the fashionable new Paine Brothers building (fig. 50).

The Jewish Community

From the start of the gold rush, a significant number of Jewish merchants and clerks moved to Walla Walla. All had come through San Francisco, where thousands of Jewish argonauts had settled since 1849. Young Jewish men made the voyage to San Francisco from cities throughout the United States and from Germanic Europe—particularly from Bavaria, the Rhineland (Alsace, Baden, etc.), and Prussian Posen. (This is known as "the German era" of Jewish immigration.[5]) In California, where they were part of the most diverse assembly of people on earth, some took to mining; however, the vast majority arrived with stocks of goods—particularly clothing—to sell to miners. Many of the Bavarians and Rhinelanders came from families with established commercial connections in the United States, and many were well educated. Among this Ashkenazi diaspora, the Eastern "Polish" Jews, who practiced more orthodox forms of Judaism, were at the bottom of the mercantile hierarchy, working, initially at least, as small-scale merchants or independent pack or cart peddlers.[6]

By 1860, the Jewish population in the Far West numbered roughly 10,000, with about half living in San Francisco. With the gold discoveries in southern Oregon, some of these family-owned merchant houses expanded northward. And with the gold discoveries at Colville and on the Clearwater, some expanded to Portland, The Dalles, Walla Walla, and the mining towns themselves. A synagogue was established in Portland in 1861.[7] As these merchants migrated northward and eastward, they behaved no differently than non-Jewish merchants: they participated in local politics, in fraternal societies, and in benevolent organizations; they embraced civic duties, for example, serving on city councils and as volunteer fire fighters. Once financially successful, they would seek (or have arranged) marriage to a Jewish woman in Portland, San Francisco, back East, or in Europe. It was common to return to Europe to accompany family members on the long voyage to the Far West. Gradually, most joined with other Jews to observe the holidays (particularly Rosh Hashanah and Yom Kippur), to arrange and celebrate marriages, and to assist in burial rites. By necessity, American Reform Judaism was practiced exclusively in Walla Walla at this time.

During the first decades in the Far West, anti-Semitism was generally limited to a few newspaper editors. If an editor did cross the line, Isidor N. Choynski, perhaps the most ferocious journalist in the Far West, was quick to call them out, "Oregon style." After losing an election in 1858, Thomas J. Dryer, editor of the *Oregonian*, accused Portland's Germans and Jews of controlling the ballot box, and accused the Jews of deceitful dealings with non-Jews. Choynski (living in Roseburg at the time) sent blistering letters to the *Oregon Statesman* (which gladly printed them as page-one features). Dryer, he declared, "is an ignoramus," "the vilest of the vile," "a mean, base scoundrel." In defense of all Jews, Choynski wrote, "Let [Dryer] point you to our prisons, and see whether there is a single Jew within its walls. Let me point you to other States and other countries, and see there whether the Jew does not stand pre-eminent as a man of honesty and integrity. . . . Where is thy shame, you ignorant puppy."[8] According to historian Howard Sachar, "In a vigorous capitalist republic, few Americans begrudged immigrant Jews their economic progress."[9] What mattered most to the vast majority of Americans at the time was that the Jews were White, hardworking, trustworthy, and they cared about the development and well-being of the place they lived. Perhaps most important of all for Walla Wallans, they tended to support the Democratic party.[10] Even the outspoken racialist William Newell of the *Statesman* expressed only respect for the Jews of Walla Walla and occasionally included articles from San Francisco's *Hebrew Observer*.

There is no standard story of Jewish entrepreneurship in the Far West, but it is worth outlining the story of the Schwabacher brothers, who established the most successful and enduring retail business in Walla Walla (1861–1910). The brothers represented their family's second generation of American immigrants. Born in the Frankish Bavarian town of Zirndorf, the brothers may have attended the local business school in neighboring Fürth, perhaps with the understanding that they would eventually be asked to assist in the businesses of one of their uncles in *Amerika*. In the 1840s, their uncles had established businesses in New York and the South. Naturally, as their webs of mercantile connections expanded, the uncles encouraged emigration of more family members (particularly these boys, after the premature deaths of their parents in 1843 and 1846). Louis, the oldest of the brothers, probably sailed for the United States shortly after completing his education in the early 1850s. He may have worked for a time at his uncle Samuel Lehrberger's cigar shop in New York. He then worked for family businesses in Alabama and Mississippi, where their maternal uncles, Henry and Isaac Bloch, had formed mercantile partnerships. Louis may also have worked in New Orleans for his future father-in-law, the Alsatian Jacob Blum. The Bloch brothers and their Alsatian business partners, Aaron and Leon Cahn, relocated to California in the early 1850s and became involved in a number of businesses, including A. Cahn & Co. in San Francisco.[11] Louis Schwabacher arrived in San Francisco in 1858 to assist in the growing Cahn-Bloch enterprises. Soon after A. Cahn & Co. expanded into Oregon in 1859, Louis was joined by his brothers, Abe and Sigmund. In 1860, Sigmund was a partner with Bloch, Miller & Co. in The Dalles. At the same time, Cahn and Bloch financed the establishment of Schwabacher Bros. & Co. in Walla Walla. One year later, the Cahn-Bloch-Schwabacher network—still anchored by A. Cahn & Co. in San Francisco—included stores in San Francisco, Portland, The Dalles, Walla Walla, Placerville, and Oro Fino. In 1863, a branch was established in Boise City.

Bailey Gatzert, the manager of the Schwabacher Bros. warehouse in Wallula, married the Schwabachers' sister, Babette, in 1862. In 1869, the Schwabachers opened a store in Seattle under the management of Gatzert, now a partner, which quickly became the most important dry goods and marine supply business in the burgeoning city. In 1872, the Schwabachers constructed Seattle's first brick building. (Three years later, Gatzert was elected mayor of Seattle.) After Sigmund married his cousin Rosa Schwabacher (born in Albany, NY) in 1871, Rosa moved to Walla Walla together with her widowed mother, her sister, and brother-in-law, Louis Goodman. Sigmund became the manager of the company's Washington and Idaho interests (which included two mills, extensive real estate, and vast tracts of farmland); Goodman became a clerk at the Walla Walla store. By the early 1880s, all three brothers were settled comfortably with their families in San Francisco.

————

Although he took a very different route to the Far West, the Alsatian Joe (known alternately as Jacob or Jacques) Bauer was also part of the Bloch-Cahn orbit. Jacob Bauer immigrated to the United States in 1855, joined the Army, and came to the Northwest with the 9th Infantry. On his discharge in 1860, he established a mercantile business with another Alsatian, M. L. Frank. In 1863, Frank became a partner in Schwabacher Bros. & Co. and ran the new branch store in Boise. The following year, using the first name "Jacques," Bauer married Leon Cahn's Alsatian sister-in-law, Julia Heyman (at the Temple Beth Israel in Portland). After Frank returned to Europe in 1864, Bauer opened his Cigar & Variety Store. Each December, Bauer's became "Santa Claus's Headquarters" and was *the* place to buy Christmas and New Year's presents. In the 1870s, Bauer—now using the name "Joe"—expanded to sell sheet music and musical instruments.[12]

In 1869, Bauer's sister Leontine arrived to marry Joseph Jacobson of Jacobson Bros. The Jacobsons were natives of Prussian Posen. By the 1860s, differences between Polish and German/Alsatian Jews were dissipating, particularly in remote corners of the Far West, where orthodox customs were necessarily relaxed.

————

All of Walla Walla was aware of Jewish holidays, because Main Street would be largely empty. From the beginning, gatherings during Jewish holidays were held at the homes of individuals. Despite the *Statesman*'s regular mocking of immigrants and ethnic minorities, it was always respectful of "our Hebrew friends." During Rosh Hashanah in 1864, for example, it noted, "The importance of the Hebrew element in our community was strikingly manifested on Monday and Tuesday last. Being the anniversary of their New Year, their stores and places of business were all closed on the days named, and as a result Main street wore a blank appearance. . . . With

Figure 22. Dusenbery & Bros., 1865, south side of Main, west of Second. Jacob, Hirsch, Nathan, and Lewis Dusenbery, natives of Rypin, Russian Poland, established a small dry goods business in Walla Walla in 1861. In summer 1864, they purchased from Dorsey Baker the 27 feet to the west of his store for $1,600 (!), and their new brick store with cast-iron façade opened for business the following spring. The brothers soon opened branches in San Francisco, Dayton, and Weston. Hirsch assumed control of the Walla Walla store in 1869. (Detail of fig. 46.)

Wednesday morning, our Hebrew friends were at their posts bright and early, and Main street once more worn its wonted cheerful appearance."[13]

With the establishment of the city cemetery in 1864, two acres were reserved for a Jewish section. The following year, the first Jewish wedding was celebrated in Walla Walla, joining Joseph Dannenbaum and Adele Loupe, the sister of his business partner. Prior to the fire of 1866, the Masonic Hall was used for Rosh Hashanah (City Councilman Bahr Scheideman was a member of the Masonic Lodge since its foundation). The city hall/firehouse was then used as a "temporary synagogue," whenever necessary. In 1867, William Newell of the *Statesman* was a guest at the Rosh Hashanah services and reported that "quite a number of Israelites came in from the neighboring settlements for the purpose of joining their brethren in the ceremonies."[14]

Germans and German Jews in Washington Territory celebrated the appointment of Gen. Edward S. Salomon as governor in 1870. The charismatic, thirty-three-year-old war hero thrilled German audiences throughout the Far West, and his commitment to bring 200 German families to the territory was widely publicized. However, to the disgust of Walla Walla's German and Jewish residents, William Newell made a slanderous accusation of Salomon appearing intoxicated in public. Newell despised Salomon as a Republican and cast him as a "Teutonic" beer-drinking stereotype. Led by the Jewish merchants, more than 100 Walla Wallans signed a denunciation of Newell's "contemptible falsehood" published in the city's rival Republican paper. Nonetheless, Newell continued to make similar accusations against (the teetotaling) Salomon and (unsuccessfully) attempted to disparage his war record. Both Republican and Democratic papers throughout Oregon and Puget Sound repeatedly chastised Newell for his slanders.

The Chinese Community

Few specifics are known of the earliest Chinese residents in Walla Walla. Like tens of thousands of miners in California and Oregon, Chinese immigrants (primarily from Guangdong province) bolted to the Idaho gold mines. Naturally, Walla Walla quickly established the largest Chinese population in Washington Territory. Yet reliable figures from the period do not exist. Only two Chinese men are listed in the 1860 census (California counted 35,000 Chinese). Beginning in 1862, Chinese men are documented in the *Statesman* as passing through town in large numbers on their way to the mines. And in 1864, when a Chinese laundry opened across the street from the *Statesman*'s office, the paper noted: "The Johns are becoming quite plenty in this much favored locality."[15] By the mid-60s, a small Chinatown had developed on the property owned by Dorsey Baker on the north side of Alder, between Second and Third (see fig. 43, #23). Most notices of this block in the *Statesman*, however, refer only to Chinese prostitution (the *Statesman* office stood on the western end of this block); references to individual Chinese residents are extremely rare.

The issue of Chinese immigration was particularly problematic in Washington Territory in the 1860s, where the governors welcomed the increased population, and well-to-do families and capitalists embraced and exploited cheap, reliable Chinese labor; yet an apparent majority of White citizens regarded the Chinese as an economic and social threat. Unfortunately, the major source for White-Chinese relations in Walla Walla is the *Statesman*, which routinely ridiculed all aspects of Chinese culture.

Nonetheless, two Chinese residents were well known to Walla Wallans. Hen Lee, a businessman with influential connections to San Francisco, lived in and ran his businesses from a log building owned by Baker, located directly behind his store. He lived there with his wife and two sons—very likely the first Chinese children born in the territory. They may also have been the only Chinese *family* in the city at the time. Lee is listed in an 1865 city directory as running one of five Chinese laundries in the city and is subsequently listed as a merchant. However, he also arranged for the movement of Chinese miners, laborers, and perhaps prostitutes from San Francisco. The *Statesman* noted in spring 1864, "Lee, one of the *tyee* [chief] Chinamen who has been engaged in the 'wholesale washing and ironing business' in the upper end of this city for the past year, left for Portland and San Francisco on Thursday last for the purpose of engaging a 'troupe' of Chinamen to go up to the Oro Fino mines. He stated that he had been employed for this object by persons in Oro Fino, and would bring up about two hundred of his people."[16] Lee apparently had connections with one of the *huiguans* in San Francisco, associations established for mutual aid and self-protection for Chinese immigrants from common Cantonese regions. (They were generally—and usually disparagingly—known to Americans as the Six Companies.[17])

In December 1869, Lee posted a notice in the *Statesman* offering a reward for the return of a Chinese girl who had run off with a Chinese man. The circumstances suggest that the girl was a prostitute; however, the *Statesman* offered only parody with no insight into the story. The goings-on in this little Chinatown were obstructed from public view by both the contents of the *Statesman* and a high board fence.[18]

Dr. Jim, AMMD, "graduate of the Imperial Medical Institute of China and formerly resident Surgeon of the Imperial Hospital in Canton," began advertising in the *Statesman* in 1863. In exchange for payment, he would occasionally have White patients write testimonials to his skills, which were then included in his ads. They usually praised Dr. Jim's herbal and holistic treatments, which were obviously a concern for some Whites. Nonetheless, he was financially successful; by May 1864, he owned at least two buildings on Main Street (at least one of which was an unlicensed "gambling house" for which he was fined in 1865). Unlike the alien land laws of Oregon and California, those of Washington Territory (1864) stipulated that any alien could own and sell land. On the other hand, the "Act to Protect Free White Labor . . . and to Discourage the Immigration of the Chinese into this Territory" was also passed by the territorial legislature in 1864. Influenced by similar laws in Oregon and California, it implemented a tax of $6 quarterly for all Chinese residents over age seventeen (similar to the taxes placed on "tolerated" Jews in Russia and Prussia).[19] Of course, with similar taxes instituted throughout the Far West, the law discouraged no one.

The 1870 census lists forty-two Chinese men and no women in the county, which represented only a fraction of the Chinese population. They are listed as laundry workers, restaurant employees, or domestics. The census indicates that most of the city's wealthier families employed either a Chinese (male) or an Irish (female) domestic. The city's Chinese population spiked with the commencement of railroad construction in the region during the 1870s and was accompanied by a rise in anti-Chinese sentiment.

Blacks in Walla Walla

Aside from one well-known family and a few notices in Far West papers, there exists little documentation regarding Blacks in the city during this period. There was a significant number of Blacks among the multitude of gold miners that passed through town, yet only a few saw the potential to earn a living in Walla Walla. Although Washington Territory lacked the exclusionary laws of Oregon and California, the 1860 census lists only 30 "free coloreds" in the territory (whereas California counted 4,086). Only one individual is listed in Walla Walla as "Black": Peter Thomas, a 54-year-old barber from Pennsylvania. Additionally, A. B. Roberts noted in 1861 that "an old negro lady" attended the birth of his daughter.[20] But nothing more is known of them. We may assume that Thomas arrived in California either as a freeman, encouraged by the abolitionist and African American press to claim his share of the gold bounty, or as a slave and managed to purchase both his freedom and his own business. Black barbers were common in American cities by the early nineteenth century (White Americans associated barbering with servitude and shunned it as a profession). They worked exclusively for a White clientele, and performed a particular role, and adhered to a particular etiquette: Black barbers could only succeed in White society by assuming a posture of deference in an atmosphere of upscale, masculine comfort. According to historian Quincy Mills, "Barbers served as clients in their own shops where White men exercised much more power as patrons."[21] Even after 1865, it was essential for the Black barber to maintain a shop free of any perception of social equality.

Many White barbers arrived with the German and Irish immigrations of the late 1840s and came to outnumber Black barbers by 1860. Yet barbering remained one of very few business opportunities available to Blacks, and every American town required at least one barbershop.

Aside from the 1860 census, Peter Thomas's name does not reappear in the city. However, the first numbers of the *Statesman* carried ads for two barbershops, one owned by W. Howard and another co-owned by J. W. Lauphus and John B. Mitchell. In March 1862, Howard may have left for the mines, and Lauphus and Mitchell moved into his larger establishment on the north side of Main between First and Second, which included baths. Lauphus seems to have also soon left town, but Mitchell became a long-term resident of the region. He was born in New York and married Jane Clay (born in Missouri) in Walla Walla in 1864. That same year, Mitchell formed a partnership with Richard A. (Dick) Bogle, a native of Jamaica, of whom far more is known. According to a biographical sketch of Bogle of 1901,

When about twelve years old, he emigrated to New York, and . . . crossed the plains to Oregon [in 1851]. He stayed three years, then moved to Yreka, California, where he learned the trade of a barber. . . . [H]e was proprietor of a restaurant and barber shop in Deadwood, California, but he subsequently engaged in mining. Returning at length to Roseburg, Oregon, he resumed his trade, and until 1862 he maintained a shop there. In that year, however, he emigrated to Walla Walla, whence he made an extensive mining tour, visiting Florence, Elk City, and Oro Fino. Upon his return, he bought an interest in a barber shop, and he has been engaged in that business unceasingly since, except for a brief period, during which he was in Oregon.[22]

The "brief period" in Oregon may refer to Bogle's marriage to America Waldo in Salem on the first day of 1863—which is known to Oregon history as the scandalous "Negro wedding." America was brought to Oregon from Missouri as a child in 1846, as the property of the Waldo family. Her wedding to Bogle was officiated and hosted by a White Congregational minister and attended by a number of judges and their families. As word of this mixed-society wedding spread (after the Bogles had left for their new lives in Walla Walla), the Democratic press attempted to frame the celebration as a political scandal.[23] The vicious exchange of editorials and published letters in Oregon could only have reinforced the correctness of the couple's decision to abandon Oregon.

Of course, Walla Walla was only marginally less uncomfortable for Blacks. Bogle later informed the historian William Lyman, "In those days [Walla Wallans] made it rather hard for men of African descent. A negro could not get a room at a hotel. He was not allowed to eat in a public dining room. He could not buy a cigar or a drink in a gin room without first taking off his hat and showing due reverence to the august vendor of the booze." Lyman continued, "Consequently it was customary for Mr. Bogle, out of the kindness of his heart, to allow colored strangers who happened to be in the town to occupy the rear of his shop, where they could keep warm and sometimes cook a meal."[24] Bogle established his own business two doors down from Joe Bauer's shop in 1865. He recalled fifteen to twenty men occupying its rear space in the 1860s.

T. M. DeSouza is listed in 1865 as proprietor of a "blacking establishment," perhaps a third Black-owned business on Main Street (bootblacking was another socially acceptable Black occupation for a White

clientele). Little is known of DeSouza aside from notices that he sub-
scribed to *The Elevator*, a Black-owned, San Francisco–based newspaper
that promoted equal rights for Blacks in the Far West. (Jane Clay was also
a subscriber.[25])

In 1871, Mitchell moved his family and business to Pendleton, Oregon, a growing town in need of a barber, and thanks to a letter printed in
The Elevator, we gain some insight into the life of one Black family in the
region. The letter was written by Lewis Walker, who had recently visited
his friend Mitchell in Pendleton, where the latter was "engaged in a controversy on the school question." (Issues concerning public education for
Black children were regularly addressed in *The Elevator*.)

> Mr. Mitchell has two children, aged nine and twelve years. He sent them
> to the public school and they were refused—but he persisted, claiming
> his right as a taxpayer and a citizen of the United States, and his children
> are now attending school, but against the strong protest of some of the
> rebel inhabitants of [Pendleton]. In a letter to Mr. Walker, he says: "How
> matters will terminate I cannot say, but I am determined to exert myself
> in every legal and honorable way, to maintain my guaranteed constitu-
> tional rights, and my integrity as a man. The rebs have found that they
> cannot scare me, so they have combined together to starve me out. They
> have started an opposition barber shop; how it will succeed I cannot say,
> but I tell them I stand firm, and don't intend to move one inch."

It seems that two school directors were responsible for the troubles, in
particular, Rev. James H. Turner, who had recently arrived from Missouri. According to one account, "Turner and Mitchell came to blows over
the dispute and the school was broken up."[26] However, the situation was
rectified in October, according to Walla Walla's (Republican) *Spirit of the
West* (est. 1872):

> The good people of [Pendleton] have at last succeeded in getting a first
> class school teacher, and will ere long have a first class school. For near
> one year, efforts have been made to establish a school, but owing to the
> obstreperous, hard headed foolishness of two of the directors all efforts
> have been futile. The trouble was brought about by these two directors
> refusing to allow colored children to attend the school. Because of this
> prejudice they refused to hire, knowing full well that the laws of the
> country would protect the colored children in their rights. The people,

however are getting tired of this foolishness and are taking the matter into their own hands—hence the success.[27]

Within a few years the Mitchells were back in Walla Walla. In 1877, the *Statesman* opined, "Mr. Mitchell is a colored man, but he is remarkable for his gentlemanly demeanor and is universally respected. We wish we could say as much for some white barbers." William Newell, who occasionally published mocking accounts of politically ambitious Black barbers, appreciated the professional façades maintained by Mitchell and Bogle, "the gentlemanly barber."[28]

The city's White-owned shaving-bath business was established in 1864 by the Baumeister brothers, Max and Ned, natives of Weimar. Their initial Oriental Bathing Saloon (next door to the Oriental Hotel, thus the name) stood directly across the street from Bogle's.

The 1867 Income Tax

The first federal income tax was enacted in 1861, as a source of revenue to support the Union war effort. In 1867, a flat tax was introduced of 5 percent on income above an exemption of $1,000. The *Statesman* published a list of taxes paid, offering a rare glimpse into the personal wealth amassed by some Walla Wallans. Taxable returns included income of all types as well as luxury goods owned. Walla Walla County contained, by far, the largest number of affluent citizens in Washington Territory. Among the county's seventy-four names are:

Sylvester Wait	$4,431
Dorsey Baker	$3,624
Abe Schwabacher	$2,241
Louis Schwabacher	$2,241
Sig Schwabacher	$2,241
Morris Brown	$2,221
Bahr Scheideman	$2,221
J. H. Day	$1,850
William Stephens	$1,659
Bailey Gatzert	$1,627[29]

To understand the relative wealth of these individuals, their assets would be measured relative to the GDP per capita of 1867, which would be roughly $350 (in 2024) per 1867 dollar. In short, these men were very wealthy.[30] To offer further perspective on this list, territorial judge J. E. Wyche, with land holdings and an annual salary of $2,500, paid $605; the blacksmith E. S. Crockett paid $253; and Chris Sturm, one of the few farmers listed, paid $3.00.[31] The vast majority of White, male residents were wage laborers, earning $25–$100/month.[32]

Sylvester Wait had built an enormously successful flour mill at the confluence of the Touchet and Coppei Creek in 1864–65. He spared the farmers in the region from having to transport their wheat to Walla Walla and made a killing by selling flour one day's transport closer to Lewiston. His $14,000 investment in the mill quickly paid off, obviously. By 1867, the town of Delta had developed near the mill, with several businesses, a post office, a hotel, and a school. The town's name was changed to Waitsburg the following year. And in 1869, the Republican-majority town attempted (but failed) to form its own county.

14

Urban Development

During his term as Indian agent, A. J. Cain remained involved in the development of Walla Walla and was a major player in both the creation of the *Statesman* and the organization of the county's Democratic Party. In June 1860, he was one of six Walla Wallans admitted to the bar by the territorial Supreme Court.[1] In April 1861, while dealing with the growing crisis on the Nez Perce reservation, he established a legal practice in Walla Walla. His ad in Olympia's *Pioneer and Democrat* noted: "Particular attention given to land and collection business." A month later, he was married in Olympia at the residence of James Tilton, the territorial surveyor general.[2] In September—nine days after his term as Indian agent expired—he received a patent for a 160-acre tract adjoining the town plat to the northeast. The warrantee for this prized piece of real estate was a sergeant stationed at Fort Vancouver, who was issued the patent under the (widely abused) Scrip Warrant Act of 1855.[3] Cain's friend James Tilton certainly could have advised him in such matters. Cain's addition to the city was platted in October, and the first lots were auctioned off in December. The *Statesman* reported, "Mr. Cain's sale of town lots on Saturday last was well attended, and quite a number of lots were sold, at reasonable prices. Persons investing money in town property in this city are sure of receiving a fair interest on their investments."[4] Cain's Addition extended Main Street across Mill Creek to the northeast, following the Nez Perce trail (map 8). Cain's "homestead" was situated between Main and Mill Creek, which contained some buildings left behind when the cantonment was abandoned. Isham T. and Martha A. Reese (fig. 25) and Cain's friend W. W. Johnson, now US deputy surveyor for donation claims, were among the first residents of the addition, and the lumberyard of Way, Bush & Co. (co-owned by A. H. Robie) was among its first businesses. However, for decades lots and blocks in Cain's Addition, as well as other parts of Walla Walla, were held as investments, frequently sold, mortgaged, and litigated over. A. J. and Emma Cain were among the most aggressive speculators of this period,

Map 8. Cain's Addition to the City of Walla Walla, *Map of the City of Walla Walla,* 1883 (detail). (Whitman College and Northwest Archives.)

although both Almos Reynolds (1864) and Dorsey Baker (1867) acquired large tracts of Cain's Addition due to mortgage defaults.

During summer 1862, another fifty lots in Cain's Addition were auctioned off. According to the *Statesman*, "all the lots advertised went off readily at fair prices."[5] At the same time, E. H. Barron and John G. Sparks were selling lots on their claims adjoining the complicated south border of the city, where the city owned triangulated sections of five blocks. Barron and Sparks (another new lawyer) entered into several years of litigation against the city and each other over disputed property lines. Sparks's case was particularly complicated because he had purchased his land from A. B. Roberts, who—under the preemption law—had no right to sell land prior to receiving a patent.[6] And Barron's case was complicated because he had already platted his claim, and prior to receiving a patent, had sold lots on which houses had been built, yet Barron himself did not have a residence on the land. Furthermore, Barron claimed most of Sparks's tract.[7]

Sparks's claim included the small church/meeting house and graveyard near Fourth and Birch. Apparently, this remained the unofficial city cemetery until 1863, when Sparks posted a threat in the *Statesman*: "Take Warning. All parties are hereby notified that all trespasses by burial or otherwise, committed on the land of J. G. Sparks, adjoining the town of Walla Walla, will be prosecuted according to the law." One year later, the city purchased a 40-acre lot 1 mile southeast of the city for the establishment of a municipal cemetery. The site was fenced, platted, lots were sold, and the graves were removed from Sparks's land.[8] The new cemetery was lovingly named the Walla Walla Cemetery.

"The Mature Proportions of a Respectable City"

The editors of the *Statesman* engaged in a running competition with those of the *Portland Times*, The Dalles's *Mountaineer*, and Lewiston's *Golden Age* to promote their city's prosperity and ideal location, and to defend it against attacks from the others. Alonzo Leland, of both the *Times* and the *Golden Age*, was most responsible for sensationalizing the Nez Perce mines. After moving to and investing heavily in Lewiston, he constantly sounded the death knell of Walla Walla as the most important launching-off point for the mines. He even published a distorted map to support his feeble claim

Figure 23. Main Street, looking west from the bridge (in the foreground) crossing Mill Creek at First, 1864. In summer 1862, Charles S. Bush of Way, Bush & Co. raised about $1,300, including $500 from the city, to construct this bridge, which integrated Cain's Addition with the city. The photographer was either William V. Brown or Phillip Castleman. (OHS Research Lib., OrHi 6213.)

that Lewiston provided a more direct route to the Boise mines. The *Moun-taineer* promoted the new town of Umatilla Landing, just downriver from Wallula, as the most direct route to the mines, via the Grande Ronde Valley (thus bypassing Walla Walla entirely). Accounts in the *Statesman*, like the following from October 1862, were not intended for Walla Wallans but for the wider mining/merchant/transportation community in the region:

> While the cry of dull times reaches us from the towns above, affairs in and about our own city manifest a tone entirely the opposite. In a walk about town the other day we counted upwards of fifty buildings which have been erected during the present season, and thirty in process of erection. . . . Main street, with its new additions, has assumed quite a city air. The new fire-proof brick of Messrs. Schwabacker Bro's, is almost completed . . . and Messrs. Brown Bro's &. Co's brick, on the opposite

side of the street, will be presenting quite as imposing an appearance in a few days. . . . Second street is also sharing in the improvements. . . . The streets as far back as Mr. Sparks' claim are dotted with new buildings, and beyond the city limits in that direction Mr. Meyer has erected a large brewery. . . . Cain's addition, which boasted of only eight dwellings last fall, has more than doubled that number, and within the next two months . . . will assume "magnificent proportions." A new warehouse just erected by Mr. Cain, adjoining his residence, gives that side of the creek a business air, and with the completion of the bridge across the creek (fig. 24), other buildings of a like character will doubtless follow. . . . [A]nd while [these improvements] evince a confidence on the part of citizens in the permanence of the town, they show that it possesses the elements of prosperity, and is rapidly marching on to a position of more than its present importance.[9]

Aside from Lewiston and The Dalles, Far West papers continued to extol Walla Walla as the most important city east of the Cascades. For example, in summer 1862, the *Oregon Statesman* observed:

Walla Walla has grown, since last year, from a very ragged country vil-lage to the mature proportions of a respectable city. Wooden buildings begin to give place to brick and stone, the sidewalks and streets are swept clean and are kept well watered, thus adding much to the health and comfort of those who domicile here. Express, Stage, and Steam Naviga-tion Co.'s offices, and large wholesale and retail mercantile establish-ments, give this all the dignified air of an old business community. Stages arrive and leave almost every day; long trains of mules and horses may be seen constantly coming in and quietly emerging with well assorted cargoes, to the different mining camps, for which this place has become the central depot. Freight wagons, with long strings of oxen and mules attached . . . literally obstruct the highways. The cheerful music of the anvil may be heard at all hours of the day from every part of the city, and the farmers add life to every branch of industry by graciously furnishing the markets with an abundance of farm and garden products of the very best quality, and in quantity, variety and price, too, that for so new a set-tlement is truly marvelous.

In this immediate neighborhood are three flouring mills, two com-pleted, with a third in process of erection; indeed, it would be difficult to picture to one's mind a community evidencing signs of greater pre-sent prosperity, or promising permanent future greatness with more certainty than this—a region possessed of large tracts of farming land with an almost boundless extent of grazing country, all well watered, and with an excellent climate and healthy location in the midst of gold mines sufficiently rich to pay well for working, extensive enough to employ many thousands of men, and durable enough that no one may conjecture when the yield of gold will reach its maximum much less when it will begin to diminish.[10]

15
Family Matters:
Homes, Schools, and Churches

During the eighteenth century, English architects published and republished numerous instruction manuals for carpenters and masons. These books usually opened with illustrated histories of Western architecture, with an emphasis on classical and renaissance stylistic principles. They went on to offer plans and elevations—patterns—of buildings, including detailed instructions on how to accomplish specific tasks (e.g., the particulars of a cornice's dimensions and individual parts). Such books were widely utilized for the design and construction of high-status buildings in colonial America. During the first third of the nineteenth century, English guidebooks were displaced by a steady stream of pattern books by American architects. The designs tended to favor Greek classicism, which became associated with a unique American, democratic ideology. The titles of the books indicate the intended audience: *The American Builder's Companion*, *The Builder's Assistant*, *The Young Builders' General Instructor*. These books underwent multiple editions and generated a widespread Greek Revival style in the 1820s and '30s, known in the United States as the Federal style. New England–trained carpenters introduced this new, austere, vernacular style to Oregon among the Methodists in the 1840s, and it remained something of an American national style throughout the century.

The gold rush brought large numbers of professional carpenters, masons, bricklayers, and even architects to the Far West. During the 1850s, thousands of men abandoned the search for gold for more secure jobs associated with the construction boom, particularly in San Francisco and Sacramento. Regular communication with the eastern states ensured that construction technologies and styles were transported quickly to California. The new "picturesque" styles—Carpenter Gothic and Italianate, in particular—were well known to both builders and their clients in the 1850s.

The styles were disseminated through numerous pattern books, including those of A. J. Downing. These designs were also widely circulated by popular magazines, such as *Godey's Lady's Book* and *American Agriculturist*.

Walla Walla's First Builders

A number of California builders gravitated to Walla Walla after 1858 and established businesses, most of which were short-lived. William Glasford and Freeman P. Allen were the city's busiest contractor-designers of the 1860s and '70s. Allen, a New Hampshirite, arrived via San Francisco in 1861. Glasford actually arrived in Walla Walla directly from Ottawa in 1862 and purchased a foreclosed building company at a sheriff's auction in 1865.

The first frame houses in Walla Walla—and the majority of houses built in the 1860s—were variations on the Federal style. The Samuel Linkton house (fig. 24), built by Freeman Allen, was a good example of this ubiquitous style. The largest residence in the city, it stood on the southwest corner of Alder and Third. It also served as the office for Linkton's lucrative lumber business. Earlier in 1864, Linkton had built a steam-powered lumber mill and a hotel on Linkton Mountain, on the new road constructed between Walla Walla and the Grande Ronde Valley (the Linkton Mill Road, funded by Linkton and other merchants). In 1866, he sold the mill and lumber business, and the following year sold his house to the county to serve as its courthouse (then took his small fortune to San Francisco). Concurrent with the construction of the Linkton house, Allen was contracted to build the Masonic Hall of similar dimensions on the northeast corner of Alder and Third (visible in fig. 21).[1]

While most Americans in the Far West sought to import the architectural styles from their hometowns (e.g., fig. 26), an increasing number embraced A. J. Downing's call for a national architecture (Downing despised the Federal style). The Downingesque cottage that Glasford built for James and Emily Lasater was based on an extremely popular design in pattern books around mid-century (figs. 27 & 28). Situated on Birch at the terminus of Third, the house façade, with its prominent, high-pitched center gable, was visible from Main Street.

Figure 24. Residence and office of Samuel Linkton, southwest corner of Alder and Third, 1864, built by Freeman P. Allen. (Detail of fig. 2.)

Figure 25. Residence of Isham T. and Martha A. Reese, ca. 1862 (purchased by Almos and Lettice Reynolds in 1869). Southeast corner of Sumach and Second (Cain's Addition). (Evans, *History of the Pacific Northwest* 2, 334.)

Figure 26. Residence of William P. and Lydia Horton, 1864. North side of Sumach, between Third and Fourth. An I-house, three bays wide and one bay deep. Although the term "I-house" was coined for the popularity of this house type in Indiana, Illinois, and Iowa, it was also common in Horton's native Kentucky. A carpenter by trade, Horton served as justice of the peace, city recorder, county road supervisor, and bridge builder. A rear ell was later added (see fig. 43, #26). (Detail of fig. 2.)

Figure 27. Residence of James and Emily Lasater, Birch Street, facing Third, ca. 1865, built by William Glasford. (Gilbert, *Historic Sketches*, opp. 32.) Raymond and Augusta Ward Rees owned a similar house on the southeast corner of Birch and First (see fig. 43, #21).

Figure 28. "Gate House in the Rustic Cottage Style." (Alexander Jackson Davis, *Rural Residences*, 1837, n.p.) Davis was a friend and collaborator of A. J. Downing.

Walla Walla's most ornate house of the 1860s belonged to Henry P. Isaacs's family. According to the 1860 census, Isaacs and his wife Lucie were the wealthiest residents of The Dalles. By 1864, he owned a successful mercantile business and the city's major hotel (the Umatilla House), as well as mercantile businesses and flour mills in Fort Colville, Walla Walla, and Boise City (the mercantiles were run by his brother, Joshua). Isaacs had his Excelsior Mill built on part of his 240 acres to the east of the city (including current Wildwood Park). His brother-in-law, Louis Scholl, may have overseen its construction. In 1864, the Isaacs family settled in Walla Walla, where Scholl (who was in charge of Isaacs's new Boise City mill) designed a house for them, christened "Brookside" (fig. 29) and based on the same Downing design as the commanding officer's house at Fort Simcoe (fig. 16).[2] Isaacs's own interest in Downing is evident from a notice posted in the *Statesman* in 1866: "The person who borrowed a book—DOWNING ON ARCHITECTURE— from the subscriber, will please return it. H. P. Isaacs."[3]

The house was fundamentally a two-story upright and ell design; its ornamentation is both Carpenter Gothic (high-pitched gables, elaborate

Figure 29. "Brookside," the Isaacs's residence, 1866, north side, likely designed by Louis Scholl. The Second-Empire-style tank house, visible behind the house, was a later addition. (Detail, undated photograph, Walla Walla Photograph Collection, Box 29, Folder 114, WCMss066, Whitman College and Northwest Archives.)

bargeboard) and Italianate (bay windows with bracketed cornices, window hoods, clapboard siding). The interior included finely carved hardwood trim and Carrara marble mantles. The *Statesman* called it "the handsomest private residence in the country. [It] is just the kind of house suited to a gentleman of means and leisure."[4]

Walla Walla's builders could provide its successful merchants with the housing style of their choice, yet most opted for conservative, familiar styles (Federal, Cape Cod, I-house). As was typical throughout the West and Far West, even those residences built in more modern, "picturesque" styles—Carpenter Gothic in the 1860s, Italianate in the 1870s, and Second Empire in the 1880s—were more popular a generation earlier back East.

Schools

The city was very slow to establish a public school—despite the existence of a superintendent of public schools since 1859. Some individuals ran private schools in their homes or in rented spaces, one of which would be declared "the District No. 1 school" by the superintendent. In 1862–63, the district school was housed in a room at the rear of Kohlhauff & Guichard's store. In 1864–65, it was housed in a hotel-saloon on Alder.

The first organized schools were established by the Catholic Church and—in response—by the Congregational Church. In 1850, Augustin Blanchet was named Bishop of Nisqually Diocese, with its seat in Vancouver. With the establishment of Washington Territory, Walla Walla became part of the diocese. In the 1860s, Blanchet's vicar general Jean-Baptiste Brouillet embarked on an aggressive campaign to establish schools on the reservations and in the cities within his jurisdiction. He was in Walla Walla in 1863, seeking support for his plan to establish schools and a church. The schools were to be run by the Sisters of Providence of Montreal. In the absence of municipal skill or initiative to realize a public school, both Catholics and non-Catholics generously supported Brouillet's plan. Edmund Barron donated four blocks adjoining the city (between Poplar and Willow, Fifth and Seventh), and an additional block was purchased from I. T. Reese, which extended the property to Alder. St. Vincent's Academy, the *Statesman* declared, "when completed, will also afford a home for destitute children, where the poor will be taught side by side with the rich; where the sisters like guardian angels will direct the footsteps of the youth of our valley."[5] During the mid-1860s, the Catholic property was the most active construction site in the city (fig. 30). A small chapel was completed in December 1863, and St. Vincent's opened three months later. Construction then began on both (the first) St. Patrick's church and St. Joseph's Academy (for boys; on its completion, St. Vincent's was exclusively for girls).

The sudden appearance of a substantial Catholic institution brought about a backlash. Peasley B. Chamberlain had been dismissed as pastor of the Congregational Church in Portland in 1862, after six years, during which time his congregation had disintegrated.[6] An ardent anti-Catholic, Chamberlain wrote that he came to Walla Walla in 1864 due to "the manifest necessity for some good school other than Catholic."[7] Like Whitman and Spalding, he saw Catholicism as a political threat that needed to

Figure 30. The Catholic property in 1875. (A): a complex of buildings incorporating St. Vincent's, the hospital, and boardinghouse; (5): St. Patrick's church; (9): St. Joseph's Academy. (Detail of fig. 3.)

be combated aggressively. Soon after his arrival in Walla Walla, he delivered an oration at the city's Fourth of July festivities that, among other things, called into question the anti-American, anti-democratic beliefs held by Catholics. One attendee described Chamberlain's speech as "a revival of 'Knownothingism' . . . an insipid, untrue, political and sectarian address."[8] In its review of the festivities, the *Statesman* did not mention the specifics of Chamberlain's oration but noted that the occasion "was remarkable for the gravity and coolness of the spectators. . . . It lacked that joyous buoyancy which ever prevailed upon occasions of 4th of July celebrations in years gone by."[9]

Chamberlain purchased a small house and a warehouse from Kyger & Reese located on the southeast corner of Rose and Second (directly behind their store, where a footbridge spanned Mill Creek). He hired William Glasford to convert the warehouse into a schoolroom/meeting hall/church. In September, Chamberlain and his wife opened their school to about thirty students (about half the enrollment of each of the other two schools).[10]

It was not coincidental that the directors of the school district (ironsmith William Phillips, saddler J. D. Cook, and photographer P. F. Castleman) took action to build a public school in fall 1864: all the city's schools combined could not satisfy the needs of the district's 203 school-age children.[11] A temporary property tax was levied to support the construction of a school building. The directors then purchased block 8 in Cain's Addition. No particular plan or pattern was required for the schoolhouse; it was a two-story, front-gable, Federal-style building, with a small bell tower. In fact, the directors had developed the "plan and

Figure 31. Public School No. 1, built by J. D. Hoffstatter, 1865–66. The school was put under the direction of Charles Moore, who was assisted by his wife Julia. Charles had followed his brother, Miles C. Moore, to Walla Walla in 1865. (Gilbert, *Historic Sketches*, opp. 322.)

specifications" prior to calling for bids to construct the building (fig. 31). When the school finally opened in March 1866, it could seat one hundred students—which was far too small for the rapidly growing city.[12]

By spring 1868, more than 400 school-age children lived within the district. That summer, superintendent Cushing Eells established a new school district (No. 34) for the southwestern part of the city. However, funding for a permanent building was even more drawn out than it had been for the "old" school. For three years, classes were held in temporary buildings in the district, including the original Catholic school building. Despite the affluence among the city's merchant class, no one was willing at this time to step up for public education as some had for the private institutions. Finally, in 1871, the directors purchased three lots on the corner of Willow and Eighth, and commissioned Freeman Allen to build a new (too-small) schoolhouse (fig. 30, #7).

The Whitman Seminary

After leaving his mission among the Spokan in 1848, Cushing Eells lived and worked as a farmer and teacher in the Willamette Valley. On visiting the graves at Waiilatpu in 1859, he determined to establish a high school in honor of the Whitmans at the mission site.[13] Later that year, he received a charter from the territorial legislature to establish "an institution of learning, for the instruction of persons of both sexes, in science and literature, to be called the 'Whitman Seminary.'" Aside from the name, no mention was made of the Whitmans nor of Christianity in the charter, yet it was to be a Congregational institution. Eells purchased the mission site from the ABCFM and moved his family there. After moving to Walla Walla in 1864, P. B. Chamberlain became a trustee and an important supporter of the seminary. Yet, while Eells imagined a Christian community growing up around his school, 6 miles to the west of the city, Chamberlain insisted that the school be located within the city and won out among the trustees.[14] Eells then put the 640-acre Waiilatpu claim up for sale "for the benefit of Whitman Seminary."

In January 1866, Henry Spalding came to town to promote himself and the seminary. At Chamberlain's church he delivered a series of bizarre, dramatic lectures titled "Early Oregon Missions: Their Importance in Securing the Country to Americans." Shortly after the killings at Waiilatpu, Spalding had concocted his own version of the causes of the incident. His multipart "History of the Waiilatpu Massacre" emphatically and incessantly claimed that the Catholic priests and the HBC orchestrated the killings.[15] Spalding's account was a hateful fantasy with little factual basis. For some reason, the *Statesman* chose to publish the lectures in nine parts—on its front page—between February and April 1866. The tale spun by Spalding was to play a major role in the identity of Whitman, the city, and the Northwest for almost a century.[16] While the heroic pioneer fantasy appealed to many Walla Wallans, its aggressive anti-Catholicism certainly troubled many others. (Yet the *Statesman* is silent regarding confessional strife in the city.) It is unclear whether there was any relationship, but while Spalding's essays were appearing in the *Statesman*, a few businessmen came to support the establishment of the seminary. In spring 1866, the trustees accepted Dorsey Baker's offer of four acres adjoining his home to the east of the city as a site for the school.[17] With Eells's mission

Figure 32. Whitman Seminary, 1866, built by Dexter & Leidy.
Photograph from the west. (Whitman College Facilities Records,
WCA067, Box 16j, Whitman College and Northwest Archives.)

claim still unsold, Chamberlain announced the establishment of the school
in the *Statesman*, citing its future location, and calling on "the friends of
true education" to fund the construction of a suitable building.[18]

The school was constructed during summer 1866 at a cost of almost
$5,000, half of which was donated by Eells. Again, there was little need
for creativity in the design of a school building in the 1860s, and similar-
sized schools had been constructed in the Willamette Valley. The hipped-
roof, two-story, 25 × 46–foot, Federal-style building did have two interesting,
eclectic features: Gothic-style pointed arches in the cupola and Italianate
window hoods (figs. 32 and 33). At the school's dedication in October,
Chamberlain reiterated Spalding's Whitman-saved-Oregon myth.[19] The
building was hailed by the *Statesman* as "possibly the most imposing structure east of the mountains."[20]

Chamberlain closed his own school and served as principal and teacher
of the seminary. Unlike other schools in the city, the seminary was open
to students of all ages. However, it was more expensive (teacher salaries
were dependent on enrollment fees). Thirty-six pupils were enrolled on the

Figure 33. The area surrounding the Whitman Seminary (10). The nearest residences were those of the Bakers and William and Mary Green to the north (not depicted), Isaacs to the northeast (upper left), and the Boyers to the west (lower right). It must have appeared to be a private school for these families. (Detail of Fig. 3.)

first day, including four Baker children (ages 5–15), their cousins, the three Boyer children, and the two sons of Almos and Lettice Clark Reynolds, soon to be their cousins.[21] However, the seminary was a financial failure, with erratic enrollment and an inability to retain faculty. Between 1872 and 1880, the school was usually closed, and the building was rented to meet the overflow of the Episcopal school.

The Episcopal Church was the most popular denomination in the country. Yet when its first rector to the city, Lemuel Wells, arrived in fall 1871, he was greeted by only six female communicants. Nonetheless, these women—Catherine Ritz, Sarah Boyer, Sarah Sharpstein, Paulina Phillips, and Annie Mix—were married to some of the wealthiest men in the city, all of whom served on the church's board of trustees. On his arrival, Wells had rented the courthouse (formerly the Linkton house) for services for his tiny congregation. By the end of the year, however, plans were in place for the construction of a church and the establishment of a boarding school for girls. In 1872, Ritz donated a lot on the northeast corner of Poplar and Third, several thousand dollars were raised and borrowed, and construction began on both buildings. Saint Paul's School for Girls opened in September with three teachers and forty students. Wells noted the school was "open to every race and color, Whites, Indians and Negroes, all being represented among its pupils." In response to demand, Wells rented the dormant Whitman Seminary building and opened St. Paul's School for Boys in December. After fire destroyed the rented boardinghouse in summer 1873, a new two-story building was rapidly constructed in time for the start of the fall term (fig. 35). Demand for the boarding school increased as Wells established churches throughout eastern Washington and Oregon. The nearby United Brethren church was used as a schoolhouse until much larger school and residence buildings were constructed on the church grounds in 1875. To the chagrin of the Congregationalists, Wells accurately advertised St. Paul's as "The only Protestant school east of the Cascades."[22]

Churches

Urban churches went through rapid stylistic transformation in the nineteenth century; however the first churches in the city and region were austere, Federal-style structures. By 1873, Walla Walla had four churches, two of which had already been rebuilt. In 1860, the county commissioners donated to the trustees of the Methodist Church two lots on the northeast corner of Alder and Fifth, across the street from the public square. The church was built at a cost of $1,000 and completed in the fall. Its design—like those of the schoolhouses—required only familiarity with country churches. Externally and structurally, there was little to differentiate one from the other: front-gable structures, three bays wide, clapboard siding, with a cupola, and perhaps a short spire, all painted white. Already by 1866, the Methodist church was described as "plain, cheap and in bad repair."[23] In 1868, desiring a more central location, the trustees purchased two lots on the southeast corner of Poplar and Second. The church was moved to the new site, repaired, and enlarged (fig. 43, #15).[24]

Once Walla Walla's Catholic congregation had outgrown the tiny chapel/meetinghouse, irregular services were held in the "schoolroom" behind Kohlhauff & Guichard's store. Immediately on receiving Edmund Barron's land donation on the southwest side of the city, Brouillet set out to establish his schools, church, and boardinghouse. A small chapel was dedicated already in December 1863.[25] St. Vincent's Academy opened in February 1864; (the first) St. Patrick's church was dedicated in August 1865; and St. Joseph's Academy for boys opened two months later (fig. 30).

After settling on the Waiilatpu site in 1860, Cushing Eells often preached at the old chapel/meetinghouse and occasionally at the Methodist church. However, he had no interest in establishing a congregation; he was focused on his school. P. B. Chamberlain was the driving force behind the formation of the Congregational Church at the start of 1865. After a fire destroyed the church on July 11, 1868, Chamberlain managed to raise $2,000 quickly and took a loan from Baker & Boyer. William Glasford, a member of the church, was hired to build an actual church on the site, which was dedicated in October (fig. 34).[26]

Chamberlain quickly established himself as one of the most controversial and divisive figures in the city. Besides Catholicism, he was outspoken against secret societies, the Masonic Order in particular. His hostile denunciations of the Masons had led to his removal from the pulpit in Portland. As he waged verbal combat with the Masons of Walla Walla, his small congregation also began to disintegrate.[27]

Figure 34. The Congregational church, built by William Glasford, southeast corner of Second and Rose, 1868. (Gilbert, *Historic Sketches*, opp. 331.)

During winter 1864–65, G. W. Adams of the United Brethren in Christ began conducting revival meetings at the Methodist church and then camp meetings on the outskirts of town. One camp meeting in summer 1866 was said to have attracted 600.[28] The following year, Adams built a church on the southwest corner of Second and Birch. However, excitement for the church dwindled rapidly. The building primarily served as a provisional schoolhouse, and Adams moved to Baker City in 1874.

For thirty years prior to the arrival of Lemuel Wells, Anglican and Episcopalian architectural theorists had been engaged in intense discussions regarding appropriate church design. Their goal was to foster the design of churches that accurately embodied the elements, functions, and atmosphere of medieval parish churches. The movement they generated came to be known as the Ecclesiological Gothic Revival. Naturally, St. Paul's Episcopal church was to look different than the four extant churches in the city. Roughly $3,500 had been raised or borrowed (from Baker & Boyer), and construction was completed during spring 1873, by which time forty-two families were connected with the congregation (fig. 35).

Figure 35. Lemuel Wells with part of his congregation outside St. Paul's Episcopal church (1872–73), school, and residence buildings (1872–75), northeast corner of Third and Poplar. (Photograph ca. 1883, Walla Walla Photograph Collection, WCMss066, Box 26, Folder 41, Whitman College and Northwest Archives.)

Like scores of Episcopal churches throughout the country, St. Paul's appears to have been based on the plan for a "Wooden Church" in Richard Upjohn's *Rural Architecture* of 1852.[29] Like Upjohn's plan, St. Paul's consisted of a nave, a chancel, and a tall, side bell tower, with the main entrance located at the foot of the tower.[30] The lancet windows and rondels were filled with stained glass (for a more "church-like" atmosphere), and the church was faced with board-and-batten siding. The nave featured three sets of varnished truss rafters, which were both functional and ornamental. The 85-foot bell tower was the tallest structure in the city. (Subsequently, the tall spires of Cumberland Presbyterian church [1876] and the second St. Patrick's church [1881] would create a distinctive skyline for the city.) Due to Wells's efforts in establishing congregations throughout the region, Bishop Benjamin Morris in Portland began calling for the establishment of a new Episcopal bishopric based in Walla Walla (when finally established in 1892, Spokane was selected as its seat).

16

Politics

In a city with such a small but influential electorate, every (man's) voice mattered in political discussions, and in the red-hot atmosphere of the 1860s and '70s, political discussions were never-ending and very public. Every election season found candidates for office speaking or debating before large audiences at the public square, at Council Grove (also known as Robert's Grove, between Birch, Park, and Alder), or in front of the courthouse. Voting blocs (primarily Democrat) were mobilized and generated as much publicity as possible. Voices of political contentment are silent in the historical record; politics was angry, hostile, and usually frustrating.

1860–61 National and Regional Politics

Although Walla Wallans were politically tied to Puget Sound, they were more closely attached to Oregon ideologically, economically, and geographically. Yet they were only spectators to the great drama played out by the Oregonians in 1860–61. The Democratic machine that dominated Oregon politics in the 1850s—the "Salem Clique"—fissured during the statehood deliberations of 1857–58. Asahel Bush, the influential editor of the *Oregon Statesman*, fell out with Joseph Lane, who had served four terms as the territory's congressional delegate. The result was a premonition of the upcoming presidential election: the fissures among Oregon's Democrats led to the election in February 1860 of Republican Edward D. Baker to one of its US Senate seats.

Out of the debacle of the Democratic national conventions of 1860, Stephen Douglas was selected as the official nominee; he was pro-Union and argued for popular sovereignty on the issue of slavery in the territories. He was challenged by breakaway, aggressively proslavery Southern

Democrats. John C. Breckinridge (Buchanan's vice president) was selected as their candidate, with Joseph Lane as his running mate. Isaac Stevens was appointed chairman of their campaign. Governor Richard Gholson left Olympia to stump for Breckinridge–Lane. Olympia's *Pioneer and Democrat* was also all in with Breckinridge–Lane. With the Democrats split into three tickets (John Bell joined the race representing the non-committal Constitutional Union Party), the Democrats hoped that no candidate would receive a majority of the electoral vote and the decision would be left to the House of Representatives, where Democrats held a majority. However, in November, Abraham Lincoln won outright, with 180 of 303 electoral votes. Not surprisingly, the Democratic votes in Oregon were split between Breckinridge (34.4 percent) and Douglas (28 percent), and Lincoln carried the state's three electoral votes with just 36.2 percent.

The political temperature in Washington Territory was mild compared to Oregon. In the elections for the territorial legislature in July 1860, the recently organized Republicans won nine of thirty-three seats, marking a new era in the territory's political complexion. In anticipation of the arrival of Lincoln's territorial appointees, a new paper appeared in Olympia: the *Washington Standard* celebrated Lincoln's victory and dedicated itself to be a strong voice for the Republican party in the territory. Similarly, in Portland, editorship of the *Oregonian* was taken over by a friend of Lincoln.[1]

The secession of South Carolina in December came as a shock in the Northwest, and many letters in the *Standard* blamed the inevitable collapse of the Union on Joseph Lane and Isaac Stevens—the "precious Siamese Twins of Secession."[2] The new legislature in Olympia, dominated by Douglas-Democrats and Republicans, dedicated itself to the support of the Union. In January, the legislature passed a resolution censuring Stevens, still the congressional delegate, for his support of the secessionists. The *Pioneer and Democrat* and the *Standard* now went to war with each other—"Oregon style"—over Stevens's reputation, legacy, and future in the territory. Some legislators accused Stevens of plotting to establish a "Pacific Republic," an accusation mentioned repeatedly in the *Standard*.

Stevens returned to Olympia in April, just as word arrived of the Confederate attack on Fort Sumter. In a series of melodramatic speeches, he asserted that he had nothing to be ashamed of, attacked his critics, and declared that he would return east to fight for the Union.[3] The May 31 issue of the *Pioneer and Democrat*, which included Stevens's final address to the legislature, was its last.

Once again Democratic division led to a Republican victory in the July election for the territory's congressional seat: Lincoln's friend William H. Wallace won with 44 percent of the vote. The Breckinridge–Lane–Stevens candidate, Edward Lander, managed only 20 percent in the territory but won 47 percent of the votes cast in Walla Walla County—the only county to give him a majority.

Joseph Lane retired to his home near Roseburg and quietly cheered on the Confederacy. Senator Baker joined the Union Army at the start of the war and was killed in battle five months later. Oregon governor John Whiteaker (unconstitutionally) filled Baker's senate seat with a proslavery Democrat. Gen. Isaac Stevens was killed at the Battle of Chantilly on September 1, 1862.

Walla Walla during the Civil War

As word of the secession spread, a number of officers at Fort Walla Walla resigned and headed east to defend their Confederate home states. After the news from Fort Sumter, the situation at the Army forts of the Far West changed dramatically. On May 10, acting governor McGill called on the men of Washington Territory to join the Union Army.[4] However, as the 9th Infantry and 1st Cavalry (formerly Dragoons) were departing from Fort Walla Walla, McGill's concern turned from defending the Union to protecting his citizens from Indian uprisings. He now pleaded with the Army to retain a sufficient number of soldiers. Gen. George Wright, now commander of the Department of the Pacific, held little hope of raising a regiment in the territory, reporting, "The sparse population and the intense excitement caused by the recent discovery of very rich gold mines may render it impossible to obtain such a large number of men."[5] In the meantime, he ordered two infantry companies of the California militia under the command of Col. Harvey Lee to occupy Fort Walla Walla. The fort's essential economic and protective bonds with the city remained unaltered as it took on the role as the center of operations in the establishment of Fort Lapwai (1862) and Fort Boise (1863). The eastward conquest continued (naturally, the first businesses in Boise City were established by Walla Walla merchants).

However, there were tensions and occasional altercations between soldiers and local Confederate sympathizers. One resident later recalled of 1862, "The gamblers and roughs at Walla Walla and all the mining camps were Rebels or rebel sympathizers . . . and these gamblers and desperadoes were the terror of the Union people. . . . Most of the large gambling houses were kept by Rebs or they showed Rebel sympathies and some would not let the soldiers or volunteers in either to play or drink." He added that soldiers were regularly mocked and that the sheriff, marshal, and their deputies were "Rebs"—as were most of the people he knew there.[6]

On April 10, 1862—the eve of the installation of the city government—a benefit was held at Robinson's theater to aid the volunteer Union Hook and Ladder Company. During the performance, according to the *Statesman*, marshal George Porter attempted to remove "a soldier who had been drinking too freely" and "marred the pleasure of the occasion by boisterous conduct . . . a fight broke out between citizens and soldiers. Pistols were drawn and fired indiscriminately." One soldier was killed and several others wounded, as were Porter and his deputy sheriff, "Cherokee Bob," a notoriously violent Georgian.[7] The *Statesman* account of misbehaving soldiers was widely noted in Far West papers, as were soldiers' accounts, which blamed the violence on Walla Walla's Confederate sympathizers. One soldier wrote,

> A small party of soldiers went to the theatre in town, and having taken a little *refreshment*, and feeling quite jubilant over the just-received intelligence of the Federal victory at Newburn, N.C., were disposed to enjoy vividly the dramatic representation of Susan Robinson *et al*. Umbrage was taken, and a quarrel sought by sundry sour secessionists (of which the town is full.). . . . The affray was premeditated, commenced and tragically consummated by a gang of rowdies and gamblers, who boldly and exultingly proclaim themselves secessionists; who have persistently annoyed and insulted the soldiers whenever opportunity offered; who look upon the volunteers with feelings of hate.[8]

The situation escalated three days later, when, in the early morning, "seventy-five or one hundred soldiers" came to town with orders from Colonel Lee to arrest Porter and Cherokee Bob. Mayor Whitman, in his third day on the job, got into a war of words with Colonel Lee, who insisted that his soldiers had acted on their own but claimed that it was a case of premeditated murder on the part of Porter.[9] Whitman affirmed that Lee had no jurisdiction within his city. One week later, the *Statesman* reported that Lee had been recalled to San Francisco.

After seven unpleasant months in Walla Walla, the California militia was replaced by two companies of the Oregon Cavalry Regiment in June 1862. Within days of their arrival, however, another flare-up occurred during a public convention to nominate candidates for county offices. Tensions ran high as various stripes of Democrats and Republicans attempted to forge a single Union ticket. According to several accounts, a secessionist attacked a soldier. In the ensuing chaos, the other soldiers present demanded that marshal Porter, who witnessed the assault, arrest the man. However, Porter took no action, and the man escaped. That evening, a group of soldiers rode into the city, demanding the arrest of Porter. According to the *Statesman*, which tried but failed to strike a neutral tone, "Shouts of 'hang him,' 'he's a d–d secessionist,' and other mob-like expressions were used." Like the Californians before them, the Oregonians considered the town to be run by secessionists and complained of being harassed in town on a regular basis. The *Statesman* accused the soldiers of only coming to town to drink and misbehave. In response to accusations that the *Statesman* itself was *secesh*, it published an elaborate editorial condemning all extremists and declaring that it was emphatically and unambiguously pro-Union and anti-abolition.[10] The same issue carried a brief notice of Porter's resignation as marshal. A correspondent for Eugene's *State Republican* noted, "Mr. George Porter, minus his Marshalship, was politely requested to leave the town and county. . . . The secesh material of this county is fast wearing away."[11]

In August 1862, the garrison was augmented by two companies of the Washington Territorial Infantry under the command of the Kentuckian Col. Justus Steinberger. Better relations were generally maintained between the garrison under Steinberger and the citizens throughout the remainder of the war. A few months later, the *Statesman* noted, "the garrison is now changed to a quiet, orderly and gentlemanly soldiery; and at no time since the establishment of the post has the management of affairs there given better satisfaction both to soldiers and citizens than now."[12]

Republicans and some Democrats came together to support the fundraising efforts of the United States Sanitary Commission, which organized field hospitals and offered services for Union soldiers. Edward E. Kelly, postmaster and owner of the City Book Store, was appointed territorial agent for the commission. As donations were tallied in local papers, individual support for the Union cause among residents quickly became clear. Dorsey Baker, a Republican and enthusiastic promoter of the commission, made an initial donation of $200. No other donation came close. Most merchants gave $25, some gave $2, but all were expected to contribute when Kelly or the wife or daughter of a prominent Republican knocked on their door. When he assumed control of the *Statesman*, William Newell supported the Sanitary fund but was far more interested in promoting rumors of graft by "Sanitary thieves." In the end, Walla Walla County, which represented more than 22 percent of the total population of the territory, contributed only 9 percent of its total receipts to the fund.[13]

The Sanitary Commission may have generated some hostility among those who opposed "Lincoln's war." The Union League, on the other hand, aggressively attempted to bring the war to the territory. This fraternal organization arrived from the East in 1863 to loudly promote the Union cause, to expose and attack *Copperhead* (anti-war) Democrats, and to ensure Lincoln's reelection. The Walla Walla group was headed by Holon Parker, a land agent/speculator. All the editors of the *Statesman* were Copperheads. In some cities, the Union League convinced the Army to shut down Copperhead or pro-Confederate papers. The editors of the *Statesman* regularly defended themselves against attacks on their patriotism and on their brutal treatment of Lincoln. In turn, they accused the Union League of treasonous, anti-constitutional activity. This came to a head when the popular Colonel Steinberger was removed from command of Fort Walla Walla in winter 1864. The *Statesman* attributed his removal to "the schemes of the Union League" and focused their venom on Joseph J. McGilvra, the Lincoln-appointed territorial attorney, "a little sqirrel-headed [sic] hypocrite and meddler." The paper published two letters of praise and gratitude to Steinberger, one from the mayor and the city council, the other signed by seventy-two individuals and businesses.[14] (The city felt vindicated when Steinberger was reinstated in August.) As territorial attorney, McGilvra was part of a constantly traveling district court that was regularly housed at Army forts. He later took pride in having assisted in cleansing the Pacific forts of Confederates:

At the beginning and all through the war of the Rebellion, there were a great many Southern men and Southern sympathizers scattered all through this country, and they belonged to the aggressive element of frontier life, loud-mouthed, defiant and threatening. Among the leaders of this element were several Army officers from the South [who] would openly curse the government that fed them, and were loud in their expressions of sympathy for the rebels. Abraham Lincoln was cursed, and toasts were drank to Jeff. Davis in the presence of the commanding officers of the military posts without rebuke. This was particularly the case in all the region of Eastern Oregon and Washington. . . . [I]t was not until the winter of 1863–64 that the military posts on this coast were thoroughly cleansed of this rebel element. . . . It was the writer's privilege to assist in this good work, for which he was soundly rated by a portion of the rebel sympathizing press of the country at the time.[15]

Throughout the war, editors, politicians, and cities (e.g., Walla Walla) were regularly accused of being *secesh*. General Wright aggressively sought to remove *secesh* officers and to suppress *secesh* papers, which further encouraged the Union League and Republican papers to make accusations against Democratic papers, like the *Statesman*. As the war spiraled to its inevitable end, the *Statesman* focused on the Lincoln administration's mismanagement of the war and its enormous costs in men, wealth, and lost opportunities.

Annexation Schemes

"The Walla Wallans seem to have secession and annexation 'on the brain.'"
—*Seattle Weekly Gazette*, November 4, 1865

The relationship between Walla Walla County and Olympia fluctuated between cold and frostbite during the 1860s and '70s. The Democratic Party stronghold resented both Olympia's remoteness and its growing Republican complexion. Already in 1861, a movement arose to establish an independent Walla Walla Territory, with Walla Walla as its capital. Olympia responded to the threat of secession by breaking up Walla Walla County: the counties of Stevens (north of the Snake) and Ferguson (current Yakima) were formed in 1863. At the same time—against the objections of both Walla Walla and Olympia—Congress established Idaho Territory, thus weakening both Olympia's desire for statehood and Walla Walla's hope of becoming the centerpiece of an overwhelmingly Democratic territory.

The following year, Idaho's capital was removed from Lewiston to Boise City, which was almost inaccessible from Lewiston. And the establishment of Montana Territory in 1864 left Idaho a geographic absurdity of natural and imaginary borders. In 1865, the citizens of Lewiston proposed the establishment of a new territory by joining the Idaho panhandle with eastern Washington Territory and Western Montana Territory (to be called Columbia Territory). No action was taken by Congress. With the end of the war and the start of Andrew Johnson's presidency, some prominent Walla Wallans devised a plan of their own. These individuals were determined to break free from distant, "black republican" Olympia, which they claimed was plagued by political warfare and corruption. Puget Sound's economy was indeed stagnant and required Walla Walla's taxes. These Walla Wallans desired more political clout.[16] In October, they drafted resolutions of annexation:

> Whereas, the County of Walla Walla is separated from the other inhabited portion of the Territory of Washington by extensive tracts of barren and uninhabited country, and the Columbia and Snake Rivers, which form a natural boundary line, and,
>
> Whereas, The boundary line between the County of Walla Walla and the State of Oregon is artificial and divides the fertile portions of the Walla Walla Valley between the State of Oregon and the Territory of Washington . . . therefore,
>
> *Resolved,* That we earnestly request the Senators and Representatives of the State of Oregon, and the Hon. A. A. Denny, Delegate to Congress from this Territory, to propose and to use all honorable means to induce the Congress of the United States to pass an act to annex the County of Walla Walla to the State of Oregon in accordance with the Boundary of said State as originally proposed to the people of Oregon in their constitution and voted for by them on the adoption thereof.[17]

The supporters of the resolution regarded Walla Walla as something of an orphaned sibling of Portland, Salem, and The Dalles.

In response, eighty-five individuals and businesses affixed their names to a call for a public meeting for the citizens "opposed to the scheme of hungry office seekers to procure the annexation of the County of Walla Walla to the . . . bankrupt State of Oregon."[18] The issue of taxation, in particular, aroused the opposition: Oregonians paid their taxes in gold coin; Walla Wallans did so in Civil War–era greenbacks (which were generally valued around $0.70). A few anonymous lawyers carried on a war of words for and against annexation in the *Statesman*, each claiming to speak for the majority of the county (at least one pretended to be a farmer). Coincidentally, at this moment William Newell arrived from The Dalles to assume control of the *Statesman* and to press his opinions—"Oregon style"—on his readership. In only his third edition, Newell suddenly appeared as a forceful proponent of annexation:

> With the Sound country we have no identity of interests, and as a consequence have little sympathy. On the other hand, we are only separated from Oregon by an imaginary line, and all our interests harmonise with that part of Oregon east of the mountains. The section of the State to which we are so nearly allied already polls one-third the vote of the State, and with the addition of Walla Walla Valley, will be able to control the legislation and shape the policy of the State. It is thus the inducement presented is not only an escape from Territorial vassalage, but the still higher privilege of controlling a sovereign State, and with that control an influence in the Congress of the Nation from which we are now entirely excluded. . . . [T]he Sound country . . . is in torpid condition, and at the present rate of growth, will require half a century to reach the proportions of a State. To chain a rich and growing county like Walla Walla to the half dead carcase of Puget Sound is a condition not to be endured.[19]

The urgency of this appeal had much to do with the new Republican majority in the Oregon state legislature. Regardless of the actual opinions of the majority of the county's residents, and despite the political complexion of the Salem legislature, it enthusiastically passed the resolution and sent a memorial to Congress.[20] The legislature in Olympia quickly responded with its own resolution: "[O]ur delegate in Congress is hereby instructed to resist any and all attempts to diminish the area of the Territory of Washington, by annexing Walla-walla county to the State of Oregon. [I]t is our firm belief that such proposed scheme of annexation meets with the earnest disapprobation of a large majority of the citizens of said county."[21] As the lawyers continued to debate in the pages of the *Statesman,* the memorials from Salem and Olympia were referred to the House Committee on Territories, where they languished. At the end of 1866, the *Statesman* declared the annexation to Oregon "A Dead Issue. . . . [A]t this time we know of no one who favors annexation to Oregon."[22]

Other scenarios for transforming boundaries in the Northwest were proposed, including a division of Oregon and Washington at the Cascades, uniting Puget Sound with Portland and the Willamette Valley, and supposedly making Walla Walla the capital of the eastern territory. These discussions all fizzled away. Finally, in 1868, the Boise and Olympia legislatures jointly petitioned Congress to annex northern Idaho to Washington Territory. However, Republican delegate Alvan Flanders, fearing the overwhelming Democratic majority of the proposed territory, opposed the petition in Congress, and no action was taken. At the same time, the legislature in Olympia rewarded the Republican majority of Clickitat County by extending its eastern boundary to the mouth of the Yakima River (thus cutting the western boundary of Walla Walla County back to the Columbia). Citizens in northern Idaho continued to fight for independence from Boise while Walla Wallans continued to grumble.

17

Community and Entertainment

Public and private events afforded members of the community, who on arrival may have had little in common, opportunities to mix and mingle and identify with one another, to come together as Walla Wallans. Prior to the arrival of a substantial number of families, Fort Walla Walla served as the entertainment center of the valley, where the community gathered, danced, and celebrated. The garrison band performed at all public celebrations; their regular dress parades were always well attended, and the fort's "Grand Balls" were seasonal highlights (held on New Year's Eve, Washington's birthday, and Fourth of July). The presence of more families in the city brought about an increase in the number of formal balls. The Fire Company held popular benefit balls on New Year's Eve and Fourth of July. The Masons, Odd Fellows, and other organizations hosted semiannual balls. In advance of the events, merchants advertised the arrival of the latest seasonal fashions. Dancing schools were available to get everyone up to speed. Some new businesses hosted balls to mark their grand openings. The Buckley's Saloon/the Oriental Hotel, the City Hotel, and the Bank Exchange Hall were all refitted with large dance halls. The Walla Walla Brass Band, Joe Bauer's Walla Walla String Band, and Mr. Huson's Quadrille Band were hired to provide regular dancing entertainment at these venues.

The Idaho gold rush put Walla Walla on the Far West theater circuit. In August 1861, the J. B. Robinson Family Troupe, one of the most celebrated theatrical groups in the region, arrived in Walla Walla and established a theater on the lower part of Main Street. Robinson had moved his family from Chicago to San Francisco in 1851 and traveled to mining towns up and down the coast. By 1855, his ten-year-old daughter Susan, billed as the "Fairy Star," was a theatrical sensation. Robinson established Portland's first theater in 1859.[1] Yet two years later, he decided that Walla Walla was the ideal home base for his troupe. Thanks to his connections with the major performers in the Far West, Walla Walla became something of an entertainment center for a few years. Several times each week, Robinson featured musical acts, dramatic troupes (always Shakespeare, and usually Macbeth), ventriloquists, magicians, and minstrel acts (which often did comical versions of Shakespeare, usually Macbeth). After fire destroyed the theater in 1862, the Robinsons performed regularly at Buckley's Saloon until 1863, when Robinson and his wife relocated to La Grande and Susan Robinson joined the Irwin Theatrical Troupe, based in Boise City.

Between 1864 and its destruction in 1866, the Masonic Hall played host to the Irwin troupe and other major touring companies. The hotels and the Bank Exchange then hosted the smaller traveling troupes that stopped in town; for example, the National Troupe of Glass Blowers, who dazzled audiences throughout the Far West with their glass spinning.

In 1870–71, a private association of citizens invested in the construction of a two-and-a-half-story frame building on the north side of First and Main, known as the City Hall or Public Hall (fig. 36). Its ground floor was occupied by a saloon; the upper floors contained offices and a large space for public gatherings and theatrical events. The theater could seat

Figure 36. Main Street, looking west from First, 1875. The City Hall/Public House is the first building on the right. (Walla Walla Photograph Collection, WCMss066, Box 25, Folder 19, Whitman College and Northwest Archives.)

400—about a quarter of the city's population in 1871. The Pixley Sisters were among the most popular acts to visit in the 1870s. During her time in Walla Walla in September 1871, women's rights activist Susan B. Anthony caught their show at the City Hall and noted in her daybook, "City Hall engaged to the Pixley Sisters . . . manage their own business & hire men to fill up plays." Anthony, hosted by Annie Mix and Lucie Isaacs, spoke to a woman-only audience at the City Hall the following day.[2]

Unlike the theatrical troupes, the circus arrived with its own portable theater. Circus performers were more famous than actors and drew much larger crowds. A number of circuses had arrived in San Francisco since 1849. Performers and managers came and went, and circuses were reconstituted, renamed, and took to the road continuously. They featured clowns (many of whom performed Shakespeare), acrobats, gymnasts, remarkable equestrians, intelligent horses, mules, pigs, and "human oddities." In 1860, the world-famous promoter Dan Rice sent the most celebrated circus yet to San Francisco. Rice remained back East, but his name at the top of the bill guaranteed quality performers and packed houses.

Dan Rice's Great Show made it to Walla Walla in September 1864 and set up its big tent on John Sparks's land. It was a scaled-down version of the California troupe, lacking above all the elephants (which had trouble with ferry crossings). Nonetheless, it featured many famous performers, including the clown and ringmaster William Aymar, The Educated Mules ("trained by Dan Rice himself"), and William Franklin, the somersault rider. At the top of the bill was Ella Zoyara, the world-famous and scandalous "equestrienne" (soon to be sensationally outed as a man, Omar Kingsley). The ad for the Great Show promised: "Single and Double Acts of Horsemanship; Daring Break Neck Acts! Terrific Feats of Vaulting! All the Modern Feats of the Cirque."[3] The attendance for the three nights was reported to be 1,500–1,800—which represented about half the population of the county.

Naturally, the completion of the transcontinental railroad in 1869 offered circuses and theater troupes from the East easier access to the Far West. The first circus to tour the country via the railroad, Dan Castello's Overland Circus and Menagerie (1869), would perform at depot towns, travel the old dirt roads to reach as many towns as possible, then return to the rails, and repeat. Very soon, however, it became far more profitable for circuses to perform exclusively for railroad cities.[4] Omar Kingsley's New York Circus (organized in Portland, with no connection to New York), visited Walla Walla in June 1871, but this may have been the last circus to visit the city via steamer and dirt road.

The most unforgettable circus experiences of the time occurred July 26, 1876. During the matinee performance of the Great Italian Circus, a violent hailstorm pummeled the tent, increased in intensity, then collapsed the tent. During the evening show, lightning, thunder, and a sudden "tornado" again drove the audience from the tent in panic. Some watched as the storm flattened the tent "like a pancake." Remarkably, no injuries were reported.[5]

Voluntary Organizations

The country's major fraternal mutual aid organizations were quickly established in the Far West; a Masonic lodge was organized in Oregon City in 1848, and a lodge of the Independent Order of Odd Fellows in San Francisco received a charter in 1849. As members relocated, they came together with other relocated "brothers" to organize new lodges, which served as lifelines for the members as they navigated their new uprooted lives in remote and insecure lands.[6] Above all, they provided life insurance and social and business contacts with local and distant members. Under the leadership of A. B. Roberts, a Masonic lodge (Walla Walla Lodge No. 7) was organized already in 1859. Membership ignored political ideology (initially) and religion (the Jewish merchants Bahr Scheideman and Julius Friedman were charter members, as was the Catholic James McAuliff), yet it was predominantly a White, Protestant, merchant-class organization. During its celebration of John the Evangelist in December 1863, forty-six members, led by the Walla Walla Brass Band, paraded up Main and down Alder to the Methodist church. However, due to a split within the lodge over loyalties during the Civil War and extrajudicial activities (see chapter 19), a second lodge (Blue Mountain Lodge No. 13) was organized in 1868 under the leadership of the blacksmith Fred Stine. Advanced York Rite and Scottish Rite lodges were organized in the 1870s.

James McAuliff led the organization of an Odd Fellows lodge in 1863 (Enterprise Lodge No. 2), and just three years later, a second lodge was chartered (Jefferson Lodge No. 2). All these lodges shared meeting spaces during these years, including the Masonic Hall and, on its completion in

1869, the upper floor of Oswald Brechtel's brick building. Their parades, in full regalia like those of the fire companies, may not have thrilled the city like those of the circus, but they punctuated the seasons.

A lodge of the Independent Order of Good Templars was established in 1867 (Mountain Gem Lodge No. 8). The local arm of the temperance movement, it focused—with little success—on lobbying for the enactment of Sunday laws. Its national bylaws opened membership to everyone, so a number of married couples were involved, including Lydia and William Horton. The photographer P. T. Shupe held the highest rank among its forty-seven members.

Of course, people quickly came together publicly for numerous causes. The most important were the fire engine companies (Tiger Engine Company No. 2 was formed in 1872), which—when not fighting with each other or with the city council—were celebrated by the city. The most active women's organizations of the time were dedicated to raising funds for the Catholic and Presbyterian schools. Their "Ladies' Fairs," held over several days prior to Christmas, included dinners, performances, dancing, and the sale of Christmas gifts.

———

Horse racing—and gambling on horse races—had probably been popular in the valley as soon as two people acquired horses in the eighteenth century, and horse racing remained the most popular sport in the region throughout the century. Marshall George Porter had laid out a race track 3 miles west of the city by 1862, and two years later the Walla Walla County Jockey Club was formally established. The fall races, with rules and purses regulated by the club, comprised 1-mile dashes and trotting races, which were always well attended. After Charles S. Bush purchased the Phinney-Craig property to the east of the city in the early 1870s, he transformed it into a racecourse, offering a more central location to train and congregate. In 1875, he added a grandstand (with seating for 1,000) and prepared the site to hold the annual Agricultural Fairs (which were ultimately asides to the races).

———

Concerned about the intellectual life of the city, a group of citizens, including A. J. Thibodo, John H. Day, and James Lasater, organized the

Walla Walla Library and Literary Association in 1865. They established a collection of books and magazines, housed it in the office of the clerk at the courthouse, and made it available for a nominal fee. W. W. Johnson served as librarian. The literary wing of the association, called the Calliopean Society, hosted a lecture series during its first year. Enthusiasm appears to have faded within a couple of years, but the enterprise was revived in 1874 with the establishment of the Walla Walla Lyceum and Library Association. Women's rights advocate Abigail Scott Duniway was among its first speakers.

In summer 1867, the *Statesman* noted, "There is scarce a one horse town in Oregon that has not one or more base ball clubs. The practice of these clubs afford healthful exercise—something required by young men too closely confined to workshops and stores. In view of this advantage, cannot we have a base ball club in Walla Walla? In these dull times an organization of the kind would serve to drive away the blues." Two weeks later, the paper announced the organization of two clubs: "Our young men have caught the contagion." The Excelsior Club and the Walla Wallas played their first game at "the ball grounds" on September 7. Excelsior, led by the saddler J. D. Cook, won 85–60, then won a rematch two weeks later.[7] The civic spirit evoked through baseball may or may not have resonated in the community; only sporadic notices of baseball in the region appeared over the next decade.

18

Disasters and Near Disasters

Fire

The residents of a tinderbox town like Walla Walla were fully aware of the risk of fire, particularly during the region's long, dry summers. Nonetheless, they continued to fill up Main Street with side-by-side frame buildings. Reports of town fires spread rapidly in the papers of the Far West and were usually accompanied by estimated financial losses and mention of whether or not the properties were insured. Once commercial properties filled up Main streets, fires were rarely contained to one building, and the risk of entire blocks of buildings being destroyed only increased.

The volunteer Union Hook and Ladder Co. No. 1, which organized in 1862, had "hooks and ladders placed at . . . convenient distances in the town, and also some thirty or forty buckets, which have been distributed among the various stores and saloons." This was done at the cost of the volunteers themselves, a fact that the *Statesman* found embarrassing, and called for the support of the city's property owners.[1] (The riot at the Robinson theater in April of that year occurred during a benefit for the Hook and Ladder Co.) Fires could start anywhere a flame was present—a lamp, a stove, a faulty chimney—however, arson seems to have been a common source of fires in the 1860s and '70s.

On June 17, 1862, the city witnessed its first catastrophic fire. Robinson's theater was completely destroyed together with the Robinsons' adjoining house. The Hook and Ladder Co., with the assistance of soldiers from the garrison, managed to save the neighboring buildings by tearing down the burning buildings. "[T]here is no doubt it was the work of an incendiary," noted the *Statesman*.[2] After the Robinson fire, an attempt was made to organize a more formal fire company, Washington Fire Company No. 1, and to raise funds for a fire engine. By the end of the year, the company had purchased both a hand-pumped Hunneman tub and a lot on the east side of Third, between Main and Alder—adjoining the *Statesman* office— and began lobbying for funds to build a proper engine house. During 1863, the city ran a water pipe from Mill Creek along Main, connecting to cisterns on each corner.

The fire company had a more significant test on the evening of Monday, May 9, 1864. A fire began at Fred Stine's blacksmith shop and spread to the adjoining buildings on the north side of Main between Third and Fourth. Mill Creek was running low, so the cisterns were of little value. Fearing that fire spreading to the City Hotel, the largest building in town, would have resulted in possible destruction of the entire business community, the fire was fought (with the assistance of citizens, farmers, and soldiers) by tearing down all eight frame buildings between the City Hotel (in the middle of the block) and the corner of Fourth. James McAuliff's saloon, which had been used as the city hall and courthouse, was destroyed, but the records were removed in time. An estimated $12,000 in property was lost.[3]

In spring 1865, the fire company was reincorporated by the city. Among the members were some of the city's most prominent businessmen, including Kohlhauff, Bauer, Brechtel, Abe Schwabacher, Bahr Scheideman, the Rees brothers of the *Statesman*, and Freeman Allen. Allen, whose planing mill stood directly across Third from the *Statesman* building and behind the Oriental Hotel, played a leading role in the first years of the company's existence. In June, the city council selected Allen's bid for the design and construction of the engine house ($2,450). A large front room on the second floor was to be reserved for the firemen, and a large rear room was intended for the city council and other civic meetings.

On August 3, 1865—as construction was commencing on the engine house/city hall—the greatest fears during the fire of 1864 were realized. By the time any fireman arrived to the sound of the fire bell just after midnight, the roof of the City Hotel was ablaze. Flames spread quickly to all the buildings on the block—many of which had been rebuilt just months earlier. A decision was made to focus on protecting the buildings on the south side of Main; however, they were quickly engulfed in flames. According to the *Statesman*, "It was but a few seconds now until both sides of

Main street was a solid sheet of roaring crackling flames, sweeping along to the North and South. A light breeze sprang up blowing down Main, and carried the fire from building to building with astonishing rapidity. Nothing now could save the lower part of town." The flames from the Oriental Hotel were scorching the *Statesman* building across Third, where the Rees brothers and their assistants protected their building with wet blankets. Eventually, numerous citizens and soldiers arrived, but chaos prevailed. "The wind had shifted around, and was blowing to the North; but the Oriental had tumbled to the ground, as had Kohlhauff and Guichard's store." The fire engine had managed to keep the fire from crossing Third. However, all the buildings on Main between Third and Fifth were destroyed. All the city records were now destroyed in McAuliff's rebuilt saloon. "Nearly one-third of Walla Walla City lay in a heap of fire and ashes. Many who were quietly sleeping beneath the roofs of their homes an hour or two previously, now found themselves in the streets houseless and homeless."[4] Remarkably, no lives were lost. Property losses were estimated at $164,500.

The day after the fire, Kohlhauff and Guichard had lumber hauled to their site, and the following day, carpenters were erecting a new store. At the same time, lumber was being delivered to the site of Joe Bauer's destroyed cigar and novelty shop next door.[5] Two doors from Bauer's, Dick Bogle soon rebuilt his barbershop, and across the street, the Baumeister brothers' Oriental Bathing Saloon was soon back in business (albeit without the Oriental Hotel). C. Jacobs & Co. was quickly back in at their same location, as were the saloons of Frank Orselli, William Terry, Frank Stone, and several others. The new buildings were designed according to the current city ordinance: a 100-foot-wide Main Street (façade to façade) and 8-foot sidewalks (fig. 37). Main Street took on a more unified appearance. Another ordinance required chimneys to be fireproofed.

After the fire, work also continued on the engine house/city hall on Third. Freeman Allen was now also appointed foreman of the fire company. On its completion in December 1865, the *Statesman* gushed: "Of the new Engine House it is safe to say that there is not a more elegant or imposing structure of the kind this side of San Francisco."[6] This was certainly the most prestigious commission for any Walla Walla carpenter, and Allen wanted to ensure it would be the most visually impressive building in town. He designed a crenellated castle with two turrets and lancet windows. The

Figure 37. The City Hotel, rebuilt 1865–66. The destroyed City Hotel had been the city's largest building. The new building was much larger. The new Bank Exchange Hall is visible two doors to the right. William Kohlhauff sold out his dry goods business in 1870 and purchased the City Hotel, which he renamed the St. Louis Hotel (for the city where he met his wife). Photograph, 1882. (Walla Walla Photograph Collection, Box 32, Folder 61, WCMss066, Whitman College and Northwest Archives.)

---

siding was broken into faux-stone sections and painted white. It is safe to assume that Allen scoured pattern books in preparation for this design. He would have been acquainted with numerous illustrations of buildings and designs that similarly incorporated Gothic façade elements.[7]

On January 1, 1866, the city officials and the uniformed fire company staged a spectacle during which the mayor formally granted the company charge of the engine house (fig. 38). The city council then attempted to establish a permanent fire company. Little was accomplished. Volunteers peeled away, many heading to the Montana mines in search of either gold or miners with gold to spend. By June, the company had dwindled to about a dozen—an insufficient number to manage the engine. Perhaps in an attempt to force the hand of the city council, the remaining officers

Figure 38. Washington Engine Co. No. 1 and City Hall, 1865, east side of Third between Main and Alder, designed by Freeman P. Allen. Photograph prior to 1882. (*The Walla Wallan*, December 30, 1948.)

announced that the company had disbanded and returned the engine house and its supplies to the city. The city officials, perhaps distracted by the local elections and the preparations for the Fourth of July festivities, formed a committee to draft a plan for the regulation of the engine house. Had the Rees brothers still been involved with the *Statesman*, the paper may have rung a tone of urgency. However, William Newell, the new editor, was far more concerned with national politics, the local vigilance committee, and the Fourth of July celebrations. On June 22, the *Statesman* carried a front-page ad for "Fire Works! . . . a large assortment of Fire Works!"

The city celebrated the 90th Independence Day with a grand parade culminating at Council Grove. The afternoon was filled with speeches and food, the evening was to feature a spectacular fireworks show, and the city was without a fire company. In the early afternoon, a fire broke out—of all places—at Freeman Allen's planing mill, directly across the street from the engine house. Wood shavings had been ignited by "the careless use of firecrackers." By the time the crowds from the Grove arrived, the large, Masonic hall across the street was engulfed in flames. The *Statesman* reported, "Soon all the buildings on the south side of Alder street, between First and Third streets, were on fire, and all hope of saving anything within the district named was given over. By the most strenuous and heroic exertions on the part of the firemen and citizens the fire was prevented from crossing Alder Street, and thus the main business portion of the city saved from destruction."[8] Aside from the Masonic hall, twenty-three houses and businesses were destroyed. Property losses were estimated at $40,000. After all the chaos, the fireworks show went on as planned. Again, reconstruction of destroyed buildings commenced within days of the fire.

In April 1867, another fire destroyed several rebuilt structures on Alder and was only extinguished thanks to the leadership of two visitors from San Francisco. The following week, the fire company with forty-two volunteers was re-formed, with Allen as foreman. As incentive to retain the company, legislation was passed by the city council exempting firemen from jury duty, poll taxes, and road taxes. Fires, like the ones that destroyed the Congregational church or the "Cain Mansion" in 1868, tended to be contained to only one or two buildings, which was all that could be expected from the single volunteer fire company.

In 1871, the city purchased a state-of-the-art Silsby steam fire engine that could potentially propel a stream of water 200 feet. In spring 1872, the city's second fire company, Tiger Engine Company No. 2, was formed to man the old Hunneman pump. Almost immediately, the two companies were called on to deal with a large warehouse fire in Cain's Addition, which was contained to two buildings. Another large fire broke out in the lower part of the city in August 1873. The two companies, assisted by hundreds of citizens and soldiers, struggled to confine the flames, which were fanned by high winds, to one (entire) block. Yet the greatest challenge arrived in October 1875. A small fire began in the (new) Oriental Hotel on the north side of Main between First and Second. With no filled water buckets, the fire spread rapidly, engulfing the neighboring buildings. Flames reached across Main; the cornice of the brand new brick Reynolds-Day building was in flames, as was the façade of J. B. Mitchell's barbershop. All the wooden structures between the City Hall building on First and the brick store of Johnson, Rees & Winans on the corner of Second (formerly Kyger & Reese) were destroyed (i.e., most of the buildings visible on the right side of fig. 36).[9]

Flood

New arrivals quickly came to understand the effect that winter Chinook winds could have on the rivers and creeks in the valley. Yet many purchased property with water access and built homes close to the water. Almost every winter, Mill Creek would overflow its banks, damaging mills and gardens, sometimes washing away outbuildings, occasionally reducing the size of some properties and augmenting others. After the completion of the Main Street bridge in 1864, the city commissioned the construction of a timber bulkhead to stabilize the creek bank as it crossed Main. The bulkhead was partially undermined during its first real test: the freshet of January 24–25, 1866. The creek ran high enough to threaten the bridge. The planing mill of Dovell & Massam was shifted off its foundation. The *Statesman* reported, "Chicken-coops, lumber, timber, etc., were to be seen . . . sailing down the rapid current, much to the delight of careless boys, and gratification of the red-skins who had a very 'good thing' in catching and appropriating the drifting articles."[10]

The flood of January 27–29, 1867, however, was unlike any ever experienced in the city. A warm rain caused snow in the Blue Mountains to melt rapidly on Sunday. On Monday, typical freshet damage occurred along the banks of the creek. By Tuesday morning, "Mill Creek was found to have assumed the proportions of a river." It overflowed its banks at Alder, and Alder became a torrent. The foundation of Sam Linkton's house on Third was washed away. The *Statesman* reported, "All day Tuesday and the greater part of Wednesday this portion of the town presented the appearance of a lake, and persons living beyond Alder street could only reach their homes by fording a stream waist-deep. . . . All along the line of Mill Creek outbuildings were being carried away, and the piles which were put down, at great cost, for the purpose of confining the creek to its channel, were being forced up and drifted away."[11] Ground floors and cellars of businesses on Alder and Main were flooded. Two houses were entirely washed away. The rear section of the new courthouse building at First and Main collapsed and washed away (county documents, however, were removed in advance). The Main Street bridge withstood the torrent, as did the bulkhead at the bend toward Rose Street. But all the city's downstream bridges were washed away (except one at a point where the river had changed its course). Bridges on the Walla Walla and lower Touchet were also washed away. For several days, all roads out of the city were impassable. Six families in town had lost their homes.

Within weeks, Linkton had repaired his large house and agreed to sell it to the county commissioners (for thirty monthly installments of $100; fig. 39).[12] Linkton then moved to San Francisco. His departure was part of an exodus of businessmen from Walla Walla to the boom towns of Idaho and Montana, and to the big-city comfort of San Francisco.

Every subsequent freshet resulted in unanticipated damage. Bridges and bulkheads were replaced or reinforced annually. The flooding and extensive damage of 1867 recurred in 1870, 1871, and 1875. As properties improved, losses increased. (Some Cayuse, recalling the siting of their lodges in proximity to Mill Creek, must have been amused by this repetitive damage to property.)

Fort Walla Walla

In August 1865, rumors circulated of the impending abandonment of Fort Walla Walla. This came as a shock to everyone in the region. They counted

Figure 39. The courthouse, ca. 1881. After purchasing Sam Linkton's house, the county hired John Dovell to raise the roof by 5 feet to accommodate a second-floor courtroom; the building was also extended by two bays to the rear, and a staircase leading to the courtroom was added to its west side. (Gilbert, *Historic Sketches*, opp. 297.)

on the security of the fort; in fact, it was a major factor in the decisions of many to settle in the region. The rumors also posed an economic threat to the local businesses that relied on the soldiers' hard currency and to regional farmers and ranchers who relied on government contracts to supply the fort with provisions. Additionally, the city was threatened with the loss of a central core of its social life; the balls, the parades, and the musical performances were essential components of "civilization" in such a remote location. The rumors made little sense to the residents; just before the war, the fort was declared the central supply depot east of the Cascades. William Newell seemed interested in generating a sense of panic by suggesting that the abandonment of the fort would encourage a general Indian uprising.[13] On August 25, the *Statesman* confirmed the rumors and began a series of personal attacks against Col. George B. Currey of the Oregon militia, who had been named acting commander of the Department of the Columbia following the death of Gen. George Wright.[14] Newell referred to the outspoken Republican as "the accidental Commander," "His Accidency," "Dirty Currey," "Col. Dirty," and the "short-sighted simpleton." He accused Currey of retaliating against the "Walla Walla Secessionists" and quoted him as saying that Walla Walla was "nothing but a d–d secesh hole anyhow and deserved no favors at the hands of Uncle Sam."[15] The quartermaster was charged with overseeing the fort until the government officially abandoned it. The fort's wood and hay reserves were sold, and its surplus possessions were gradually auctioned off. An inspection report of 1866 concluded: "The necessity for this post, on account of Indians, has passed away. This rich valley is too well settled, but there are advantages in keeping it . . . as a depot, repair post, &c."[16] Of the aesthetically remarkable Fort Dalles, on the other hand, the report concluded: "This post is useless."

During the Army's campaign against the Paiute, Bannock, and Shoshone bands throughout the Great Basin (1866–67), Fort Walla Walla served a similar role as the HBC's Fort Walla Walla had for the Snake brigade (instead of collecting pelts, however, the hunt was for human beings). Soldiers and provisions passed through the region, and occasionally Walla Wallans received government contracts for provisions. However, an auction of the fort's surplus goods including "a lot of stoves" in March 1867 signaled the nail in the coffin.

On February 24, 1871, the secretary of war was authorized by Congress to transfer the military reservation of "Walla-Walla, in the State of Oregon" to the secretary of the interior "for disposition for cash . . . to the highest bidder."[17] The closure of the fort marked the beginning of a series of economic setbacks for the city.

19

Law and Order

Accounts are plentiful of the city's rowdy character during the mining years. An overlander of 1863, for example, noted, "The dirty streets were crowded with freighting wagons and teams and pack animals and a considerable army of rough men. One would naturally conclude, to judge from the numerous places where gambling was in progress, day and night, with an orchestra and free lunch as additional attractions in each establishment, that this was the chief occupation, other things and exorbitant prices only ordinary adjuncts; all the games known to the guild were running in full blast unceasingly."[1] Beginning with City Ordinance No. 6 of May 1862, the municipal coffers were primarily dependent on license fees for "All buildings, houses, rooms, or places where one or more females are kept, reside, or remain for the purpose of open and promiscuous fornication or adultery" and "Drinking saloons, bar-rooms or tippling houses." Initially, these fees were set at $75 quarterly, but they were increased regularly. (Merchant licenses, by contrast, cost only $10–$80 annually.) Despite increasing concern for such "vices" (as families settled in large numbers), the city had an economic incentive to be tolerant.

Prostitution

The *Statesman* seems to have gone out of its way to avoid mentioning Walla Walla's bustling demimonde. Reports of shootings and assaults in town usually alluded to the saloons. The big fire of 1864 was reported to have "originated in a house occupied by a Spanish courtezan."[2] There were some references to Chinese prostitutes on the property owned by Dorsey Baker on the north side of Alder, between Second and Third; the *Statesman* stated that Baker "has enjoyed the monopoly of renting houses to lewd China women [in] the Chinese rookery in the rear of his store."[3] The city council actually banned prostitution in January 1864 (Ordinance No. 20): "No person or persons shall keep or cause to be kept any dance house, room or cellar, or place where public prostitutes or lewd women live or assemble for the purpose of dancing with the public." The *Statesman* applauded the law, noting that "A Spanish fandango house at the lower end of the city, which has of late been a source of much annoyance to the residents of that vicinity, has been closed under the law."[4] However, a newly elected city council looked over the municipal debt that summer and decided to repeal the ban. Ordinance No. 26 of September 1864 required, instead, license fees totaling $1,000 annually to run such establishments. Apparently, this law caused no hardship in town; in 1866, it was amended to require *quarterly* license fees of $1,000! Such businesses could have avoided the fee by relocating to one of the unincorporated additions to the city; however, the *Statesman* mentions only one "hurdy gurdy establishment" to have done so (in Cain's Addition).[5] Business license fees accounted for more than two-thirds of the city's income at this time.

Unfortunately, general knowledge of prostitution in the first decades of the city has been limited to Bill Gulick's romanticized story of Josephine Wolfe, who ran at least one brothel in the city from 1861 until her death in 1909.[6] Some long-term resident prostitutes, like Wolfe, or Bridget Gallagher in Portland, became well known locally. Newspaper accounts following Wolfe's death are far less entertaining than Gulick's historical fiction, but they are more reliable. Wolfe, a native of Baden, was part of the large German emigration to California during the gold rush. Like Dick Bogle, Fred Stine, and others, she came to Walla Walla via Yreka, California.[7] According to an obituary, "since her arrival into this section of the country [she] has been widely known as one of the town characters. . . . [S]he soon became well known for her many benevolent acts and kindnesses, always taking the greatest care that no one should hear of these things."[8] Wolfe owned two adjoining houses on the south side of Alder between Second and Third (map 9 and fig. 43, #22). The census records sometimes include the names of single women living with, or next door to, Wolfe; however, these names never reappear in the census records or city directories.[9] At least two brothels on this block were owned by a John Meduna, who, in 1863, got into a shooting affray with Raffaella Acosta, "a 'nymph of the pave' of the Spanish persuasion."[10]

Wolfe's houses stood directly across Alder from Chinatown, location of most of the *Statesman*'s references to prostitution. Yet no women are

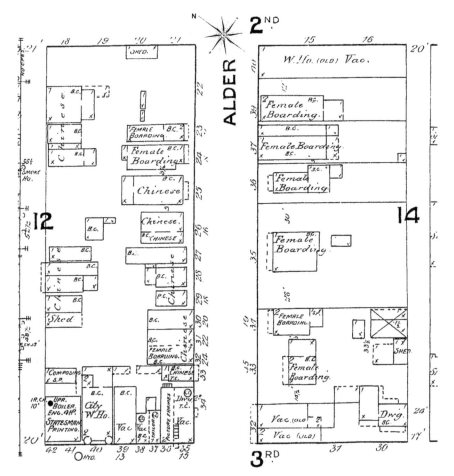

Map 9. *Sanborn Fire Insurance Map for Walla Walla*, 1888, page 2, detail depicting every building and its function on Alder between Second and Third. "Female Boarding" or "FB" were Sanborn's designations for buildings dedicated to prostitution. Josephine Wolfe's house is the large one at #35 on block 14. (Library of Congress Geography and Map Division, Sanborn Maps Collection. https://loc.gov/item/sanborn09361_002/.)

recorded as residing on this block in the early censuses. Sociologist Lucie Cheng Hirata noted that Chinese prostitution "remained a semifeudal organization."[11] Chinese prostitutes were indentured or owned and lacked the freedom to leave town or to marry, while the prostitutes in Jo Wolfe's house would have been among the best protected and the best compensated in the city. There would have been a sense of luxury in Wolfe's house, and women would have entertained clients in a formal receiving room and bedroom. The Chinese prostitutes, on the other hand, may have worked from "cribs": rows of tiny sheds only large enough to fit a bed and a chair, with access often from an alley.[12] They may have been indentured to one of the San Francisco tongs, and numerous men would have had a share of their income, including the White property owners.[13] And they would have held the lowest social status in the city. At saloons, "hurdy-gurdies," and "Fandango houses" non-Chinese women would have been paid to sit or dance with men, and small rooms or curtained-off areas would have been available for privacy. They would have been employed by the proprietors of the establishment, for whom alcohol sales were prioritized.

The Hurdy Gurdy Girl [*Drehleiermädchen*] was a German phenomenon. Large numbers of young girls from impoverished families in the Rheinland Pfalz region were brought to San Francisco during the 1850s and '60s to increase saloon profits through dancing, encouraged drinking, and prostitution. Theodor Kirchhoff, a German merchant in The Dalles, published an influential essay in a popular German magazine in 1865, calling on German officials to take action against the "soul merchants" [*Seelenverkäufern*] behind the practice.[14] In a rare bit of insightful journalism, the *Statesman* noted, "These hurdys are generally regarded as a nuisance, but business men regard them otherwise, claiming that they retain and throw into circulation a large amount of money that otherwise would be carried out of the country."[15]

In the 1860s, the number of prostitutes in Walla Walla would have fluctuated with the comings and goings of the miners.[16] It is safe to assume that the prostitutes in the early mining towns of Idaho and Montana had passed through Walla Walla. While some Far West towns and cities developed "red-light districts" separate from the business center, prostitution in Walla Walla was located in several downtown areas: on both sides of Alder between Second and Third; inside, above, and behind the saloons and dance halls on Main west of Third; and in Cain's Addition.

The first couple of decades following the gold rush were remarkable in terms of wealth and property ownership among prostitutes in the Far West, where they "constituted a kind of businesswomen's network." As the hordes of transient miners and pilot-fish gamblers dissipated in the 1870s, cities increasingly moved to curb prostitution, and the number of prostitutes with the social and economic status of Wolfe dwindled.[17]

The Vigilance Committee

Among the army of miners and gamblers that wintered in Walla Walla during the 1860s was also a sizable number of thieves. Most worked in organized groups. When the weather got warmer and the transients departed, some of the most valuable cattle and horses in the valley would go missing. Additionally, organized bands of highwaymen or "road agents" presented a constant danger on the roads radiating from the city. The situation was increasingly dangerous as one traveled within the mining districts. The *Statesman* and its contributors regularly reported on robberies in the region. It noted on November 1, 1862: "Scarcely a day passes that we [do] not hear of a robbery or an attempt at one."[18] Two weeks later, it reported that three men who had been accused of highway robbery were hanged at Lewiston.

Vigilantism had been widespread in the United States since the 1830s. In the Far West, "vigilance committees" took control of San Francisco and other regions during periods of crisis in the 1850s. Vigilantes either had no faith in the principles of due process or acted in regions where the population was dispersed far from the seats of justice. Their sense of mission was frequently accompanied by elements of ethnic or racial hatred. Attitudes regarding vigilantism were often colored by one's place of birth; the strongest supporters of the rule of law, for example, were concentrated in the Northeast.[19]

At the end of 1863, some resident Masons in Idaho Territory established at least one vigilance committee. It is likely that some of their members had been involved in prior vigilante action, in Iowa (1857), San Francisco (1851, 1856), or Oregon (1855–56), for example. Throughout 1864, Northwest papers covered a long series of lynchings in Idaho and Montana territories, particularly when they involved notorious criminals. The Idaho papers were split on the actions of the vigilantes. The editors of the *Statesman* embraced both positions at first. Correspondents from the mines also expressed mixed opinions. There were reports of lawyers who were intimidated or chased from regions for attempting to defend those accused of committing crimes. And there were regular accusations that the vigilantes had executed innocent people. There were also notices that some of the thieves chased from Montana and Idaho would winter in Walla Walla. The *Statesman* noted on February 3, 1865, "It is common talk about town this week, that a score or two of individuals possessed with thieving propensities and road agency proclivities, were granted permanent leave of absence from this city and vicinity, by some resident citizens who assumed to speak and act by authority. . . . The mysterious outpouring and lively skeedaddling of the light-fingered gentry from the city, has excited much public comment, and given rise to innumerable stories about an organized Vigilance Committee existing in town. . . . We hope the committee will act with due deliberation and do nothing rash."[20] Although Walla Walla was the seat of the district court, there were constant concerns regarding the structural integrity of the city and county jail. The county commissioners had a jailhouse built on the public square in 1862. However, on its completion, it was already deemed to be insufficient in terms of security and capacity. Escapes were almost comically frequent. In December 1864, two convicted murderers escaped from the county jail, including

George Porter, the former marshal. Within days, improvements were made. Yet two months later, two accused thieves—"Six-toed Pete" and "Waddingham"—escaped from the jail, with the assistance of "Slim Jim from the Hook." According to a letter from a vigilante printed in the next edition of the *Statesman* (March 3), a group of 700 (!) vigilantes hunted the 3 men down and turned them over, safely, to the sheriff. The author recommended specific improvements be made to the jail. Within days, the city commissioned reinforced walls for the jailhouse, the addition of an upstairs room for a jailer, and the construction of a 12-foot fence around an 80 × 84–foot yard, the latter to keep the prisoners' friends away (fig. 40).

In an April 14 editorial, the *Statesman* (still edited by the Rees brothers) demonstrated a keen understanding of the mindset of the local vigilantes. Bands of thieves, chased from the eastern territories, had, as feared, gravitated to Walla Walla:

> When from any cause the guilty go unpunished, in whatever locality, the lawless will find it out and flock toward that (to them) favored region. It is but natural that thieves should congregate to the localities where there is little or no chance for punishment. . . . The Walla Walla valley had no Vigilance organization, nor no jail, certainly none worthy [of] the name. The desperadoes were not long in discovering that this was

Figure 40. The City/County Jail, 1862–65. (Gilbert, *Historic Sketches*, detail, opp. 297.)

a suitable region for their operations, and they swarmed here in large numbers. . . . [T]here was scarcely a resident of the valley who had not lost property of one kind or other. No community, under such circumstances, could be expected to remain in a state of tranquility, and ours did not. Known thieves were pointed out on every hand, and soon a Vigilance Committee was organized, but for a while it seemed to have no terrors for the thieving fraternity. Within the last week or so, however, we judge that the Vigilantes have been very active, for light fingered gentry have thinned out wonderfully. We guess the rogues discovered at last that they couldn't establish "law and order" here to suit their own feelings, and so took their leave. All the honest people in the valley will rejoice at their departure.[21]

The next night the vigilantes began lynching people in and around Walla Walla. An accused cattle thief was found hanging from a tree near the racetrack one morning. Two men "were caught by the Committee last week near Wallula, tried and convicted of horse stealing and brought up on to the Walla Walla river and hung." Their bodies were visible to the passengers on the stagecoach to Wallula, who then brought the news to Portland. "The tall, thick-lipped negro, known as 'Slim Jim,' . . . was found on Tuesday, hanging to a tree about three-fourths of a mile east of town. He has been known in the community as a thief, and several petty larcenies have been traced to him."[22] (The editors made no comment regarding the suitability or unsuitability of the penalty for "several petty larcenies.") According to Dick Bogle, Slim Jim was sleeping with about fifteen other Black men in his barbershop when he was violently abducted by a heavily armed group.[23] The *Statesman* insisted that only four men had been executed. However, an eyewitness, who traveled to Portland, reported seeing fifteen lynchings.[24] In another story about the executions, the *States-man* made a joke of the hanging of "nigger Jim." (This edition also carried the news of Lincoln's assassination.)

The vigilantes also carried out revenge executions and undertook favors for friends. In July, a Black farmer named Green got into an altercation with a White man, during which the White man's forearm was lacerated. Green fled his farm but was found hanged the next morning. An Irish farmhand, who had been acquitted of charges of "insulting a woman," was abducted at work and found months later having been castrated and lynched.[25]

Cushing Eells was living and farming at the Waiilatpu site, in the vicinity of much of the vigilante activity. His son Myron later wrote, "Eells was not a member of [the vigilance committee], but only because he was too old. His oldest son [Edwin] was . . . and all knew that the father's sympathies were with the committee, for it seemed that there was no safety in any other resource. . . . [W]e were surrounded by vigilantes, and they were good, brave, determined men. They waited for the law to do what it ought to until long after patience ceased to be a virtue, and then they went to work."[26]

In February 1866, Thomas Donohue shot Ferdinand Patterson, a notorious gambler, in Dick Bogle's barbershop. Donohue pursued Patterson outside and shot him four more times. In Idaho one year earlier, Patterson had shot and killed the ex-sheriff of Boise City for singing an anti-Secessionist song ("We'll hang Jeff Davis to a sour apple tree.").[27] This seemed to be a clear case of premeditated murder of an unarmed man. However, Donohue's trial for murder in April ended in a hung jury. While awaiting a new trial, the prison doors were mysteriously unlocked, Donohue was set free, and given forged papers of acquittal. Several days later, the *Statesman* published a self-righteous letter "By Order of the Vigilance Committee." The following week, the backlash began. A citizen (perhaps a lawyer) submitted a letter demanding responses to a series of due process questions.[28] The next issue carried not a response from the vigilantes but a letter from "Law-Abiding Citizen," who chastised the vigilantes for damaging the reputation of the people of the Walla Walla Valley: "There is no difference whatever in the treason that seeks to overthrow a government, and that which tramples the laws of the commonwealth under foot. . . . The vigilance committee of Walla Walla County . . . are as guilty of treason as was either John Brown or Jefferson Davis. . . . I hope, Mr. Editor, that your columns will not, hereafter, be disgraced with any more notices of vigilance committees."[29] In July, a grand jury rather timidly recommended "that the Vigilence Committee, if such an organisation exists, be disbanded."[30] Nonetheless, William Newell retained a soft spot for the vigilantes: "Thanks to the Vigilance Committe, Walla Walla Valley is clear of cattle thieves."[31]

The vigilante activities came to an end in spring 1867, when a large group convened at the Engine House to "repudiate and condemn" the actions of the vigilantes, and to formulate a memorial intended to eradicate the vigilantes' intimidation methods from the courts and the ballot. The group established a long list of charges against the vigilantes and agreed to form a bipartisan ticket for the upcoming election, dedicated to the rule of law. The document was signed by 119 men "and fifty others," unnamed. At its next meeting, the group elected a ticket and christened itself "The Law and Order Party." The lawyer James D. Mix was named president, and the former editor Raymond Rees was appointed secretary.[32]

Something of a firestorm was ignited when the chairman of the Democratic Party publicly demanded to know whether those already on the Democratic ticket would accept their Law and Order nominations. (The Republican ticket had no such issues.) The Democrats focused their attack on Mayor James McAuliff. William Newell, who stood for a seat on the territorial council on the Democratic ticket, described the Law and Order Party as the "half-breed party" and, prior to the election, warned his readers, "The loafers, bummers, gamblers, and pimps, without exception, support the 'half-breed' ticket."[33] The elections of 1867 were the bitterest to date in the valley. Newell seemed to go out of his way to generate friction, even after the election, in his call for a return to "respectful behavior."[34] None of the Law and Order candidates won an appointment, yet thanks to the hostility within the Democratic Party, Republicans won a handful of county and territorial seats. And a Republican merchant from Wallula, Alvan Flanders, was elected congressional delegate. Newell won his election seat, and—less than two years since moving to the territory—was on his way to Olympia to go face-to-face with the despised "clam-eaters."

Around the time of the burning of the Masonic Hall on July 4, 1866, the fraternity seems to have been inactive, split by the issue of vigilantism. Following a special meeting on August 31, calls for meetings ceased to appear in the *Statesman*. The division within the lodge was so deep that a second lodge (Blue Mountain No. 13) was organized in spring 1868.

———

The first legal execution by hanging in the county was carried out in 1873. A Chinese man, Lung Yow, was convicted of murdering another Chinese man. After being sentenced, he escaped, was captured, then granted a reprieve by Governor Elisha P. Ferry, but Ferry rejected appeals to commute the sentence to life in prison.

20

Forging Lives in a Hostile Landscape

When we had as agent, Barnhard . . . when my people died, a coffin was made for them, and they were put in naked, and had no clothes to cover them. When Barnhard was agent, he had a blacksmith here; we thought he was here for us, but when an Indian went to have anything fixed he was driven out of the shop. Was that right? It is the same when an Indian takes a gun to be fixed; it is taken to the shop, they are told to leave it, and there it stands until it rots, and they do not see it any more. There are some Indians have wagons; when they break them they take them to the shop to have them fixed. They stay there weeks and months, and are never repaired. If a white man comes along with a broken wagon it is repaired at once, they do not have to wait. Yet these very men who repair them are working for us and not for the white man. . . . When Barnhard was agent I used to see twenty hogs in a pen, fed with wheat that grew on the reservation, and I never knew what became of the hogs. I think he did not take good care of us.

—Howlishwanpum, 1871[1]

William H. Barnhart, Indian Agent (1861–62, 1863–69)

Barnhart, a Portland merchant, was appointed agent to the reservation on recommendation of his friend Sen. James Nesmith. He served until 1869, except for a nine-month period in 1862–63, during which he was suspended. Initially, his top priority seems to have been the establishment of a private mercantile business on the road passing through the reservation. In his 1862 report, he estimated that at least 4,000 miners and packers had traversed the reservation in the previous four months. Additionally, he noted, "The reservation is closely surrounded by white settlers, among whom there are a few wretched men, whose chief ambition is to sell whiskey to Indians and despoil them of their property." The Indians, he stated, assumed that the Whites would eventually claim the reservation. And yet he was at a loss as to why so many refused to move to the reservation. "Many of these Indians have never been removed to the reservation, and they declare by message to the agent that they never will live on it. . . . These tribes are bold and haughty, and boast they have never been conquered, and occupy the reservation simply because it belongs to them, and not from any wholesome fear of the government."[2] No mention was made of the fact that Barnhart had responded to the murder of a Cayuse woman by a high-status Cayuse man (a relative of both Hyumhowlish and Howlishwanpum) by executing the assailant. Howlishwanpum, who by all accounts was a brilliant orator, backed by a cavalry detail from Fort Walla Walla, may have saved Barnhart's life and may have prevented further violence.[3] This was the first of three deadly incidents involving the Cayuse in 1862. As Barnhart was writing his report in August, some Sahaptians were at their annual summer camps in the Grande Ronde Valley. The few settlers in the valley felt threatened. Some prospective settlers were told they could not settle there because the Indians claimed it was reservation land. The headmen on the reservation insisted to Superintendent William H. Rector that "they did not sell the Grande Ronde valley" in 1855. When Rector attempted to convince the incredulous headmen that this was explained to them by Stevens and Palmer, "They said that the record lied, but their ears did not lie."[4] Barnhart called on Colonel Steinberger at Fort Walla Walla, who "ordered a detachment to proceed forthwith."[5] Captain Currey led the detachment to the Grande Ronde to arrest "certain leaders of the tribe." Among the leaders was "Dreamer," according to Currey. The Army report continued: Dreamer fired a shot at Currey, who then killed Dreamer; "fifty or more" Indians then fired on Currey's men, and three Indians were killed and "one or two wounded." The *Statesman* applauded the action. Of course, the details of the account are absurd, as there were no reports of injuries among the soldiers from the rounds of "fifty or more" Indians. (Regional papers picked up the "Dreamer" story and celebrated the killing, but were disappointed to learn eventually that it was not the infamous Smohalla, known as The Dreamer.)

Accounts and rumors of Indian-on-White violence on the plains continued to be sensationalized and misrepresented in Far West papers. Despite the agents' assurances of the peaceful disposition of the Indians, the papers equated all Indians with the most violent stories and rumors. It comes as no surprise that the *Statesman* concluded its report on "the Killings of the Grande Ronde Indians" with the warning: "a descent upon the settlers is liable to occur at any time."[6]

The third incident occurred in November, when a packer was shot and wounded in an altercation while crossing the reservation. When soldiers arrived to arrest the accused men, Howlishwanpum refused to turn them over. The chief was arrested instead, and Steinberger threatened to hang him. The alleged assailants were eventually captured and turned over to the fort, where they were declared guilty by Steinberger, without a trial, and hanged, to the dismay of the soldiers.[7] (Following the incident, Howlishwanpum was stripped of his title as head chief.)

A "feature" on Main street of late has been bands of roving Indians, some on horse-back arrayed in gaudy attire; others sauntering around the store doors and street corners. They are mostly made up of Cayuses, and Nez Perces, a few Spokanes and Palouses—with renegades and stragglers from the Umatilla and Nez Perces Reservations. They look on in amazement at the wonderful progress the valley has made since they roamed at large over the domain, "monarchs of all they surveyed."

—*Walla Walla Statesman*, September 30, 1864

Few Whites respected the rights of the reservation. The agents were unable to limit the presence of non-Indians due to the busy road running through the reservation. And the traffic in whiskey could not be checked. The Umatilla area was so rapidly populated that the Oregon legislature formed Umatilla County in 1862. And settlers regularly exploited the reservation's ambiguously defined borders.[8] Soon the county began to agitate for opening the prized reservation land for settlement. Walla Wallans joined in the clamor. The *Statesman* noted in 1863, "The land comprising [the reservation] constitutes nearly all the good agricultural land in Umatilla county, and if purchased and opened to settlement will undoubtedly become a rich producing region."[9] (This was shortly after the government reduced the Nez Perce reservation by 90 percent.) Gov. William Pickering of Washington Territory declared at the same time: "It is highly important to the people of the eastern and south-eastern portion of our Territory that the Indian title to all lands between [the Rockies] and the Columbia river should be extinguished."[10]

In 1864, Congress passed a bill, sponsored by Oregon's senators, enabling the president to relinquish the rights of "the confederated tribes of Indians . . . to fish, hunt, gather roots and berries, and to pasture stock outside of their reservation."[11] However, no action was taken on this bill, and a majority of "government wards" continued to cautiously follow their seasonal rounds or to live off the reservation entirely. Once off the reservation the Indian had few rights, however. According to Davenport, only the wealthiest families were able to remain on the reservation year-round. The reservation's only thriving business was the trade in horses and cattle. However, only the families of Tintinmitse (head chief between 1862 and his death in 1868) and Howlishwanpum (his predecessor and successor) owned large numbers of horses and cattle. Barnhart reported in 1866, "It is generally understood that most of the Indians here are wealthy; that is a mistake. A large majority of them are poor indeed. The numerous herds of horses and cattle in their possession are owned by thirty or forty men, who know how to take care of their property as well if not better than white people."[12]

One schoolhouse was finally built (of green cottonwood logs) in 1866, and—through Howlishwanpum's insistence—a Catholic priest, the Belgian Gustave Vermeersch, was assigned its teacher. However, the vast majority of school-age children remained with their families, spending much of the year off-reservation. In 1866, for example, Vermeersch reported that an average of twenty-five children attended school—about one-tenth of school-age children. Given its location and its Catholic instructor, the school seems to have been exclusively for Howlishwanpum's band. Throughout the 1860s and '70s, education took place primarily in the lodge, as it always had. Many families certainly kept their children away from the school as acts of resistance. Understanding this, Vermeersch (unsuccessfully) called for the establishment of "a regular boarding school, by which the children should be taken from the control of the parents."[13]

In spring 1865, Shoshone warriors attacked a band of Umatillas while fishing on the John Day River and stole their horses. After Barnhart reported the attack to Fort Walla Walla, Colonel Currey led a cavalry detachment, augmented by seventy Cayuse and Umatilla, led by Hyum-howlish, to recover the horses. This was neither the first nor the last time the Army would call on the Cayuse for assistance as scouts. After the Cayuse again assisted the Army in its pursuit of the Northern Paiute in 1867, even the *Statesman* applauded their service and recommended that they be established as a permanent unit.[14] However, the paper's stance on Indians in general had not softened; an editorial from 1866 stated: "In the Indian character the element of progress does not exist, and hence the effort made in his behalf has been labor lost. Totally worthless and without one redeeming trait of character, the sooner he disappears from the earth the better."[15] Stories of violence in Shoshone or Lakota or Apache territory continued to be attributed to universal "Indian character." At the same time, Americans generally anticipated the inevitable, providential dying off of all Indigenous people.

Agitation for removal of the reservation may have heated up statewide in 1865, when crops produced on the reservation began receiving awards at the Oregon State Fair.[16] Whether true or not, Oregonians began to claim that the reservation possessed the richest soil in the state and that it could only fully be exploited by Whites. Oregon's congressional representatives relentlessly pressed for elimination of the reservation. Barnhart's reports of 1865–69 emphasized the Indians' great insecurity and constant anxiety over rumors and threats that they would be removed from their reservation. In 1866, Oregon's legislators embraced a petition of the citizens of Umatilla County to remove the Indians to other reservations. At the same time, the BIA asked J. W. Perit Huntington, Superintendent of Indian Affairs for Oregon (1863–69), to estimate the cash value of the reservation. He concluded, "[T]he reservation could be sold for $150,000 to $200,000. Its perpetual possession has been guaranteed to the Indians by treaty, and it would be the grossest of bad faith to take possession of it without their consent. That consent will be obtained with the greatest difficulty, if at all." On the other hand, Huntington requested funding to hold another treaty council to strip the three tribes of "the right to fish, hunt, gather roots and berries, and pasture their stock on land outside the reservation." He added, "This privilege is simply equivalent to giving them permission to roam at will over the country, and is demoralizing to them and damaging to the White settlers."[17] No details were offered.

The *Statesman* launched an aggressive campaign against the reservation in 1867. James Vansyckle, the opinionated owner of most of Wallula, anointed himself the paper's authority on Indian affairs in general. Writing under the name "Cumtux"—Chinook Wawa, meaning "information"—Vansyckle had been a contributor to the paper from its inception. Aside from the usual critiques of the corruption within the BIA, the laziness of the Indians, the great and imminent threat posed by Smohalla, and the enormous expenses of the federal government, Cumtux always slipped in a bit of alarmist rhetoric, usually about Indians purchasing weapons in the area.[18] Barnhart responded indirectly to Cumtux's insistence of an impending uprising in a letter to the *Statesman*, "[A]s far as I know, there is no cause for alarm. The Indians are perfectly quiet, and have given me no trouble for a long time. They have made a large crop considering the dry season, and most of them are now engaged in harvesting their grain. The Indians in my charge know well that they have the most vital interest in remaining at peace with the Whites, and I do not believe that the slightest idea of hostilities is entertained by them."[19] On the same page, Newell printed his own alarmist and paranoid critique of Indian affairs:

> Not only are white travelers and settlers being remorselessly slaughtered and their dead bodies shockingly outraged every day, but the Indians have stopped telegraphic communication almost entirely, intercepted the mails, and captured railroad trains. . . . A war of extermination against the Indians would be better for all, than the merciless and continuous butcheries that have been going on. Weak sentimentalists may object to this as barbarous, but those who are acquainted with the Indian character, and know how utterly worthless he is, will endorse it as right and proper. Those "wards of the Government" have recently made themselves troublesome in this quarter, and have shown a strong disposition to inaugurate a war.[20]

Newell's fear-mongering was directly related to the Army's impending abandonment of Fort Walla Walla. On the following page, he addressed Barnhart's letter directly and continued his rant:

> That the Indians are disaffected and mean mischief, is too evident to admit of argument. . . . Some ten miles below here, on the Walla Walla, they have appeared in large numbers, and by their threatening demonstrations greatly alarmed the settlers, some of whom have removed their families to town as a place of safety. [A] general feeling of uneasiness has seized upon our people, and the conviction is growing that we are to

have another Indian war, with all the attendant horrors. . . . Our people have endured their outrages and insolence about long enough, and if the authorities fail to afford them protection, they will make such measures as will effectually relieve them of the presence of the vagabond Indians who now infest the country.[21]

Certainly, many Walla Wallans were influenced by the opinions of Vansyckle and Newell, and many others arrived in the valley holding such opinions; nonetheless, it would be interesting to hear more about these "threatening demonstrations." Would it be surprising to learn that some readers of the *Statesman* became alarmed whenever they *saw* a group of Indians, particularly if they were doing Indian things, like singing, dancing, fishing, racing horses, assembling a tipi, or striking a tipi? Barnhart reported the following summer, "The fears of the whites were utterly groundless. . . . The Indians . . . committed *none* of the various crimes and depredations attributed to them by the fervid diatribes of the local press and the distempered fancies of those who were governed alone by their vivid imaginations, or a morbid desire to surreptitiously possess themselves of the Indian lands."[22] The Oregon Superintendent of Indian Affairs Alfred B. Meacham (1869–72) noted, "Under the treaty with these Indians, they are to enjoy the privilege of hunting and grazing on the public domain in common with citizens; but this right is scarcely acknowledged by the settlers of places they visit, under the treaty."[23] As historian Gray Whaley succinctly writes, "Native people went back and forth from the reservations, as individual circumstances dictated, trying to forge lives in a hostile landscape."[24] Whites, on the other hand, traversed the reservation and consumed its resources at will.

Not all Indian–non-Indian interactions were negative, however. Accounts of early Walla Walla settlers include numerous references to peaceful interactions, particularly related to the horse trade on Main Street in Walla Walla and Pendleton. White gamblers with fast horses would often visit the reservation racetrack. And the Walla Walla Jockey Club was regularly invited to the reservation by Howlishwanpum, who boasted owning the fastest horses in the world and who loved fleecing his challengers. According to Meacham, who was also a local businessman, large crowds of Whites and Indians would attend these races.[25]

21

Agriculture, Horticulture, Infrastructure

Those that had long praised the Walla Walla Valley as ideal ranchland had no idea what a bonanza ranchers would experience in the early 1860s. Despite the terrible winter of 1862, beef, bacon, and mutton prices were so high and in such demand in the mining towns that ranchers were quickly able to replenish their livestock via the Willamette Valley. After fattening their livestock in the valley during the winter, ranchers began driving enormous numbers of cattle and sheep into Idaho and Montana territories. However, these regions became increasingly self-reliant during the decade.

The belief that only limited sites in the valley were conducive to farming grain was a thing of the past by 1866. Farmers were surprised by the rich grain harvest that followed the drought of 1864. The *Statesman* noted that September, "Some of our farmers have raised excellent wheat crops this season from high and dry hill ground. One farmer informs us that from a field of fifty acres of this hill land, sown in wheat early last fall, he got the average yield of thirty-three bushels per acre [which] shows that the hill lands will produce good wheat crops, even when the seasons are unusually dry, like the past one."[1] The era of dryland (unirrigated) wheat farming in the region had begun. J. C. Isaacs began advertising new horse-drawn self-raking reapers, mowers, threshing machines, and harvesters. Baker & Co. became agents for Knapp, Burrell & Co. of Portland, the major manufacturer of agricultural machinery in the Northwest. William Phillips, a native of Shrewsbury, Shropshire, established the Walla Walla Foundry in 1867 (Main and Eighth), which repaired farm machinery and replaced parts.

By 1866, the quality of the flour produced by Walla Walla's five mills was considered to be at least equal to that of the Willamette Valley. For their part, the first editors of the *Statesman* had repeatedly urged farmers not to abandon their farms for the gold mines and assured profits from their labor. Occasionally, the paper would report on a visit to the home of a prosperous farmer. In fall 1863, four years before the rise of the Grange movement, the editors called for the establishment of an agricultural society: an organization that would facilitate communication among farmers, ranchers, orchardists, millers, and merchants.[2] Until such an entity could be organized, the paper served as such a forum.

The orchardist, Philip Ritz, relocated to Walla Walla from Corvallis in 1862 and quickly established himself as a strident advocate for an agricultural organization. Early in 1863, he began advertising his Columbia Valley Nursery in the *Statesman*: "the most complete and reliable assortment of Every Variety of Tree, Shrub and Flower north of Sacramento." The *Statesman* heavily publicized Ritz's nursery and encouraged homeowners to plant trees, shrubs, and gardens, and for farmers to plant fruit trees (fig. 41). Ritz was particularly successful in persuading people throughout the region to plant Lombardy poplars, which he assured could reach 40 feet in only ten years. Images of the city and region from the 1870s and

Figure 41. Farm residence of John and Eliza Tracy, on Mill Creek, 8 miles east of the city, ca. 1866. Tracy emigrated from Ireland in 1849, served with the 9th Infantry, and staked this claim on his discharge in 1860. A homesteader's first house was often a crude log structure, like the one visible in the middle background. The new house was most likely built around the time of Tracy's marriage to Eliza Hendricks in 1865. It may have begun as a 1½ -story center-gable structure (which was popular among the early farmhouses), with the 2-story ell at the rear added as the family grew. Obviously, Tracy embraced Philip Ritz's call for farmers to cultivate orchards. (Gilbert, *Historic Sketches*, opp. 168.)

'80s illustrate the popularity of the Lombardy poplar along sidewalks and as windbreaks on urban and rural properties. The trees grew particularly well in the Northwest. (However, with widespread use, they often succumbed to disease within twenty years.)

In summer 1866, the county commissioners took the initiative in forming the County Agricultural Society (with Henry Isaacs as president) and arranged the first county fair in the fall.[3] Held October 4–6 at Council Grove, it was a very local affair, and it remained so for years. Prizes were awarded for livestock, grain, flour, vegetables, dairy products, flowers, manufactures, domestic manufactures, equestrianism, and so on. Since it ran during racing season, the highlights of this and subsequent fairs were the races (run according to the rules of the Jockey Club and dominated by its members). In 1870, the society was reorganized as the Washington Territory Agricultural Fair and Industrial Exhibition, and entries were opened to anyone from the territory, from eastern Oregon, or from western Idaho (with mixed results). The 1871 fair was a letdown due to a smallpox outbreak.[4] Nonetheless, it was well covered in the press due to the presence in the city of both Susan B. Anthony and the Pixley Sisters. (Visitors invariably complained of the dusty 3-mile trip to the fairgrounds.)

Over the next three years, the Society disintegrated, and the fair devolved into a livestock market with races; interest outside the region diminished. The society was reorganized in 1875, holding a "First Annual Fair" at Charles Bush's Trotting Park (with its new grandstand), but the venue only put greater emphasis on the races.

Transportation on the Columbia

With the sudden increase in traffic along the Columbia in 1860 (particularly miners and freight), a group of ambitious steamship owners, portage road controllers, and Portland-based investors incorporated the Oregon Steam Navigation Company (OSN) to coordinate and monopolize transportation along the Columbia and Willamette. The Columbia was broken into three navigable portions, connected by portage roads on both its north and south sides. Passengers and freight moving from Portland to Walla Walla: (1) traveled on an OSN steamer to a wharf at Cascades on the north side of the river (65 miles); (2) transferred to the OSN's 5-mile-long,

mule-drawn, portage railroad to a wharf above the cascades; (3) transferred to an OSN steamer to The Dalles (38 miles); (4) transferred to the
OSN's 14-mile long, mule-drawn, portage railroad on the south side of
the river to a wharf above Celilo Falls; and (5) transferred to an OSN
steamer to Wallula (110 miles).[5] (From that point, independent teamsters
carried freight, and passengers traveled with saddle trains or with John
Abbott's stagecoach to Walla Walla.) If all went well, the trip took three
days. The OSN was initially celebrated by everyone in the Northwest.

Between 1858 and 1862, Wallula was primarily the site of an Army
warehouse within the ruins of old Fort Walla Walla. One steamer, the
Colonel Wright, traversed this upper section of the river at the time. Despite
the lack of vegetation in the Wallula area, the ambitious capitalist James
Vansyckle purchased 400 acres of sand encompassing the old fort, the
mouth of the Walla Walla River, and a riverbank on the west side of the
Columbia.[6] Determined to cash in on the expansion of the OSN, in 1862,
he platted the town of Wallula and soon built a hotel, saloon, general store,
livery business, and warehouse. The *Statesman* initially mocked Vansyckle
for believing that his town could replace Walla Walla as the main supply
station for the mines. Instead—thanks to a new county road linking them—
Wallula quickly developed into the port of Walla Walla; the city's major
merchant houses built warehouses there. Even the OSN built a hotel and
warehouse there. At the same time, Dorsey Baker procured a large tract
immediately to the north of Wallula to fully capitalize on its potential
importance. As a place of residence, however, Wallula offered no incentives. Frances Fuller Victor wrote of her visit there in 1870, "The sand of
Wallula is something to be dreaded. It insinuates itself everywhere. You
find it scattered over the plate on which you are to dine; piled up in little
hillocks in the corner of your wash-stand; dredged over the pillows on
which you thoughtlessly sink your weary head, without stopping to shake
them; setting your teeth on edge with grit, everywhere."[7]

The *Statesman* enthusiastically supported the OSN at first. By May 1862,
however, it advised merchants to hire local teamsters to carry their freight
from The Dalles instead of paying the OSN's storage and commission
fees.[8] At the same time, in an attempt to break the OSN's monopoly on
the Columbia, Dorsey Baker joined with some Portland capitalists to
establish the Merchant Transportation Line and built a steamer to work
the upper section of the river. Other companies formed with the same

intention. In 1863, the OSN bought out the Merchant Line and by the end of the year had reestablished its monopoly (and allowed Baker—$27,895 richer—to expand his businesses, including the first flour mill in the Grande Ronde Valley). Meanwhile, the OSN was in the process of converting its railroads from mule to steam power. Its celebrated Cascades and Dalles-Celilo railroads—the first true steam railroads in the Northwest—debuted in April 1863.

Walla Walla Rail Road Company

The logistics of railroad building in the Northwest were usually insurmountable, yet there was no shortage of ambitious and/or wealthy men willing to attend meetings and to invest in railroads through the region's remote and uncompromising terrain. Enormous capital was necessary (and at great risk); federal, territorial, and private land subsidies needed to be granted; and large teams of civil engineers and armies of laborers needed to be hired. For every actual American railroad there were dozens of "paper railroads," chartered, incorporated railroads that never laid a single crosstie.

During fall 1861, a group of Walla Walla businessmen and lawyers held a series of meetings to discuss the establishment of a railroad to carry goods between Wallula and Walla Walla. Above all, they sought a cheaper alternative to the fees charged by teamsters. Thirty-three men were named in the articles of incorporation of the Walla Walla Rail Road Company, which received a charter in January 1862.[9] The railroad was to be surveyed by November 1863 and completed by November 1868. In December, the *Statesman* carried a letter from Lt. John Mullan in New York City assuring that Wall Street investors would subscribe $250,000 of stock in the company.[10] Prominent businessmen were assigned to solicit subscriptions in Far West cities. Mullan was responsible for New York and Congressman William H. Wallace for Washington, DC.

Editorials on the "Railroad to Wallula" appeared regularly in the *Statesman*. Its May 3, 1863, edition carried a strong appeal to support the railroad to ensure the city's prosperity. "A railroad," it concluded, "will make us the center of supply for the Grande Ronde valley and its tributaries, as well as the Nez Perces and Colville countrys; will deliver the goods needed for home consumption at ten dollars a ton less freight, and although it may cost $750,000 or even a million of dollars to build it, still it will save that amount of money in the course of the next ten years."[11] The March 1863 edition of *American Railroad Journal* featured a letter by John Mullan describing the economic virtues of the Walla Walla Valley and the objectives of the company.[12] However, after resigning from the Army, Mullan was on his way back to Walla Walla to oversee his business interests. Lobbying in New York had come to an end.[13] The company's charter was reamended in 1864; however, no action was taken during the next four years.

The Walla Walla Water Company

The 1862 charter for the City of Walla Walla called for "the erection of water works to supply the city with water." However, nothing was accomplished for four years. Following the first big fires, plans were finally set in motion by Henry Isaacs in 1866. He, Alpheus Kyger, J. D. Cook, and the hotelier M. Hartman were contracted by the city council to supply Main Street with water piped in from Mill Creek. In November, the *Statesman* noted,

> A large gang of workmen are engaged in getting out the timbers preparatory to erecting a reservoir for the use of the city water works. The reservoir will be placed at the head of Main street, and will have an elevation of 50 feet above the highest point in the city. The reservoir will be filled by means of two force-pumps. . . . The intention is to put down a six-inch iron pipe, running the length of Main street, from which smaller pipes will be used to conduct water to all parts of the city.[14]

By summer 1867, the 6-inch pipe had extended to Third, and the company was installing individual service pipes for a fee.[15] However, given the inconsistent flow of Mill Creek, the system was unreliable for fighting fires. Some business owners installed more reliable force pumps behind their buildings in case of fire. For drinking water, Walla Wallans, like most Americans, relied on iron lift pumps. (Both lift and force pumps were produced at the foundry and sold at Phillips & O'Donnell's hardware store.)

The Mullan Road

The immediate postwar years were particularly stressful for Walla Wallans. The economic loss resulting from the closing of Fort Walla Walla was amplified by the rapid disappearance of the miners, who, by 1867, wintered in cities much closer to the gold fields. Additionally, the debt assumed by the Lincoln administration during the war grew astronomically (to more than $2 billion), adding to a long period of national and international financial instability. Prices for all goods were down, as were salaries. Wheat prices, in particular, plummeted: from $1.25/bushel in 1865 to a low of $.40 in 1868. Walla Walla businesses also faced increasing competition and decreasing demand in supplying the new gold mining areas of Montana, which boomed in 1865–66. Some merchants and ranchers permanently departed for the new boomtowns. A number of Montana cities already possessed larger populations than Walla Walla. Walla Walla's merchants suddenly found themselves poorly situated, geographically, to fully capitalize on this trade. The 642-mile Mullan Road linked Walla Walla to Montana, yet the sections through the mountains became impassable for wagons due to fallen trees and damaged bridges shortly after its completion in 1862. Only pack trains could navigate these sections of the "wagon road." To the outrage of Walla Wallans, merchants from Portland and San Francisco funded new routes to Montana that bypassed Walla Walla entirely. Above all, in fall 1865, they established a steamer dock at White Bluffs on the Columbia and soon put a steamer on Lake Pend Oreille.

———

In 1866, the farmers of Walla Walla County produced 550,000 bushels of wheat, 250,000 bushels of oats, 225,000 bushels of barley, and 150,000 bushels of corn.[16] Impressive, but without the garrison and with growing competition from all sides, millers, merchants, and freighters needed to be aggressive in exporting surplus grain, crops, and livestock. The necessity of exporting goods expediently and aggressively was accentuated by news of regular shipments of California grain to Liverpool, of food shortages in the postwar South, and of crop failures back East and in Europe. The geographer Donald Meinig noted, "It was ironic that the glimpse of a vastly greater potential production coincided with a sharply contracting market."[17]

The Mullan Road was the gateway not only to Montana but also potentially to Southern and Eastern markets via the Missouri River. On the heels of the 1866 Agricultural Fair, Walla Wallans held a mass meeting regarding the Mullan Road. The *Statesman* pressed the urgency of the matter: "All know that our prosperity depends upon securing outlets for our surplus products, and certainly Montana must be one of our principal markets. . . . [L]ooking to this development it becomes us to seek new outlets, and thus be prepared for the changes that are soon to be upon us. A community to be permanently prosperous cannot afford to stand still, and it is in obedience to this law of progress that we should constantly endeavor to extend the area of country dependent upon us for supplies."[18] In December, the territorial legislature (unsuccessfully) petitioned Congress on behalf of Walla Walla County to invest in reopening the road.

A disheartening reality became clear in 1867: Walla Walla and its mercantile rivals in the Northwest—including the OSN—were at a disadvantage in the competition for the Montana trade with Salt Lake City, Omaha, and St. Louis, which had vastly improved their wagon roads and steamer service to Montana. "Dull times" became the theme of the next few years in cities across the Northwest. The *Statesman* looked around at less dull cities and concluded: "The present depression of business interests in this immediate section, is mainly due to the fact that our productions have not been sufficiently diversified. The demand for wheat, has fell off and that being our one great staple, all branches of industry suffer."[19] Each edition of the *Statesman* carried gloomy economic reports and pessimistic forecasts from Eastern papers. In summer 1867, it noted, "On the principle that misery loves company, we are glad to hear that our town isn't the dullest place in the world." Some joy was taken in the fact that a quarter of Portland's commercial buildings were unoccupied.[20]

In October 1866, Philip Ritz departed for Washington to lobby Congress to support the Mullan Road bill. However, in his native Philadelphia and in Washington, he made the acquaintance of people associated with Jay Cooke, the financier behind the planned Northern Pacific Railroad (NPR), and was struck with a case of railroad fever. He became a lobbyist for the NPR instead and returned East annually. In 1868, he produced for the NPR an elaborate study on the agricultural and mineral resources of the Northwest, which was published, and discussed, in several Eastern papers.[21] He remained one of the railroad's major advocates in Walla Walla for the next two decades.

The Walla Walla and Columbia River Railroad

During 1867–69, Americans were fixated on the progress of the transcontinental railroad. Updates appeared in papers weekly, as did reports of the incorporation of branch lines connecting to the Union Pacific and Central Pacific railroads, and news of the rapid growth of depot towns on the completed sections. Various plans appeared to construct railroads connecting the Columbia or Puget Sound to Salt Lake City or Montana. William Newell moved to Walla Walla in 1865, after the initial railroad plans had abated. In fall 1867, he embraced the rekindled railroad fever and used the *Statesman* to rally support for the construction of the Walla Walla–Wallula railroad.[22] Railroad meetings resumed in March 1868 and were well attended by businessmen, farmers, and lawyers. Newell, Vansyckle, and the lawyers James Lasater and James Mix emphasized that the future of agricultural development, economic expansion, and population growth was dependent on this railroad. They spoke of increased real estate value in the valley and assured that the railroad would ultimately become part of the main branch of the NPR. Estimating the total cost to be $500,000, they announced that the OSN had already offered to invest $100,000 toward the project. Aside from selling $1,000 shares, they were confident that the county and the city (despite their running deficits) would be large shareholders. Articles of incorporation were drafted and a board of trustees elected, comprising Baker, Lasater, Reynolds, Kyger, Reese, Elisha Ping (of Patit Creek), and Anderson Cox (of Waitsburg).

The April 10 issue of the *Statesman* was loaded with optimistic reports regarding the Walla Walla and Columbia River Railroad (WWCRR); a growing number of capitalists in Oregon were interested in the project; real estate prices were already rising in the valley. In subsequent numbers, Ritz wrote from Washington of the NPR's interest in running its main line through the Walla Walla Valley.

In May, congressional representative Alvan Flanders introduced a bill granting right of way for the WWCRR. However, as the bill was held up in the House Committee on Public Lands, election season was heating up in Washington Territory. Some of the major figures behind the railroad project threw their hats in the ring to succeed Flanders: Democrats Newell, Mix, Frank Dugan, and Ben Sharpstein; and Republicans Baker, Reynolds, Cox, and Ritz. The candidates canvassed the territory during a particularly contentious spring; both political camps were determined to have a representative from Walla Walla County. To their dismay, none of its candidates received their party's nomination in April 1869. The June election was won by Selucius Garfielde, a Republican (and former Democrat), who was regarded by many Republicans as little more than a charismatic political opportunist. Democrats, now unified, made a clean sweep of all county positions.

The appearance of the Republican *Walla Walla Union* in April 1869 dramatically increased the level of political animosity in the county. Perhaps due to this political division, public meetings of the WWCRR ceased. The railroad bill had been approved on March 3, but with an amendment calling for a special county election on the question of whether or not to allow the county commissioners to own stock and to issue bonds. The bill required an unattainable 75 percent majority.

In summer 1869, Jay Cooke sent an expedition to the Northwest to evaluate potential routes for the NPR. Director Thomas H. Canfield, chief civil engineer W. Milner Roberts, and Cooke's confidant R. Bethell Claxton spoke before a large, enthusiastic audience in Walla Walla and urged the business community to construct the railroad. "[T]here is not a particle of danger contracting a debt in so doing," Roberts assured. "Railroads always double the production of any country and enhance the population from three to ten fold. . . . [A railroad] to the Columbia river [would] lay the foundation for a railroad system that would eventually fully develop the vast sources of this country."[23]

The report published by the NPR party offered a glowing image of the Walla Walla Valley; the visitors were amazed by the fertility of the soil and by the orchards of Roberts and Ritz.[24] Above all, the report included a preliminary map of the NPR route passing directly through Walla Walla. Nonetheless, this report was not followed by another railroad meeting; the collapse of the gold market on September 24—the original Black Friday— silenced such ambitious projects everywhere.

The *Walla Walla Union*

Politics in the Walla Walla Valley changed forever on April 17, 1869, with the appearance of the first issue of the *Union*. Its first editorial noted, "Of course, as is suspected, ours will be a Republican paper, a RADICAL Republican paper." The project had been in the works for five months. Dorsey Baker purchased all its equipment and, according to Newell, was always at the head of the "*Onion*." During 1869, as Baker played a more prominent role in the Republican Party, Newell attacked him regularly and made several references to Baker's ownership of buildings used as Chinese brothels. When a fire broke out in one of these buildings in June, Newell reminded his readers, "The building is owned by Dr. Baker, and is occupied by a lot of degraded Chinawomen. . . . Certainly no individual for the purpose of lining his own pocket has the right to endanger the lives and property of the whole community." Baker replied with a card in the *Union* suggesting that Newell knew so much about the occupants of the building because he spent so much time there.[25] And so it continued. Newell responded to the threat of the *Union* by publishing a triweekly *Statesman*. Nonetheless, by the end of the year, the *Union* boasted the "Largest Circulation in the Territory."

The *Union* was originally printed in the second floor of the new frame building erected by the Baumeister brothers in 1869, literally feet from the *Statesman* office on Third. The paper's impact is evident in the increasing Republican gains in the city and county during the following decades.

Telegraph

With an extensive telegraphic network in the Eastern states and the establishment of the Pony Express between California and Missouri, news of the attack on Fort Sumter reached Portland in three weeks. The news then reached Walla Walla a week later. With the completion of the first transcontinental telegraph line in October 1861, cities in California were in almost instant communication with the East. Yet Walla Wallans were still at least three weeks away (and only when the roads were open). They could only wait for the California State Telegraph Company (CSTC) or some other company to run lines to Portland and then up the Columbia. Progress was far too slow, particularly for newspaper editors. In 1863, thanks to the monopolistic strength of the CSTC, Portland was linked to California and to the rest of the country. The following year, the lines were extended to the Puget Sound. As Walla Wallans waited impatiently, the transatlantic telegraph cable was successfully completed in 1866. In the same year, the CSTC was absorbed into the Western Union Telegraph Company, the national monopoly. However, Western Union was focused on linking to Europe via Alaska and Russia. The *Statesman* lamented in 1867, "Helena, a city . . . less than three years old, is in telegraphic communication 'with all the world and the rest of mankind.' [. . .] A town without telegraph now-a-days is out of the world, and really belongs to the antedeluvian period."[26] In 1868, the Oregon and Idaho Telegraph Co. was incorporated. A subsidiary of the OSN, it offered the first real telegraph opportunity for Walla Walla. However, their plan to connect Portland to the transcontinental telegraph line via Boise bypassed Walla Walla. The city was asked to raise $5,000 to connect to the network. Walla Walla was finally connected to the world, with fanfare, on June 1, 1870. The first transmission from the city was sent from Mayor Frank Stone to Mayor Bernard Goldsmith of Portland: "Allow me to congratulate you on the completion of the telegraph that places the first city of Oregon in connection with the metropolis of Washington, and to express the hope that it is but the precursor of the iron rail that is to unite us still more indissolubly in the bonds of interest and affections."[27]

22

Bird's-Eye Views

P hotographers tended to move regularly in the Far West. Even when a photographer owned a studio, it was often occupied by a visiting photographer while the host was out of town occupying the studio of another photographer, or setting up a temporary shop. Walla Walla's first photographic gallery was run during 1861–62, by Edward M. Sammis, who had just relocated from Olympia and who then moved on to Seattle. Phillip Castleman and William V. Brown established their "Melainotype and Photograph Rooms" shortly after Sammis's departure. Little is known of Brown; however, Castleman was something of a celebrity in the Northwest. He could be regarded as an itinerant photographer, although photographer was just one of his many professions. Since leaving Kentucky for the gold rush, he had worked as a miner, baker, hotelier, miller, and teamster in California and Oregon. According to his (auto)biography, in 1853, he trekked back to New York, where he learned the daguerreotype process.[1] He purchased equipment and the following year established a studio in Eugene. With Eugene as a home base, he lived the life of an itinerant photographer throughout southern Oregon and Northern California. He settled in Walla Walla in 1862 and soon partnered with Brown.

In spring 1864, Castleman and Brown purchased a small, two-story frame building next door to Schwabacher Bros. and launched both the Ice Cream Saloon (the city's first candy manufacturer) and the Daguerrean Gallery (upstairs). Both men were already established as prominent businessmen and Masons. After Brown returned to his native Nova Scotia in October, Castleman ran both businesses and served on the school board.

Around this time, Castleman undertook a subscription drive to produce a lithograph of the city and the valley based on photographs (fig. 2). The genre was already popular. The producers of such prints sought to tap into the citizens' pride in the city's progress and sense of permanence, but also to allow them to promote or celebrate their own material success. By the 1850s, two basic types of city views were published. Bird's-eye views, the older tradition, were created from numerous drawings of buildings overlaid onto a map of the city, in two-point perspective. The result was an idealized view of the city from an imaginary perspective, high above the ground. The availability of transportable photographic equipment brought about the second type, around mid-century. The source of the images was left to the earthbound photographer and his camera. The panoramas were thus limited to the highest available viewpoint. Usually, vignettes of individual houses or businesses framed the central image. In the Far West, the photo-based process was most popular in the 1850s and '60s. The lithographic firm of Kuchel & Dresel in San Francisco, for example, had a traveling artist visit a city, advertise their project in a local paper, meet with clients desiring to have buildings included in the print, and then produce photographs of the buildings and panoramic views of the city. Back at the home office (or at an outsourced printing house) the print would be designed, lithographs would be produced from the photographs, and a specified number of images would be printed and delivered to the individuals and merchants of the city.[2] The fees paid for the vignette images (about $10) generally covered the costs of production. Additional profits were made on the production side from subscriptions for the prints ($2.50–$5.00 each). Local merchants could order any number of prints and, in turn, sell them at a profit. Castleman could undertake such a project only because he had connections with the lithographer Grafton Tyler Brown in San Francisco— in fact, Brown, one of the first Black business owners in the city, had inherited the firm of Kuchel & Dresel.[3]

Castleman's project was already well known to the business community by May 5, 1865, when it was first outlined (by Castleman himself) in the *Statesman*:

> Mr. P. F. Castleman is engaged in taking photographic views of the city and of the principal business houses, with a view of sending them to San Francisco and having them lithographed. The design is to have a view of the city printed on the center of a card 24 × 32 inches, with . . . the principal business houses in the city in the margin. It is being gotten up by subscription, those who have their places of business or residences printed paying a stipulated sum for the same. The chances for having business houses, &c., printed are all, or nearly all, taken, but persons wishing to

subscribe for a picture can have an opportunity to do so by calling upon Mr. Castleman, at his daguerrean gallery.[4]

The photograph of the city (fig. 42) was taken from the highest point in the city: the roof of I. T. Reese's new mill on Mill Creek between Eighth and Ninth (visible in the right foreground of fig. 3). From this perspective, looking toward the southeast, the city has little sense of order. Nonetheless, this was the best attainable photograph of the city and the valley. In fact, Brown the lithographer needed to be creative to present a more orderly city.[5]

The central identifiable building—in fact, the only architecturally unique building in the image—is the turreted engine house/city hall. It is symmetrically flanked by two large, front-gable buildings. To the right, Samuel Linkton's house on the southwest corner of Third and Alder; to the left, the City Hotel, the largest building in the city. The Methodist church is depicted to the right, albeit with a fictional spire. In front of the church is the public square with the walled-in jailhouse. Although the image is based on a photograph, the buildings of the subscribers were sometimes exaggerated or depicted at an optimum angle, and buildings were sometimes idealized (which seems to be the case with the church). St. Vincent's Academy is depicted far off to the right, perhaps to better balance the composition.

The design is identical to many Kuchel & Dresel prints. Around the central image are twenty-nine vignettes depicting thirty-one businesses and six residences. Eight of the buildings illustrated in the vignettes had been destroyed and rebuilt after the August 3rd fire. In fact, the vignette of the side-gable City Hotel is based on a pre-fire photograph; the central image depicts the larger, front-gable structure that was still under construction when Castleman departed for San Francisco with his photographs (it did not reopen until July 1866).

There is no notice of the arrival of Castleman's prints in the *Statesman*. However, the *Daily Alta California* noted "the receipt of a fine lithographic picture of Walla Walla" by Grafton Brown on July 21, 1866. Castleman may not have been active as a photographer again in Walla Walla. By 1867 he had relocated to Eugene.

In March 1866, P. T. Shupe and T. M. Wood, recently of La Grande and The Dalles, respectively, took over Castleman's studio. Among other

Figure 42. *Walla Walla, 1866.* (Detail of fig. 2.)

things, they advertised, "Views and pictures of deceased persons taken at short notice." Wood moved on after eight months, and Shupe managed to keep his business afloat until 1868, when his equipment was lost in litigation, and he returned to La Grande.

———

Eli S. Glover was among the most prolific urban viewmakers in the West during the last third of the nineteenth century. Unlike Castleman, he employed the older tradition of idealized views depicted from imaginary perspectives, high above the ground, as if from a hot-air balloon. (In fact, the location from which Castleman took his photograph—Reese's flour mill—appears to be hundreds of feet below in Glover's image.) Glover arrived in Walla Walla on October 29, 1875, via Montana, where he had prepared views of Helena, Bozeman, and Virginia City. He found most of the north side of Main Street between First and Second razed by the fire just eleven days earlier. Glover had made prior arrangements with the furniture manufacturers Charles Abel and Emil Eversz to produce the print. Over the next nineteen days, he and an assistant made extensive sketches of the city's buildings and setting, studied the city plat, and arranged the buildings into a two-point perspective grid. Unfortunately, Glover's travel diary contains no mention of his work while in town. His notes on the appearance of the city are limited to: "The city . . . is regularly laid out with wide streets and well shaded. Thousands of Lombardy Poplars and cottonwood trees ornament the walks, and the yards about the houses are filled with fruit trees."[6] This was a business trip. Glover then made his way to Salem, where he prepared drawings for another image, and finally sailed from Portland to California.

Glover's image (figs. 3, 30, 33, & 43) was lithographed in San Francisco, and prints were delivered to Eversz & Abel for sale and distribution in February 1876. They sold for $5 each or three for $10, and Eversz & Abel also furnished frames specifically for the prints. The *Statesman* noted that "suitably framed," the 19 × 28½–inch print "will make an excellent parlor ornament," adding, "Every property holder in the city should secure a copy, and if he can afford it, a second copy to send to a distant friend, who may desire to know what Walla Walla looks like."[7]

The bottom margin of the print includes some general information about the city (population about 3,000, three weekly papers, two banks,

Figure 43. The business district on Main Street (November 1875) is framed by the city's largest brick structures: the Reynolds-Day building near Second (6) and the Stine House on Fourth (12). The most opulent residence in the city had just been constructed for Michael B. and Amelia E. Ward on the site of A. B. Roberts' 10-acre orchard and residence (19). Ward had made a small fortune raising livestock. The Italianate residence was built by William Glasford based on a design from John Riddell's *Architectural Designs for Modern Country Residences* (1861).

———

numerous mercantile establishments, center of a fine agricultural district with a railroad to Wallula). Instead of the vignette images of the Castleman print, Glover designed a numerical legend identifying the locations of ten churches and schools, twelve public buildings and factories, the railroad depot (with an imaginary train, at Twelfth and Rose), the fairgrounds, and the hospital. Most of the burned-out section remains vacant.

Unlike the Castleman print, Walla Wallans would have recognized many city landmarks and could have pointed to the location of their own houses. Some would have regarded the print as visual evidence of sixteen

Key: 1: Fire House/City Hall; 2: Courthouse; 3: City/County Jail; 4: Glasford's lumber mill; 5: "City Hall" building; 6: Reynolds-Day building; 7: Stephens building; 8: Johnson; Rees & Winans; 9: Baker building; 10: Brechtel building; 11: St. Louis Hotel; 12: Stine House; 13: Stahl residence and City Brewery; 14: Congregational church; 15: Methodist church; 16: Episcopal church; 17: Episcopal school; 18: United Brethren church; 19: Ward residence; 20: Schwabacher residence; 21: Rees residence; 22: Josephine Wolfe residence; 23: "Chinatown"; 24: Lasater residence; 25: Baker-Moore residence; and 26: Horton residence. (Detail of fig. 3.)

———

years of remarkable progress and wealth. Others would have seen it as the complete conquest of *Pašxápa*, demographically, architecturally, and economically.

23
The End of the Reservation?

With the very best intentions, there must be failure of great expectations in this matter of civilizing the Indians in a generation. But with little or no effort in this direction, with dishonest and avaricious agents to stand between the Government and the Indians, only evil results may be anticipated.

—Frances Fuller Victor, 1871[1]

The Council of 1871

The bill "To vacate and sell the Umatilla reservation in the State of Oregon" (sponsored by George H. Williams [R-OR]) passed both houses of Congress in 1868 but was not acted on. The BIA responded by simply neglecting the reservation. No improvements were made. The agent and the employees resided in the growing town of Pendleton on the western side of the reservation; the road traversing the reservation only became more permanent; attendance dropped at the unheated, leaky school; and about half of the Walla Wallas and Umatillas continued to follow Smohalla and refused to even visit the reservation.

———

Hoping to clean up and improve the running of the BIA at the start of his administration, President Grant appointed as its commissioner Col. Ely S. Parker (1869–71), a Tonawanda Seneca, and civilian agents were replaced by Army officers. After eight years of neglect, Barnhart was replaced by Lt. William H. Boyle (1869–71), who had experience with neither Indian affairs nor the Northwest. (Barnhart quickly established himself as the "sheep king" of Umatilla County.) The new Oregon Superintendent, Alfred B. Meacham (1869–72), owned a hotel, saloon, and mercantile business on the road on the southeast section of the reservation (current Meacham). He was well aware of the value of the reservation, and with the support of his congressmen, was determined to finally remove its inhabitants. However, the Grant administration also instituted the Board of Indian Commissioners, comprising non-salaried philanthropists and charged with, among other things, ensuring that the government treated Indians humanely and that it met its treaty obligations.

In 1871, the Grant administration chose to act on another Senate resolution to negotiate the removal of the Umatilla reservation. A survey was finally commissioned in anticipation of subdividing it for sale. The commission went to deputy surveyor Z. F. Moody, who had business interests in the region.[2] Like the *Statesman*, the *Union* welcomed the survey: "It is estimated there is good land enough to make two thousand good farms of one hundred and sixty acres each." If the country is opened to settlement, it continued, "Umatilla will soon become one of the most wealthy counties in the State of Oregon."[3] Parker instructed Felix R. Brunot, chairman of the Board of Commissioners, to ascertain "on what terms [the] Indians will relinquish to the United States all their claims or rights to said reservation and remove to some other reservation."[4]

The council took place on the reservation August 7–13, 1871. Brunot was joined by Meacham, new agent Narcisse Cornoyer (1871–80), interpreters Donald McKay (step-grandson of John McLoughlin) and P. B. Pambrun (grandson of Pierre Pambrun), and a group of journalists. On the third day, they were joined by a large audience of both Indians and non-Indians. Based on the record of the council, this was indeed a humane affair—aside from some threats by Meacham and Sen. Henry W. Corbett (R-OR), who sponsored this resolution. Unlike the Stevens–Palmer council, the chiefs were fully aware of the decision they were asked to make. In fact, they regularly criticized Stevens and Palmer for their false promises. Howlishwanpum (who Brunot noted "in dress, personal appearance, and bearing, [is] superior to the average American farmer") was most concerned with the broken promises of the 1855 treaty. And he stayed on message throughout the council. When observing the transformation of his Walla Walla Valley homeland, he may have remembered Stevens and Palmer's inability to "talk straight" at the council ("We don't come to steal your lands, we pay you more than it is worth"). Howlishwanpum spoke first on day three:

I came here and have been here eleven years. Of all that was promised I have seen none. It must have been lost. I heard what you said about our lands, and I understood what you said. We like this country and don't want to dispose of our reservation. I look at this land, this earth; it is like my mother, as if she was giving me milk, for from it I draw the food on which I live and grow. I see this little piece of land; it is all I have left; I know it is good land. . . . I don't know whether you will fulfil your promise if I accept your promises for my land. I did not see, with my own eyes, the money that was promised me before. . . . The large country I gave Governor Stevens, and you have not paid for it. The white man has settled on it. . . . The same I said before I say again, I cannot let my reservation go. That is what I have to say now to your commissioners.[5]

To an even greater extent than in 1855, *tamálwit* formed the basis of the chiefs' arguments. The following day, Homli, the Walla Walla head chief and nephew of Peo-Peo-Mox-Mox, gestured to his band, saying, "You see those Indians, they have all heard what has been said. For a great many years they have listened to your teachings. These peoples' fathers were not without instruction. The earth was their teacher. That is the true teacher. That is where the Indian first discovered that he was a human being." (Homli, a follower of Smohalla, lived primarily on the Columbia.)

Several statements were made by Meacham and Corbett about how much more productive the land would be in the hands of White farmers, to which some headmen took offense. Some of them emphasized the great amount of labor their people had invested into the land—with little or no assistance. Winampsnut, the Umatilla head chief, stated, "I see our reservation, how little work has been done on it. The [agents] did very little of it; all the rest the Indians have done. They learned [agriculture] themselves, and did the best they could. They learned very slowly, but, seeing what we have done, we love it." He concluded by gesturing to Meacham, saying, "You make speeches too long. All day yesterday you talked. We cannot remember what you say."

On day four, Howlishwanpum returned to the broken promises of 1855:

All that was promised me I kept in my heart, and brought with me onto this reservation. This is what was told me: 'You [the three chiefs] are going to live well, to have a house like white men.' That is what I heard. That is one thing that was promised. Another thing that was promised, when we went on the reservation, that we should have a white man for a doctor, a good one; and we were to have a good blacksmith, & good schoolteacher to teach our children, and a man to teach us religion, a good man. And we should have a flour-mill as soon as we got to the reservation, and a good man to show us how to farm, and a good sawyer to attend to the saw-mill. Now I want to show all of you white chiefs that none of these things that were promised to us can we see. . . . I will tell you all that I see on this reservation. I see a small church; some of my children go to school at the church. And all of us . . . do not see any of the houses they promised us. I see a house that was supposed to have been built for me. It is about five feet high, made out of round cottonwood logs. It is all rotten and falling down. There is Wenap Snoot's house, down below; it is as if it had been made for a pig-sty. Hom-li's house, up the river, is made out of cottonwood logs, and looks like a house for pigs. . . . I see my real house over there; it is out of mats; that is the one the chief lives in. He was promised a good house with glass windows and doors in it.

Young Chief of the Cayuse reinforced Howlishwanpum's statement: "The red man and the white man held a council in Walla-Walla. . . . Both you and me know what was talked about at that council. What was promised was not done. It was as if you had taken the treaty as soon as it was made and torn it up. . . . The treaties made with the Indians on all the reservations have never been kept; they have all been broken." Like Young Chief and several others, Winampsnut noted that he had visited the other reservations, concluding, "I have seen all them with my own eyes, and none of these countries would suit me."

On the sixth day of the council, all the chiefs stated that they fully understood the proposal put before them, and each in turn rejected it. Brunot then made a remarkable speech, addressed indirectly to the senator and the White neighbors in attendance:

I know that there are many persons within reach of this reservation, and other reservations, who suppose that the Indians will be removed, and they are waiting for places on them. These men will be told by their candidates for Congress that they will get the Indians removed. If they should ever succeed, and I do not believe they ever will, it will be with the certainty that the Indians will get the full value of their lands, and I

Figure 44. Indian camps, Umatilla Indian Reservation, July 4, 1903 (cropped). Once bison hides became inaccessible, tipis were covered with either mats or government-issued canvas. (Lee Moorhouse photographs, PH036 5923, University of Oregon Libraries, Special Collections and University Archives.)

believe the man who waits here to get a pre-emption claim on this land will die a poor man still waiting.

Equally remarkable perhaps, was the *Union*'s sympathetic assessment of the outcome: "While we could have wished it otherwise, all must admit that the Indians have an undoubted right to use their pleasure in the matter." The paper also printed Brunot's speech in full, concluding, "We would commend it to all as just in sentiment and correct in principle."[6] Of course, this council was the work of a Republican administration, and it was only applauded by the Republican press—and we may assume by a portion of Walla Walla's Republican minority (Newell's "weak sentimentalists"). The council received nationwide coverage, with the (Republican) *New-York Tribune* commenting, "These unsophisticated savages have learned something of the white man's untrustworthiness; they will not take the word of the white man's Government any more; they have settled down for life, and will not be lured away by specious promises. What a commentary is this on the good faith of the Government!"[7]

Brunot concluded his report to the President,

In view of the maladministration of agents and the misapplication of funds, the failure of the Government to perform the promises of the treaty, and the fact that the Indians have been constantly agitated by assertions that the Government intended their removal, and that their removal was urged for several years in succession in the reports of a former agent, (thus taking away from them all incentives to improve their lands,) it must be admitted that the progress these Indians have made in ten years has been wonderful. [N]othing remains but to do them simple justice and protect them in their rights.[8]

The Cayuse headmen had performed a remarkable and heroic service for their people at the council of 1855 in retaining a large reservation of their traditional territory, and the headmen of the Confederated Tribes did the same in 1871 (fig. 44). According to the popular agent Cornoyer, the Indians were far less anxious immediately after the council. The respite was to be brief.

24

New Economic Realities

*The Walla Walla business firms are now doing a rushing business—that is,
rushing into bankruptcy.*

—*State Rights Democrat* (Albany, Oregon), May 2, 1873

A s the national economy stagnated at the close of the 1860s, the *Statesman* observed that most of the businesses and individuals that advertised with the paper in 1863 had since left town.[1] On the other hand, in
anticipation of the construction of the NPR in 1869–73, emigration to the
valley increased, and real estate values spiked. Many Walla Walla businesses wisely adapted by turning their focus to the growing home market
and catering exclusively to the needs of the city and the valley (population
about 1,500 and 4,600, respectively, in 1870). In fall 1869 alone, Johnson
& (Raymond) Rees, Paine Bros. & Moore, Wertheimer Bros., and Kim-
ball & Day opened general stores specifically for the local, domestic
market—clothing, "family" groceries, housewares, stationery, and farmers' exchanges for crops and dairy products. They did not sell miners' supplies, nor were they interested in sending pack trains to the mining towns.
Both Dorsey Baker and James McAuliff sold off their mules and packing
equipment in 1869. Many freighters and packers to the mines moved to
other occupations.[2] (Of course, freight service to and from Wallula remained
a vital enterprise.) In summer 1868, Eversz and Abel opened the city's first
business exclusively dedicated to residential furniture. In 1869 they expanded
to offer all aspects of interior décor, including wallpaper, window shades,
mirrors, and picture frames. The success of these local merchants was made
visible in the increasing number of brick buildings lining Main Street and
in the number of large, Italianate residences throughout the city by the late
1870s. Despite the regular complaints of "dull times" and the onset of a
global depression, business in Walla Walla was usually more active than in
other Northwest cities during the 1870s. Visitors were universally impressed

by the city, the region, and the residents. Frances Fuller Victor reported for the *Oregonian* in 1870, "During my stay in Walla Walla I noticed ample evidences of prosperity of a sure and steady kind. Although, comparatively, times are said to be 'hard,' there seemed to be more money in circulation than in the Wallamet Valley, and more trade between the farming community and the merchants."[3] The *Oregon Republican* (Dallas) noted one year later,

> Walla Walla is now the richest and most populous county in Washington Territory, and in natural resources is not excelled by any equal area in this or any other section of the United States. It is now rapidly filling up with emigrants from Oregon and the Atlantic States. With a railroad connection with the Northern Pacific Railroad, or even with the navigable waters of the Columbia River, from the head of the valley, opening a ready market for its abundant crops of wheat, corn, fruit and other products, there is no part of the far-famed Willamette Valley which could count upon a more brilliant future.[4]

The steadily growing population was aided by the establishment of a Land Office in Walla Walla in 1871 (to which William Stephens was appointed receiver). However, unless they had the means to purchase expensive land near the city, new arrivals were forced to locate homesteads in remote parts of the county.

The increased population supported two additional newspapers in the early 1870s. A. J. Cain launched the monthly *Real Estate Gazette* in 1869, which documented the increasing demand and real estate values in the region, and *Spirit of the West* was established in 1872 as a more moderate Republican voice. (The latter changed ownership several times and was renamed the *Walla Walla Watchman* by Charles Besserer in 1876.)

———

Walla Walla began to look city-like in 1869, with the erection of its first two-story brick buildings—both of which were geared to the home market: Oswald Brechtel's Walla Walla Bakery (fig. 45) and Dorsey Baker's "Bank Place" (fig. 46). Earlier in the year, Baker & Co. had sold its mercantile business to three ambitious young men: Frank and John Paine and Miles C. Moore. Paine Bros. & Moore took over the ground floor, and Baker and Boyer dedicated themselves to banking and real estate on

Figure 45. Southeast corner of Third and Main, 1872: from the left: Fred Colman's drugstore; Brechtel building (1869, upstairs were offices and a meeting room for the fraternal organizations); the Baumeister brothers' building (1869, their Oriental Baths occupied one-half of the ground floor; the *Union* was printed upstairs); Adams Bros. (1862, bought out Brown Bros. in 1868). (Kemble Col, Neg. No. 2884; California Historical Society.)

Figure 46. Southwest corner of Second and Main, 1872: from the left: Frank Orselli's grocery store (1857), Baker building (1869), and Dusenbery Bros. (1865). The Italianate façade designs of the Brechtel and Baker buildings were nearly identical. Miles C. Moore married Baker's daughter Mary in 1873 and became increasingly involved in Baker's business ventures. At the time of the photograph, the city had installed nine oil lamps along Main Street. (Walla Walla Photograph Collection, WCMss066, 025 013 003, Whitman College and Northwest Archives.)

the second floor. This was the city's second bank; John Day and Almos Reynolds had opened a bank next door to Day's drug store the previous summer. These banks assisted in the establishment of the new businesses.

The city and county continued to be the wealthiest and most populous in the territory into the 1880s. Yet, despite steady population growth and increased real estate values, the county's assessed value of property for 1867–74 shows remarkably little growth:

Assessed Property Values	Population
1867: $1,748,663	2,943
1868: $1,988,198	4,612
1869: $1,900,858	—
1870: $2,548,530	4,583
1871: $3,101,790	5,572
1873: $2,943,970	—
1874: $2,571,185	7,379[5]

Wealth and real estate were increasingly concentrated in the hands of an elite group of merchants, bankers, ranchers, and millers. The newcomers to the region must have marveled at the material wealth accumulated by these individuals in just one decade.

These newcomers were primarily farmers lured to the region by reports of recent crop yields. However, agricultural overproduction was already a growing problem in the region. Even during the drought years of the late 1860s, production far outpaced local needs. In 1873, the valley produced an estimated surplus of 1 million bushels of grain, but only 100,000 could be shipped out. This became national news. The *Statesman* pointed out, "To team this surplus grain to the river is out of the question, and so for the present, or at least until the railroad is complete, the prospect for our farmers is rather gloomy."[6] Wheat was selling at the time for just $0.40/bushel, which was almost half of what farmers expected. The suppressed prices were a result of overproduction combined with the fees for moving freight to Wallula and down the Columbia. Many farmers—particularly new arrivals who lived farther from the cities and mills—were forced to wait until spring to sell their grain.

Frances Fuller Victor concluded her study of 1870 Walla Walla: "Nothing is lacking except railroad communications with the Columbia River and the East, to establish its importance; and that is what its citizens are now struggling to obtain."[7] Given its location—which had been selected by the Army strictly to control Indians—the city had no future as an industrial center; it could only aspire to be the hub of an agricultural and horticultural region. At present, however, it faced an ever-increasing need to move its products economically and efficiently to distant markets. Continued, sustainable economic growth would require enormous investment, self-sacrifice, and civic cooperation and coordination. At the time of Victor's visit, Walla Walla's most affluent citizens showed little aptitude for these requirements. Partisan politics had divided the community. Despite the growing population, greater profits and security continued to lure some ambitious merchants to Boise and other burgeoning cities that would soon be connected to the transcontinental railroad.

The Walla Walla and Columbia River Railroad, Again

Walla Walla's future prospects changed regularly throughout this period. In 1870, the NPR slowly commenced construction from Duluth and from the newly created town of Kalama on the Columbia to Puget Sound. Fearing that the NPR created Kalama specifically to bypass Portland, businessmen there, led by William W. Chapman, incorporated the Portland, Dalles and Salt Lake Railroad Co. with the goal of connecting Oregon to the transcontinental railroad. Perhaps inspired by Chapman, a former business partner of Dorsey Baker, WWCRR meetings (with smaller attendance) resumed in November 1870. In March, the NPR offered to prepare a survey of the route from Walla Walla to Wallula if the city would fund it ($1,835). If they chose to build the route, the city would be refunded; if they declined to build, all survey documentation would be turned over to the city. After the completion of the survey in May, the NPR announced that its main line would come no closer to Walla Walla than Wallula. The papers immediately began lobbying for local construction of the 31½-mile branch line to Wallula. The first obstacle, as stipulated in the railroad bill passed by Congress in 1869, was to convince 75 percent of the county voters that the county commissioners should back the project by guaranteeing payment of 8 percent interest on $300,000 in bonds for twenty years ($24,000 annually). The county would retain exclusive authority to regulate fees and would control the proceeds of all freight to Wallula. The *Orego-nian* was particularly enthusiastic about the project: "By this branch the rich valley of Walla Walla will be able to pour the products of its industry into the channels of commerce. A valley which will ultimately be home to 100,000 people will thus be opened, and a new career for it will begin."[8]

Baker and others canvassed aggressively, but only 49 percent supported the proposition in the September 18 election. Within two weeks of the vote, Baker, president of the company and wealthiest person in the valley, determined to oversee the project largely by himself and in conjunction with Chapman's proposed Portland, Dalles and Salt Lake Railroad.[9] The endeavor called for superhuman energy and coordination, especially for a capitalist with no experience in railroad building—and particularly during such economically unstable times. Determined to build a narrow-gauge railroad for $300,000 and to complete it within one year, Baker first lob-bied for $75,000 in local subscriptions—unsuccessfully. Undaunted, he proceeded to hire civil engineer Sewell Truax to oversee construction, imported crews of Chinese laborers, and sent teams to collect and float timber down the Yakima River to Wallula. Baker then traveled east. He studied narrow-gauge and wooden strap-iron railroads, ordered two small locomotives and parts for freight cars in Pennsylvania, visited with the president of the NPR, investigated prices for shipping rail to the Northwest, and met with bankers and congressmen.[10]

On his return to the Northwest in March 1872, Baker built a saw-mill, engine house, and small village on his plat near Wallula, and purchased rights of way from farmers along the route (which was certainly facilitated by William Stephens, who was both treasurer of the railroad and receiver at the Land Office). Yet, despite the labors of Baker and Truax, the lack of actual railroad construction prior to the promised completion date of November 1, 1872, combined with the deepening economic malaise, disheartened many Walla Wallans. Additionally, Baker's lack of popularity in the region—thanks largely to the *Statesman*—plagued him throughout the planning and construction process. A Walla Walla correspondent wrote to a Seattle paper in October, "[T]he dark angel of discord seems hovering near, having driven away that spirit of contentment which usually held full sway and with it the bustle, confusion and busy life which has heretofore characterized the everyday existence of the city. Dull times and complaining merchants. The failure of

Dr. Baker & Co. to complete the construction of the Railroad between here and Wallula has somewhat discouraged the merchants, farmers and mechanics for this season and they now have little faith in the scheme."[11] Some shareholders began selling their stock back to Baker. Above all, I. T. Reese, the company's vice president, who came into serious financial difficulties with his Portland creditors in 1872, was forced to sell all of his stock back to Baker.[12] The following year, Reese lost his little commercial empire to bankruptcy.

Reese's was one of the most public financial failures of this period of bankruptcies and foreclosures. The most public was the collapse of Alpheus Kyger, Reese's original partner in the booming mercantile business of the 1860s. While serving as county treasurer in 1872, Kyger chose to settle with his creditors by staging a robbery of $19,000 from the treasury. (Robberies were occurring regularly at the time; in 1873, William Phillips of the Walla Walla Foundry was killed during a robbery.) Within months, the truth had been revealed, and Kyger was forced into bankruptcy (but not prison, thanks to a friendly grand jury; disgraced, he moved to Los Angeles). A. B. Roberts also experienced a humiliating, well-publicized bankruptcy. He moved to Baker City in 1873. Reports of businessmen fleeing town to escape their creditors became commonplace.

Ominous reports from Eastern papers of imminent financial difficulties appeared in Far West papers increasingly during 1871–73. The *Real Estate Gazette* noted in June 1873,

> Never in the history of this Valley has business been so poor as so far this season. Many causes have combined to produce this. . . . Lavish expenditures of money and time have been made for things that brought forth no particular good during the past few years, when all supposed that trade would continue for all to flow into our city and valley. But a change came, and with it failures, as a matter of course followed, causing depression in all branches of business, naturally making business men suspicious, thus hastening on the calamities that might have been averted.[13]

After Tacoma was selected as the western terminus of the NPR in July 1873, outraged Seattle businessmen cobbled together plans for a narrow-gauge railroad from Seattle to Walla Walla via Snoqualmie Pass. Arthur Denny and Joseph McGilvra pitched the $4.5 million plan to a large audience in Walla Walla in September 1873 and initially found some enthusiasm (far more than Baker was finding).[14] The *Statesman*, always looking to take a shot at Baker, stated, "The outlet by way of the Columbia, improved as it may be, will never meet the wants of the great interior basin, and so it is our people join hands with the Seattleites in favor of an all-rail line to tide-water."[15] The *Real Estate Gazette* energetically supported the Seattle plan, "That the people of Seattle are alive their late action proves. That they are entitled to our support, and that of all who reside along the line of the proposed road, it is scarcely necessary to affirm. That a hearty and determined co-operation will, beyond any doubt, result in success, not even the skeptical can question."[16]

However, such enthusiasm soon evaporated. On September 18, Jay Cooke & Co., the financier of the NPR, failed, setting off a chain reaction of bank closures. The New York Stock Exchange closed for eleven days. The Panic of 1873 initiated what became known at the time as the Great Depression (1873–79). The NPR ceased all operations. Railroad plans across the country dissolved, including Chapman's. The WWCRR asked Walla Wallans to support a bond to complete construction to the city, but the plan was rejected. The *Real Estate Gazette* was among the country's 18,000 failed businesses. Soon, fifteen buildings on Main Street were unoccupied.[17] During 1872–73, the county had approved the construction of a grand new courthouse and jail. Freeman Allen designed an extravagant $75,000 building. The commissioners then debated, mismanaged, and fought over the project until the economy put an end to the plans. Throughout 1874–75, the sheriff held regular auctions of city lots and parcels of land due to foreclosure or failure to pay taxes (forty-four properties were auctioned off in a single day in July 1875). The *Statesman* observed in January 1875 something unthinkable a few years earlier: several saloons had recently shut down. "The reason assigned is the high rate for licenses exacted by the city and county and the general depression in business."[18] Perhaps the most distressing portrait of the region appeared in Boise's *Idaho Statesman* that summer. In order to pay their taxes, it noted, a significant number of Walla Walla farmers sought work, primarily as teamsters, at Boise—300 miles away from their farms. It accused Walla Walla's journalists and businessmen of pursuing "a foolish policy" of luring vast numbers of farmers to their region, where "they raise ten times as much as they can consume and have no market. The trouble is they pursue no industry there only farming. . . .

To speak plainly, it is the poorest country for a farmer, that we know of on the Pacific coast." The *Walla Walla Statesman* found the article "only too true."[19]

Instead of addressing this serious issue, however, the territorial press focused its condemnation on the NPR for its exploitation and manipulation of the largest land grant in US history and for crushing the dreams and fortunes of countless regional investors. Gradually, support for the Seattle-Walla Walla Railroad was revitalized. Despite the economic situation, it was now widely promoted as a regional endeavor, free of monopolistic abuse—"our railroad," with profits remaining in "our territory." Actual construction began in Seattle on May 1, 1874, with great fanfare. But progress was slow, and the railroad never developed beyond King County.

Fort Walla Walla, Again

In August 1873—as the economic situation looked bleaker with every week—Walla Wallans received a shot in the arm: Fort Walla Walla was to be regarrisoned. Back in February 1871, Congress had approved the sale of the fort reservation. However, because the bill located the fort in *Oregon*, it required amendment, which dragged on until June 1872. The fort was transferred to the Interior Department for disposal, but during the prolonged Indian hostilities in Northern California and southern Oregon (the "Modoc War," 1872–73) the Department of the Columbia requested suspension of the sale of the fort. The fort was then transferred back to the War Department and reactivated as a permanent post for eight cavalry companies in August 1873. All thanks to a clerical error. Although the garrison now comprised a much smaller percentage of the city's population, Walla Wallans certainly appreciated the security provided by the fort, the return of local government contracts, the return of the 1st cavalry brass band, and above all, the return of the paymaster.

The Grange

American farmers finally had a national advocacy organization with the establishment in 1867 of the National Grange of the Order of Patrons of Husbandry. Energized by the Grange's message of cooperation, protection, and collective political clout—and above all by its focus on lobbying federal and state legislatures for lower shipping and warehouse rates for agricultural goods—the movement spread rapidly throughout the North-west during 1873. (The term "Grange fever" was common during 1873–75.) A deputy of the National Grange arrived in Walla Walla in August and within a few weeks had organized Granges in Waitsburg, Dayton, Dixie, and two in Walla Walla.[20] Farmers were united in their contempt for monopolies—in particular, the OSN and NPR, which became the targets of all their economic anxieties. And Baker's railroad was criticized as just another monopoly by supporters of the Seattle-Walla Walla Railroad, including the Grangers.

The Granges urged farmers to withhold their support for political party tickets and instead to back candidates who supported their cause regardless of party affiliation. In 1874, the Walla Walla lawyer and three-term state legislator B. L. Sharpstein ran unsuccessfully as the Democratic candidate for congressional delegate, a defeat that *Spirit of the West* attributed to his connection to the WWCRR: "We are satisfied that the chief cause which led to that result was the uncharitable belief which many entertained that because of his ownership of stock in the Walla Walla and Columbia River Railroad, Mr. Sharpstein must of necessity be opposed to the building of the Seattle-Walla Walla Railroad. There is a strong sentiment here in favor of the latter enterprise, and reports of the character having once been put in circulation, many lost sight of everything else in their zeal for this road and voted for [the Republican candidate, Orange] Jacobs."[21]

Completion of the WWCRR

Baker, far behind schedule, nonetheless trudged along at great personal expense. The wooden strap-iron railroad reached Touchet in 1874 and began shipping wheat 16 miles to Wallula. Finally, in 1875, with barely perceptible progress on the Seattle railroad, Walla Wallans agreed to purchase $25,000 of stock in the WWCRR, and construction—with iron rails—reached the city in October 1875. A depot was built on Eleventh and Rose, which was soon joined by a number of warehouses. Eli Glover was among the first passengers on the WWCRR, departing with his draw-ings of the city on November 18. He noted in his diary: "It is a narrow gauge road, very poorly equipped. . . . [T]he road is doing good business, shipping grain, fruit and stock. But the shippers complain of the prices."[22] Under pressure from the Granges, in December 1874, the OSN had dra-matically reduced its rate for grain to Portland to $6.00/ton. In summer 1875, Baker had assured the merchants that shipping rates for grain to Wal-lula would not exceed $4.00/ton. In fact, the rate was initially set at $3.50—but with a $1.00/ton transfer surcharge. The rate was lower than that charged by the teamsters (who additionally required an extra day to Wallula), yet many felt that no benefit was received from the $25,000 investment. When the WWCRR raised the rate to $4.50 (plus a $0.50 surcharge) in March 1876, all the Granges in the region declared war on Baker. Among the resolutions adopted at their various meetings: "[W]e believe it necessary that some speedy means should be adopted to release our community from the ruinous grasp of this would-be monopoly." They called on the county commissioners to immediately invest more generously in the improvement of the wagon road to Wallula.[23] Some desperate team-sters offered to carry freight at the same rate as the WWCRR, and the Granges pledged to support them exclusively. (They then distributed 500 posters around the Northwest advertising for teamsters.) They called for a boycott of any businesses that patronized the railroad and received the sup-port of fifty-three businesses. Baker responded to the Granges in mid-April with an elaborate and scathing letter to the local papers.[24] At the same time, the Granges called on the (suddenly benevolent) OSN to build a rival railroad. Once that plan fizzled away, they discussed the creation of a canal to the Columbia. Finally, in August, the WWCRR dropped its rate to $4.00 (plus a $0.50 surcharge). By this time, some teamsters needed to attend to their own harvests, and it became obvious that both the team-sters and the railroads together would be hard-pressed to handle the down-freight demand. Then it became obvious that the combination of the railroad and steamers was unable to satisfy the demand. Enormous quan-tities of grain and flour would continue to sit in warehouses during the winter as the steamers were idle.

The major beneficiaries of the WWCRR were, ultimately, its shareholders—particularly Baker, his sons, and son-in-law. In 1876, Baker

Figure 47. Residence of Dorsey S. and Lizzie H. Baker, west façade, 1876. (Baker Family Collection, WCMss040 box 3, folder 2, Whitman College and Northwest Archives.)

initiated construction of an Italianate villa adjoining his extant large house (fig. 47), which certainly attracted a good deal of resentment.[25]

Building Boom

The rate and scale of construction in Walla Walla during this Great Depression seems paradoxical. In 1873, Fred Stine opened the Stine House on the site of his former blacksmithing business on Fourth (fig. 48). The three-story, fifty-room hotel was the largest brick building in the territory. The following year, Almos Reynolds and John Day replaced their adjoining frame buildings with a double-lot, two-story brick building for their businesses, plus generous office space upstairs, all with gas lighting (fig. 43, #6).

The greatest building activity in the city occurred in 1876, when Johnson, Rees & Winans and Schwabacher Bros. replaced their brick stores with double-lot, two-story brick blocks (fig. 49); William Stephens added a brick building of similar size next door to Johnson, Rees & Winans; William

Figure 48. Stine House, 1872–73, southeast corner of Fourth and Main, built by David Ashpaugh and John Goudy. Stine initiated construction in August 1872 after coming into a large inheritance. (Walla Walla Photograph Collection, Box 32, Folder 109, WCMss066, Whitman College and Northwest Archives.)

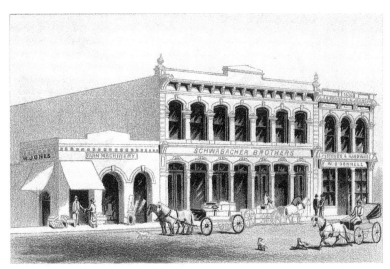

Figure 49. Northeast corner of Third and Main as it looked in 1876. During construction of its new building, Schwabacher's moved into the corner brick building (built by the late William Phillips). After its completion, Hawley, Dodd & Co., a successful Portland hardware and agricultural machinery firm, opened a branch in this building. (*The West Shore* 13, no. 3 [March 1887], 235.)

O'Donnell added a second story to his brick hardware store adjoining Schwabacher's (fig. 49); and the saddler Thomas Quinn built a two-story brick block on the northwest corner of Second and Main. At the same time, Frank and John Paine were buying up all the properties near the corner of Second and Main. In 1878, they initiated construction on the largest office building in the territory (fig. 50). All of these buildings were embellished

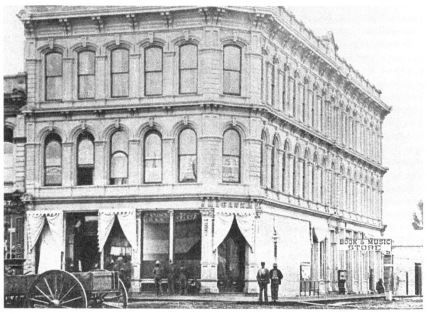

Figure 50. Paine Brothers building, 1878–79, southeast corner of Second and Main (adjoining the Reynolds-Day building) Photograph ca. 1880. Frank W. Paine arrived as part of the 1862 gold rush from California. However, he ended up working for Dorsey Baker, where he learned the safe money was in outfitting miners. Within two years, he had partnered with William Stephens, and in 1866, he and his brother John bought out Stephens. In 1869, they joined with Miles C. Moore, another ambitious twenty-something, and bought out Baker & Co. The brothers opened a branch in Waitsburg, bought up farmland and real estate, represented 40 percent of the association that built the City Hall, and put a steamer on the Snake River. The Paines initiated construction after Moore left the firm in 1878 to go into business with his father-in-law, Dorsey Baker. The 41 × 120–foot building was fitted out to house the First National Bank of Walla Walla (formerly Almos Reynolds's bank, with Levi Ankeny as president), three ground-level stores, a large meeting room, and about thirty offices. The cost of the building alone was estimated at $25,000. (Walla Walla Photograph Collection, WCMss066, Box 32, Folder 23 Whitman College and Northwest Archives.)

with ground-floor cast-iron façades (at least some of which were fabricated at the Walla Walla Foundry). Increasingly, business owners—butchers, blacksmiths, barbers, saddlers, and so on—became capitalists, involved in multiple ventures, particularly real estate. Many of these capitalists were simultaneously building impressive Italianate villas for their families. And yet the *Statesman* counted fifteen unoccupied buildings on Main Street in spring 1876. The concentration of the region's wealth into the hands of a small number of families was all too visible.

Newcomers required substantial assets to establish a business or farm in the 1870s.[26] A small improved farm within a day's trip from the city could cost $30/acre. Land in Whitman County was extensive and relatively inexpensive, but many of the prime sites were owned by Walla Wallans. Most newcomers were tenant farmers or renters of commercial properties, and much of their earnings went into the coffers of the city's Bakers, Paines, and Schwabachers.[27] Of course, none of this was unique to Walla Walla.

Annexation, Again

Global annexation schemes seem to have been discussed in every issue of every newspaper in the early 1870s: US annexation of British Columbia, US annexation of San Domingo, annexation of Alaska to Washington Territory, Prussian annexation of Alsace, and so on. And again, talk in Salem turned to the annexation of Walla Walla County. In 1871, Oregon's senators introduced a bill to return to the state its natural northeast boundary. The Republican *Oregonian* saw the new bill as an attempt to refortify the state's fading Democratic majority: "Walla Walla county, like all the districts east of the Cascade mountains, is filled up with a class of men who found it necessary to decamp from Missouri, on account of their secessionist proclivities, during the rebellion. Such persons can be relied on to vote Democratic tickets at all times and under all circumstances."[28] Naturally, the *Statesman* supported the annexation on both political and economic grounds, stating erroneously that Walla Walla County provided the territory with more than half its tax revenue (in fact, it provided less than a third). The *Union* initially opposed annexation, but by 1875 came to support it strictly on economic grounds. The *Spirit of the West/Walla Walla Watchman* consistently opposed annexation. Despite vigorous debates in the papers and on the street corners of Northwest cities, no action was taken in Congress.

The loss of Walla Walla—the largest city in the territory and the second largest in the Northwest—was unthinkable to the legislature in Olympia, which responded to the threat to its desire for statehood by regenerating talk of annexing northern Idaho, a plan overwhelmingly supported by the residents there.[29] The citizens of northern Idaho sent memorials to Congress in 1873, 1875, 1877, and 1878; Washington Territory sent its memorials in 1873, 1875, and 1877. To the dismay of many Walla Wallans, in October 1875, the elected representatives of the booming town of Dayton petitioned the territorial legislature for a division of Walla Walla County. Walla Wallans responded with a counter-petition. In what seemed to be a hostile gesture, in November, the legislature granted the new Columbia County the lion's share of the former county's acreage (map 10). Of course, the political leaders of Dayton opposed annexation to Oregon. This act only amped up hostilities between Walla Walla and Puget Sound. After 1,400 Walla Wallans petitioned for a fair adjustment of the county line, the governor granted them Waitsburg.[30]

In December 1875, Oregon's senators introduced both a revised bill to annex Walla Walla and Columbia counties and—as compensation—a bill to annex Alaska to Washington Territory. The *Union* was amused by the sudden attention Walla Walla was receiving in the Puget Sound papers:

> As we expected, the people over on the Sound are becoming greatly interested. They never took much interest in this section, except that they always looked in this direction for about twelve or thirteen thousand dollars of Territorial tax each year. . . . We were useful in furnishing from one-third to one-fourth of the whole amount that went to support the chronic office-holders and political managers of Puget Sound, and of course they do not wish to lose this money. We and our people are most anxious for a change in their political relations. In the first place they would prefer to be let out of the fight by being annexed to Oregon, and then let Idaho and the balance of Washington Territory adjust their boundaries to the best interests of the several sections of the two Territories.[31]

The county commissioners and a bipartisan group of 819 Walla Walla and Columbia county citizens (a majority of voters) then sent memorials to Congress in support of Oregon's bill. The *Statesman* was far more aggressive than the *Union* in stating its contempt for the "clam eaters"—who it believed should be united with the "seal catchers" of Alaska. It predicted: "The 1st of January, 1877 should mark the annexation of Walla Walla valley to the State of Oregon."[32] Despite the intensification of hostilities between Walla Walla and the Sound, Congress took no action on reconsidering its somewhat random, unnatural, and sometimes absurd territorial and state boundaries in the Far West.

"The Future of Our City"

The first issue of the *Statesman* to appear after the death of William Newell in November 1878 carried an editorial titled "The Future of Our City" (perhaps the last penned by Newell). It offered the example of the recent developments of Leavenworth, Kansas, and Kansas City, Missouri, since 1865. Leavenworth, the larger city, controlled the trade in Kansas. But the enterprising businessmen of Kansas City, "ceaseless in their efforts," managed to divert the trade, and theirs is now a bustling city of 50,000, while Leavenworth "is almost deserted; grass grows on its once busy streets."[33] It concluded, "What shall our future be—a Kansas City or a Leavenworth?" The editorial failed to note that Kansas City had surpassed Leavenworth as a trade hub by out-lobbying Leavenworth for a railroad bridge across the Missouri. Walla Walla had no such geographic bargaining power; it was fortunate to have a military post (like Leavenworth) and to have a little railroad to the Columbia that might someday connect to tidewater or a transcontinental railroad.[34] The immediate future of urban development in the Northwest belonged to the deep harbors and the depot cities along the NPR (which resumed construction in 1879 and would be fully completed in 1888). The future metropolis of the "Inland Empire" belonged to a sparsely populated site at Spokane Falls. Regardless of the determination of its citizens, Walla Walla's future was not a Kansas City.

25

The End of the Treaty

[T]he Umatilla reservation [is] held in reserve and prevented from settle-
ment for the benefit of a few worthless vagrants. . . . Remove as soon as
practicable these Indians to the Wallowa valley; throw open the Umatilla
reservation to settlers, and within two years it will bud and blossom with the
fruits of honest toil, its plains will be waving with golden grain; its surface
be dotted with farm houses and in place of squalid filthy wigwams, there will
be happy homes, and the talent so long hid to the earth will be reclaimed to
usefulness.

—*Walla Walla Statesman*, October 16, 1875

Indians may have been entirely dispossessed of the Walla Walla Valley by 1873, yet they were very much on the minds of the valley's occupants. In November 1872, Superintendent Meacham called upon the Army to force a band of Modoc in Northern California back onto their assigned reservation (with their longtime enemy, the Klamath). The result was a six-month-long embarrassment for the Army and for President Grant's "Peace Policy." A small band of warriors repelled increasingly larger forces, inflicting scores of casualties. In April 1873, at a council with a peace commission, the Modoc wounded Meacham and killed two commissioners, including Gen. Edward Canby, Commander of the Department of the Columbia. The Modoc continued to elude and attack the Army for several weeks, and were only defeated in June.

The violent Modoc rebellion sent shock waves throughout the Far West. The *Statesman* posted recurrent stories of the warlike intentions of the Indians in the region. It observed "clear indications" that the Umatilla reservation Indians and the Nez Perce "are in sympathy with the Modocs, and should the war in that quarter continue for any length of time, we may look for trouble." A few days later: "A week or two since, we noticed the presence of an unusually large number of Indians in this valley," where they "roam around, greatly to the disgust of honest settlers. . . . Within a day or two, we learn, that these Indians are trading their ponies whenever an opportunity offers, and that the funds thus realized are invested in revolvers and other warlike weapons. There is every reason to believe that the Indians east of the mountains expect and are preparing for an outbreak."[1] Papers throughout the region echoed the concerns of the *Statesman*. Young Joseph's band of non-treaty Nez Perce in the Wallowa Valley became involved in the rumors. Dispossessed of their land by the 1863 "Thief Treaty," Old Joseph (who died in 1871) broke with chief Lawyer and the reservation Nez Perce and insisted that he had never sold his land. The close connection between the Wallowa band and the Cayuse was a concern for many Whites. Agent Cornoyer reported that out of fear of this "renegade" connection, "white settlers in all portions of Eastern Oregon were forming military companies for their defense."[2] There were rumors of hostilities among the Palus. It was reported that the Palus had been joined by Kamiakin and a son of Peo-Peo-Mox-Mox—names certainly intended to recall the violence of the 1850s. Smohalla and chief Moses on the mid-Columbia were also supposedly making war plans. Large numbers of "renegade" Indians from the Umatilla reservation supposedly had moved into the Walla Walla Valley. Prior to the regarrisoning of the fort, Walla Wallans had petitioned the governor for Army presence in the valley.

The agent to the Yakama reservation made an extensive tour of the region and then informed the *Oregonian* that all the reports he investigated were totally unfounded. In fact, he generally found peaceful cohabitation of Indians and non-Indians.[3] Sylvester Wait, now a resident of Dayton, sent a letter to the *Oregonian* denouncing those who were publishing false reports of Indian threats. "[B]ecause the times are rather dull here just now . . . there are a few designing persons who would like to see an Indian war, in order that troops might be sent into the vicinity and help to make money a little more plentiful. . . . The truth is, the Indians are well disposed in this country; but it is not so with all the whites."[4]

To the disbelief of many Whites in the Northwest, instead of imposing further restrictions on the Indians, in June 1873, President Grant authorized the creation of a reservation in the Wallowa Valley for Joseph's band. After conflicts with the small number of White settlers there, an agreement was arranged by the superintendent to divide the valley in half, with an eastern section reserved for the Nez Perce. Many Oregonians, led by the governor, were outraged that more state territory was given to the Indians. Cornoyer's report continued, "There was also great excitement existing among the citizens in this vicinity, particularly in La Grande, during the summer, in consequence of the Government giving the Wal-low-wa Valley to the Indians. And as many of the Indians of the [Umatilla] reservation go every year to hunt, fish, and dig roots in that vicinity, I deemed it necessary to go with them, taking with me the interpreter, and it was only with great effort that difficulty was avoided, as many of the settlers were disposed to prevent the Indians from going there at all." The *Statesman* saw this as an opportunity to ramp up its call for the removal of the Indians of the Umatilla reservation to the Wallowa reservation and to finally open the land to White settlement. However, the division of the Wallowa Valley was transcribed by the BIA and made official as an absurd north-south division. Thus, the Wallowa band was assigned to the choice agricultural northern half—among an increasing number of White settlers—and the more inaccessible high valley, including Wallowa Lake, was declared public domain.[5] Instead of rectifying the error, two years later, President Grant simply rescinded the executive order that had established the reservation.

Cornoyer annually complained of the lack of appropriations to support the stipulations of the 1855 treaty. In 1874, he was still requesting a map of the reservation survey completed three years earlier. The reservation was supposed to comprise 512,000 acres. However, the survey lopped off a large section on its east side, ending up with 326,551 acres (map 10). The BIA's chronic neglect led to Cornoyer's (temporary) resignation in 1875.

In the months that Cornoyer was gone, the chiefs began discussing leaving the Umatilla for another reservation. Both Homli and the Cayuse Young Chief visited the *Statesman* office with interpreters to explain that "the Indians fully recognize the necessity of a removal." With the expiration of the treaty looming, the chiefs were hoping to visit the president to work out a new treaty.[6] At the same time, the Northwest press was confident that a new bill to close the reservation would soon be passed by Congress. Young Joseph visited the Umatilla reservation in April to encourage the chiefs to insist on joining with his band on a reestablished Wallowa reservation (an option fully supported in Walla Walla but energetically opposed in Salem).[7] However, in a series of councils during 1876–77, Gen. Oliver Howard, Commander of the Department of the Columbia, insisted that all the non-treaty Nez Perce would relocate to the Nez Perce reservation. In

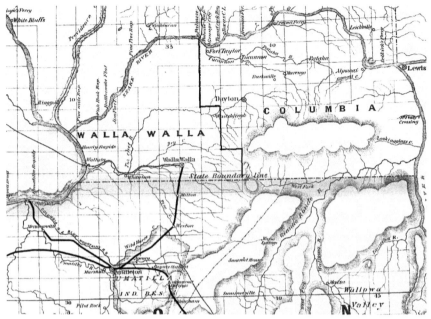

Map 10. *Washington Territory, 1878*, Portland: J. K. Gill & Co. (detail). The stage roads from Walla Walla, The Dalles, and Umatilla City to Boise City (over La Grande) are emphasized. The map includes the proposed routes of the Columbia River and Blue Mountain Railroad and the Seattle and Walla Walla Railroad. (Library of Congress Geography and Map Division. https://loc.gov/item/98687150/.)

———

response to Joseph's claim that the Americans had no right to his land, Howard cited the "doctrine of discovery": "under the law of nations the title of our government to this whole country, drained by the Columbia, by right of discovery and occupation, had been admitted by other great nations."[8]

In his record of one of these councils, David Jerome of the Board of Indian Commissioners concluded that all the Indians in the Northwest should be consolidated onto either the Nez Perce or the Yakama reservation. He was adamant that the Umatilla reservation needed to be sold off, adding bizarrely, "The Indian will never attain a knowledge of the arts of husbandry, and become independent and self-sustaining, without the advantages of good soil and other appliances deemed essential for successful farming."[9] Any hope for a Wallowa reservation was squashed at a council at Lapwai in May, when Howard forced the non-treaty Indians to select sites for their people on the Nez Perce reservation.

The ensuing desperate trek known to history as the "Nez Perce War" brought panic to Walla Walla and renewed dread to the Umatilla reservation. Settlements and farms were abandoned for the security of Walla Walla. The papers spread rumors and generated terror of a general Indian uprising: Spokan and Columbia River warriors were attacking from the north, the reservations would attack from the south; the Nez Perce were winning every skirmish with the Army; "the young men have left the Umatilla reservation, and are now far on their way to join Joseph and his hostile bands."[10] Cornoyer sent messengers to the Columbia to urge all Indians onto the reservations for protection. The movement of these families through the Walla Walla Valley generated further panic.

On June 28, Cornoyer and twenty-nine unarmed headmen from the reservation rode into Walla Walla to assure the citizens of their peaceful stance.[11] Nonetheless, alarm of an imminent Spokan attack was enough to cancel Fourth of July festivities. Instead, 200 Walla Wallans met at the courthouse to discuss the formation of a militia. Miles C. Moore informed Governor Ferry, "Walla Walla is filled with refugees, panic stricken. . . . Indians are driving off stock and committing depredations of every character." He requested weapons and authority to raise two militia companies.[12] Ferry arrived with 200 firearms a week later. Of course, no attack occurred. And Walla Wallans were relieved by reports of the eastward movement of the violence. By the time the non-treaty Nez Perce were subdued in October, Walla Wallans had settled back to business as usual. On the Umatilla reservation, people were coming to terms with the loss of their cousins and the Wallowa Valley.

––––––––

Having learned a lesson in 1877, perhaps, the papers downplayed rumors of Indian uprisings in 1878—including rumors of violence among the Bannock in faraway southern Idaho. However, this turned out to be a real threat to the city and the reservation. After the first skirmishes with the Army, the Bannock warriors moved westward toward their Paiute cousins in southeastern Oregon. Once again, isolated settlers flocked to the cities for protection. Rumors generated panic. Governor Ferry arrived in Walla Walla on July 7 to raise a militia to support the Army.

Pendleton was protected by a militia, but it refused to protect the reservation. Many Indians were harvesting and fishing off the reservation on July 14 when the Bannock-Paiutes attacked the reservation. They were led by Egan, a Cayuse who had been abducted as a child. They burned houses and agency buildings, ran off horses and cattle, and destroyed crops. Some reservation warriors had sided with Egan; however, details were unclear (three Umatillas were later executed for having done so). What is known is that a band of reservation warriors, led by the Cayuse headman Umapine, rode out that evening and returned the following morning with Egan's head, 25 scalps, and about 300 horses, thus putting an end to the greatest threat of the "Bannock War." When the dust had settled, Cornoyer reported,

> Some of the most industrious and worthy Indians on the reservation have been reduced from comfortable circumstances to poverty by their losses. . . . There is an uneasy feeling manifested among these Indians, and an anxiety to know what the policy of the government will be toward them upon the expiration of the treaty next year. They are aware that the press and people of this section of the country are clamorous for their removal, and charge them with being in sympathy with the hostiles, notwithstanding the fact of their having killed [Egan], the war chief of the hostiles. . . . In fact they showed their animosity to the hostiles by doing more damage to them while in the vicinity of the reservation than was done by all the troops that fought them during the campaign. . . .
>
> The men who rail against them do not wish to take these facts into consideration, for the simple reason that they wish to be rid of the Indians, and have the reservation thrown open for settlement. This feeling between the Indians and whites, if it continues, will lead to further trouble in the future, unless a military force is left here to protect the Indians until the question whether they are to remain here or not is definitely settled.[13]

After receiving Cornoyer's report, the Commissioner of Indian Affairs, Ezra A. Hayt (1877–80), concluded, "I deem it expedient that the tribes occupying the Umatilla Reservation be removed to [the Yakama reservation], and that the lands thus vacated be sold."[14]

The agents often pointed out that the people of the Umatilla reservation were well versed in the stipulations of the treaty. However, no one knew exactly what would happen when the treaty expired in 1879. The immediate future for reservation and non-reservation Sahaptians was no less unpredictable and insecure than it had been during the previous two decades. A new road and a telegraph line were built through the reservation. And plans were under way to construct a railroad through the reservation. The non-Indian population of the town of Pendleton—on the reservation—would soon outnumber the reservation's population. Instances of off-reservation Indians being shot were increasing. The reservation leaders met with President Hayes in April 1879 (fig. 51), and talk turned from consolidation of the reservations to dividing them into allotments. Yet absolutely no one could predict the BIA's next ideological turn. Six different commissioners would head the BIA during the 1880s.

Figure 51. Howlishwanpum, based on a photograph taken in San Francisco, March 1879. He was en route to Washington, DC, to meet with President Hayes and Secretary of the Interior Carl Schurz, accompanied by Homli, Winampsnut, Umapine, Young Chief, and Chief Moses of the mid-Columbia. In Washington, Schurz explained his post-treaty plan of dividing the Umatilla reservation into 160-acre allotments. On their return journey, the chiefs requested a visit to Chief Joseph in Indian Territory but were denied. Howlishwanpum died March 19, 1880. (*Frank Leslie's Illustrated Newspaper*, 48, no. 1231 [May 3, 1879], 133.)

Acknowledgments

I lived in Walla Walla for about a decade before I took any real interest in the region's history. My exclusive focus was European cultural history. I was inspired to study regional history through the opening of the Tamástslikt Cultural Institute and the activities of a number of local historians and preservationists (including Bob Bennett, Mary Meeker, Mark Anderson, and Joe Drazan.). The architecture of Walla Walla increasingly came to play a prominent role in my courses. In 2015, I introduced a seminar on local architecture and history, which turned my attention to the Whitman College and Northwest Archives, and to what used to be called New Western History. Before I was aware of the work of historians like Patricia Nelson Limerick, Richard White, and Eugene Moehring, I was similarly dedicated to unfixing archaic historical narratives in European cultural history. I can only hope that my debt to the work of these historians is evident.

This book started out as an architectural history of the city of Walla Walla, which is exemplary of so many small cities in the Far West. However, as I became immersed in the material, buildings increasingly became punctuations to the narrative, rather than the force driving the narrative. The city's prehistory, its establishment at its particular location, and the displaced people required far more substantial contextualization.

During the earliest parts of this project, invaluable assistance was provided by the WCNA archivists Melissa Salrin, Ben Murphy, and Dana Bronson, by Shannon Buchal of the Fort Walla Walla Museum, and by the staff at the Oregon Historical Society Research Library. My students and my friend and colleague Matt Reynolds supplied limitless encouragement and inspiration. With the lockdown and unconstrained research time, this project took on a life of its own. I became indebted to Jen Pope and the staff at the Penrose Library and to the staff at the Guin Library in Newport for supplying me with every desired publication. Lindsay Muha and Edward Singer provided unique assistance at the National Archives. As the manuscript began to take shape, my friend James Warren, wordsmith (jameswarrenediting.com), brought clarity to far too many words. Jennifer Karson Engum of Tamástslikt and Lee Micklin generously read sections.

Matt Reynolds and J. Philip Gruen gave the manuscript elaborate readings and provided essential advice. The arduous task of image gathering was made *un*arduous thanks to Alexis Hickey of the WCNA, Frances Kaplan and Debra Kaufman at the California Historical Society, Eileen Price at the Washington State Historical Society, and Nicola Woods at ROM, Toronto. I am grateful to Erin Humphrey (erinhumphreydesign .com) for generously providing last-minute image assistance. My thanks to Gary Morris, copyeditor. Thanks to all the students in my Walla Walla architecture seminars, and to Joel Gaytan and Matt Levy. Thanks to my friends and family in Walla Walla, Yachats, Tacoma, New Orleans, and Wales for patiently listening to me ramble about this stuff. A big thank you to Linda Bathgate for her faith in this project. Finally, I lack the eloquence to sufficiently express my gratitude to my wife, Susan Babilon, for reading and reading, and listening and listening, and walking and walking, and playing and playing, and for 44 years of maximum joy.

—Dennis Crockett
Wakonda Beach, Oregon

I acknowledge that I reside within the ancestral homeland of the Alsea people, whose treaty with the US government in 1855 was never ratified by Congress. In 1875, their land was opened to American settlement, without compensation, and they were coerced onto the Siletz reservation. In 1977, two decades after the termination of the Siletz reservation, the descendants of the Alsea and other Indigenous coastal people successfully regained federal recognition as the Confederated Tribes of Siletz Indians and a reservation was reestablished in 1980.

Murder is the third leading cause of death for Indigenous women in this country. The murder rate for women living on reservations is ten times higher than the national average. I urge you to become acquainted with MMIW.

Notes

Introduction

1. Isaac I. Stevens, *Narrative and Final Report of Explorations for a Route for a Pacific Railroad . . . from St. Paul to Puget Sound*, 36th Cong., 1st sess. (1859), H.R. Doc. 56, 196.
2. Hazard Stevens, *The Life of Isaac Ingalls Stevens*, vol. 2 (Boston: Houghton, Mifflin, 1900), 30–1.
3. Col. Lawrence Kip, "The Indian Council at Walla Walla, May and June, 1855," *Sources of the History of Oregon* 1, no. 2 (1897), 9–10.

Part I: "The Most Hostile Spot on the Whole Line of Communication"

1. Robert M. Netting, *Cultural Ecology*, 2nd ed. (Prospect Heights, IL: Waveland, 1986), 10.

1. The Cayuse and the Walla Walla Valley

1. See Verne F. Ray, "Native Village and Groupings of the Columbia Basin," *Pacific Northwest Quarterly* 27, no. 2 (April 1936), 99–152; Robert Suphan, *Oregon Indians II: Ethnographical Report of the Umatilla, Walla Walla and Cayuse Indians* (New York: Garland, 1974), 145–6; Theodore Stern, "Cayuse, Umatilla, and Walla Walla," in *Handbook of North American Indians 12: Plateau*, ed. William C. Sturtevant (Washington, DC: Smithsonian, 1998), 395; Robert Ruby and John Brown, *The Cayuse Indians: Imperial Tribesmen of Old Oregon* (Norman: University of Oklahoma Press, 1972), 13; and Eugene S. Hunn et al., "They Are Gathering for Winter," *Cáw Pawá Láakni/They Are Not Forgotten: Sahaptian Place Names Atlas of the Cayuse, Umatilla, and Walla Walla* (Pendleton, OR: Tamástslikt Cultural Institute, 2015), 36–7.
2. It is believed that the Sahaptin and Nez Perce languages evolved from the same Plateau Penutian family; the term "Sahaptian" encompasses both languages.
3. The Cayuse language may not have been directly related to the Sahaptian languages at all. See Bruce J. Rigsby, "On Cayuse-Molala Relatability," *International Journal of American Linguistics* 32, no. 4 (October 1966), 369–78; and "The Waiilatpuan Problem: More on Cayuse-Molala Relatability," *Northwest Anthropological Research Notes* 3, no. 1 (Spring 1969), 68–146.
4. On Cayuse-Nez Perce kinship ties, see Deward E. Walker Jr., "Nez Perce," in *Handbook of North American Indians 12: Plateau*, 420–38.
5. Confederated Tribes of the Umatilla Indian Reservation, *Comprehensive Plan* (2010, updated 2018), 20. https://ctuir.org/media/sychezsg/2018updated-2010_comprehensiveplan -webversion.pdf.
6. See E. Thomas Morning Owl, "Tamánwit," and Armand Minthorn, "On Tamánwit," in *Wiyaxayxt/Wiyaakaa'awn/As Days Go By: Our History, Our Land, Our People—The Cayuse, Umatilla, and Walla Walla*, ed. Jennifer Karson (Seattle: University of Washington Press, 2006), 3, 224; and Phillip E. Cash, "Our Storied Earth," *Cáw Pawá Láakni*, 21–4. Morning Owl notes, "It is good to remember that there is no single canonical version of a story shared by all Sahaptian-speaking people." "The Land of the Story Time," *Cáw Pawá Láakni*, 27–9.

7. Christopher L. Miller, *Prophetic Worlds: Indians and Whites on the Columbia Plateau* (New Brunswick, NJ: Rutgers University Press, 1985), 16.

8. On precontact Sahaptian cosmology, see Larry Cebula's *Plateau Indians and the Quest for Spiritual Power, 1700–1850* (Lincoln: University of Nebraska Press, 2003), chapter 1.

9. See Verne Ray, *Cultural Relations in the Plateau of Northwestern America* (Los Angeles: Southwest Museum, 1939), 102–13.

10. Hunn, "They Are Gathering for Winter," 36.

11. *Cáw Pawá Láakni*, 124.

12. Bruce Rigsby, "The Stevens Treaties, Indian Claims Commission Docket 264, and the Ancient One Known as Kennewick Man," in *The Power of Promises: Rethinking Indian Treaties in the Pacific Northwest*, ed. Alexandra Harmon (Seattle: University of Washington Press, 2008), 257, 272. Unfortunately, much knowledge of Sahaptian place names has been lost, especially in the Walla Walla Valley. See *Cáw Pawá Láakni*; in particular, Bruce J. Rigsby's "Foreword: *Iwaačanáay* 'This Is How It Was,'" xii.

13. See Stern, "Cayuse, Umatilla, and Walla Walla," 416–7.

14. See Erna Gunther, "The Westward Movement of Some Plains Traits," *American Anthropologist* 52, no. 2 (April–June 1950), 174–80; and Stern, "Cayuse, Umatilla, and Walla Walla," 397–9.

15. See Eugene Hunn, "Columbia Plateau Indian Place Names: What Can They Teach Us?," *Journal of Linguistic Anthropology* 6, no. 1 (June 1996), 3–26; and Alvin M. Josephy, *Nez Perce Country* (Lincoln: University of Nebraska Press, 2007), 7–9.

16. A coup in this context is a brilliant, sudden, and usually highly successful stroke or act. Coups were visually represented by marks—often colored stripes—displayed on various possessions of a warrior.

17. Early accounts of the treatment of slaves among the Sahaptians vary wildly. A 1920s survey of more than eighty firsthand accounts found numerous unique anecdotes but came away without a clear or consistent assessment. Elsie Frances Dennis, "Indian Slavery in Pacific Northwest," *Oregon Historical Quarterly* 31, nos. 1–3 (March, June, September 1930), 69–81, 181–95, 285–96. More recently, Ruby and Brown came to the same inconclusion in *Indian Slavery in the Pacific Northwest* (Spokane, WA: Clarke, 1993), 232–42.

18. See Robert Suphan, *Oregon Indians II*, 340–8; and Stern, "Cayuse, Umatilla, and Walla Walla," 418.

19. Daniel Lee and Joseph H. Frost, *Ten Years in Oregon* (New York: n.p., 1844), 176–7. The word "Kiuse" is misprinted throughout the book as "Kinse." Lee estimated that 500 Sahaptians would winter at Wascopam.

20. Robert Boyd, *People of The Dalles: The Indians of Wascopam Mission* (Lincoln: University of Nebraska Press, 2004), 293.

21. Thomas J. Farnham, *Travels in the Great Western Prairies, the Anahuac and Rocky Mountains, and in the Oregon Territory* (New York: Greeley & McElrath, 1843), 141. Farnham's knowledge of the Cayuse may have derived from conversations with Lee and Perkins that were only partly understood or recalled.

22. Robert Boyd, *People of The Dalles*, 63–8; Eugene S. Hunn, *Nch'i-Wána, 'The Big River': Mid-Columbia Indians and Their Land* (Seattle: University of Washington Press, 1991), 64–5.

23. Meriwether Lewis, May 5, 1806, *The Journals of the Lewis and Clark Expedition*, ed. Gary Moulton (Lincoln: University of Nebraska Press, 2002). https://lewisandclarkjournals.unl.edu/item/lc.jrn.1806-05-05#lc.jrn.1806-05-05.02.

24. See Harry Holbert Turney-High, *The Flathead Indians of Montana* (Menasha, WI: American Anthropological Association, 1937), 97–104; Herbert J. Spinden, *The Nez Perce Indians* (Lancaster, PA: American Anthropological Association, 1908), 196; Ray, *Cultural Relations*, 102–13; Luther S. Cressman, *The Sandal and the Cave: The Indians of Oregon* (Portland, OR:

Beaver, 1962), 38–9; and Gerald A. Oetelaar, "Beyond Activity Areas: Structure and Symbolism in the Organization and Use of Space inside Tipis," *Plains Anthropologist* 45, no. 171 (February 2000), 35–61.

25. Robert Boyd, ed., *Indians, Fire, and the Land in the Pacific Northwest* (Corvallis: Oregon State University Press, 1999), 2–3. See also William G. Robbins, *Landscapes of Promise: The Oregon Story, 1800–1940* (Seattle: University of Washington Press, 2009), 42–7.

26. See Robert Boyd, *The Coming of the Spirit of Pestilence: Introduced Infectious Diseases and Population Decline among Northwest Coast Indians, 1774–1874* (Seattle: University of Washington Press, 1999), chapter 1.

27. Hunn, *Nch'i-Wána, "The Big River,"* 237–41.

28. See Elizabeth Vibert, "'The Natives Were Strong to Live': Reinterpreting Early-Nineteenth-Century Prophetic Movements in the Columbia Plateau," *Ethnohistory* 42, no. 2 (Spring 1995), 197–229; Miller, *Prophetic Worlds*, 15–21; and Cebula, *Plateau Indians and the Quest for Spiritual Power*, chapter 2. Many of the prophesies of the time were later associated with subsequent events, like the coming of the Whites or Christianity. Jarold Ramsey refers to this as "retroactive prophecy" in *Reading the Fire: Essays in the Traditional Indian Literatures of the Far West* (Seattle: University of Washington Press, 1999), 194–207.

29. Alexander Mackenzie, *Voyages from Montreal to the Frozen and Pacific Oceans* (Philadelphia: Morgan, 1802), 388, 391.

30. Barbara B. Oberg, ed., *The Papers of Thomas Jefferson 40, 4 March–10 July 1803* (Princeton, NJ: Princeton University Press, 2013), 177–80.

31. Meriwether Lewis and William Clark, May 1, 1806; Patrick Gass, July 4, 1806; and William Clark, April 27, 1806, *The Journals of the Lewis and Clark Expedition*.

32. Clark, June 6, 1806; and Lewis, June 8, 1806, *The Journals of the Lewis and Clark Expedition*.

33. See David J. Peck, *Or Perish in the Attempt: The Hardship and Medicine of the Lewis and Clark Expedition* (Lincoln: University of Nebraska Press, 2011), chapter 16.

2. The Fur Trade in the Walla Walla Region

1. T. C. Elliott, ed., "Journal of David Thompson," *Quarterly of the Oregon Historical Society* 15, no. 1 (March 1914), 57–8.

2. See Robert J. Miller, *Native America, Discovered and Conquered: Thomas Jefferson, Lewis and Clark, and Manifest Destiny* (Lincoln: University of Nebraska Press, 2008).

3. Gabriel Franchère, *Narrative of a Voyage to the Northwest Coast of America in the Years 1811, 1812, 1813, and 1814*, trans. J. V. Huntington (New York: Redfield, 1854), 123–4.

4. Alexander Ross, *Adventures of the First Settlers on the Oregon or Columbia River* (London: Smith, Elder, 1849), 87–8.

5. The fur trade companies brought their own unique corporate hierarchies to the region. With major decisions in the hands of boards of shareholders in the companies' home cities, chief factors, chief traders, or junior partners were assigned to oversee regional operations from "factories"—central collection centers. These well-educated men—usually Anglo-Scottish—received shares of their post's profits. Each trading post included at least one clerk, and smaller posts were overseen by clerks or postmasters. With distinguished service, these men could be elevated to chief traders. The vast majority of company employees were salaried under contract: trappers, guides, interpreters, laborers, and *voyageurs* (transporters of furs, people, and supplies by canoe). They were primarily Canadien and Métis but also included Iroquois, Delawares, and Hawaiians.

6. The term *les dalles* was used by the *voyageurs* for rapids through deep rocky ravines. The area above the current city of The Dalles was known as *les grand dalles de la Columbia*.

7. Ross, *Adventures of the First Settlers*, 126–7, 128–9, 131.

8. Alexander Ross, *Fur Hunters of the Far West*, vol. 1 (London: Smith, Elder, 1855), 218–9. Some Cayuse did trap beaver; however, those that traded pelts were primarily intermediaries, obtaining them from others.

9. Ross, *Adventures of the First Settlers*, 216–7.

10. Ross, 225–6.

11. Ross, *Fur Hunters of the Far West*, 175.

12. Ross, *Fur Hunters of the Far West*, 251. The Northern Shoshone, Bannock, and Northern Paiute were known collectively to the fur traders as the Snake Indians.

13. The Iroquois had established a reputation as excellent hunters and trappers. The NWC also hired a large number of Hawaiians in 1816 to fill a labor shortage. See Richard S. Mackie, *Trading beyond the Mountains: The British Fur Trade on the Pacific, 1793–1843* (Vancouver: University of British Columbia Press, 1997), 20.

14. The NWC began trading weapons with the Sahaptians at this time. It was a particularly aggressive period for the Sahaptians, who carried out raids against the Northern Shoshone and on the villages of the Narrows. Gray H. Whaley suggests that the latter may have been carried out on behalf of the fur traders. *Oregon and the Collapse of Illahee: U.S. Empire and the Transformation of an Indigenous World, 1792–1859* (Chapel Hill: University of North Carolina Press, 2010), 59–63.

15. Ross, *Fur Hunters of the Far West*, 175–6.

16. Ross, 214–7.

17. George Simpson, *Narrative of a Journey round the World, during the Years 1841 and 1842*, vol. 1 (London: Colburn, 1847), 160; John Kirk Townsend, *The Narrative of a Journey across the Rocky Mountains to the Columbia River* (Philadelphia, 1839), 155; and W. H. Gray, *History of Oregon, 1792–1849* (Portland: Harris and Holman, 1870), 144.

18. Ross, *Fur Hunters of the Far West*, 176.

19. Ross, 185.

20. The HBC was organized on the lines of a colonial government.

21. John Dunn, *History of the Oregon Territory and British North-American Fur Trade* (London: Edwards & Hughes, 1844), 154.

22. The English referred to Pacific Islanders in general as "Kanakas," which was derived from the term by which the Hawaiians identified themselves (*kānaka maoli*). The number of Hawaiian laborers in the Northwest increased after the establishment of a British consulate in Hawaii in 1825. See Jean Barman and Bruce McIntyre Watson, *Leaving Paradise: Indigenous Hawaiians in the Pacific Northwest, 1787–1898* (Honolulu: University of Hawai'i Press, 2006).

23. Charles Wilkes, *Narrative of the United States Exploring Expedition during the Years 1838, 1839, 1840, 1841, 1842*, vol. 4 (Philadelphia: Lea and Blanchard, 1844), 419.

24. Theodore Stern, *Chiefs and Chief Traders: Indian Relations at Fort Nez Percés, 1818–1855* (Corvallis: Oregon State University Press, 1993), 102–3.

25. E. E. Rich, ed., *Simpson's 1828 Journey to the Columbia* (London: Champlain Society, 1947), 51.

26. Frederick Merk, ed., *Fur Trade and Empire: George Simpson's Journal . . . 1824–1825* (Cambridge, 1831), 104.

27. Ross, *Fur Hunters of the Far West*, 230–1.

28. Merk, 127–8, 137.

29. "The Character Book of George Simpson, 1832," in *Hudson's Bay Miscellany, 1670–1870*, ed. Glyndwr Williams (Winnipeg: Hudson's Bay Record Society, 1975), 192–3.

30. Stern, 211, n. 25.

31. E. E. Rich, ed., *McLoughlin's Fort Vancouver Letters: First Series 1825–38* (London: Champlain Society, 1941), 196.

32. Larry Cebula argues that the Sahaptians were far more interested in the traders' "spirit power"—their immunity from disease—than in the weapons and other goods that they traded. *Plateau Indians and the Quest for Spiritual Power* (Lincoln: University of Nebraska Press, 2003), chapter 3. Cebula refers to the new syncretic forms of devotion on the plateau of the 1830s as the "Columbian Religion."
33. Merk, 108.

3. American Colonization of Oregon 1832–40

1. At the convention, among other things, they agreed to recognize joint occupancy for a period of ten years. The Columbia and Snake rivers were recognized as the unofficial borders, pending a formal treaty. (This article was extended for an additional twenty years.) The United States further secured a foothold in the Far West with the Adams-Onís Treaty with Spain in 1819–21, which established the 42nd parallel north as the border between Alta California and the Oregon Country.
2. Hall Kelley, "Manual of the Oregon Expedition" (Charlestown, MA: Wheildon & Williams, 1831), 8–11.
3. Curtis J. Lyons noted in 1892, "People in these days can hardly realize how important an element [adobe] was in the early building up of Honolulu." "Traces of Spanish Influence in the Hawaiian Islands," *Papers of the Hawaiian Historical Society*, no. 2 (1892), 25–7.
4. Cited in Edmond Mallett, "The Origin of the Flathead Mission of the Rocky Mountains," *Records of the American Catholic Historical Society of Philadelphia* II (1886–88), 188–9.
5. G. P. Disoway, "The Flat-Head Indians," *The Christian Advocate and Journal* (March 1, 1833), 1. Josephy detailed the Nez Perce understanding of the "Macedonian Call" in *The Nez Perce Indians and the Opening of the Northwest* (New York: Houghton Mifflin Harcourt, 1997), 93–8.
6. Wilbur Fisk, "Proclamation," *The Christian Advocate and Journal* (March 22, 1833), 118.
7. "Diary of Reverend Jason Lee II," *Quarterly of the Oregon Historical Society* 17, no. 3 (September 1916), 242, 258.
8. Daniel Lee and Joseph H. Frost, *Ten Years in Oregon* (New York: n.p., 1844), 100, 127; and "Diary of Jason Lee II," 264.
9. "Address of the Prudential Committee," *Missionary Herald* 23, no. 12 (December 1827), 396–7.
10. Samuel Parker, *Journal of an Exploring Tour beyond the Rocky Mountains* (Ithaca, NY: Andrus, 1838), 13, 48, 76–8; and F. G. Young, ed., "Journal and Report by Dr. Marcus Whitman of His Tour of Exploration with Rev. Samuel Parker in 1835 beyond the Rocky Mountains," *Oregon Historical Quarterly* 28, no. 3 (September 1927), 247–9.
11. Washington Irving, *Adventures of Captain Bonneville: Or, Scenes beyond the Rocky Mountains of the Far West*, vol. 1 (London: Routledge, 1837), 171.
12. J. B. A. Brouillet, *Protestantism in Oregon: Account of the Murder of Dr. Whitman, and the Ungrateful Calumnies of H. H. Spalding, Protestant Missionary* (New York: Cozans, 1853), 10–1.
13. In a letter to the ABCFM in 1839, Whitman excoriated Parker for his complete lack of preparation for their arrival in 1836: "he neglected even to write a single letter containing any information concerning the country, Indians, prospects, or advice of any kind whatever." Clifford M. Drury, *Marcus and Narcissa Whitman and the Opening of Old Oregon*, vol. 1 (Glendale, CA: Clark, 1973), 282.
14. T. C. Elliott, "The Coming of the White Women, 1836 (II)," *Oregon Historical Quarterly* 37, no. 3 (September 1936), 186–7.

15. Clifford M. Drury, ed., *The Mountains We Have Crossed: Diaries and Letters of the Oregon Mission, 1838* (Lincoln: University of Nebraska Press, 1999), 157.
16. Whitman also believed he was grooming the Nez Perce boy Richard into his personal interpreter. However, he soon expelled the boy from the house for stealing and gambling.
17. See Genevieve McCoy, "The Difficulties of Translating Mission Theory into Practice: The Whitman-Spalding Nez Perce Mission," *The Journal of Presbyterian History* 77, no. 3 (Fall 1999), 181–94.
18. Drury, *Marcus and Narcissa Whitman*, 1, 261–2.
19. Theodore Stern, *Chiefs and Change in the Oregon Country: Indian Relations at Fort Nez Percés, 1818–1855* (Corvallis: Oregon State University Press, 1996), 56.
20. "Spalding and Whitman Letters, 1837," *Oregon Historical Quarterly* 37, no. 2 (June 1936), 123.
21. Elliott, 52.
22. Elliott, 58–61.
23. Myron Eells, *Father Eells* (Boston: Congregational Publishing Society, 1894), 62.
24. Drury, ed., *The Mountains We Have Crossed*, 109.
25. Drury, *Marcus and Narcissa Whitman*, 1, 388.
26. "Letters Written by Mrs. Whitman to Her Relatives in New York," *Transactions of the Nineteenth Annual Reunion of the Oregon Pioneer Association for 1891* (Portland: n.p., 1893), 134.
27. "Letters Written by Mrs. Whitman," 133–4.
28. Lyman Beecher, *A Plea for the West* (Cincinnati: Truman and Smith, 1835), 11, 142–3.
29. On his second visit to French Prairie in 1839, Blanchet discovered that the Methodists had circulated copies of *Maria Monk* among the Canadien settlers. Francis Norbert Blanchet, *Historical Sketches of the Catholic Church in Oregon, during the Past Forty Years* (Portland: n.p., 1878), 90–1.
30. Blanchet, 26–7.
31. Blanchet took great joy in discussing the failures of the Protestant missions in Oregon. Blanchet, 18.
32. Stern, 62.
33. Drury, *Marcus and Narcissa Whitman*, 2, 526.
34. All three had married daughters of the Nez Perce headman Thunder Eyes, known to the missionaries as James.

4. Oregon Fever

1. F. G. Young, ed., "Journal of Medorem Crawford: An Account of His Trip across the Plains with the Oregon Pioneers of 1842," *Sources of the History of Oregon* 1, no. 1 (1897), 20.
2. Alvin M. Josephy, *The Nez Perce Indians and the Opening of the Northwest* (New York: Houghton Mifflin Harcourt, 1997), 229.
3. For details on White's council, see Gustavus Hines, *Oregon: Its History, Condition and Prospects* (Buffalo: Derby, 1851), chapter 9; and Theodore Stern, *Chiefs and Change in the Oregon Country: Indian Relations at Fort Nez Percés, 1818–1855* (Corvallis: Oregon State University Press, 1996), chapters 14 and 15. According to A. B. Roberts, Five Crows stood 6'5" tall and was "at least" 250 lb. "Reminiscences of a Life in the Far West," 6, WCMss055, Box 1, Roberts Family Papers, Whitman College and Northwest Archives.
4. W. M. "St. Louis, April 14, 1843," *New York Herald*, April 26, 1843.
5. "From Oregon," *New York Daily Tribune*, February 21, 1843.
6. "Arrival from Oregon," *New York Weekly Tribune*, March 30, 1843.
7. "The Far West—The Rocky Mountains," *New York Herald*, September 18, 1843.

8. Clifford M. Drury, *Marcus and Narcissa Whitman and the Opening of Old Oregon*, vol. 2 (Glendale, CA: Clark, 1973), 106.

9. Drury, 117.

10. J. Henry Brown, *Brown's Political History of Oregon*, vol. 1 (Portland: W. B. Allen, 1892), 148–54.

11. P. J. de Smet, *Letters and Sketches with a Narrative of a Year's Residence among the Indian Tribes of the Rocky Mountains* (Philadelphia: Fithian, 1843), 231–3.

12. The Catholic ladder was a pictorial catechism adapted by Jesuit missionaries in the seventeenth century. In its crudest form, a long, flat stick was marked with horizontal dashes representing the centuries from Genesis to the birth of Christ, read from the bottom up; another thirty-three dashes represented the life and Resurrection of Christ. The remaining vertical section generally led to the present day with symbols for various relevant historical events and people, and concluded with the path to salvation. The Catholic ladders developed by Blanchet always emphasized the Protestants losing their way. De Smet's ladder included text and elaborate engravings.

13. William Augustus Mowry, *Marcus Whitman and the Early Days of Oregon* (New York: Burdett, 1901), 262–3.

14. Robert Fleming Heizer, "Walla Walla Indian Expeditions to the Sacramento Valley," *California Historical Society Quarterly* 21, no. 1 (March 1942), 1–7.

15. Overton Johnson and William H. Winter, *Route across the Rocky Mountains* (Lafayette, IN: Semans, 1846), 109–13. The authors also expressed concern over the mutual animosities of the Protestant and Catholic missionaries.

16. On the other hand, Joel Palmer's overland party of 1845 found only friendly, eager trade partners among the Cayuse. *Journal of Travels over the Rocky Mountains to the Mouth of the Columbia River* (Cincinnati: James, 1852), 53–6.

17. Drury, 164–7.

18. Section 1; Article 3. La Fayette Grover, ed., *The Oregon Archives* (Salem: n.p., 1853), 29.

19. "Dr. White's Letters," *Oregon Spectator*, November 12, 1846.

20. John D. Unruh Jr. notes that only 4 percent of the estimated 10,000 overlander deaths were the result of Indian violence. *The Plains Across: The Overland Emigrants and the Trans-Mississippi West, 1840–60* (Urbana: University of Illinois Press, 1993), 408.

21. Fred Wilbur Powell, *Hall Jackson Kelley, Prophet of Oregon* (Portland: Ivy Press, 1917), chapter 7.

22. See Benjamin Madley, *An American Genocide: The United States and the California Indian Catastrophe, 1846–1873* (New Haven: Yale University Press, 2017), chapter 2.

23. John Beeson, *A Plea for the Indians* (New York: n.p., 1858), 15–6.

24. The most popular racialist publication of the mid-century was Gliddon and Nott's *Types of Mankind or Ethnological Researches* of 1854, which underwent ten editions. See Reginald Horsman, *Race and Manifest Destiny: The Origins of American Racial Anglo-Saxonism* (Cambridge: Harvard University Press, 1981), chapter 7; Robert E. Bieder, *Science Encounters the Indian, 1820–1880: The Early Years of American Ethnology* (Norman: University of Oklahoma Press, 1986); and Gray H. Whaley, *Oregon and the Collapse of Illahee: U.S. Empire and the Transformation of an Indigenous World, 1792–1859* (Chapel Hill: University of North Carolina Press, 2010), chapter 5.

25. John L. O'Sullivan, "Annexation," *United States Magazine and Democratic Review* 17, no. 85 (July–August 1845), 5–10. O'Sullivan was concerned primarily with Mexican annexation but alluded to Oregon.

26. "Letter from M. M. M. [Morton M. McCarver]," *Oregon Spectator*, May 14, 1846.

27. "Fourth of July Celebration at Salem," *Oregon Spectator*, July 23, 1846.

28. "Annexation," *Oregon Spectator*, July 23, 1846.

5. 1847–48

1. J. B. A. Brouillet, *Protestantism in Oregon: Account of the Murder of Dr. Whitman, and the Ungrateful Calumnies of H. H. Spalding, Protestant Missionary* (New York: Cozans, 1853), 81.
2. Joseph Warren Revere, *A Tour of Duty in California* (New York: Francis, 1849), 147–8, 154, 162. See also Robert Fleming Heizer, "Walla Walla Indian Expeditions to the Sacramento Valley," *California Historical Society Quarterly* 21, no. 1 (March 1942), 1–7.
3. See "The War," *Californian*, November 21, 1846.
4. Clifford Drury, *Marcus Whitman, M. D.: Pioneer and Martyr* (Caldwell, ID: Caxton, 1937), 373. In August, seventeen-year-old Perrin Whitman and Alanson Hinman and his family (overlanders of 1844) were sent to take possession of Wascopam.
5. Francis Norbert Blanchet, *Historical Sketches of the Catholic Church in Oregon, During the Past Forty Years* (Portland: n.p., 1878), 159.
6. See Robert Boyd, "Pacific Northwest Measles Epidemic of 1847–1848," *Oregon Historical Quarterly* 95, no. 1 (Spring 1994), 6–47.
7. Boyd, 17.
8. Brouillet, *Protestantism in Oregon*, 17–8, 41–4. McKay embodied the history of the Oregon fur trade: as a teenager in 1811, he had voyaged to Astoria on the *Tonquin* with his father (who was later killed); he had been employed in succession by the PFC, the NWC, and the HBC; and his mother married John McLoughlin.
9. "Trial of Cayuse Murderers," *Oregon Spectator*, May 30, 1850.
10. Many of the witnesses later published accounts of the incident; however, they are all tainted by time and prior publications.
11. See Henry Spalding's letter to the *Spectator*, January 20, 1848; and William Craig's testimony to Chief Justice Peter Burnett of July 11, 1848, in Brouillet, 33–6. The messenger stated that 197 Cayuse had died since the arrival of the first overlanders in September.
12. In an apparent attempt to have his life spared, the teacher Andrew Rogers declared that he had, in fact, heard Whitman and Spalding discuss plans for poisoning the Indians to take their land. He was later killed.
13. "The Massacre at Waiilatpu," *Oregon Spectator*, January 20, 1848.
14. J. Henry Brown, *Brown's Political History of Oregon*, vol. 1 (Portland: W. B. Allen, 1892), 356.
15. "News from the Army: Gilliam to Abernethy, Fort Walla Walla, February 29, 1848," *Oregon Spectator*, March 23, 1848.
16. Theodore Stern, *Chiefs and Change in the Oregon Country: Indian Relations at Fort Nez Percés, 1818–1855* (Corvallis: Oregon State University Press, 1996), 197–8.
17. Brown, 390.
18. Brown, 416.
19. Letters, H. A. G. Lee, July 6, 1848, *Oregon Spectator*, July 13, 1848.
20. "Return of Volunteers," *Oregon Free Press*, September 30, 1848.

6. Oregon Territory

1. "California," *Oregon Spectator*, August 10, 1848.
2. "The California 'Fever,'" *Oregon Free Press*, August 19, 1848.
3. "Gold," *Oregon Free Press*, September 2, 1848.
4. "Governor's Message," *Oregon Spectator*, October 4, 1849. This was the first issue of the *Spectator* since it went on gold rush hiatus in February.
5. "The Indian Difficulties," *Placer Times*, April 28, 1849.
6. "The Governor's Message," *Sacramento Transcript*, January 10, 1851.
7. Colonel Loring reported meeting with "several chiefs of the Cayuse and Nez Percé Indians" in the Grande Ronde Valley and "found them friendly and intelligent." Raymond W. Settle,

ed., *The March of the Mounted Riflemen . . . as Recorded in the Journals of Major Osborne Cross and George Gibbs and the Official Report of Colonel Loring* (Lincoln: University of Nebraska Press, 1989), 228–9, 339.

8. McBean wrote to Lane that Tawatoy had "planned to decoy all of [the accused] into his village to capture them—his nephew included." "Spitefully," Stern wrote, Tawatoy also wanted Lane to know that "Tomahas and his brother, Frank Escaloom, were in fact Nez Percés." Theodore Stern, *Chiefs and Change in the Oregon Country: Indian Relations at Fort Nez Percés, 1818–1855* (Corvallis: Oregon State University Press, 1996), 223.

9. The source for this anecdote is Frances Fuller Victor, *The Early Indian Wars of Oregon* (Salem: Baker, 1894), 249. However, it is unclear who among "his captors" could have interpreted and recorded his words.

10. For a thorough account of the trial and executions, see Ronald B. Lansing, *Juggernaut: The Whitman Massacre Trial, 1850* (San Francisco: Ninth Judicial Circuit Historical Society, 1993).

11. Robert H. Ruby and John A. Brown, *The Cayuse Indians: Imperial Tribesmen of Old Oregon* (Norman: University of Oklahoma Press, 1972), 168–9. Zachary Taylor (Whig), who succeeded James Polk (Democrat) as president in 1848, replaced Lane (in October 1849) with John P. Gaines. Gaines—who was offered the position after it had been declined by Abraham Lincoln—arrived in Oregon in August 1850 (after the death of Taylor).

12. Thurston held an almost obsessive contempt for John McLoughlin and the HBC. His lobbying efforts also resulted in the government refusing to recognize McLoughlin's land claim at Oregon City. Thurston died on his return voyage five months later.

13. Donald W. Meinig, *The Great Columbia Plain: A Historical Geography, 1805–1910* (Seattle: University of Washington Press, 1995), 154–8.

14. See Charles Wilkinson, *The People Are Dancing Again: The History of the Siletz Tribe of Western Oregon* (Seattle: University of Washington Press, 2010).

15. Roberta Stringham Brown and Patricia O'Connell Killen, eds., *Selected Letters of A. M. A. Blanchet: Bishop of Walla Walla and Nesqualy (1846–1879)* (Seattle: University of Washington Press, 2013), 54–5.

16. Lt. Sylvester Mowry, quoted in Priscilla Knuth, *"Picturesque" Frontier: The Army's Fort Dalles*, 2nd ed. (Portland: Oregon Historical Society, 1987), 11.

17. Among the first residents of what became the city of The Dalles was the family of Elizabeth Lord, who provided a remarkable memoir of the period: *Reminiscences of Eastern Oregon* (Portland: Irwin-Hodson, 1903). Her father was among the first civilians hired by the army.

7. Washington Territory

1. See Robert E. Ficken, *Washington Territory* (Pullman: Washington State University Press, 2002), chapter 1.

2. "Washington Territory—'All's Well That Ends Well,'" *The Columbian*, April 23, 1853.

3. Manypenny to Stevens, May 9, 1853, *Report of the Commissioner of Indian Affairs*, 33d Cong., 2d sess. (1854), S. Doc. 1, 453, 456.

4. Between his service in the Mexican War and his appointment as governor, Stevens headed the US Coast Survey Office. On Stevens, see Kent D. Richards, *Isaac I. Stevens: Young Man in a Hurry* (Pullman: Washington State University Press, 2016).

5. Stevens, 131–2.

6. Eugène-Casimir Chirouse was one of the five oblates that traveled from France to join Augustin Blanchet on his overland trek in 1847.

7. Stevens to Manypenny, December 29, 1853, *Communications from the Commissioner of Indian Affairs*, 33d Cong., 1st sess. (1853–54), S. Doc. 34, 13. Stevens stated much of the same in his

inaugural address to the people of Puget Sound. "Governor's Message, Feb 28, 1854," *Pioneer and Democrat*, March 4, 1854.

8. Stevens to Manypenny, September 16, 1854, *Report of the Commissioner of Indian Affairs* (1854), 455–6. On Stevens's treaties, see the special issue of *Oregon Historical Quarterly* devoted to "The Isaac I. Stevens and Joel Palmer Treaties, 1855–2005" (106, no. 3 [Fall 2005]); and Suann M. Reddick and Cary C. Collins, "Medicine Creek Remediated: Isaac Stevens and the Puyallup, Nisqually, and Muckleshoot Land Settlement at Fox Island, August 4, 1856," *Pacific Northwest Quarterly* 104, no. 2 (Spring 2013), 80–98.

9. The opening of the Panama Railroad in January 1855 accelerated communication with Washington; the Medicine Creek Treaty was ratified within ten weeks.

10. Hazard Stevens, *The Life of Isaac Ingalls Stevens* (Boston: Houghton, Mifflin, 1900), 2, 38.

11. Barbara Monroe, *Plateau Indian Ways with Words: The Rhetorical Tradition of the Tribes of the Inland Pacific Northwest* (Pittsburgh: University of Pittsburgh Press, 2014), 49. Monroe emphasizes the Sahaptians' concerns regarding translation and their insistence on understanding and being understood.

12. Source of all quotations from the council: Darrell Scott, ed., *A True Copy of the Record of the Official Proceedings at the Council in the Walla Walla Valley, 1855* (Fairfield, WA: Ye Galleon Press, 1985).

13. According to A. B. Roberts, "Reminiscences of a Life in the Far West," 6, WCMss055, Box 1, Roberts Family Papers, Whitman College and Northwest Archives.

14. Monroe attempts to retrieve some of the ironic tone in the transcriptions of the speeches at the Walla Walla council in *Plateau Indian Ways with Words*, chapter 3.

15. The first reference is to the young man hanged by John Clarke in 1813; the second is to the death of The Hat, a Nez Perce warrior who had accompanied William Gray on his eastward trek in 1837 but was killed in an attack by the Lakota.

16. Stevens possessed, at best, a sketchy understanding of the occupants of the vast "Yakama country." See Andrew H. Fisher, *Shadow Tribe: The Making of Columbia River Indian Identity* (Seattle: University of Washington Press, 2011), chapter 2.

17. Lawrence Kip, "The Indian Council at Walla Walla, May and June, 1855," *Sources of the History of Oregon* 1, no. 2 (1897): 17–8.

18. Kip, 18.

19. Stevens, *The Life of Isaac Ingalls Stevens* 2, 47.

20. Kip, 22.

21. On treaties and reservations in general, see Francis Paul Prucha's *The Great Father: The United States Government and the American Indians*, 2 vols. (Lincoln: University of Nebraska Press, 1984); and *American Indian Treaties: The History of a Political Anomaly* (Berkeley: University of California Press, 1994).

22. *Topographical Memoir and Report of Captain T. J. Cram, on Territories of Oregon and Washington*, 35th Cong., 2d sess. (March 3, 1859), H.R. Doc. 114, 81–4.

8. The Governor Stevens Wars

1. *Topographical Memoir and Report of Captain T. J. Cram, on Territories of Oregon and Washington*, 35th Cong., 2d sess. (1859), H. Doc. 114, 86.

2. "Maj. Haller driven in to the Dalls!—The Indians swarming in Great Numbers!!—Attack on the Settlements feared!!! [sic]," *Oregon Argus*, October 20, 1855.

3. "War—The Yakima Indians, &c.," *Pioneer and Democrat*, October 19, 1855.

4. "Indian Character—Political Malignity," *Oregon Argus*, November 10, 1855.

5. "Progress of Indian Difficulties," *Pioneer and Democrat*, October 19, 1855; and "Indian Difficulties," *Oregon Argus*, October 20, 1855.

6. "Maj. Haller driven in to the Dalls!" Original emphasis.
7. Letter, Olney to Curry, October 12, 1855, *Oregon Argus*, October 27, 1855.
8. Lieutenant Withers to Colonel Cooper, November 12, 1855, *Indian Hostilities in Oregon and Washington*, 34th Cong., 1st sess. (1856), H. Doc. 93, 11–2.
9. According to A. J. Splawn, in 1854, Kamiakin, Peo-Peo-Mox-Mox, and Looking Glass called for council of all plateau leaders at the Grande Ronde to discuss plans for a unified resistance. They agreed to attend a council with Stevens, if called, but to surrender no land Of all the headmen, only Lawyer, Itstikats, and Spokane Garry were in favor of making treaties with Stevens. The others agreed to support each other in the event of war. *Ka-mi-akin: The Last Hero of the Yakimas* (Portland: Kilham, 1917), 21–8. Alvin M. Josephy believed the Grande Ronde council was held after the Walla Walla council. *Nez Perce Country* (Lincoln: University of Nebraska Press, 2007), 305–6.
10. *Indian Affairs on the Pacific*, 34th Cong., 3rd sess. (1857), H. Doc. 76, 213.
11. The seventy-one-year-old Wool had participated in almost every military action of the century and had served as commander of the Department of the East (1847–54) and the Department of the Pacific since 1854.
12. Wool to Army Headquarters, December 13, 1855, *Indian Hostilities* (1856), 15.
13. Quoted in Geneva D. Lent, *West of the Mountains: James Sinclair and the Hudson's Bay Company* (Seattle: University of Washington Press, 1963), 281. A. B. Roberts claimed he buried Peo-Peo-Mox-Mox's 6′6″ body. A. B. Roberts, "Reminiscences of a Life in the Far West," WCMss055, Box 1, Roberts Family Papers, Whitman College and Northwest Archives, 6, 9.
14. Stevens to Manypenny, December 22, 1855, *Indian Disturbances in Oregon and Washington*, 34th Cong., 1st sess. (1856), H. Doc. 48, 6.
15. "Governor's Message," *Pioneer and Democrat*, January 25, 1856.
16. Wool to Stevens, February 12, 1856, *Indian Hostilities* (1856), 45.
17. "Gen Wool and the War," *Pioneer and Democrat*, February 15, 1856.
18. Wright to Capt. Jones, June 11, 1856, *Report of the Secretary of War*, 34th Cong., 3d sess. (1856), H. Doc. 1, 160–1.
19. Wright to Mackall, July 18, 1856, *Report of the Secretary of War* (1856), 177–8.
20. Mackall to Wright, July 3, 1856, *Report of the Secretary of War* (1856), 165–6.
21. Stevens to Jefferson Davis, June 8, 1856, *Indian Affairs on the Pacific* (1857), 173. Stevens was becoming unhinged at this time. He responded to a series of attacks by the Puget Sound Indians by arresting the former HBC employees in the region, in fear that they would conspire with the Indians. When the territorial judge ordered their release, Stevens had the judge arrested, and on May 12 declared a state of martial law in Pierce and Thurston counties.
22. Near current intersection with 5 Mile Road.
23. Steptoe to Wright, September 18, 1856, *Indian Affairs on the Pacific* (1857), 197–8.
24. Wright to Mackall, October 30, 1856, *Indian Affairs on the Pacific* (1857), 230–1.
25. Howlishwanpum is interpreted as having said: "The chiefs were absent when Colonel Shaw approached. He sent Captain John, a friendly Nez Perce, to open a communication with the Cayuses. No persons authorized to talk were in the Cayuse camp. The women and children became alarmed at the advance of the volunteers, and commenced packing up. The volunteers then charged the camp." Wright to Mackall, October 31, 1856, *Indian Affairs on the Pacific* (1857), 233.
26. Stevens to Davis, November 21, 1856, *Indian Affairs on the Pacific* (1857), 236–7.
27. Charles M. Gates, ed., *Messages of the Governors of the Territory of Washington to the Legislative Assembly, 1854–1889* (Seattle: University of Washington Press, 1940), 28–47.
28. Wool to Col. L. Thomas, January 3, 1857, *Indian Affairs on the Pacific* (1857), 244.
29. Kurt R. Nelson, *Treaties and Treachery: The Northwest Indians' Resistance to Conquest* (Lincoln: University of Nebraska Press, 2011), 204.

30. *Report of J. Ross Browne . . . Indian Affairs in the Territories of Oregon and Washington*, 35th Cong., 1st sess. (1858), H. Doc. 40, 2–13. Steptoe to Mackall, October 19, 1857, *Indian Affairs in Oregon and Washington Territories*, 35th Cong., 1st sess. (1858), H. Doc. 112, 4. Lawyer had traveled to Salem to introduce himself to Joseph Lane.

31. Steptoe to Mackall, April 17, 1858, *Indian Affairs in Oregon and Washington Territories* (1858), H. Doc 112, 344.

32. It is also known as "the Battle of Tohotonimme" and "the Battle of Pine Creek."

33. Stevens wrote to a friend in Olympia: "I quietly observed *The Indians who whopped Steptoe, the Volunteers whipped.*" Ronald Todd, ed., "Letters of Governor Isaac I. Stevens, 1857–1858," *Pacific Northwest Quarterly* 31, no. 4 (October 1940), 442–3.

34. Mackall to Wright, July 4, 1858, *Report of the Secretary of War*, 35th Cong., 2d sess. (1858), H. Doc. 2, 363–4.

35. Wright to Mackall, August 31, 1858, *Report of the Secretary of War* (1858), 385–6. Steptoe was soon sent home on sick leave and resigned in 1861. See also Clifford Trafzer and Richard Scheuerman, *The Snake River-Palouse and the Invasion of the Inland Northwest* (Pullman: Washington State University Press, 2016), 89–108. Wright formed an agreement of cooperation with twenty-one Nez Perce headmen at Fort Walla Walla on August 6. The warriors were armed and uniformed as part of the agreement and, led by Lieutenant John Mullan, formed the advance unit.

36. Wright to Mackall, September 30, 1858, *Report of the Secretary of War* (1858), 402.

37. Wright to Mackall, September 30, 1858, *Report of the Secretary of War* (1858), 203–4.

38. The Army maintained a hostile relationship with the BIA since it was transferred from the War Department to the Department of the Interior in 1849. Wool, Clarke, Wright, and Steptoe each firmly insisted that the BIA belonged under the control of the Army rather than in the hands of "civilians."

39. Clarke to Army Headquarters, October 29, 1858, *Report of the Secretary of War* (1858), 411–2.

40. Harney to Army Headquarters, November 5, 1858, *Report of the Secretary of War*, 36th Cong., 1st sess. (1860), H. Doc. 93, 92.

9. US Army Forts on the Plateau

1. Formerly, 10-square-mile reserves were claimed by the War Department for forts. However, in 1853, as this policy came into conflict with the Donation Land Act, the reservations were reduced to 1 square mile.

2. Lawrence Kip, *Army Life on the Pacific* (New York: Redfield, 1859), 23.

3. Wool to Wright, January 29, 1856, *Report of the Secretary of War*, 34th Cong., 1st sess. (1856), H. Doc. 93, 62.

4. A native of Baden, Scholl had studied civil engineering in his native Karlsruhe. He emigrated to the United States after the failed revolution in 1848, made his way to California, then Salt Lake City, where he began working as a civilian clerk and cartographer for Major Steptoe. Louis Scholl, "Recollections of Sixty Years," *Up-to-the-Times Magazine* 1, no. 12 (October 1907), 531–5; and vol. 2, no. 2 (December 1907), 51–4.

5. See Alison K. Hoagland, *Army Architecture in the West: Forts Laramie, Bridger, and D. A. Russell, 1849–1912* (Norman: University of Oklahoma Press, 2004), chapter 3.

6. Priscilla Knuth, *"Picturesque" Frontier: The Army's Fort Dalles* (Portland: Oregon Historical Society, 1987), 56–62, 84–5; and Louis Scholl, "Recollections of Sixty Years," 533.

7. Alexander Jackson Downing, *Architecture of Country Houses* (New York: Appleton, 1851), 301.

8. Scholl to Angelina Bowman, March 26, 1857, Mss300, folder 2, Louis Scholl papers, 1852–1920, Oregon Historical Society. The recipient of this letter had lived at the fort prior to her husband's death in 1856.

9. Wool to Wright, January 29, 1856, *Report of the Secretary of War* (1856), 62.

10. Wright to Mackall, October 30, 1856, *Indian Affairs on the Pacific*, 34th Cong., 3d sess. (1857), H. Doc. 76, 230–1.

11. "Fort Walla Walla in 1857," *Up to the Times Magazine* 1, no. 7 (May 1907), 352–4. Ron McFarland attributes the original drawing to Eugène de Girardin. *Edward J. Steptoe and the Indian Wars: Life on the Frontier, 1815–1865* (Jefferson, NC: McFarland, 2016), 137, 152. Girardin, a French illustrator, had accompanied Stevens to Washington Territory in 1853.

12. "An Indian War Veteran's Tale," *Up-to-the-Times Magazine* 1, no. 2 (December 1906), 20–4.

13. McFarland, *Edward J. Steptoe*, 130. Like Captain Jordan, Steptoe was a Virginian.

14. Mackall to Steptoe, January 1, 1857, *Indian Affairs on the Pacific* (1857), 255–6.

15. Knuth, 42.

16. Knuth, 43–4.

17. Knuth, 44.

18. Knuth, 69–72.

19. Heister Dean Guie, *Bugles in the Valley: Garnett's Fort Simcoe*, rev. ed. (Portland: Oregon Historical Society, 1977), 132–3.

20. U.S. Army Corps of Engineers Seattle District, "Context Study of the United States Quartermaster General Standardized Plans 1866–1942" (1997). The *Regulations*, however, were never universally accepted. It was not until the 1880s that army fort architecture became standardized.

21. Knuth, 72.

22. Scholl to Steptoe, April 12, 1857, Louis Scholl papers, Oregon Historical Society.

23. Current site of the Jonathan M. Wainwright Memorial VA Medical Center.

24. T. C. Elliott, "The Dalles-Celilo Portage: Its History and Influence," *Quarterly of the Oregon Historical Society* 16, no. 2 (June 1915), 152.

25. Scholl to George H. Himes, July 6, 1904, Louis Scholl papers, Oregon Historical Society. Details of the fort's buildings are included in War Department, *Outline Description of U.S. Military Posts and Stations in the Year 1871* (Washington, DC: Government Publishing Office, 1872), 114–5; and War Department, *A Report on the Hygiene of the U.S. Army, with Description of Military Posts* (Washington, DC: Government Publishing Office, 1875), 490–2.

26. Based on plans in the National Archives Cartographic Section (RG 77-Miscellaneous Fort File, Walla Walla, Fort, Washington).

27. Quoted in Knuth, 66.

10. Steptoeville 1857–59

1. "Colville and Walla Walla," *Pioneer and Democrat* (August 5, 1859); and Howard S. Brode, ed., "Diary of Augustus J. Thibodo of the Northwest Exploring Expedition, 1859," *Pacific Northwest Quarterly* 31, no. 3 (July 1940), 345.

2. *Preliminary Topographical Memoir of Colonel George Wright's Campaign, Prepared . . . by Lieutenant John Mullan*, 35th Cong., 2d sess. (1859), S. Doc. 32, 10.

3. Isaac I. Stevens, "Northwest America," *Journal of the American Geographical and Statistical Society* 1, no. 1 (January 1859), 5.

4. Grace G. Isaacs, "Some Historical Data," *Up-to-the-Times Magazine* 1, no. 8 (June 1907), n.p.; and "Henry P. Isaacs and Josh C. Isaacs," *Idaho State Historical Society Reference Series*, no. 579 (1981).

5. "Removal of an Old Landmark," *Walla Walla Statesman*, January 12, 1878.

6. "History of Walla Walla," *Walla Walla Statesman*, October 28, 1882; and "Methodists in Banquet at Semi-Centennial," *Evening Statesman*, October 12, 1909.

7. Roberts published numerous reminiscences of the town ca. 1859.

8. The Bounty-Land Acts (of 1850, 1852 and 1855) allowed for veterans to claim 40- to 160-acre tracts, depending on their length of service.

9. General Harney to Lieutenant Colonel Thomas, April 25, 1859, *Report of the Secretary of War* (1860), 96.

10. In a letter to Colonel Steptoe dated April 12, 1857, Scholl noted that he was sending him seeds along with Charles Russell's freight. Mss300, folder 2, Louis Scholl papers, Oregon Historical Society. In a letter to George Himes dated July 6, 1904, Scholl noted that he had brought bluestem wheat seeds to Walla Walla in 1858 (Mss300, folder 7).

11. "Interesting Personages in and around Walla Walla by Lewis McMorris," *Evening Statesman*, July 10, 1909.

12. "Close of Long Life," *Walla Walla Weekly Union*, April 27, 1889. Dent, brother-in-law of Ulysses S. Grant, was reassigned at the outbreak of the Civil War and never returned to the Northwest.

13. U.S. Census Bureau, 1860, U.S. Federal Census, Walla Walla County, Washington State Archives, Digital Archives, digitalarchives.wa.gov.

14. "Our Portland Correspondence," *Daily Alta California*, August 27, 1859.

15. "Diary of Hamet Hubbard Case, June–September 1859," WCMss207, Hamet Hubbard Case Papers, 1859, Whitman College and Northwest Archives.

16. Already in December 1858, acting governor Mason expressed his concern for individuals who had yet to receive patents for land that they had settled under the Donation Land Act. Charles M. Gates, Charles M., ed., *Messages of the Governors of the Territory of Washington to the Legislative Assembly, 1854–1889* (Seattle: University of Washington Press, 1940), 61–6.

17. Samuel Phinney, who married Craig's daughter Adeline in 1861, received title to the 160-acre claim in 1865.

18. It stretched from Craig's claim (roughly current Clinton street, north to Mill Creek) to current Fourth Ave., and from Alder to Garrison Creek.

19. A. B. Roberts, "Walla Walla Fifty-One Years Ago," *Up-to-the-Times Magazine* 4, no. 3 (January 1910), 2416.

20. In fact, the city of Walla Walla did not formally receive its Trustee Townsite from the District Land Office until 1869.

21. See Henry Nash Smith, *Virgin Land: The American West as Symbol and Myth* (Cambridge, MA: Harvard University Press, 1950/1978), chapter 18.

22. The legislature actually appointed officials from among the dozen or so residents that Isaac Stevens encountered during his journey to Olympia. Needless to say, it was never formally organized.

23. "An Act Appointing Officers for Walla-Walla County," *Acts of the Legislative Assembly of the Territory of Washington . . . December 6th, A.D. 1858* (Olympia, 1859), 61–2.

24. Untitled, *Pioneer and Democrat*, February 11, 1859.

25. "Walla-walla County Democratic Convention," *Pioneer and Democrat*, April 29, 1859.

26. *Petition and Papers of Toussaint Mesplié*, 43d Cong., 1st sess. (1874), H. Doc. 97, 10.

27. "History of Walla Walla."

28. Roberts, 2416–7.

29. Bordered by current Colville, Palouse, Alder, and Birch.

30. Lewis A. McArthur, "The Oregon State Boundary," *Oregon Historical Quarterly* 37, no. 4 (December 1936), 301–2.

31. "Is Walla Walla in Oregon?," *Walla Walla Statesman*, June 23, 1865.

32. *Population of the United States in 1860* (Washington, DC, 1864), 580–3. https://census.gov/library/publications/1864/dec/1860a.html.
33. "Interesting Personages . . . Lewis McMorris." In diary entries from December 1859, A. J. Thibodo noted a stag dance and dances with a few women and "men innumerable." "Diary of Augustus J. Thibodo," 343–5.
34. "Walla Walla," *Pioneer and Democrat*, December 21, 1860.
35. Based on the "child-ladder," the age and birthplace of the children.

11. The Cayuse in Limbo 1858–61

1. "Indian Appropriation Bill," *Congressional Globe*, Senate, 37th Cong., 2d sess. (1862), 2095.
2. Report of A. P. Dennison, August 1, 1858, *Report of the Commissioner of Indian Affairs*, 35th Cong., 2d sess. (1858), H. Doc. 1, 997, 262.
3. Theodore Stern, *Chiefs and Chief Traders: Indian Relations at Fort Nez Percés, 1818–1855* (Corvallis: Oregon State University Press, 1993), 60.
4. The order in which the seven Cayuse headmen signed the 1855 treaty indicates their rank within the Cayuse hierarchy at the time. Howlishwanpum signed after Weatenatemany, Qemátspelu, and Itstikats, but ahead of Five Crows; Tintinmitse signed after Five Crows and Hyumhowlish. According to Stern, Tintinmitse was a Flathead, married to a Cayuse woman. Theodore Stern, *Chiefs and Change in the Oregon Country: Indian Relations at Fort Nez Percés, 1818–1855* (Corvallis: Oregon State University Press, 1996), 176–7.
5. Cain had accompanied his father, John, from Indiana to the Northwest, where the elder Cain served the Washington superintendent of Indian Affairs in various capacities from 1855 to 1858.
6. "Report of A. J. Cain, August 2, 1859, *Report of the Commissioner of Indian Affairs*, 36th Cong., 2nd sess. (1860), S. Doc. 2, 413–4.
7. Cain to Geary, October 31, 1859, Washington Superintendency of Indian Affairs, roll 21, 1859–1860, Yakima Valley Libraries, Relander Collection, https://archives.yvl.org/handle/20.500.
8. Report of A. J. Cain, September 30, 1860, *Report of the Commissioner of Indian Affairs* (1860), 208, 210.
9. Report of Edward R. Geary, October 1, 1860, *Report of the Commissioner of Indian Affairs* (1860), 178–9.
10. T. W. Davenport, "Recollections of an Indian Agent," *Quarterly of the Oregon Historical Society* 8, no. 2 (June 1907), 110.
11. Report of Geo. H. Abbott, November 5, 1860, *Letter from the Secretary of the Treasury, Transmitting Estimates of Additional Appropriations*, 37th Cong., 1st sess. (1861), H. Doc. 1, 21–2. Abbott requested an additional $9,500.
12. Smohalla was attracting hundreds of Sahaptians to his large village at Priest Rapids. He called for a rejection of selling land, of farming, of whiskey, and of all assimilation of white culture. Above all, he insisted that the sacred bond between the people and their particular place on the earth remain unbroken. His influence surged with BIA attempts to corral Sahaptians onto the reservations in the 1860s and lasted until his death in 1895. Although he preached a form of passive resistance, Smohalla was increasingly regarded as an enemy of the government for refusing to recognize its authority. He unwaveringly and peacefully frustrated the many attempts by various government agencies to control him and his large band. See Clifford E. Trafzer and Margery Ann Beach, "Smohalla, the Washani, and Religion as a Factor in Northwestern Indian History," *American Indian Quarterly* 9, no. 3 (Summer 1985), 309–15; and Robert H. Ruby and John A. Brown, *Dreamer-Prophets of the Columbia Plateau: Smohalla and Skolaskin* (Norman: University of Oklahoma Press, 1989), 19–50.

13. Report of G. H. Abbott, July 30, 1860, *Report of the Commissioner of Indian Affairs* (1860), 219–20.
14. Records of the Oregon Superintendency of Indian Affairs, letters received 1861, No. 22, Yakima Valley Libraries, Relander Collection, https://archives.yvl.org/handle/20 .500.11867/6776.
15. Records of the Oregon Superintendency of Indian Affairs.
16. Report of G. H. Abbott, September 10, 1861, *Report of the Commissioner of Indian Affairs,* 37th Cong., 2nd sess. (1861), S. Doc. 1, 164–6.
17. Elizabeth Vibert, *Traders' Tales: Narratives of Cultural Encounters in the Columbia Plateau, 1807–1846* (Norman: University of Oklahoma Press, 1997), 183–6.
18. Report of Wm. H. Rector, September 2, 1862, *Annual Report of the Commissioner of Indian Affairs,* 37th Cong., 3rd sess. (1862), H. Doc. 1, 258–9.
19. Davenport, "Recollections," 14. Davenport, like Rector, was a prominent Republican. However, like Lincoln's crony Commissioner William P. Dole, Rector soon embraced the BIA's corruption. On Dole, see David Allen Nichols, *Lincoln and the Indians: Civil War Policy and Politics* (St. Paul Minnesota Historical Society, 2012), chapter 2. Democrats and Republicans alike in Oregon lobbied for Rector's removal.

12. The Gold Rush Town

1. Cain to Geary, May 8, 1860, Washington Superintendency of Indian Affairs, roll 21, 1859–1860, Yakima Valley Libraries, Relander Collection, https://archives.yvl.org/handle/20.500.
2. "From the Skimmtik [sic] Mines," *Oregon Argus,* May 12, 1860. The hottest gold mining site in the Northwest at the time was on the Similkameen River.
3. Charles E. Mix, Acting Commissioner of Indian Affairs, to Geary, July 2, 1860; Cain to Geary, August 21, 1860, BIA, Washington Superintendency of Indian Affairs.
4. *Portland Advertiser,* November 6, 1860. "Bostons" is Chinook Wawa for Americans.
5. Cain to Steen, November 25, 1860; Steen to Cain, November 26, 1860; Cain to Geary, November 27, 1860, Washington Superintendency of Indian Affairs.
6. "Legislative Proceedings," *Washington Standard,* December 22, 1860.
7. "Nez Perce Gold Country," *Daily National Democrat* [Marysville, CA], January 25, 1861.
8. "The Nez Perces Mines," *Sacramento Union,* February 8, 1861. Similar reports, attributed to Portland sources, appeared throughout Oregon and California.
9. On the eastward spread of urbanism, see Eugene P. Moehring, *Urbanism and Empire in the Far West, 1840–1890* (Reno: University of Nevada Press, 2004).
10. "Letter from Washington Territory," *Daily Alta California,* April 3, 1861.
11. According to Frank T. Gilbert, $1,750,000 in gold dust was shipped from the region in 1861. *Historic Sketches of Walla Walla, Whitman, Columbia and Garfield Counties, Washington Territory, and Umatilla County, Oregon* (Portland: A. G. Walling, 1882), 227.
12. On the events of 1860–63, see Alvin M. Josephy Jr., *Nez Perce Country* (Lincoln: University of Nebraska Press, 2007), chapter 6.
13. "Treaty," *Pioneer and Democrat,* April 26, 1861; and *Washington Standard,* April 27, 1861.
14. "Nez Perce Mines—Report of Dr. Thibodo," *Portland Times,* April 24, 1861.
15. Josephy, *Nez Perce Country,* 86.
16. The chiefs who stood to be dispossessed of their lands (including Old Joseph of the Wallowa Valley) left the council without signing the treaty.
17. It was edited by Rees and Northrop until Northrop's death at age twenty-nine in 1863. Raymond and S. G. Rees then published the paper until they sold it to William Newell in 1865. The most reliable account of the origin of the *Statesman* is Raymond Rees's obituary for Northrop: "Died: Northrop," *Washington Statesman,* February 28, 1863. Northrop and the

Rees brothers were friends of A. B. Roberts in Portland. A.B. Roberts, "Reminiscences of a Life in the Far West," 6, WCMss055, Box 1, Roberts Family Papers, Whitman College and Northwest Archives, 4.

18. Unlike many papers in the West, the *Statesman* did not subscribe to patent pages, which were supplied by companies to fill the first and fourth pages with news and advertisements.
19. "The 'Good Time' Has Come," *Washington Statesman*, December 13, 1861.
20. Harvey K. Hines, *An Illustrated History of the State of Washington* (Chicago: Lewis, 1893), 271.
21. George Hunter, *Reminiscences of an Old Timer*, 4th ed. (Battle Creek, MI: Review and Herald, 1889), 256. See also B. F. Manring, "Recollections of a Pioneer of 1859—Lawson Stockman," *Quarterly of the Oregon Historical Society* 11, no. 2 (June 1910), 168–72.
22. "From Our Walla Walla Correspondent," *Oregonian*, November 18, 1861; and "News from Walla Walla," *Oregonian*, December 18, 1861.
23. "Our Society," *Washington Statesman*, January 10, 1862.
24. "The Weather," *Washington Statesman*, December 20, 1861.
25. "The Weather," *Washington Statesman*, January 10, 1862.
26. "Farmers Should Prepare for Winter," *Washington Statesman*, January 10, 1862.
27. "The Cold Winter—Loss of Stock," *Washington Statesman*, February 22, 1862. The agent on the reservation estimated that at least 2,000 horses and 500 head of cattle had perished. Report of W. H. Barnhart, August 5, 1862, *Report of the Commissioner of Indian Affairs* (1862), 269.
28. "Oregon Items," *Washington Statesman*, January 25, 1862.
29. "From Below," *Washington Statesman*, March 22, 1862.
30. "The Mayor's Message," *Washington Statesman*, April 19, 1862.

13. Commerce

1. Baker had relocated from Portland to personally oversee his business in 1861. He had trained as a physician at Jefferson College in Philadelphia before gold fever lured him to California. He took his gold earnings to the Calapooya Valley in Oregon, where he established a grist mill and a mercantile business. In 1858, he relocated to Portland, where he established a mercantile business. In 1860, Baker estimated the value of his businesses, property, livestock, and so on at $43,014.12. W. W. Baker, *Forty Years a Pioneer: Business Life of Dorsey Syng Baker, 1848–1888* (Seattle: Lowman & Hanford, 1934), 53.
2. Frank T. Gilbert, *Historic Sketches of Walla Walla, Whitman, Columbia and Garfield Counties, Washington Territory, and Umatilla County, Oregon* (Portland: Walling, 1882), appx. 11–12.
3. Baker seems to have acted as his own contractor: during summer 1861 he recorded in his notebook the receipt of brick ($708), lumber ($500), and building tools ($45.89). Diary of Dorsey S. Baker, Volume 5, 1859–1861, WCMss040, Baker Family Collection, Whitman College and Northwest Archives.
4. On women-owned millinery and dressmaking businesses, see Wendy Gamber, *The Female Economy: The Millinery and Dressmaking Trades, 1860–1930* (Urbana: University of Illinois Press, 1997).
5. In the decades following the Napoleonic wars, every state within the German Confederation debated the issue of Jewish emancipation, and each state slowly extended (or extended and then rescinded) rights—but always with restrictions. In Bavaria, for example, the number of Jewish residents in each locale was limited by law (*Judenmatrikel*), which often forced children to relocate on completion of their studies or apprenticeships. Restrictions were particularly harsh in the Polish regions of Prussia and Russia, where most Jews were impoverished, and their movement, choice of profession, and ability to marry were strictly controlled. The Alsatian Jews in France had been granted rights of citizenship during the

Revolution, but most remained impoverished. See David Sorkin, *Jewish Emancipation: A History across Five Centuries* (Princeton, NJ: Princeton University Press, 2019), chapter 12. With the failure of democratic revolutions throughout Europe in 1848, Jews joined the multitude of Germans to emigrate to the United States.

6. On Jewish identity and activities during the gold rush, see Fred Rosenbaum, *Cosmopolitans: A Social and Cultural History of the Jews of the San Francisco Bay Area* (Berkeley: University of California Press, 2011), chapter 1.

7. On early Jewish population and society in Portland, see Scott Cline, "Creation of an Ethnic Community: Portland Jewry, 1851–1866," *Pacific Northwest Quarterly* 76, no. 2 (April 1985), 52–60; and "The Jews of Portland, Oregon: A Statistical Dimension, 1860–1880," *Oregon Historical Quarterly* 88, no. 1 (Spring 1987), 4–25.

8. I. N. Choynski, letter, and "We Know What We Say," *Oregon Statesman*, August 17, 1858, and October 19, 1858. In 1859, Choynski became a journalist for the *Weekly Gleaner*, a Jewish paper in San Francisco.

9. Howard M. Sachar, *A History of the Jews in America* (New York: Knopf, 1992/2013), 43. See also Eric L. Goldstein, *The Price of Whiteness: Jews, Race, and American Identity* (Princeton, NJ: Princeton University Press, 2008), 1–6. Historians Robert Rockaway and Arnon Gutfeld note "the German Jews achieved unparalleled success in the economic sphere and many commentators praised them for their sobriety, work ethic, low crime rate and family ties," yet they emphasize, "uncertainty about their place in Christian America beset many of them." They note that Jews were conditioned to ignore slights and stereotypes in the press. "Demonic Images of the Jew in the Nineteenth Century United States," *American Jewish History* 89, no. 4 (December 2001), 369.

10. Sachar, 53, 72.

11. This information is culled from newspaper notices, census documents, Julia Niebuhr Eulenberg's dissertation "Jewish Enterprise in the American West: Washington, 1853–1909" (University of Washington, 1996); Fred Lockley's "Reminiscences of Colonel Henry Ernst Dosch," *Quarterly of the Oregon Historical Society* 25, no. 1 (March 1924), 60–5; and Jean Roth's "The Schwabacher Family of Washington State," *Jewish Genealogical Society of Washington State*, 2015, https://jgsws.org/schwabacher.php.

12. "Julia" Bauer offered language instruction in French and German. On the Bauers' remarkable daughters, see Susan E. Pickett, *Marion and Emilie Frances Bauer: From the Wild West to American Musical Modernism* (Morrisville, NC: Lulu Publishing, 2014).

13. "Hebrew New Year," *Walla Walla Statesman*, September 14, 1864.

14. "Hebrew New Year," *Walla Walla Statesman*, October 4, 1867. Newell did, however, make the distinction, "With the Israelites, as with our own people." Such a slight may only have been perceptible to a Jewish reader.

15. "New Firm," *Washington Statesman*, June 3, 1864.

16. "Importing Chinese Laborers," *Washington Statesman*, April 9, 1864. Lee "supplied almost all the Chinese mining camps in eastern Washington and northern Idaho." "The Old Log Cabin," *Walla Walla Union* (March 31, 1884). Lee's sons became respected businessmen in the city.

17. See Yucheng Qin, "A Century-old 'Puzzle': The Six Companies' Role in Chinese Labor Importation in the Nineteenth Century," *Journal of American-East Asian Relations* 12, no. 3/4 (Fall-Winter 2003), 225–54.

18. "Elopement," *Walla Walla Statesman*, December 4, 1869; Baker, *Forty Years a Pioneer*, 52.

19. "Tax upon Chinamen," *Washington Statesman*, February 6, 1864. See Mark L. Lazarus III, "An Historical Analysis of Alien Land Law: Washington Territory & State 1853–1889," *University of Puget Sound Law Review* 12 (1989), 197–212.

20. Letter to Elizabeth Caseday, February 11, 1861, A. B. Roberts's letter book, 1856–77, WCMss055, Box 1, Roberts Family Papers, Whitman College and Northwest Archives.

21. Quincy T. Mills, *Cutting along the Color Line: Black Barbers and Barber Shops in America* (Philadelphia: University of Pennsylvania Press, 2013), 61–2. Douglas Walter Bristol Jr. notes, "These men catered to white vanity in order to wrest from a repressive society a significant degree of control over their own lives." *Knights of the Razor: Black Barbers in Slavery and Freedom* (Baltimore: Johns Hopkins University Press, 2009), 41.

22. William D. Lyman, *Illustrated History of Walla Walla County* (San Francisco: Lever, 1901), 342–6.

23. Egbert S. Oliver, "Obed Dickinson and the 'Negro Question,'" *Oregon Historical Quarterly* 92, no. 1 (Spring 1991), 4–40.

24. Lyman, *Illustrated History of Walla Walla County*, 242.

25. Eleven Walla Walla residents are listed as "mulatto" in the 1870 census, including the Bogles and their three children and the Mitchells and their two daughters.

26. William Parsons, *An Illustrated History of Umatilla County* (San Francisco: Lever, 1902), 262.

27. "From Idaho," *The Elevator* (December 20, 1873). Walker had included the article from *Spirit of the West*, October 24, 1873, with his letter.

28. "J. B. Mitchell," *Walla Walla Statesman*, July 14, 1877; "Dick Bogle," *Walla Walla Statesman*, February 5, 1876.

29. "Washington Territory Incomes—1867," *Walla Walla Statesman*, July 31, 1868.

30. On the other hand, the purchasing power of $1.00 in 1867—relative only to the purchase of household goods—is equivalent to about $22 in 2024. In 1860, before the wartime inflation, it would have been around $37. "Purchasing Power Today of a US Dollar Transaction in the Past," *MeasuringWorth, 2023.* https://measuringworth.com/ppowerus/.

31. Crockett, a native of Tennessee, was a distant cousin of the author.

32. Bureau of Statistics, *Special Report on Immigration* (Washington, DC: Government Publishing Office, 1871), 198. A small cottage in town could be rented for $10–$20/month (or built for $500); however, there was always a housing shortage during this period.

14. Urban Development

1. These six were followed by, among others, William Langford (1863), James Lasater (1863), James Mix (1863), Benjamin Sharpstein (1865), and Nathan Caton (1867). Arthur S. Beardsley and Donald A. McDonald, "The Courts and Early Bar of the Washington Territory," *Washington Law Review* 17, no. 2 (April 1942), 74–5.

2. "Married," *Washington Standard*, June 1, 1861. Tilton became infamous in the Far West during his well-publicized, unsuccessful legal battle to reclaim a slave who had escaped to Canada.

3. General Land Office Records, Bureau of Land Management, https://glorecords.blm.gov /details/patent/default.aspx?accession=0466-103&docClass=MW&sid=4ib0xicl.1xa. Despite repeated attempts by Congress to remedy abuses of the Scrip Warrant Act, fraudulent claims were regularly filed, and speculators managed to accumulate large numbers of warrants. See Paul W. Gates, "Military Bounty Land Policies," in *History of the Public Land Law Development* (Washington, DC: Government Publishing Office, 1968), 274–84.

4. Untitled, *Washington Statesman*, December 20, 1861.

5. "Sale of Town Lots," *Washington Statesman*, July 12, 1862. Cain auctioned another fifty lots in 1863.

6. The Land Office noted, "*A settler must acquire the right of pre-emption by virtue of his own acts, and not by the acts of another.*" "Decision of the Register and Receiver: Barron vs. Sparks,

and Sparks, vs. The City of Walla Walla," *Washington Statesman*, October 11, 1862. Original emphasis.

7. See "Decision of the Register and Receiver: E. H. Barron vs. The City of Walla Walla," *Washington Statesman*, December 27, 1862; "The City Land Case," *Walla Walla Statesman*, April 22, 1864; and "The Walla Walla Land Case," *Walla Walla Statesman*, June 23, 1865.

8. "Public Burying Ground," *Washington Statesman*, April 25, 1863; and "City Cemetery," *Washington Statesman*, March 26, 1864.

9. "City Improvements," *Washington Statesman*, October 18, 1862. Cain's warehouse was soon purchased by Schwabacher Bros.

10. Quoted in G. Thomas Edwards, "Walla Walla: Gateway to the Pacific Northwest Interior," *Montana: The Magazine of Western History* 40, no. 3 (Summer 1990), 35. During 1862, Almos Reynolds built his own mill, Frontier Mills, on his property on Yellowhawk Creek.

15. Family Matters

1. "The Masonic Hall," *Washington Statesman*, April 29, 1864; and "New Buildings," *Walla Walla Statesman*, September 2, 1864.

2. Isaacs later explained that the decision to move to Walla Walla was made after it became evident that the establishment of Umatilla Landing would bring about a decline in trade at The Dalles. "I wanted [the people of The Dalles] to make a road directly from the Dalles to Boise, in order to keep the trade, but they could not see as far as I could." Henry P. Isaacs, "Trading in the Upper Columbia Basin," interview by Frances Fuller Victor, 1879, WCMss639, Whitman College and Northwest Archives.

3. "Lost Book," *Walla Walla Statesman*, June 29, 1866.

4. "City Improvements," *Walla Walla Statesman*, November 16, 1866.

5. "The Education of Youth," *Washington Statesman*, December 19, 1863.

6. Harvey Whitefield Scott, *History of Portland, Oregon* (Portland: Mason, 1890), 350.

7. "Historical Sketch . . . of the First Congregational Church of Walla Walla" (1910), 2. WCMss 111, First Congregational Church of Walla Walla Records, Whitman College and Northwest Archives. Chamberlain had studied at the Bangor Theological Seminary under one of the most prolific anti-Catholics of the time, Enoch Pond, author of *No Fellowship with Romanism* (1843).

8. Letter by E. H. M. [Edward H. Massam], *Washington Statesman*, July 15, 1864.

9. "The Celebration," *Washington Statesman*, July 8, 1864.

10. "The Select School," *Walla Walla Statesman*, September 23, 1864.

11. "District School," *Walla Walla Statesman*, September 9, 1864; "The District Schools," *Walla Walla Statesman*, September 30, 1864; "Report of School Superintendent," *Walla Walla Statesman*, December 30, 1864; and "The District School," *Walla Walla Statesman*, December 2, 1864.

12. In November 1865, the nearly completed building was "blown down" by a hurricane. "Hurricane," *Walla Walla Statesman*, November 24, 1865. The cost of the building, including the storm damage, was $2,300.

13. G. Thomas Edwards, *The Triumph of Tradition: The Emergence of Whitman College, 1859–1924* (Walla Walla: Whitman College, 1992), 6.

14. Edwards, 9–10.

15. Brouillet had published a series of rebuttals to Spalding's initial account of the killings in 1853, which were subsequently collected into the booklet *Protestantism in Oregon* (1853). Brouillet defended himself and his fellow clergymen against Spalding's accusations, and also disparaged Spalding and Whitman for having failed in their duties as missionaries. J. Ross Browne included Brouillet's pamphlet in his report for the BIA in 1857, to demonstrate the

interconfessional hostility generated by the missionaries among the Indians. Thus, *Protestant-ism in Oregon* was published by Congress. On learning of Brouillet's government-sanctioned publication, Spalding elaborated on his own account of the history of the missions and the Whitman killings. His story first appeared in the Congregational journal *The Pacific* in 1865. In 1871, he managed to get his story also published by Congress.

16. Among other things, Spalding claimed that God had determined that the gold mines of the West should be opened exclusively by Americans, that God *selected* the Whitmans and Spaldings to establish the overland route from the states to the gold fields; that the purpose of Whitman's trek across the country in 1842 was to (successfully) stop President Tyler from trading the Oregon Territory to Britain in exchange for "a codfishery"; that Whitman organized and led the largest party of Americans across the Oregon trail, making him responsible for having initiated American immigration to Oregon and for having *saved* Oregon for the United States. The Whitman killings, he claimed, were carried out by the Cayuse in coordination with the Catholics—above all, "General Brouilette, Vicar General for the Pope of Rome on this coast"—and the HBC. William McBean, who was accused of being an accomplice to the killings, sent two letters to the *Statesman* denouncing Spalding. After publishing the final part of Spalding's story, the *Statesman* published "by special request" a letter written by Brouillet on March 2, 1848, offering his account of the events following the killings.

17. A. B. Roberts, James Lasater, and Philip Schauble all offered proposals for land. According to the deed, the property with its improvements would revert back to Baker were the educational mission to fail. WCA088, Whitman Seminary Records, Whitman College and Northwest Archives.

18. P. B. Chamberlain, "Whitman Seminary," *Walla Walla Statesman*, June 8, 1866.

19. "Address Delivered by Reverend P. B. Chamberlain at the Opening of Whitman Seminary, October 13, 1866," Whitman Seminary Records, Whitman College and Northwest Archives.

20. Eells needed to borrow $1,000 from Baker, which put the institution in debt from the start. Edwards, 23.

21. In 1867, Dorsey Baker married the sister of Lettice Clark Reynolds, Elizabeth Millican. Lettice's first husband, Ransom Clark, died in 1859 after staking his homestead on Yellow-hawk Creek. She married her neighbor Almos Reynolds in 1861.

22. Lemuel H. Wells, *A Pioneer Missionary* (Seattle: Progressive, 1931), chapters IX and XI; and "Minute Book for 1872–1892," WCMss062, Saint Paul's School Collection, 1875–1968, Whitman College and Northwest Archives.

23. "Walla Walla" [reprinted from *The Pacific Christian Advocate*], *Walla Walla Statesman*, June 15, 1866.

24. "First M. E. Church," *Up-to-the-Times Magazine* 3, no. 32 (June 1909), 1985–6.

25. See "New Chapel," *Washington Statesman*, December 12, 1863; and "Extension," *Washington Statesman*, May 6, 1864.

26. "New Congregational Church," *Walla Walla Statesman*, October 30, 1868. The loan was only paid off after Chamberlain's death in 1889. T. C. Elliott, "The Organization and First Pastorate of the First Congregational Church of Walla Walla, Washington," *Washington Historical Quarterly* 6, no. 2 (April 1915), 95–6.

27. Elliott, "The First Congregational Church," 97–8. The church, under Chamberlain, closed in 1879.

28. "Camp Meeting," *Walla Walla Statesman*, July 6, 1866.

29. An Army officer from Fort Walla Walla may have designed the church. See "A Visitation in Eastern Oregon and Washington Territory," *Spirit of Missions* 40 (July 1875), 479. Capt. William H. Winters, Capt. David Perry, and Col. William Russell Parnell were all

congregants. Minute Book for 1872–92, Saint Paul's School Collection, Whitman College and Northwest Archives.

30. The chancel was deemed essential by the ecclesiologists; it housed the altar and was reserved exclusively for the clergy during services.

16. Politics

1. On Lincoln's influence on the Northwest, see Richard W. Etulain, *Lincoln and Oregon Country: Politics in the Civil War Era* (Corvallis: Oregon State University Press, 2013).

2. "Preserve Me from My Friends," *Washington Standard*, March 9, 1861.

3. "Democratic Precinct Meeting," *Pioneer and Democrat*, May 3, 1861; "Sancho Panza Addresseth Ye Faithful," *Washington Standard*, May 11, 1861; "The Secession Convention at Vancouver," *Washington Standard*, May 25, 1861; and "Speech of Gov. Stevens," *Pioneer and Democrat*, May 31, 1861.

4. "Proclamation by the Governor," *Washington Standard*, May 18, 1861. On the other hand, Governor Whiteaker had no interest in raising companies of Union soldiers in Oregon; the responsibility was assigned to a citizen committee.

5. Wright to Lorenzo Thomas, December 10, 1861, *The Official History of the Washington National Guard*, vol. 3 (Tacoma: n.d.), 19–20. https://mil.wa.gov/official-history-of -washington-national-guard.

6. Doyce B. Nunis Jr., ed., *The Golden Frontier: The Recollections of Herman Francis Reinhart, 1851–1869* (Austin: University of Texas Press, 1962), 205.

7. "Shooting Affray," *Washington Statesman*, April 12, 1862.

8. J. W. Scobey, "Walla Walla Correspondence," *Placer Herald*, May 3, 1862. This account is supported by Herman Francis Reinhart in *The Golden Frontier*, 203–7.

9. "Riot at the Theater" and "Correspondence between Mayor Whitman and Col. Lee," *Washington Statesman*, April 19, 1862; and "Military," *Washington Statesman*, April 26, 1862.

10. "Rant versus Cant" and "A Malicious Assault," *Washington Statesman*, June 28, 1862.

11. "Washington State Correspondence," *State Republican*, July 26, 1862.

12. "Col. Steinberger's Regiment," *Washington Statesman*, November 8, 1862.

13. Charles Janeway Stillé, *History of the United States Sanitary Commission* (Philadelphia: Lippincott, 1866), 544.

14. "Removal of Col. Steinberger," *Washington Statesman*, January 9, 1864; and "Reinstated," *Washington Statesman*, August 19, 1864.

15. H. K. Hines, *An Illustrated History of the State of Washington* (Chicago: Lewis, 1893), 278.

16. See Robert E. Ficken, *Washington Territory* (Pullman: Washington State University Press, 2002), chapter 5.

17. [In pursuance of a call], *Walla Walla Statesman*, October 20, 1865.

18. [The citizens of Walla Walla County], *Walla Walla Statesman*, October 20, 1865; and "Opposition Meeting," *Walla Walla Statesman*, October 27, 1865.

19. "The Annexation Question," *Walla Walla Statesman*, November 24, 1865. See C. S. Kingston, "The Walla Walla Separation Movement," *Washington Historical Quarterly* 24, no. 2 (April 1933), 95–6.

20. "Memorial of the Legislature of Oregon, in Favor of Incorporating the County of Walla-Walla, Washington Territory, into the State of Oregon," 39th Cong., 1st sess. (1866), S. Doc. 83.

21. "Resolution Protesting against the Disintegration of Washington Territory," *Statutes of the Territory of Washington, 1865–66* (Olympia, 1866), 242–3.

22. "A Dead Issue," *Walla Walla Statesman*, December 28, 1866.

17. Community and Entertainment

1. See Carolyn Grattan Eichin, *From San Francisco Eastward: Victorian Theater in the American West* (Reno: University of Nevada Press, 2020), chapter 2; and Chad Evans, *Frontier Theatre: A History of Nineteenth-Century Theatrical Entertainment in the Canadian Far West and Alaska* (Victoria: Sono Nis Press, 1983), 34, 43–4.
2. She also addressed audiences at the new schoolhouse and the Bank Exchange. Susan B. Anthony Papers: Daybook and Diaries, 1856–1906; Diaries; 1871, Library of Congress, MSS 11049005–139, https://crowd.loc.gov/campaigns/susan-b-anthony-papers/. Annie Mix was named vice president of the Territorial Woman Suffrage Association, established in Olympia in November 1871.
3. Ad, *Walla Walla Statesman*, September 2, 1864.
4. In 1871, Castello's circus was renamed for his new business partner, P. T. Barnum.
5. "Panic," *Walla Walla Statesman*, July 29, 1876.
6. For example, when the physician and Mason A. J. Thibodo arrived in December 1859, "Brother Mason" James McAuliff invited him to set up his practice in his general store. Howard S. Brode, ed., "Diary of Augustus J. Thibodo of the Northwest Exploring Expedition, 1859," *Pacific Northwest Quarterly*, 31, no. 3 (July 1940), 343.
7. "Base Ball Clubs," *Walla Walla Statesman*, July 26, 1867; and "Base Ball Club," *Walla Walla Statesman*, August 16, 1867.

18. Disasters and Near Disasters

1. "Union Hook and Ladder Co. No. 1," *Washington Statesman*, February 1, 1862.
2. "Burning of the Theater Building," *Washington Statesman*, June 21, 1862.
3. "Fire," *Washington Statesman*, May 13, 1864. Two of the destroyed buildings belonged to Dr. Jim.
4. "Destructive Fire," *Walla Walla Statesman*, August 4, 1865.
5. "Rebuilding," *Walla Walla Statesman*, August 4, 1865. The next week's edition noted that nine buildings in the decimated area were under construction.
6. "The New Engine House," *Walla Walla Statesman*, January 5, 1866.
7. Perhaps the best-known examples would have been the New York University Building (1833–34) and the Louisiana State Capitol in Baton Rouge (1847–52). The latter had been widely illustrated in magazines after it was captured by the Union Army in 1862.
8. "Destructive Fire," *Walla Walla Statesman*, July 6, 1866.
9. "Destructive Fire," *Walla Walla Statesman*, October 23, 1875. The paper criticized the fire companies for poor coordination and noted that during the fire, Hen Lee and other Chinese men were beaten "by a lot of worthless boys."
10. "The Freshet," *Walla Walla Statesman*, January 26, 1866.
11. "Great Freshet," *Walla Walla Statesman*, February 1, 1867.
12. "Rebuilding," *Walla Walla Statesman*, March 1, 1867; and "New Court House," *Walla Walla Statesman*, March 15, 1867.
13. "Fort Walla Walla," *Walla Walla Statesman*, August 18, 1865.
14. Wright and his wife perished in a shipwreck en route to assume command in Vancouver.
15. E.g., "Fort Matters," *Walla Walla Statesman*, October 6, 1865; and "Precaution Extraordinary, against Secession," *Walla Walla Statesman*, December 8, 1865. Currey was discharged in November 1865; however, the *Statesman*'s attacks continued for months.
16. *A Report of Inspection of Military Posts*, 39th Cong., 2d sess. (1867), H. Doc. 20, 3, 11.
17. Henry Norris Copp, *Public Land Laws Passed by Congress from March 4, 1869, to March 3, 1875* (San Francisco: Bancroft & Co., 1875), 93. The city was usually identified as "Walla Walla, Oregon" in the national press.

19. Law and Order

1. Randall H. Hewitt, *Across the Plains and over the Divide: A Mule Train Journey from East to West in 1862, and Incidents Connected Therewith* (New York: Broadway, 1906), 463.

2. "Fire," *Washington Statesman*, May 13, 1864.

3. "A Monopoly," *Walla Walla Statesman*, June 4, 1869. Actually, Baker would have rented buildings to Chinese men for whom the prostitutes worked. See also "Fire," *Walla Walla Statesman*, June 25, 1866; and "The Chinese Quarter," *Walla Walla Statesman*, July 2, 1869.

4. "Dance Houses," *Washington Statesman*, January 23, 1864.

5. "Among other improvements, we notice that Mr. Van Wormington is putting up a large building at the upper end of Main Street, to be used as a hurdy gurdy establishment. The building is located beyond the Bridge, in order to avoid the heavy tax imposed by the city authorities." "A Hurdy Establishment," *Walla Walla Statesman*, November 23, 1866. Martin Van Buren Wormington was one of the founders of Milton, Oregon.

6. Bill Gulick, "Josephine Wolfe, Walla Walla's Genteel Madam," in *Outlaws of the Pacific Northwest* (Caldwell, ID: Caxton, 2000), 55–65. Anne M. Butler writes, "The experiences of a few notorious, but prosperous, madams have clouded the realities of urban prostitution and prompted some cities to exalt their infamous and wealthy locals as scintillating examples of the fun-filled life of the prostitute." *Daughters of Joy, Sisters of Misery: Prostitutes in the American West, 1865–90* (Chicago: University of Illinois Press, 1985), 3–4.

7. A large fire in Yreka in October 1859 destroyed "Every China house of ill fame," and Josephine Wolfe lost $1,500 worth of property. "Fire at Yreka," *Sacramento Daily Union*, October 24, 1859.

8. Wolfe's estate was valued at $32,811.15; most was bequeathed to St. Patrick's church. See "Notorious Woman Dead of Pneumonia," *Evening Statesman*, April 15, 1909, 5; "'Dutch Joe's' Will," *Evening Statesman*, May 21, 1909, 5; and "Dutch Joe's Will Unique Document," *Yakima Herald*, April 21, 1909, 8. In the 1870 census, Wolfe is listed as owning $2,500 in real estate.

9. Nine single women, ages twenty to thirty, with no occupation noted, are listed together with Wolfe on the 1887 census.

10. Meduna was fined $5 for "firing pistol within the city limits." Acosta was fined $40 and taxed $25. "Recorder's Court," *Washington Statesman*, December 5, 1863. Meduna lost two houses in the 1866 fire. "Destructive Fire."

11. Lucie Cheng Hirata, "Free, Indentured, Enslaved: Chinese Prostitutes in Nineteenth-Century America," *Signs* 5, no. 1 (Autumn 1979), 4.

12. Dorsey Baker made at least one reference to "China alley." Diary of Dorsey S. Baker, vol. 24, 1878, WCMss040, Baker Family Collection, Whitman College and Northwest Archives.

13. Cheng Hirata pointed out that prostitution "provided Chinese entrepreneurs one of the few opportunities to accumulate capital in a hostile society." "Free, Indentured, Enslaved," 4.

14. Theodor Kirchhoff, "Die rheinischen Hurdy Gurdys in Amerika: Noch ein Kapitel vom deutschen Menschenhandel," *Die Gartenlaube: Illustriertes Familienblatt*, no. 20 (1865), 311–3.

15. "The City Makes a Raise," *Walla Walla Statesman*, November 30, 1866.

16. For example, a correspondent from the Powder River mines noted on the population there, "There is also several 'ladies of pave' here—one or two from your city." *Washington Statesman*, September 13, 1862. See also Butler, chapter 1; Benson Tong, *Unsubmissive Women: Chinese Prostitutes in Nineteenth-Century San Francisco* (Norman: University of Oklahoma Press, 1994); Alexy Simmons, "Red Light Ladies in the American West: Entrepreneurs and Companions," *Australian Journal of Historical Archaeology* 7 (1989), 63–9; Catherine Holder Spude, "Brothels and Saloons: An Archaeology of Gender in the American West," *Historical Archaeology* 39, no. 1 (2005), 89–106; and Paula Petrik, "Capitalists with Rooms: Prostitution

in Helena, Montana, 1865–1900," *Montana: The Magazine of Western History* 31, no. 2 (Spring 1981), 28–41.

17. In her study of prostitution in Helena, Montana, Paula Petrik shows that prostitutes reporting wealth and/or property dropped from 45 percent in 1870 to 0 percent in 1900. "Capitalists with Rooms," 30.

18. "Highway Robbery," *Washington Statesman*, November 1, 1862.

19. See Michael J. Pfeifer, *The Roots of Rough Justice: Origins of American Lynching* (Chicago: University of Illinois Press, 2011), chapter 2.

20. "Leave of Absence Granted," *Walla Walla Statesman*, February 3, 1865.

21. "Law and Order," *Walla Walla Statesman*, April 14, 1865.

22. "Hung by the Vigilance Committee," *Walla Walla Statesman*, April 21, 1865.

23. William D. Lyman, *Illustrated History of Walla Walla County* (San Francisco: Lever, 1901), 242–5.

24. "Fifteen Men Hung at Walla Walla," *Oregonian*, April 21, 1865. This report circulated throughout the Far West.

25. The discovery of his rotted body, partly devoured by animals, repulsed William Newell, who advised, "If we are to have any more executions of this character, we trust that the volunteer hangmen will at least have the decency to bury their dead. In our horror of crime let us not forget the dictates of common humanity." "Horrible Affair," *Walla Walla Statesman*, July 20, 1866.

26. Myron Eells, *Father Eells: Or, The Results of Fifty-Five Years of Missionary Labors in Washington and Oregon* (Boston: Congregational Publishing Society, 1894), 185–7.

27. "Assassination of Ferd. Patterson," *Walla Walla Statesman*, February 16, 1866; and "The Killing of Pinkham," *Walla Walla Statesman*, August 25, 1865.

28. Letter from "Reform," *Walla Walla Statesman*, June 22, 1866.

29. Letter from "Law-Abiding Citizen," *Walla Walla Statesman*, June 29, 1866.

30. "Grand Jury Report," *Walla Walla Statesman*, July 13, 1866.

31. "A Scamp," *Walla Walla Statesman*, October 5, 1866.

32. "Citizens' Meeting," *Walla Walla Statesman*, May 10, 1867; and "Mass Convention," *Walla Walla Statesman*, May 17, 1867.

33. "A Sign," *Walla Walla Statesman*, May 24, 1867.

34. "A Respite," *Walla Walla Statesman*, June 7, 1867.

20. Forging Lives in a Hostile Landscape

1. "Record of Council at the Umatilla Indian Reservation, Eastern Oregon, August 7 to 13, 1871," *Third Annual Report of the Commissioner of Indian Affairs*, 42d Cong., 2d sess. (1871), H. Doc. 1, 524.

2. Report of W. H. Barnhart, August 5, 1862, *Report of the Commissioner of Indian Affairs* (1862), 269.

3. See T. W. Davenport, "Recollections of an Indian Agent," *Quarterly of the Oregon Historical Society* 8, no. 1 (March 1907), 29–30. Davenport was asked to step in temporarily when Barnhart was suspended and ordered to Washington to address accusations of a number of crimes, including the use of government funds to run his mercantile business. "The Umatilla Agency," *Washington Statesman*, August 30, 1862.

4. The Grande Ronde Valley and river were discussed repeatedly at the Walla Walla council seven years earlier. Both Weatenatemany and Itstikats had emphatically demanded retention of the valley. In outlining his plans for the reservation, Stevens ambiguously defined the respective western and eastern boundaries as the foothills and valleys encircling the Grande Ronde Valley, yet he may never have stated that the valley itself was to be ceded to the government.

5. Report of Wm. H. Rector, September 2, 1862, *Report of the Commissioner of Indian Affairs,* 37th Cong., 3d sess. (1862), H. Doc. 1, 260.
6. "Particulars of the Killing of the Grande Ronde Indians," *Washington Statesman,* August 30, 1862.
7. Davenport, "Recollections," 33–4.
8. On the ambiguities of the original boundary, see E. Thomas Morning Owl and Roberta L. Conner, "They Are Cutting Up the Marked Land," *Čáw Pawá Láakni/They Are Not Forgotten: Sahaptian Place Names Atlas of the Cayuse, Umatilla, and Walla Walla* (Pendleton, OR: Tamástslikt Cultural Institute, 2015), 49–53. Pending an 1866 survey, the Oregon–Washington border itself remained an approximation.
9. "The Umatilla Reservation," *Washington Statesman,* November 28, 1863.
10. "Governor's Message," *Washington Statesman,* January 3, 1863.
11. "Indian Treaty," *Washington Statesman,* July 29, 1864.
12. Report of W. H. Barnhart, August 4, 1866, *Report of the Commissioner of Indian Affairs for the Year 1866,* 39th Cong., 2nd sess. (1866), H. Doc. 2, 87.
13. Report of Father Warneersch [sic], August 1, 1866, *Report of the Commissioner of Indian Affairs,* 39th Cong., 2d sess. (1866), H. Doc. 2, 88.
14. "Indian Warriors," *Walla Walla Statesman,* November 15, 1867.
15. "Right," *Walla Walla Statesman,* July 13, 1866.
16. The "Umatilla Indians" won first premium for best display of both onions and cauliflower, and second premium for display of vegetable. "Fourth Annual State Fair," *Oregon Statesman,* October 9, 1865.
17. Report of J. W. Perit Huntington, October 15, 1866, *Report of the Commissioner of Indian Affairs* (1866), 76.
18. Cumtux, "The Indian Question: How it Can Be Settled," *Walla Walla Statesman,* July 5, 1867; "Indian Affairs—Folly of Treating with the Red Skins," *Walla Walla Statesman,* June 28, 1867; and "Indian Treaties—Swindling Systematized," *Walla Walla Statesman,* July 12, 1867.
19. Wm. H. Barnhart, "Indian Affairs," *Walla Walla Statesman,* August 30, 1867.
20. "Indian Outrages," *Walla Walla Statesman,* August 30, 1867. Newell's successor at the *Daily Mountaineer*—no friend of Indians—had earlier taken a shot at Newell for his fixations on Indians and mail contracts: "We wonder when folks will get sense enough to cease their grumbling about such trifles as the mails and Indian difficulties!" "Useless Grumbling," *Daily Mountaineer,* March 28, 1866.
21. "The Indians," *Walla Walla Statesman,* August 30, 1867.
22. Report of W. H. Barnhart, July 25, 1868, U.S. Congress, House, *Report of the Commissioner of Indian Affairs for the Year 1868,* 40th Cong., 3d sess. (1868), H. Doc. 2, 113.
23. A. B. Meacham, *Wigwam and War-Path: Or, The Royal Chief in Chains* (Boston: Dale, 1875), 206.
24. Gray H. Whaley, *Oregon and the Collapse of Illahee: U.S. Empire and the Transformation of an Indigenous World, 1792–1859* (Chapel Hill: University of North Carolina Press, 2010), 236.
25. See Meacham, chapter 13. Meacham established *The Council Fire* in 1878, a journal dedicated to Indian rights and criticism of the BIA.

21. Agriculture, Horticulture, Infrastructure

1. "The High Lands Good for Wheat Raising," *Walla Walla Statesman,* September 16, 1864. On the origins of wheat farming in the region, see Richard Scheuerman and Alexander McGregor, *Harvest Heritage: Agricultural Origins and Heirloom Crops of the Pacific Northwest* (Pullman: Washington State University Press, 2013), chapter 4.
2. "Agricultural Society," *Washington Statesman,* November 7 and 14, 1863.

3. "Agricultural Society," *Walla Walla Statesman*, June 22, 1866; and "Agricultural Fair" and "Agricultural Meeting," *Walla Walla Statesman*, July 13, 1866.
4. Papers nationwide noted a smallpox outbreak at "Walla Walla, Oregon."
5. The village of Cascades was destroyed by flood in 1894.
6. See G. Thomas Edwards, "Town Boosterism on Oregon's Mining Frontier: James Vansyckle and Wallula, Columbia Riverport, 1860–1870," *Oregon Historical Quarterly* 106, no. 1 (Spring 2005), 76–97.
7. Frances Fuller Victor, *All Over Oregon and Washington* (San Francisco: Carmany, 1872), 104.
8. "Freighting from the Dalles," *Washington Statesman*, May 31, 1862.
9. "An Act to Incorporate the Walla Walla Rail Road Company," *Session Laws of the Territory of Washington . . . 9th Session of the Legislative Assembly Held at Olympia, 1861–62* (Olympia: n.p., 1862), 119–23.
10. "Railroad to Wallula," *Washington Statesman*, December 20, 1862.
11. "Railroad to Wallula," *Washington Statesman*, May 3, 1862.
12. Capt. John Mullan, "Walla Walla Rail Road Company," *American Railroad Journal* 19, no. 13 (March 28, 1863), 285–6.
13. Keith Petersen suggests that the railroad plans collapsed with Mullan's return to Walla Walla. *John Mullan: The Tumultuous Life of a Western Road Builder* (Pullman: Washington State University Press, 2014), 189–93.
14. "City Water Works," *Walla Walla Statesman*, November 9, 1866.
15. The city water works would turn out to be a thirty-year headache for Isaacs and the city. See William D. Lyman, *Lyman's History of Old Walla Walla County*, vol. 1 (Chicago: Clarke, 1918), 149–50, 301–2.
16. "Productiveness of Walla Walla Valley," *Walla Walla Statesman*, November 30, 1866.
17. Donald W. Meinig, *The Great Columbia Plain: A Historical Geography, 1805–1910* (Seattle: University of Washington Press, 1995), 225.
18. "Public Meeting," *Walla Walla Statesman*, October 12, 1866.
19. "Sheep Raising," *Walla Walla Statesman*, March 8, 1867. For years, the *Statesman* encouraged the development of a wool industry in the region as one means of diversification.
20. "Dull Times," *Walla Walla Statesman*, August 30, 1867.
21. Philip Ritz, *Letter upon the Agricultural and Mineral Resources of the North-western Territories, on the Route of the Northern Pacific Railroad* (Washington, DC: Chronicle Print, 1868).
22. "The Railroad," *Walla Walla Statesman*, November 15, 1867.
23. "Northern Pacific Railroad Meeting," *Walla Walla Statesman*, July 23, 1869.
24. W. Milnor Roberts, *Special Report of a Reconnoissance [sic] of the Route for the Northern Pacific Railroad* (Philadelphia: n.p., 1869), 18.
25. "Fire," *Walla Walla Statesman*, June 25, 1869; and "We Can Stand It," *Vancouver Register*, July 31, 1869.
26. "Telegraphic," *Walla Walla Statesman*, November 1, 1867.
27. "The Telegraph to Walla Walla," *Oregonian*, June 2, 1870.

22. Bird's-Eye Views

1. Elwood Evans, *History of the Pacific Northwest: Oregon and Washington*, vol. 2 (Portland: North Pacific History Co., 1889), 246–9. Individuals paid to have biographical sketches included in such publications.
2. The most important study of these lithographic urban views remains John W. Reps's *Views and Viewmakers of Urban America: Lithographs of Towns and Cities in the United States and Canada* (Columbia: University of Missouri, 1984). Reps estimated that 5,000 sets of these prints were produced for 2,400 North American cities between 1825 and 1925 (p. 3).

3. Robert J. Chandler, *San Francisco Lithographer: African American Artist Grafton Tyler Brown* (Norman: University of Oklahoma Press, 2014), 41–7.
4. "Lithographic View of the City," *Walla Walla Statesman*, May 5, 1865.
5. Brown's biographer claims, "When he worked from a photograph, he transformed the scene and intensified his 'feel' for the town." Chandler, 116.
6. "The Diary of Eli Sheldon Glover," Eli Sheldon Glover papers, Mss 2721, Oregon Historical Society Research Library.
7. "Bird's Eye View of Walla Walla," *Walla Walla Statesman*, February 12, 1876. A wood engraving of the images was subsequently produced and illustrated in several local publications.

23. The End of the Reservation?

1. Frances Fuller Victor's "The Oregon Indians, Part I," *Overland Monthly* 7, no. 4 (October 1871), 350.
2. Moody served as governor of Oregon, 1882–87.
3. "Umatilla Indian Reservation," *Walla Walla Union*, May 27, 1871.
4. E. S. Parker to Felix R. Brunot, May 31, 1871, "Record of Council at the Umatilla Indian Reservation, Eastern Oregon, August 7 to 13, 1871," *Third Annual Report of the Commissioner of Indian Affairs*, 42d Cong., 2d sess. (1871), H. Doc. 1, 94. Parker soon resigned, believing the Board of Commissioners had usurped his authority.
5. All quotations from "Record of Council at the Umatilla Indian Reservation," 89–107.
6. "The Umatilla Indian Council," *Walla Walla Union*, August 19, 1871.
7. "No Room for Red Men," *New-York Tribune*, September 23, 1871, 4. The *Tribune* had printed a full report of the council two days earlier.
8. Brunot, November 15, 1871, "Record of Council at the Umatilla Indian Reservation," 89.

24. New Economic Realities

1. "Six Years' Changes," *Walla Walla Statesman*, April 23, 1869.
2. See James W. Watt, "Experiences of a Packer in Washington Territory Mining Camps during the Sixties," *Washington Historical Quarterly* 20, no. 1 (January 1929), 39, 49.
3. F. F. Victor, "Summer Wanderings," *Oregonian*, June 27, 1870.
4. "Walla Walla Branch N. P. Railroad," *Oregon Republican*, June 3, 1871.
5. Frank T. Gilbert, *Historic Sketches of Walla Walla, Whitman, Columbia and Garfield Counties, Washington Territory, and Umatilla County, Oregon* (Portland: Walling, 1882), 296. Granted, these assessments were often underestimated.
6. "Grain Crop," *Walla Walla Statesman*, August 9, 1873.
7. Frances Fuller Victor, *All Over Oregon and Washington* (San Francisco: Carmany, 1872), 118.
8. "The Walla Walla Railroad," *Oregonian*, June 8, 1871.
9. See "Railway Aid," *Oregonian*, October 2, 1871; and "Supplementary Articles of Incorporation," *Oregonian*, October 7, 1871. In 1871, the board consisted of I. T. Reese, vice president; H. M. Chase, secretary; William Stephens, treasurer; and John Boyer, B. L. Sharpstein, and Lew McMorris, trustees. In all, 24 stockholders purchased 1,738 shares; Baker took on 5,262 shares. W. W. Baker, *Forty Years a Pioneer: Business Life of Dorsey Syng Baker, 1848–1888* (Seattle: Lowman & Hanford, 1934), 168–9.
10. Narrow-gauge railroads were attracting a great deal of interest around 1871. Baker ordered one (0-4-0T) locomotive in Pittsburgh and then ordered a second, identical one in 1872. He named them "Walla Walla" and "Wallula."
11. "Walla Walla Correspondence," *Puget Sound Dispatch*, October 24, 1872.
12. Diary of Dorsey S. Baker, vols. 19–20, 1871–72, Baker Family Collection, Whitman College and Northwest Archives.

13. "Business," *Puget Sound Dispatch*, June 12, 1873.
14. Schwabacher Bros. was among the major supporters in Walla Walla. When it was organized in 1874, Sigmund Schwabacher and Bailey Gatzert sat on the railroad's board of directors.
15. "Seattle Railroad," *Puget Sound Dispatch*, August 21, 1873. This was part of a page-one feature hyping the railroad.
16. "Seattle and Walla Walla Railroad," *Puget Sound Dispatch*, August 14, 1873. See Kurt E. Armbruster, *Orphan Road: The Railroad Comes to Seattle, 1853–1911* (Pullman: Washington State University Press, 1999), chapter 5.
17. "Vacant Buildings," *Walla Walla Statesman*, March 25, 1876. On the collapse of the NPR, see Richard White, *Railroaded: The Transcontinentals and the Making of Modern America* (New York: W. W. Norton, 2011), chapter 2. White notes that twenty-five *actual* railroads collapsed between September 18 and the end of 1873 (p. 84).
18. "Hard Times," *Walla Walla Statesman*, January 16, 1875.
19. "What Is Said of Us," *Walla Walla Statesman*, August 7, 1875.
20. See Ezra S. Carr, *The Patrons of Husbandry on the Pacific Coast* (San Francisco: Bancroft & Co., 1875). The organization of the Granges was based on Masonic tradition, but, like the Good Templars, women were admitted, and they advocated temperance and women's suffrage.
21. "Walla Walla for the Railroad," *Puget Sound Dispatch*, November 19, 1874.
22. "The Diary of Eli Sheldon Glover," Eli Sheldon Glover papers, Mss 2721, Oregon Historical Society Research Library. Above all, Glover was fascinated by the colorful stories of Baker's "penuriousness" as told by the railroad employees.
23. During the winter, the commissioners had allocated $5,000 toward improving the road—largely due to damage caused by the construction of the railroad. C. C. Cram and Frank Louden were both commissioners and Grangers.
24. "The Freight Question," *Walla Walla Statesman*, March 25, April 1, April 15, 1876.
25. The total cost of the railroad was $356,134.85. The sale of Baker's stock in the WWCRR in 1878 (to the OSN) and 1880 (to Henry Villard) made him a millionaire.
26. The brewer John Stahl (1870 from Canyon City, Oregon) and the rancher/entrepreneur William Kirkman (1871 from San Francisco), for example, arrived in the city flush after having sold successful businesses. Stahl purchased the City Brewery for $7,500. After his house was lost to fire in 1872, he immediately had a two-story brick house built. Kirkman's grand, brick Italianate mansion, built by Freeman Allen (1879–80) at a cost of $7,000, is still standing.
27. Farmland rent varied, but commonly the owner would supply the seed or stock and ask for a percentage of the produce, often one-third.
28. "Adjusting Our Boundaries," *Oregonian*, February 10, 1871.
29. In 1880, northern Idahoans voted 1216 to 7 in favor of annexation. Kingston, "The North Idaho Annexation Issue," *Washington Historical Quarterly*, 24, no. 2 (April 1933), 213–7.
30. "Democratic Meeting," *Daily Intelligencer*, September 27, 1876. The annexation movement was led by Democrats B. L. Sharpstein and Nathan Caton.
31. "The Annexation Project," *Albany Register*, January 7, 1876.
32. "Alaska," *Walla Walla Statesman*, December 25, 1875; and "Annexation," *Walla Walla Statesman*, July 17, 1876.
33. "The Future of Our City," *Walla Walla Statesman*, December 15, 1878.
34. According to the 1880 US census, the most populous cities in the Northwest were Portland (17,577), Walla Walla (3,588), Seattle (3,533), Salem (2,538), and The Dalles (2,232).

25. The End of the Treaty

1. "The Territories," *Oregonian*, April 25, 1873; and "Indian Troubles East of the Mountains," *Oregonian*, April 28, 1873.

2. Report of Narcisse Cornoyer, September 4, 1873, *Report of the Commissioner of Indian Affairs,* 43rd Cong., 1st sess. (1873), H. Doc. 1, 318. The citizens of Pendleton (successfully) petitioned the governor for weapons in April.

3. "The Indians of Eastern Oregon," *Oregonian,* May 9, 1873.

4. [S. M. Wait], "Further Assurances from East of the Mountains," *Oregonian,* May 10, 1873.

5. Alvin M. Josephy Jr., *The Nez Perce Indians and the Opening of the Northwest* (New York: Houghton Mifflin Harcourt, 1997), 456–7.

6. "Umatila Reservation," *Walla Walla Statesman,* February 19, March 4, April 15, 1876.

7. "Umatila Reservation," *Walla Walla Statesman,* April 15, 1876.

8. "Report of Civil and Military Commission to Nez Perce Indians Washington Territory and the Northwest," *Annual Report of Commissioner of Indian Affairs for the Year 1877* (Washington, DC: Government Publishing Office, 1877), 212.

9. "Report of Civil and Military Commission to Nez Perce Indians," 215.

10. "The Umatillas," *Walla Walla Statesman,* June 23, 1877.

11. "Major N. Cornoyer," *Walla Walla Statesman,* June 30, 1877. Cornoyer and his entourage were praised for this. They did the same in Pendleton and Weston.

12. "From the Seat of War," *Weekly Pacific Tribune,* July 13, 1877.

13. Report of N. A. Cornoyer, August 23, 1878, *Annual Report of the Commissioner of Indian Affairs for the Year 1878* (Washington, DC: Government Publishing Office, 1878), 122.

14. Report of N. A. Cornoyer, xxxvii.

Bibliography

Archives

National Archives, Cartographic and Architectural Section
Oregon Historical Society
Oregon State Archives (records.sos.state.or.us)
Whitman College and Northwest Archives
Yakima Valley Libraries, Relander Collection

Newspapers

Albany Register
California Star
Californian
Christian Advocate and Journal (New York)
The Columbian (Olympia)
Daily Alta California
Daily Intelligencer (Seattle)
Daily National Democrat (Marysville, CA)
The Elevator (San Francisco)
The Evening Statesman (Walla Walla)
The Missionary Herald (Boston)
New York Daily Tribune
New York Herald
New-York Tribune
Oregon Argus (Oregon City)
Oregon Free Press (Oregon City)
Oregon Republican
Oregon Spectator (Oregon City)
Oregon Statesman (Salem)
The Oregonian (Portland)
Pioneer and Democrat (Olympia)
Placer Times (Sacramento)
Portland Advertiser
Portland Democratic Standard
Portland Times
Puget Sound Dispatch (Seattle)
Puget Sound Herald (Steilacoom)
Real Estate Gazette (Walla Walla)
Sacramento Transcript
Sacramento Union
The Spirit of Missions (Gambier, Ohio)
The State Republican (Eugene)
State Rights Democrat (Albany)
United States Magazine and Democratic Review (Washington, DC)
Vancouver Register

Walla Walla Union
Walla Walla Union-Bulletin
Walla Walla Weekly Union
Washington Standard (Olympia)
Washington Statesman/Walla Walla Statesman
Weekly Pacific Tribune (Olympia)
Yakima Herald

Ackerman, Lillian Alice. *A Necessary Balance: Gender and Power among Indians of the Columbia Plateau.* Norman: University of Oklahoma Press, 2003.

Armbruster, Kurt E. *Orphan Road: The Railroad Comes to Seattle, 1853–1911.* Pullman: Washington State University Press, 1999.

Baker, W. W. *Forty Years a Pioneer: Business Life of Dorsey Syng Baker, 1848–1888.* Seattle: Lowman & Hanford, 1934.

Barman, Jean, and Bruce McIntyre Watson. *Leaving Paradise: Indigenous Hawaiians in the Pacific Northwest, 1787–1898.* Honolulu: University of Hawai'i Press, 2006.

Beardsley, Arthur S., and Donald A. McDonald. "The Courts and Early Bar of the Washington Territory." *Washington Law Review* 17, no. 2 (April 1942): 56–82.

Beecher, Lyman. *A Plea for the West.* Cincinnati: Truman and Smith, 1835.

Beeson, John. *A Plea for the Indians.* New York: n.p., 1858.

Bennett, Robert A. *Walla Walla: Portrait of a Western Town, 1804–1899.* Walla Walla: Pioneer Press, 1980.

Bieder, Robert E. *Science Encounters the Indian, 1820–1880: The Early Years of American Ethnology.* Norman: University of Oklahoma Press, 1986.

Blanchet, Francis Norbert. *Historical Sketches of the Catholic Church in Oregon, During the Past Forty Years.* Portland: n.p., 1878.

Boyd, Robert. "Pacific Northwest Measles Epidemic of 1847–1848." *Oregon Historical Quarterly* 95, no. 1 (Spring 1994): 6–47.

Boyd, Robert. "Commentary on Early Contact-Era Smallpox in the Pacific Northwest." *Ethnohistory* 43, no. 2 (Spring 1996): 307–28.

Boyd, Robert. *The Coming of the Spirit of Pestilence: Introduced Infectious Diseases and Population Decline among Northwest Coast Indians, 1774–1874.* Seattle: University of Washington Press, 1999.

Boyd, Robert, ed. *Indians, Fire, and the Land in the Pacific Northwest.* Corvallis: Oregon State University Press, 1999.

Boyd, Robert. *People of the Dalles: The Indians of Wascopam Mission.* Lincoln: University of Nebraska Press, 2004.

Bristol, Douglas Walter, Jr. *Knights of the Razor: Black Barbers in Slavery and Freedom.* Baltimore: Johns Hopkins University Press, 2009.

Brode, Howard S., ed. "Diary of Augustus J. Thibodo of the Northwest Exploring Expedition, 1859." *Pacific Northwest Quarterly* 31, no. 3 (July 1940): 287–347.

Brouillet, J. B. A. *Protestantism in Oregon: Account of the Murder of Dr. Whitman, and the Ungrateful Calumnies of H. H. Spalding, Protestant Missionary.* New York: Cozans, 1853.

Brown, J. Henry. *Brown's Political History of Oregon.* Vol. 1. Portland: W. B. Allen, 1892.

Brown, Roberta Stringham, and Patricia O'Connell Killen, eds. *Selected Letters of A. M. A. Blanchet: Bishop of Walla Walla and Nesqualy (1846–1879).* Seattle: University of Washington Press, 2013.

Butler, Anne M. *Daughters of Joy, Sisters of Misery: Prostitutes in the American West, 1865–90.* Chicago: University of Illinois Press, 1985.

Carr, Ezra S. *The Patrons of Husbandry on the Pacific Coast.* San Francisco: Bancroft & Co., 1875.

Cebula, Larry. *Plateau Indians and the Quest for Spiritual Power, 1700–1850*. Lincoln: University of Nebraska Press, 2003.

Chandler, Robert J. *San Francisco Lithographer: African American Artist Grafton Tyler Brown*. Norman: University of Oklahoma Press, 2014.

Clark, Keith, and Donna Clark. "William McKay's Journal, 1866–67: Indian Scouts." *Oregon Historical Quarterly* 79, no. 3 (Fall 1978): 268–333.

Cline, Scott. "Creation of an Ethnic Community: Portland Jewry, 1851–1866." *Pacific Northwest Quarterly* 76, no. 2 (April 1985): 52–60.

Cline, Scott. "The Jews of Portland, Oregon: A Statistical Dimension, 1860–1880." *Oregon Historical Quarterly* 88, no. 1 (Spring 1987): 4–25.

Confederated Tribes of the Umatilla Indian Reservation. *Comprehensive Plan*. 2010/2018. https://ctuir.org/media/sychezsg/2018updated-2010_comprehensiveplan-webversion.pdf.

Copp, Henry Norris. *Public Land Laws Passed by Congress from March 4, 1869, to March 3, 1875*. San Francisco: Bancroft & Co., 1875.

Cressman, Luther S. *The Sandal and the Cave: The Indians of Oregon*. Portland: Beaver Books, 1962.

Davenport, T. W. "Recollections of an Indian Agent." *Quarterly of the Oregon Historical Society* 8, nos. 1–2 (March, June 1907): 1–41, 95–128.

Davis, Alexander Jackson. *Rural Residences*. New York: n.p., 1837.

de Smet, P. J. *Letters and Sketches with a Narrative of a Year's Residence among the Indian Tribes of the Rocky Mountains*. Philadelphia: M. Fithian, 1843.

Dennis, Elsie Frances. "Indian Slavery in Pacific Northwest." *Oregon Historical Quarterly* 31, nos. 1–3 (March, June, September 1930): 69–81, 181–95, 285–96.

Disoway, G. P. "The Flat-Head Indians." *Christian Advocate and Journal* (March 1, 1833): 1.

Downing, Andrew Jackson. *The Architecture of Country Houses*. New York: Appleton, 1850.

Drury, Clifford M. *Marcus Whitman, M. D.: Pioneer and Martyr*. Caldwell, ID: Caxton, 1937.

Drury, Clifford M. *Marcus and Narcissa Whitman and the Opening of Old Oregon*. Glendale, CA: Clark, 1973.

Drury, Clifford M., ed. *The Mountains We Have Crossed: Diaries and Letters of the Oregon Mission, 1838*. Lincoln: University of Nebraska Press, 1999.

Dunn, John. *History of the Oregon Territory and British North-America Fur Trade*. London: Edwards & Hughes, 1844.

Edwards, G. Thomas. "Walla Walla: Gateway to the Pacific Northwest Interior." *Montana: The Magazine of Western History* 40, no. 3 (Summer 1990): 28–43.

Edwards, G. Thomas. *The Triumph of Tradition: The Emergence of Whitman College, 1859–1924*. Walla Walla: Whitman College, 1992.

Edwards, G. Thomas. "Town Boosterism on Oregon's Mining Frontier: James Vansyckle and Wallula, Columbia Riverpont, 1860–1870." *Oregon Historical Quarterly* 106, no. 1 (Spring 2005): 76–97.

Eells, Myron. *Father Eells: Or, The Results of Fifty-Five Years of Missionary Labors in Washington and Oregon*. Boston: Congregational Publishing Society, 1894.

Eichin, Carolyn Grattan. *From San Francisco Eastward: Victorian Theater in the American West*. Reno: University of Nevada Press, 2020.

Elliott, T. C., ed. "Journal of David Thompson." *Quarterly of the Oregon Historical Society* 15, no. 1 (March 1914): 39–63.

Elliott, T. C. "The Fur Trade in the Columbia River Basin Prior to 1811." *Quarterly of the Oregon Historical Society* 15, no. 4 (December 1914): 241–51; 6, no. 1 (January 1915): 3–10.

Elliott, T. C. "The Organization and First Pastorate of the First Congregational Church of Walla Walla, Washington." *Washington Historical Quarterly* 6, no. 2 (April 1915): 90–9.

Elliott, T. C. "The Dalles-Celilo Portage: Its History and Influence." *Quarterly of the Oregon Historical Society* 16, no. 2 (June 1915): 133–74.

Elliott, T. C. "The Coming of the White Women, 1836." *Oregon Historical Quarterly* 37, no. 3 (September 1936): 171–91; 38, no. 1 (March 1936): 44–62.

Etulain, Richard W. *Lincoln and Oregon Country: Politics in the Civil War Era.* Corvallis: Oregon State University Press, 2013.

Eulenberg, Julia Niebuhr. "Jewish Enterprise in the American West: Washington, 1853–1909" (PhD diss., University of Washington, 1996).

Evans, Chad. *Frontier Theatre: A History of Nineteenth-Century Theatrical Entertainment in the Canadian Far West and Alaska.* Victoria: Sono Nis Press, 1983.

Evans, Elwood. *History of the Pacific Northwest: Oregon and Washington.* Vol. 2. Portland, OR: North Pacific History, 1889.

Farnham, Thomas J. *Travels in the Great Western Prairies, the Anahuac and Rocky Mountains, and in the Oregon Territory.* New York: Greeley & McElrath, 1843.

Ficken, Robert E. *Washington Territory.* Pullman: Washington State University Press, 2002.

Ficken, Robert E. "After the Treaties: Administering Pacific Northwest Indian Reservations." *Oregon Historical Quarterly* 106, no. 3 (Fall 2005): 442–61.

Fisher, Andrew H. *Shadow Tribe: The Making of Columbia River Indian Identity.* Seattle: University of Washington Press, 2011.

Fisk, Wilbur. "Proclamation." *Christian Advocate and Journal* (March 22, 1833): 118.

Franchère, Gabriel. *Narrative of a Voyage to the Northwest Coast of America in the years 1811, 1812, 1813, and 1814.* Translated by J. V. Huntington. New York: Redfield, 1854.

Gamber, Wendy. *The Female Economy: The Millinery and Dressmaking Trades, 1860–1930.* Urbana: University of Illinois Press, 1997.

Garth, Thomas R. "Archaeological Excavations at Fort Walla Walla." *Pacific Northwest Quarterly* 43, no. 1 (January 1952): 27–50.

Garth, Thomas R. "Early Nineteenth Century Tribal Relations in the Columbia Plateau." *Southwestern Journal of Anthropology* 20, no. 1 (Spring, 1964): 43–57.

Gates, Charles M., ed. *Messages of the Governors of the Territory of Washington to the Legislative Assembly, 1854–1889.* Seattle: University of Washington Press, 1940.

Gibson, James R. *Farming the Frontier: The Agricultural Opening of the Oregon Country, 1786–1846.* Vancouver: University of British Columbia Press, 2011.

Gilbert, Frank T. *Historic Sketches of Walla Walla, Whitman, Columbia and Garfield Counties, Washington Territory, and Umatilla County, Oregon.* Portland: Walling, 1882.

Gilliam, Washington Smith. "Reminiscences of Washington Smith Gilliam." *Transactions of the 29th Annual Reunion of the Oregon Pioneer Association for 1901.* (Portland: n.p., 1902): 202–20.

Goldstein, Eric L. *The Price of Whiteness: Jews, Race, and American Identity.* Princeton, NJ: Princeton University Press, 2008.

Gray, W. H. *History of Oregon, 1792–1849.* Portland: Harris and Holman, 1870.

Guie, Heister Dean. *Bugles in the Valley: Garnett's Fort Simcoe.* Portland: Oregon Historical Society, 1977.

Gulick, Bill. *Outlaws of the Pacific Northwest.* Caldwell, ID: Caxton, 2000.

Gunther, Erna. "The Westward Movement of Some Plains Traits." *American Anthropologist*, New Series 52, no. 2 (April–June 1950): 174–80.

Heizer, Robert Fleming. "Walla Walla Indian Expeditions to the Sacramento Valley." *California Historical Society Quarterly* 21, no. 1 (March 1942): 1–7.

Hewitt, Randall H. *Across the Plains and over the Divide: A Mule Train Journey from East to West in 1862, and Incidents Connected Therewith.* New York: Broadway, 1906.

Hines, Gustavus. *Oregon: Its History, Condition and Prospects*. Buffalo, NY: Derby, 1851.

Hines, Harvey K. *An Illustrated History of the State of Washington*. Chicago: Lewis, 1893.

Hirata, Lucie Cheng. "Free, Indentured, Enslaved: Chinese Prostitutes in Nineteenth-Century America." *Signs* 5, no. 1 (Autumn 1979): 3–29.

Hoagland, Alison K. *Army Architecture in the West: Forts Laramie, Bridger, and D. A. Russell, 1849–1912*. Norman: University of Oklahoma Press, 2004.

Horsman, Reginald. *Race and Manifest Destiny. The Origins of American Racial Anglo-Saxonism*. Cambridge, MA: Harvard University Press, 1981.

Hunn, Eugene. *Nch'i-Wána, "The Big River": Mid-Columbia Indians and Their Land*. Seattle: University of Washington Press, 1991.

Hunn, Eugene. "Columbia Plateau Indian Place Names: What Can They Teach Us?" *Journal of Linguistic Anthropology* 6, no. 1 (June 1996): 3–26.

Hunter, George. *Reminiscences of an Old Timer*. Battle Creek, MI: Review and Herald, 1889.

Idaho State Historical Society Reference Series, "Henry P. Isaacs and Josh C. Isaacs." No. 579. 1981.

Irving, Washington. *Adventures of Captain Bonneville: Or, Scenes beyond the Rocky Mountains of the Far West*. Vol. 1. London: Routledge, 1837.

Isaacs, Grace G. "Some Historical Data." *Up-to-the-Times Magazine* 1, no. 8 (June 1907): n.p.

Johnson, Overton, and William H. Winter. *Route across the Rocky Mountains*. Lafayette, IN: Semans, 1846.

Josephy, Alvin M., Jr. *The Nez Perce Indians and the Opening of the Northwest*. New York: Houghton Mifflin Harcourt, 1997.

Josephy, Alvin M., Jr. *Nez Perce Country*. Lincoln: University of Nebraska Press, 2007.

Kane, Paul. *Wanderings of an Artist among the Indians of North America*. London: Longman, 1859.

Karson, Jennifer, ed. *Wiyaxayxt/Wiyaakaa'awn/As Days Go By: Our History, Our Land, Our People—The Cayuse, Umatilla, and Walla Walla*. Seattle: University of Washington Press, 2006.

Kelley, Hall Jackson. "Manual of the Oregon Expedition." Charlestown, MA: Wheildon & Williams, 1831.

Kingston, C. S. "The Walla Walla Separation Movement." *Washington Historical Quarterly* 24, no. 2 (April 1933): 91–104.

Kip, Lawrence. *Army Life on the Pacific*. New York: Redfield, 1859.

Kip, Lawrence. "The Indian Council at Walla Walla, May and June, 1855." *Sources of the History of Oregon* 1, no. 2 (1897): 9–10.

Kirchhoff, Theodor. "Die rheinischen Hurdy Gurdys in Amerika: Noch ein Kapitel vom deutschen Menschenhandel." *Die Gartenlaube: Illustriertes Familienblatt* 20 (1865): 311–3.

Knuth, Priscilla. *"Picturesque" Frontier: The Army's Fort Dalles*. Portland: Oregon Historical Society, 1987.

Lansing, Ronald B. *Juggernaut: The Whitman Massacre Trial, 1850*. San Francisco: Ninth Judicial Circuit Historical Society, 1993.

Lazarus, Mark L. "An Historical Analysis of Alien Land Law: Washington Territory and State 1853–1889." *University of Puget Sound Law Review* 12 (1989): 197–246.

Lee, Daniel, and Joseph H. Frost. *Ten Years in Oregon*. New York: n.p., 1844.

Lee, Jason. "Diary of Reverend Jason Lee II." *Quarterly of the Oregon Historical Society* 17, no. 3 (September 1916): 240–66.

Lent, Geneva D. *West of the Mountains: James Sinclair and the Hudson's Bay Company*. Seattle: University of Washington Press, 1963.

Limerick, Patricia Nelson. *The Legacy of Conquest: The Unbroken Past of the American West*. New York: Norton, 1987.

Lockley, Fred. "Reminiscences of Colonel Henry Ernst Dosch." *Quarterly of the Oregon Historical Society* 25, no. 1 (March 1924): 53–71.

Lord, Elizabeth. *Reminiscences of Eastern Oregon*. Portland: Irwin-Hodson, 1903.

Lyman, William D. *Illustrated History of Walla Walla County*. San Francisco: Lever, 1901.

Lyman, William D. *Lyman's History of Old Walla Walla County*. 2 vols. Chicago: Clarke, 1918.

Lyons, Curtis J. "Traces of Spanish Influence in the Hawaiian Islands." *Papers of the Hawaiian Historical Society* 2 (1892): 25–7.

Mackenzie, Alexander. *Voyages from Montreal to the Frozen and Pacific Oceans*. Philadelphia: Morgan, 1802.

Mackie, Richard S. *Trading beyond the Mountains: The British Fur Trade on the Pacific, 1793–1843*. Vancouver: University of British Columbia Press, 1997.

MacLoed, R. C. "Fort Walla Walla in 1857." *Up-to-the-Times Magazine* 1, no. 7 (May 1907): 352–4.

MacLoed, R. C. "History of Catholic Church in the Walla Walla Valley." *Up-to-the-Times Magazine* 2, no. 6 (April 1908): 227.

Madley, Benjamin. *An American Genocide: The United States and the California Indian Catastrophe, 1846–1873*. New Haven: Yale University Press, 2017.

Mallett, Edmond. "The Origin of the Flathead Mission of the Rocky Mountains." *Records of the American Catholic Historical Society of Philadelphia* II (1886–88): 174–205.

Manring, B. F. "Recollections of a Pioneer of 1859—Lawson Stockman." *Quarterly of the Oregon Historical Society* 11, no. 2 (June 1910): 162–76.

McArthur, Lewis A. "The Oregon State Boundary." *Oregon Historical Quarterly* 37, no. 4 (December 1936): 301–7.

McCoy, Genevieve. "The Difficulties of Translating Mission Theory into Practice: The Whitman-Spalding Nez Perce Mission." *Journal of Presbyterian History* 77, no. 3 (Fall 1999): 181–94.

McFarland, Ron. *Edward J. Steptoe and the Indian Wars: Life on the Frontier, 1815–1865*. Jefferson, NC: McFarland, 2016.

McLoughlin, John. "Copy of a Document Found among the Private Papers of the Late Dr. John McLoughlin." In *Transactions of the Eighth Annual Re-Union of the Oregon Pioneer Association for 1880*, 46–55. Salem, OR, 1881.

McLoughlin, John. *McLoughlin's Fort Vancouver Letters, First Series 1825–38*. London: Champlain Society, 1941.

Meacham, A. B. *Wigwam and War-Path: Or, The Royal Chief in Chains*. Boston: Dale, 1875.

Meany, Edmond S. "Newspapers of Washington Territory." *Washington Historical Quarterly* 14, no. 4 (October 1923): 269–90.

Meinig, Donald W. *The Great Columbia Plain: A Historical Geography, 1805–1910*. Seattle: University of Washington Press, 1995.

Merk, Frederick, ed. *Fur Trade and Empire: George Simpson's Journal . . . 1824–1825*. Cambridge: Harvard University Press, 1831.

Meyer, Bette E. "The Pend Oreille Routes to Montana, 1866–1870." *Pacific Northwest Quarterly* 72, no. 2 (April 1981): 76–83.

Miller, Christopher L. *Prophetic Worlds: Indians and Whites on the Columbia Plateau*. New Brunswick, NJ: Rutgers University Press, 1985.

Miller, Robert J. *Native America, Discovered and Conquered: Thomas Jefferson, Lewis & Clark, and Manifest Destiny*. Lincoln: University of Nebraska Press, 2008.

Mills, Quincy T. *Cutting along the Color Line: Black Barbers and Barber Shops in America*. Philadelphia: University of Pennsylvania Press, 2013.

Moehring, Eugene P. *Urbanism and Empire in the Far West, 1840–1890*. Reno: University of Nevada Press, 2004.

Monroe, Barbara. *Plateau Indian Ways with Words: The Rhetorical Tradition of the Tribes of the Inland Pacific Northwest.* Pittsburgh: University of Pittsburgh Press, 2014.

Moulton, Gary, ed. *The Journals of the Lewis and Clark Expedition.* Lincoln: University of Nebraska Press, 2002. https://lewisandclarkjournals.unl.edu/item/lc.jrn.1806-05-05#lc.jrn.1806-05 -05.02.

Mowry, William Augustus. *Marcus Whitman and the Early Days of Oregon.* New York: Burdett, 1901.

Mullan, Capt. John. "Walla Walla Rail Road Company." *American Railroad Journal* 19, no. 13 (March 28, 1863): 285–6.

Nagae, Peggy. "Asian Women: Immigration and Citizenship in Oregon." *Oregon Historical Quarterly* 113, no. 3 (Fall 2012): 334–7.

Nelson, Kurt R. *Treaties and Treachery: The Northwest Indians' Resistance to Conquest.* Lincoln: University of Nebraska Press, 2011.

Netting, Robert McC. *Cultural Ecology,* 2nd ed. Prospect Heights, IL: Waveland, 1986.

Nichols, David Allen. *Lincoln and the Indians: Civil War Policy and Politics.* St. Paul: Minnesota Historical Society, 2012.

Nunis, Doyce B., ed. *The Golden Frontier: The Recollections of Herman Francis Reinhart, 1851–1869.* Austin: University of Texas Press, 1962.

Oberg, Barbara B., ed. *The Papers of Thomas Jefferson 40, 4 March–10 July 1803.* Princeton, NJ: Princeton University Press, 2013.

Oetelaar, Gerald A. "Beyond Activity Areas: Structure and Symbolism in the Organization and Use of Space inside Tipis." *Plains Anthropologist* 45, no. 171 (February 2000): 35–61.

Oliver, Egbert S. "Obed Dickinson and the 'Negro Question.'" *Oregon Historical Quarterly* 92, no. 1 (Spring 1991): 4–40.

O'Sullivan, John L. "Annexation." *United States Magazine and Democratic Review* 17, no. 85 (July–August 1845): 5–10.

Oviatt, Alton B. "Pacific Coast Competition for the Gold Camp Trade of Montana." *Pacific Northwest Quarterly* 56, no. 4 (October 1965): 168–76.

Palmer, Joel. *Journal of Travels over the Rocky Mountains to the Mouth of the Columbia River.* Cincinnati: James, 1852.

Pambrun, Andrew Dominique. *Sixty Years on the Frontier in the Pacific Northwest.* Fairfield, WA: Ye Galleon Press, 1978.

Parker, Samuel. *Journal of an Exploring Tour beyond the Rocky Mountains.* Ithaca, NY: Andrus, Woodruff, & Gauntlett, 1838.

Parsons, William. *An Illustrated History of Umatilla County.* San Francisco: Lever, 1902.

Peck, David J. *Or Perish in the Attempt: The Hardship and Medicine of the Lewis and Clark Expedition.* Lincoln: University of Nebraska Press, 2011.

Petersen, Keith. *John Mullan: The Tumultuous Life of a Western Road Builder.* Pullman: Washington State University Press, 2014.

Petrik, Paula. "Capitalists with Rooms: Prostitution in Helena, Montana, 1865–1900." *Montana: The Magazine of Western History* 31, no. 2 (Spring 1981): 28–34.

Pfeifer, Michael J. *The Roots of Rough Justice: Origins of American Lynching.* Chicago: University of Illinois Press, 2011.

Pickett, Susan E. *Marion and Emilie Frances Bauer: From the Wild West to American Musical Modernism.* Morrisville, NC: Lulu Publishing, 2014.

Powell, Fred Wilbur. *Hall Jackson Kelley, Prophet of Oregon.* Portland: Ivy Press, 1917.

Prucha, Francis Paul. *The Great Father: The United States Government and the American Indians.* 2 vols. Lincoln: University of Nebraska Press, 1984.

Prucha, Francis Paul. *American Indian Treaties: The History of a Political Anomaly.* Berkeley: University of California Press, 1994.

Qin, Yucheng. "A Century-Old 'Puzzle': The Six Companies' Role in Chinese Labor Importation in the Nineteenth Century." *Journal of American-East Asian Relations* 12, no. 3/4 (Fall–Winter 2003): 225–54.

Ramsey, Jarold. *Reading the Fire: Essays in the Traditional Indian Literatures of the Far West.* Seattle: University of Washington Press, 1999.

Ray, Verne F. "Native Village and Groupings of the Columbia Basin." *Pacific Northwest Quarterly* 27, no. 2 (April 1936): 99–152.

Ray, Verne F. *Cultural Relations in the Plateau of Northwestern America.* Los Angeles: Southwest Museum, 1939.

Ray, Verne F. "The Columbia Confederacy: A League of Central Plateau Tribes." In *Culture in History: Essays in Honor of Paul Radin,* edited by Stanley Diamond, 771–89. New York: Columbia University Press, 1960.

Reddick, Suann M., and Cary C. Collins. "Medicine Creek Remediated: Isaac Stevens and the Puyallup, Nisqually, and Muckleshoot Land Settlement at Fox Island, August 4, 1856." *Pacific Northwest Quarterly* 104, no. 2 (Spring 2013): 80–98.

Reps, John W. *Views and Viewmakers of Urban America: Lithographs of Towns and Cities in the United States and Canada.* Columbia: University of Missouri, 1984.

Revere, Joseph Warren. *A Tour of Duty in California.* New York: Francis & Co., 1849.

Rich, E. E., ed. *McLoughlin's Fort Vancouver Letters: First Series 1825–38.* London: Champlain Society, 1941.

Rich, E. E., ed. *Simpson's 1828 Journey to the Columbia.* London: Champlain Society, 1947.

Richards, Kent D. *Isaac I. Stevens: Young Man in a Hurry.* Pullman: Washington State University Press, 2016.

Rigsby, Bruce J. "On Cayuse-Molala Relatability." *International Journal of American Linguistics* 32, no. 4 (October 1966): 369–78.

Rigsby, Bruce J. "The Waiilatpuan Problem: More on Cayuse-Molala Relatability." *Northwest Anthropological Research Notes* 3, no. 1 (Spring 1969): 68–146.

Rigsby, Bruce J. "The Stevens Treaties, Indian Claims Commission Docket 264, and the Ancient One Known as Kennewick Man." In *The Power of Promises: Rethinking Indian Treaties in the Pacific Northwest,* edited by Alexandra Harmon, 244–76. Seattle: University of Washington Press, 2008.

Ritz, Philip. *Letter upon the Agricultural and Mineral Resources of the North-western Territories, on the Route of the Northern Pacific Railroad.* Washington, DC: Chronicle Print, 1868.

Robbins, William G. *Landscapes of Promise: The Oregon Story, 1800–1940.* Seattle: University of Washington Press, 2009.

Roberts, A. B. "Fragments of Early History: The City of Walla Walla in 1859." *Up-to-the-Times Magazine* 3, no. 3 (May 1909): 1936.

Roberts, A. B. "Walla Walla Fifty-One Years Ago." *Up-to-the-Times Magazine* 4, no. 3 (January 1910): 2414–7.

Roberts, W. Milnor. "Special Report of a Reconnoissance [sic] of the Route for the Northern Pacific Railroad between Lake Superior and Puget Sound, via the Columbia River." Philadelphia: n.p., 1869.

Rockaway, Robert, and Arnon Gutfeld. "Demonic Images of the Jew in the Nineteenth Century United States." *American Jewish History* 89, no. 4 (December 2001): 355–81.

Rosenbaum, Fred. *Cosmopolitans: A Social and Cultural History of the Jews of the San Francisco Bay Area.* Berkeley: University of California Press, 2011.

Rosoff, Nancy B., and Susan Kennedy Zeller, eds. *Tipi: Heritage of the Great Plains.* Seattle: University of Washington Press, 2011.

Ross, Alexander. *Adventures of the First Settlers on the Oregon or Columbia River.* London: Smith, Elder, 1849.

Ross, Alexander. *Fur Hunters of the Far West.* Vol. 1. London: Smith, Elder, 1855.

Roth, Jean. "The Schwabacher Family of Washington State." *Jewish Genealogical Society of Washington State.* 2015. https://jgsws.org/schwabacher.php.

Ruby, Robert H., and John A. Brown. *The Cayuse Indians: Imperial Tribesmen of Old Oregon.* Norman: University of Oklahoma Press, 1972.

Ruby, Robert H., and John A. Brown. *Dreamer-Prophets of the Columbia Plateau: Smohalla and Skolaskin.* Norman: University of Oklahoma Press, 1989.

Ruby, Robert H., and John A. Brown. *Indian Slavery in the Pacific Northwest.* Spokane: Arthur H. Clark, 1993.

Sachar, Howard M. *A History of the Jews in America.* New York: Knopf, 1992/2013.

Scholl, Louis. "Recollections of Sixty Years." *Up-to-the-Times Magazine* 1, no. 12 (October, 1907): 531–35; 2, no. 2 (December 1907): 51–4.

Scott, Darrell, ed. *A True Copy of the Record of the Official Proceedings at the Council in the Walla Walla Valley, 1855.* Fairfield, WA: Ye Galleon Press, 1985.

Scott, Harvey Whitefield. *History of Portland, Oregon.* Portland: Mason & Co., 1890.

Settle, Raymond W., ed. *The March of the Mounted Riflemen . . . as Recorded in the Journals of Major Osborne Cross and George Gibbs and the Official Report of Colonel Loring.* Lincoln: University of Nebraska Press, 1989.

Simmons, Alexy. "Red Light Ladies in the American West: Entrepreneurs and Companions." *Australian Journal of Historical Archaeology* 7 (1989): 63–9.

Simpson, George. *Narrative of a Journey round the World, during the Years 1841 and 1842.* London: Colburn, 1847.

Smith, Henry Nash. *Virgin Land: The American West as Symbol and Myth.* Cambridge: Harvard University Press, 1950/1978.

Sorkin, David. *Jewish Emancipation: A History across Five Centuries.* Princeton, NJ: Princeton University Press, 2019.

"Spalding and Whitman Letters, 1837." *Oregon Historical Quarterly* 37, no. 2 (June 1936): 111–28.

Spinden, Herbert J. *The Nez Perce Indians.* Lancaster, PA: American Anthropological Association, 1908.

Splawn, A. J. *Ka-mi-akin: The Last Hero of the Yakimas.* Portland: Kilham, 1917.

Spude, Catherine Holder. "Brothels and Saloons: An Archaeology of Gender in the American West." *Historical Archaeology* 39, no. 1 (2005): 89–106.

Stern, Theodore. *Chiefs and Chief Traders: Indian Relations at Fort Nez Percés, 1818–1855.* Corvallis: Oregon State University Press, 1993.

Stern, Theodore. *Chiefs and Change in the Oregon Country: Indian Relations at Fort Nez Percés, 1818–1855.* Corvallis: Oregon State University Press, 1996.

Stevens, Hazard. *The Life of Isaac Ingalls Stevens.* Boston: Houghton, Mifflin, 1900.

Stevens, Isaac I. "Northwest America." *Journal of the American Geographical and Statistical Society* 1, no. 1 (January 1859): 5.

Stillé, Charles Janeway. *History of the United States Sanitary Commission.* Philadelphia: Lippincott, 1866.

Sturtevant, William C., ed. *Handbook of North American Indians 12: Plateau.* Washington, DC: Smithsonian, 1998.

Suphan, Robert. *Oregon Indians II: Ethnographical Report of the Umatilla, Walla Walla and Cayuse Indians.* New York: Garland, 1974.

Tamástslikt Cultural Institute. *Cáw Pawá Láakni/They Are Not Forgotten: Sahaptian Place Names Atlas of the Cayuse, Umatilla, and Walla Walla*. Pendleton, OR: Tamástslikt Cultural Institute, 2015.

"The Isaac I. Stevens and Joel Palmer Treaties, 1855–2005." [Special Issue] *Oregon Historical Quarterly* 106, no. 3 (Fall 2005).

Todd, Ronald, ed. "Letters of Governor Isaac I. Stevens, 1857–1858." *Pacific Northwest Quarterly* 31, no. 4 (October 1940): 403–59.

Tong, Benson. *Unsubmissive Women: Chinese Prostitutes in Nineteenth-Century San Francisco*. Norman: University of Oklahoma Press, 1994.

Townsend, John Kirk. *The Narrative of a Journey across the Rocky Mountains to the Columbia River*. Philadelphia: Perkins, 1839.

Trafzer, Clifford, and Richard Scheuerman. *The Snake River-Palouse and the Invasion of the Inland Northwest*. Pullman: Washington State University Press, 2016.

Trafzer, Clifford E., and Margery Ann Beach. "Smohalla, the Washani, and Religion as a Factor in Northwestern Indian History." *American Indian Quarterly* 9, no. 3 (Summer 1985): 309–15.

Turney-High, Harry Holbert. *The Flathead Indians of Montana*. Menasha, WI: American Anthropological Association, 1937.

Unruh, John D., Jr. *The Plains Across: The Overland Emigrants and the Trans-Mississippi West, 1840–60*. Urbana: University of Illinois Press, 1993.

Vibert, Elizabeth. "'The Natives Were Strong to Live': Reinterpreting Early-Nineteenth-Century Prophetic Movements in the Columbia Plateau." *Ethnohistory* 42, no. 2 (Spring 1995): 197–229.

Vibert, Elizabeth. *Traders' Tales: Narratives of Cultural Encounters in the Columbia Plateau, 1807–1846*. Norman: University of Oklahoma Press, 1997.

Victor, Frances Fuller. "The Oregon Indians, Part I." *Overland Monthly* 7, no. 4 (October 1871): 344–52.

Victor, Frances Fuller. *All Over Oregon and Washington*. San Francisco: Carmany, 1872.

Victor, Frances Fuller. *The Early Indian Wars of Oregon*. Salem: Baker, 1894.

Walla Walla 2020. https://ww2020.net/.

Walla Walla Valley, Washington Territory: Its Resources, Climate, River and Railroad Systems . . . . Walla Walla: Statesman, 1879.

Watt, James W. "Experiences of a Packer in Washington Territory Mining Camps during the Sixties." *Washington Historical Quarterly* 20, no. 1 (January 1929): 36–53.

Wells, Lemuel H. *A Pioneer Missionary*. Seattle: Progressive, 1931.

Whaley, Gray H. *Oregon and the Collapse of Illahee: U.S. Empire and the Transformation of an Indigenous World, 1792–1859*. Chapel Hill: University of North Carolina Press, 2010.

White, Richard. *"It's Your Misfortune and None of My Own": A New History of the American West*. Norman: University of Oklahoma Press, 1991.

White, Richard. *Railroaded: The Transcontinentals and the Making of Modern America*. New York: Norton, 2011.

Whitman, Narcissa. "Letters Written by Mrs. Whitman to Her Relatives in New York." In *Transactions of the Nineteenth Annual Reunion of the Oregon Pioneer Association for 1891*, 79–179. Portland: n.p., 1893.

Wilkinson, Charles. *The People Are Dancing Again: The History of the Siletz Tribe of Western Oregon*. Seattle: University of Washington Press, 2010.

Williams, Glyndwr, ed. *Hudson's Bay Miscellany, 1670–1870*. Winnipeg: Hudson's Bay Record Society, 1975.

Wright, Mary C. "The Woman's Lodge: Constructing Gender on the Nineteenth-Century Pacific Northwest Plateau." *Frontiers: A Journal of Women Studies* 24, no. 1 (2003): 1–18.

Young, F. G., ed. "Journal of Medorem Crawford: An Account of His Trip across the Plains with the Oregon Pioneers of 1842." In *Sources of the History of Oregon* 1, pt. 1, 3–26. Eugene, 1897.

Young, F. G., ed. "Journal and Report by Dr. Marcus Whitman of His Tour of Exploration with Rev. Samuel Parker in 1835 beyond the Rocky Mountains." *Oregon Historical Quarterly* 28, no. 3 (September 1927): 239–57.

Young, F. G., and Joaquin Young, "Ewing Young and His Estate: A Chapter in the Economic and Community Development of Oregon." *Quarterly of the Oregon Historical Society* 21, no. 3 (September 1920): 171–315.

Government Publications (chronological)

Wilkes, Charles. *Atlas of the Narrative of the United States Exploring Expedition during the Years 1839, 1840, 1841, 1842.* Philadelphia: Sherman, 1844.

Grover, La Fayette, ed. *The Oregon Archives.* Salem: n.p., 1853.

U.S. Congress. Senate. *Communications from the Commissioner of Indian Affairs.* 33d Cong., 1st sess. 1853–54. S. Doc. 34.

U.S. Congress. Senate. *Annual Report of the Commissioner of Indian Affairs.* 33d Cong., 2d sess. 1854. S. Doc. 1.

U.S. Congress. House. *Indian Disturbances in Oregon and Washington.* 34th Cong., 1st sess. 1856. H. Doc. 48.

U.S. Congress. House. *Report of the Secretary of War.* 34th Cong., 1st sess. 1856. H. Doc. 93.

U.S. Congress. House. *Report of the Secretary of War.* 34th Cong., 3d sess. 1856. H. Doc. 1.

U.S. Congress. House. *Indian Affairs on the Pacific.* 34th Cong., 3d sess. 1857. H. Doc. 76.

U.S. Congress. Senate. *Report of J. Ross Browne . . . Indian Affairs in the Territories of Oregon and Washington.* 35th Cong., 1st sess. 1858. S. Doc. 40.

U.S. Congress. House. *Indian Affairs in Oregon and Washington Territories, &c.* 35th Cong., 1st sess. 1858. H. Doc. 112.

U.S. Congress. House. *Report of the Commissioner of Indian Affairs.* 35th Cong., 2d sess. 1858. H. Doc. 1.

U.S. Congress. House. *Report of the Secretary of War.* 35th Cong., 2d sess. 1858. H. Doc. 2.

U.S. Congress. Senate. *Preliminary Topographical Memoir of Colonel George Wright's Campaign, Prepared . . . by Lieutenant John Mullan.* 35th Cong., 2d sess. 1859. S. Doc. 32.

U.S. Congress. House. *Topographical Memoir and Report of Captain T. J. Cram, on Territories of Oregon and Washington.* 35th Cong., 2d sess. 1859. H. Doc. 114.

Acts of the Legislative Assembly of the Territory of Washington . . . December 6th, 1858. Olympia: n.p., 1859.

Stevens, Isaac I. *Reports of Explorations and Surveys . . . for a Railroad from the Mississippi River to the Pacific Ocean* 12. Washington, DC: Ford, 1860.

U.S. Congress. House. *Report of the Secretary of War.* 36th Cong., 1st sess. 1860. H. Doc 93.

U.S. Congress. Senate, *Annual Report of the Commissioner of Indian Affairs.* 36th Cong., 2d sess. 1860. S. Doc. 2.

U.S. Congress. House. *Letter from the Secretary of the Treasury, Transmitting Estimates of Additional Appropriations.* 37th Cong., 1st sess. 1861. H. Doc. 1.

U.S. Congress. Senate. *Annual Report of the Commissioner of Indian Affairs.* 37th Cong., 2d sess. 1861. S. Doc. 1.

Session Laws of the Territory of Washington . . . 9th Session of the Legislative Assembly Held at Olympia, 1861–62. Olympia: n.p., 1862.

U. S. Congress. Senate. *Congressional Globe.* "Indian Appropriation Bill." 37th Cong., 2d sess. 1862. 2095.

U.S. Congress. House. *Annual Report of the Commissioner of Indian Affairs.* 37th Cong., 3d sess. 1862. H. Doc. 1.

U.S. Congress. Senate. *Report of Captain John Mullan [Construction of a Military Road from Fort Walla-Walla to Fort Benton].* 37th Cong., 3d sess. 1863. S. Doc. 43.

U.S. Congress. House. *Annual Report of the Commissioner of Indian Affairs.* 38th Cong., 1st sess. 1863. H. Doc. 1.

U.S. Congress. House. *Annual Report of the Commissioner of Indian Affairs.* 38th Cong., 2d sess. 1864. H. Doc. 1.

Population of the United States in 1860. Washington, DC, Government Publishing Office, 1864. https://census.gov/library/publications/1864/dec/1860a.html.

U.S. Congress. House. *Annual Report of the Commissioner of Indian Affairs.* 39th Cong., 1st sess. 1865. H. Doc. 1.

Statutes of the Territory of Washington, 1865–66. Olympia: McElroy, 1866.

U.S. Congress. Senate. *Memorial of the Legislature of Oregon, in Favor of Incorporating the County of Walla-Walla, Washington Territory, into the State of Oregon.* 39th Cong., 1st sess. 1866. S. Doc. 83.

U.S. Congress. House. *Report of the Commissioner of Indian Affairs for the Year 1866.* 39th Cong., 2d sess. 1866. H. Doc. 2.

U.S. Congress. House. Orville Elias Babcock. *A Report of Inspection of Military Posts.* 39th Cong., 2d sess. 1867. H. Doc. 20.

U.S. Congress. House. *Report of the Commissioner of Indian Affairs for the Year 1867.* 40th Cong., 2d sess. 1867. H. Doc. 1.

Evidence for the United States in the Matter of the Claim of the Hudson's Bay Company . . . Washington, DC: Government Publishing Office, 1867.

U.S. Congress. House. *Report of the Commissioner of Indian Affairs for the Year 1868.* 40th Cong., 3d sess. 1868. H. Doc. 2.

U.S. Congress. House. *Report of the Commissioner of Indian Affairs for the Year 1869.* 41st Cong., 2d sess. 1869. H. Doc. 1.

U.S. Congress. House. *Report of the Commissioner of Indian Affairs for the Year 1870.* 41st Cong., 3d sess. 1870. H. Doc. 1.

Bureau of Statistics. *Special Report on Immigration.* Washington, DC: Government Publishing Office, 1871.

U.S. Congress. House. *Third Annual Report of the Commissioner of Indian Affairs, 1871.* 42d Cong., 2d sess. 1871. H. Doc. 1.

U.S. Congress. House. *Report of the Commissioner of Indian Affairs, 1871.* 42d Cong., 2d sess. 1872. H. Doc. 1.

War Department. *Outline Description of U.S. Military Posts and Stations in the Year 1871.* Washington, DC: Government Publishing Office, 1872.

Ninth Census: Volume 1. The Statistics of the Population of the United States. Washington, DC, Government Publishing Office, 1872. https://census.gov/library/publications/1872/dec/1870a.html.

U.S. Congress. House. *Report of the Commissioner of Indian Affairs, 1872.* 42d Cong., 3d sess. 1872. H. Doc. 1.

U.S. Congress. House. *Annual Report of the Commissioner of Indian Affairs.* 43d Cong., 1st sess. 1873. H. Doc. 1.

U.S. Congress. House. *Petition and Papers of Toussaint Mesplié.* 43d Cong., 1st sess. 1874. H. Doc. 97.

U.S. Congress. House. *Annual Report of the Commissioner of Indian Affairs.* 43d Cong., 2d sess. 1874. H. Doc. 1.

U.S. Congress. House. *Annual Report of the Commissioner of Indian Affairs.* 44th Cong., 1st sess. 1875. H. Doc. 1.

War Department. *A Report on the Hygiene of the U.S. Army, with Description of Military Posts.* Washington, DC: Government Publishing Office, 1875.

U.S. Congress. House. *Annual Report of the Commissioner of Indian Affairs.* 44th Cong., 2d sess. 1876. H. Doc. 1.

Annual Report of Commissioner of Indian Affairs for the Year 1877. Washington, DC: Government Publishing Office, 1877.

Annual Report of the Commissioner of Indian Affairs for the Year 1878. Washington, DC: Government Publishing Office, 1878.

Abbott, T. O. *Real Property Statutes of Washington Territory, from 1843 to 1889.* Olympia: State Publishing, 1892.

Washington Military Department. *The Official History of the Washington National Guard,* vol. 3. Tacoma: n.d. https://mil.wa.gov/official-history-of-washington-national-guard.

Gates, Paul W. *History of the Public Land Law Development.* Washington, DC: Government Publishing Office, 1968.

U.S. Army Corps of Engineers Seattle District. *Context Study of the United States Quartermaster General Standardized Plans 1866–1942.* Seattle: n.d., 1997.

General Land Office Records. Bureau of Land Management. https://glorecords.blm.gov/search/default.aspx.

U.S. Census Bureau. U.S. Federal Census. Walla Walla County. Washington State Digital Archives. https://digitalarchives.wa.gov.

Index

About the Author

Dennis Crockett grew up on the Brooklyn-Queens border in New York City. He attended college while traveling around the United States, ultimately completing an M.A. in art history at Queens College and a Ph.D. at the City University of New York. As a professor of art history and visual culture at Whitman College (Walla Walla, WA) for three decades, he taught numerous courses in visual culture and served as department chair from 1999 to 2014. Among the honors and awards he received during his career are the Thomas D. Howells Award for Distinguished Teaching in the Humanities and Arts, Whitman College (2016); an Andrew W. Mellon Foundation grant (2010); the Arnold L. and Lois S. Graves Award (2000); and a Henry Luce Foundation grant (1999–2000). His research and teaching have ranged from medieval European art to the houses down the block. In addition to *Becoming Walla Walla*, he is the author of *German Post-Expressionism: The Art of the Great Disorder, 1918–1924.*

Printed in the USA
CPSIA information can be obtained
at www.ICGtesting.com
JSHW010048101224
75129JS00002B/3